THEORY AND PRACTICE
IN SOCIOLOGY

PEARSON
Education

We work with leading authors to develop the strongest
educational materials in Sociology bringing cutting-edge
thinking and best learning practice to a global market.

Under a range of well-known imprints, including
Prentice Hall, we craft high-quality print and electronic
publications which help readers to understand and
apply their content, whether studying or at work.

To find out more about the complete range of our
publishing please visit us on the World Wide Web at:
www.pearsoned.co.uk

THEORY AND PRACTICE
IN SOCIOLOGY

Edited by Ian Marsh

PEARSON
Prentice
Hall

Harlow, England • London • New York • Boston • San Francisco • Toronto
Sydney • Tokyo • Singapore • Hong Kong • Seoul • Taipei • New Delhi
Cape Town • Madrid • Mexico City • Amsterdam • Munich • Paris • Milan

Pearson Education Limited
Edinburgh Gate
Harlow
Essex CM20 2JE
England

and Associated Companies throughout the world

Visit us on the World Wide Web at:
www.pearsoned.co.uk

First published 2002

© Pearson Education Limited 2002

ISBN 0 13 0 26553 5

British Library Cataloguing-in-Publication Data
A catalogue record for this book can be obtained from the British Library

Library of Congress Cataloging-in-Publication Data
Theory and practice in sociology / edited by Ian Marsh.
     p. cm.
   Includes bibliographical references and index.
   ISBN 0-13-026553-5 (alk. paper)
   1. Sociology—Philosophy.   2. Sociology—Methodology.   I. Marsh, Ian, 1952–
HM585 .T4785 2002
   301′.01—dc21   2002071553

10 9 8 7 6 5 4 3 2
07   06   05   04   03

Typeset in 10/12.5pt Sabon by 35
Printed in Malaysia, CLP

Contents

92

137

177

220

Preface

Theory and Practice in Sociology aims to provide students (and tutors) with a comprehensive, clear and accessible introduction to the different methods and practice of social research and the main theoretical approaches in sociology. By covering both research methods and theory, students and tutors have a text that examines the two areas that are generally compulsory, core elements of sociology undergraduate degrees. Sociological methods and theories – in some guise (such as sociological analysis; methods of research in sociology; sociological knowledge and practice) – are invariably compulsory parts of level 2 (usually year 2) programmes in sociology. And, if not compulsory, there are modules or courses on methods and theories in all such degree programmes.

Theory and Practice in Sociology reviews and examines ideas, issues and arguments in greater depth than is possible through the summaries provided in specific chapters in large, all-encompassing sociology textbooks. It provides more detailed and fuller examples and case studies of specific methodological and theoretical approaches; and an opportunity for students to reflect on these. While each of the two main areas – methods and theories – could be covered in separate texts, and while the two areas are distinct and we would not look for artificial links between them for the sake of it, covering both in one book enables regular cross-referencing between practice and theory – with particular studies referred to in one section re-examined from a range of theoretical and methodological viewpoints in different parts of the book. It also enables students to get a fuller flavour of original arguments than they can from general introductory texts. At the same time, they are not faced with a massively detailed tome.

Structure and features

A key characteristic of *Theory and Practice in Sociology* is its interactive approach which encourages students to react to the material covered and to think for themselves. The active engagement of students with the material helps to distinguish this from other texts in the area and provides a real teaching resource for tutors. We have not included questions for the sake of it, but there are a number of **Discussion Questions** in each chapter which provide reflective breaks and will encourage students to consider perhaps a case study or the discussion and respond to questions on it. In particular, these questions will try to stimulate them to relate general issues to their own situations and lives.

In addition to these 'mini-activities', at the end of each chapter are fuller **Exercises**, which could be used as groupwork exercises or undertaken by students as individual pieces of work. These exercises usually involve students reflecting on the material in the chapter and possibly undertaking some additional research and reading of their own.

As regards the contents, there are two main parts to the book: Sociological Practice and Sociological Theory. In Part 1, Sociological Practice, social research is considered as an active process in which the researcher aims to get close to the social world to which we all belong. Chapter 1 looks at the history of social research and the principles behind such research. The emergence of the 'modern' world view is related to the philosophical thinking that characterised the eighteenth-century Enlightenment. After a consideration of the ways in which different philosophies affect how social research is conducted and of the balance between theory and methods, the chapter finishes by looking at two key methodological approaches used in sociology: the scientific method and the interpretive method. Chapter 2 focuses on the practical issues involved in doing social research and describes the major stages of the research process. The issues examined include: the choice of research topic and the formulation of research questions and hypotheses; the strengths and weaknesses of the different research techniques and methods available; the interpretation and analysis of research data; and the publicising of research findings.

Part 2, Sociological Theory, provides a broadly chronological discussion of sociological theorising. Chapter 3 considers what it is that characterises social theory and assesses its relevance and 'worth' through evaluating some of the typical criticisms of such theory. The emergence and development of social theory is described in Chapter 4. In particular it describes the intellectual origins of social theory in the Enlightenment and then examines the work of five key nineteenth-century social theorists: Comte, Spencer, Durkheim, Marx and Weber. It is argued that studying these classic social theorists cannot be divorced from studying the Enlightenment, as the work of these great thinkers was a debate with the issues raised by that movement. Among the major developments of the Enlightenment that prompted the emergence of social theory were an emphasis on intellectual rigour, a conception of society as composed of individuals, an attempt to rationally understand their behaviour, a concern with social interconnection, a rational approach to the state and a stress on classification and typology.

Chapter 5 traces the emergence of 'modern society' and 'modern social theory' in the early twentieth century. It considers the relationship of the Enlightenment and classic social theorists to these developments and, in particular, to the work of four 'modern' theorists: Simmel, Tonnies, Nietszche and Freud. Each of these writers (it is not really appropriate to describe Freud and Nietzsche, at least, as sociologists) tried to explain the nature of modern urban/industrial society and, to varying degrees, compared this form of society unfavourably with pre-modern social structures.

The social theories looked at so far offered grand theoretical explanations – meta-narratives – of social development. In the mid-twentieth century a new direction and perspective emerged in American sociology in particular with a focus on the individual as of key importance in social analysis. Chapter 6 examines this development in American sociology between the 1920s and 1960s. Of course this work did not develop in a vacuum and the link between aspects of early modern theorising, in particular the work of Simmel, and this fascination with individual behaviour as a basis for social theorising is explored. The chapter then considers the rise and role of the Chicago School of Sociology: a number of key theorists are examined including Thomas, Cooley, Mead and Blumer. The continuing impact of the Chicago School in postwar sociology is demonstrated by the massive influence of Erving Goffman, whose position as a modern classic social theorist is assessed.

The final two chapters look at contemporary social theory. Postmodernism is the focus of Chapter 7 which starts by considering what postmodernism is and what encouraged the move from modern to postmodern society. The argument that we live in postmodern times has transformed the ways that sociologists have theorised about the social world, and this chapter examines and assesses the work of three of the theorists most closely associated with postmodernism: Baudrillard, Lyotard and Jameson. After exploring their analyses of the implications of the emergence of postmodern society for the development and status of social theory, the chapter concludes by reflecting on the theoretical and the political consequences of postmodern sociology for the enterprise of sociology as a whole. Chapter 8 looks at the development and continuing impact of feminist theory. Rather than providing a run through of the various strands of feminist theory, the focus here is on the dynamic nature of feminism, especially as it relates to changing conceptualisations of power and oppression. Both standpoint theory and the role of dichotomous thinking are used to illustrate the link between theory and lived experience, and to encourage students to reflect more widely upon the process of sociological theorising.

The diverse spread of writers looked at in Part 2 of this book demonstrates that social theory encompasses a wide range of perspectives and arguments. However, the text has been necessarily selective in its choice of theorists and theories and would make no claims to providing a definitive account and who's who of social theory. It does, though, provide a reasonably comprehensive discussion and assessment of many writers whose work has influenced (and still does) the development of sociological theory. Some important writers and perspectives which students may well have come across in their studies have been omitted. All of the chapters in Part 2 have tried to provide a detailed enough coverage of particular writers and theories to give students a real flavour of such work.

Theory and Practice in Sociology has been written by a team of established sociology tutors based at Liverpool Hope University College, each covering areas they have experiences of teaching or researching in. Their main aim has been to excite and interest students in sociological theory and research and the debates within them. As a consequence of this it is hoped that those students will look at other areas of sociology that they study with a greater theoretical and methodological awareness.

Ian Marsh
January 2002

Acknowledgements

Theory and Practice in Sociology has been a collective endeavour between the team of writers and Pearson Education. Everyone involved has tried to produce a text that is both thorough and accessible. It is conventional to thank friends, families and generations of students who have had to put up with the writers' personal and professional practices and habits. The editor and authors of this text are happy to stick with that convention. They would also like to record their thanks to Matthew Smith at Pearson for his support from start to finish and to Jill Birch for overseeing the production of the text.

Publisher's Acknowledgements

We are grateful to the following for permission to reproduce copyright material:

Dea Birkett for her article 'Voyage of self-discovery' published in *The Guardian* 28 July 1998 © Dea Birkett 1998; Bob Dylan Music Company for the lyrics to 'Positively 4th Street' by Bob Dylan © 1965 by Warner Bros Inc., renewed © 1993 by Special Rider Music (all rights reserved, international copyright secured); Guardian Newspapers Limited for extracts from 'Special report: May day 2001' by Seamus Milne published in *The Guardian* 2 May 2001 © The Guardian 2001, 'Interview with Tony Blair' by Polly Toynbee, Michael White and Patrick Wintour published in *The Guardian* 14 August 2001 © The Guardian 2001, and 'Reloca-tion of refugees "should not be rushed"' by Lucy Ward published in *The Guardian* 14 August 2001 © The Guardian 2001; The Random House Group Limited for an extract from *Captain Corelli's Mandolin* by Louis de Bernières published by Secker & Warburg; Lennie St Luce for her poem 'You are not alone' published in 'Violence against women: experiences of South African domestic workers' by B.M.M. Sexwale from *The Dynamics of 'Race' and Gender* ed. H. Afshar; and Times Newspapers Limited for extracts from 'Virgin in deal with Sing Tel' by Chris Ayres, and 'Blair is facing exodus of his women MPs' by Roland Watson both pub-lished in *The Times* 20 May 2000 © Times Newspapers Limited 2000. Page 279 cartoon from '*Dot*' series published by Paperlink Ltd., London, England (Daphne David, 1994); Page 288 cartoon captioned, '*I wandered lonely as a cloud . . .*' copy-right Jacky Fleming, 1997 (www.jackyfleming.co.uk).

In some instances we have been unable to trace the owners of copyright material and we would appreciate any information that would enable us to do so.

Part 1

Sociological Practice

Chapter 1

The nature of social research and social knowledge

JULIE F. SCOTT

Chapter outline

- Early social research
- Sociology the empirical 'science'
- The sociological perspective
- The method–theory relationship
- Ways of knowing
- Epistemology
- Hermeneutics
- Methodology
- Epistemological revolutions or crises?
- Exercises

> The outcome of any serious research can only be to make two questions from where only one grew before.
>
> (T. Veblen, *The Place of Science in Modern Civilization*, 1919)

Imagine you run a business which is about to launch a new product, and before you spend millions on marketing it you want to know if it will sell. What do you do? Or picture yourself in charge of the budget for the National Health Service and you need to decide what to spend it on. How do you make such decisions when everything seems to be a priority? Or what if you were managing a big football club, which keeps losing and needs an injection of 'new blood'. How do you decide whom to sign? The answer to all these questions is 'research'. Of course it might not be called that, rather in business terms it becomes 'market research', in health policy it is known as 'policy review' and in the football world 'scouting'. Whatever the name, it involves the principles of research, that is individuals or groups of people systematically and in a variety of ways trying to find answers to specific questions. All areas of life involve research, and the research skills gained in one area can often be applied in others.

Research is particularly associated with academia and is at the heart of all academic disciplines. Sociology is no exception. Different academic subjects often use very different types of research, while many share the same research techniques. Sociology, for example, shares many of its types of research with psychology and social anthropology. Social research involves the investigation of all types of social phenomena. Sociologists are trying to understand how society works and why people do the things that they do, in the way that they do them. Social research provides the evidence with which sociologists can formulate theories of society and hopefully provide a better understanding of how we live. Sociology is a diverse subject and this is reflected in the almost endless list of potential research topics, including religion, crime, racism, gender, media and family life. Our image of the researcher might involve someone wearing a white coat in a laboratory or standing in the centre of town with a clipboard asking questions. However, research can take many forms and is just as likely to involve the researcher joining a religious cult or standing in the audience at a pop concert watching crowd behaviour, or interviewing people in an online chatroom. Whatever type of research they do, all sociologists take research for granted as part of their professional role and are actively engaged to some degree in research at all times. It can be surprising to reflect upon just how much research one does, whether gathering sources for an essay or a report, analysing data for a book or preparing a presentation or a lecture.

Research is often described as an adventure, an encounter or a journey, which reflects the fact that research is an active process in which the researcher will experience a range of emotions from excitement to boredom, enthusiasm to lethargy. Whatever emotions may be experienced during research, the experience is rarely dull and often at the end of research the researcher will feel changed, intellectually or even personally. Much of sociology involves writing about, theorising and discussing the social world around us. While this can at first sight appear lifeless and dull, separated off from the 'real world', research allows us to get up close to the social world to which we belong and can bring colour and life to social theory, making it relevant and lively.

Discussion questions

1 Consider the subjects you studied at school or college. What were the most common types of research associated with each subject?

2 Account for the different approaches to research within different academic subjects.

3 Reflect upon the types of research experiences (at school/college or in a non-academic sphere) you have had. What research skills did you develop and what did you learn about conducting research?

4 List other areas of life (aside from academic studies) where research is important and suggest the most appropriate or usual form of research in these areas.

This chapter starts by looking at the history of social research, a history that pre-dates the establishment of sociology as an academic discipline in its own right. When sociology was founded as an academic discipline particular research techniques were used, but since the mid-nineteenth century the nature and role of social research has changed. Additionally the relationship between data gathering and theory formulation has also shifted in more recent times. After consideration of the development of social research, the chapter discusses the philosophy behind research. How we view and understand the world around us affects how research is conducted, and it is important that researchers reflect upon this in their work. Different philosophical perspectives have given rise to a variety of approaches to research, most of which are intrinsically linked to the different theories explored in Part 2 of this book.

EARLY SOCIAL RESEARCH

This book is focused on the researching and theorising of society since the advent of a distinct academic discipline for the study of society, i.e. sociology. However, this is not to say that people did not study their own societies before sociology's arrival in the early nineteenth century. We can locate early attempts at theorising society typically within the field of philosophy. In a similar vein, we can also find examples of social research being conducted throughout history. Pre-sociology, 'social research' can be divided into two types: counting and measuring surveys and cultural descriptions.

Counting and measuring surveys

Throughout history and across cultures it is possible to find evidence of social surveys giving historians and archaeologists rich information on the size and constitution of particular societies. It could be viewed as the norm for large, literate ancient cultures, such as the Egyptians, Mayans and the Babylonians, to conduct regular surveys of people, land and resources. Such surveys were essential for the bureaucratic organisation and, often, imperial expansion of these cultures. A civil-servant type class of professional information collectors would conduct them. Such surveys were introduced into European practice by the Romans and were adopted into regular use by the Christian Church in Europe as a way of ensuring church wealth, power and expansion. Expanding European nation states adopted such surveys to keep note of acquisitions within Europe (see, for example, the Domesday Book of William the Conqueror) and abroad. The first thing many colonial powers did on annexing overseas colonies was to conduct a survey to record resources (people, land and raw materials). This pragmatic use of surveys was purely administrative and developed in tandem with the emergence of more bureaucratic practices within Europe, for example with the keeping of detailed parish records of births, marriages and deaths. The data produced from such surveys provides a useful historical record for us today but does not really provide us with much insight, in a sociological sense, into these cultures. For example, knowing the number of slaves kept by the average Roman merchant does not explain the practice of slavery or Roman views of it, let alone the experience of slavehood for the individuals themselves.

Cultural descriptions

Just as societies have always utilised surveys to provide administrative information about their own and other cultures, they have also produced cultural descriptions of societies they encounter or conquer. Such descriptions were produced by a variety of writers, including soldiers, missionaries, civil servants, professional writers and travellers. Most were done in the spirit of expanding information. However, such accounts are highly descriptive and subjective, dwelling less on the social mechanics of the 'foreign' culture and more on exotic customs and ethnic difference. Most such descriptions must be viewed in relation to the ideology of imperialism or at least through the visor of ethnic superiority. For example, the Romans typically portrayed the cultures they encountered as cannibalistic *barbari* (the Latin word describing the primitive speech of non-Roman cultures from which we derive the word 'barbarian'). One infamous example is found in the work of the Greek historian Strabo (c.63BC–AD23) who produced a detailed account of the ancient Irish whom he portrayed as bloodthirsty cannibals, stating that 'they count it an honourable thing, when their fathers die, to devour them'. These accounts are strikingly similar to those produced by medieval European writers about Islamic culture, and later European portrayals of their encounters with colonial peoples in Africa, Asia and the Americas. In all of them we find accounts of savagery, barbarity and often lewd sexual detail. 'Natives' were either infantile and innocent or barbaric savages.

> The people are thus naked, handsome, brown, well shaped in body, their heads, necks, arms, private parts, feet of men and women are little covered with feathers. The men also have many precious stones in their faces and breasts. No one also has anything, but all things are in common. And the men have no wives those who please them be they mothers, sisters, or friends, therein make they no distinction. They also fight with each other. They also eat each other even those who are slain, and hang flesh of them in smoke. They become a hundred and fifty years old.
> (From a sixteenth century Portuguese account of contact with South American Indians)

Accounts such as the one above fuelled and justified imperialist ideologies, old and new. We might find such accounts useful today not as accurate records of how societies once lived but rather as interesting insights for exploring colonialism, past and present, and its incumbent ideological tools.

Both of the above types of research can be labelled 'social' in that they were studying society, often in ways people of that time felt were scientific, systematic and accurate. However, they are flawed in our eyes because they are not truly empirical and are not backed by a specific theoretical perspective on society.

SOCIOLOGY THE EMPIRICAL 'SCIENCE'

The way we view and understand the social and physical world around us is radically different from how people in the past viewed it. Before the eighteenth century, people's worldview was dominated by the Christian Church and religious ways of understanding and viewing the world. One obvious example of Christian beliefs dominating worldview can be seen in the fields of science and medicine. In science, the view that God was at the centre of the universe and God's creation (Earth and mankind) close to this centre resulted in the view that the Sun and all the other planets in our solar system revolved around the Earth. Scientists such as Copernicus (1473–1543) and Galileo (1564–1642) faced church persecution for presenting opposing (and ultimately accurate) models. Similarly, in a time before microbiology, illness was often seen as the result of sinful living and a punishment from God. This worldview dominated by religion is referred to as the pre-modern.

The pre-modern worldview gave way to the modern as a result of a number of social and philosophical revolutions. The point when the modern era is seen as having emerged is known as the Enlightenment, a philosophical movement of the eighteenth century. The Enlightenment had a profound effect on western ways of thinking, viewing and exploring the world, both physical and social. However, it is important to understand that the Enlightenment was not an isolated, unique event but rather the product of a number of profound ideological revolutions and important social events that had interacted with each other since the fourteenth century to fragment and then shatter the pre-modern worldview. The two key 'revolutions' in this process of change were the Renaissance and the Reformation.

The Renaissance began in Italy in the fourteenth century and soon spread throughout western Europe. It was an artistic movement, which saw the development of new ways of picturing and portraying the world as exemplified in the work of artists such as Leonardo da Vinci (1452–1519) and Michelangelo (1475–1564). One of the driving forces of this era was the re-emergence and reappraisal of once forbidden (by the church) classical writings. Ancient works of art and literature produced not only a great artistic outpouring but also scientific developments and innovations, which can be seen in the work of scientists such as Galileo. The foundations for what we can now call modern science were laid at this time. The Renaissance also saw the emergence of notions of the self and the importance of the individual which would become key to modern ways of thinking.

While the Renaissance was entering its final period a second ideological revolution occurred in Europe known as the Reformation. The Reformation began in 1517 with the German theologian Martin Luther's (1483–1546) criticisms of the Roman Catholic Church and, in particular, papal indulgence and corruption. The ensuing attacks and counter-attacks split the Christian Church in western Europe and opened up the notion of a multiplicity of ways of viewing the world. Instead of a single, unified church with a unified doctrine ('truth'), there emerged a number of strands of Christianity all offering a slightly different interpretation of this once unified doctrine. The one 'truth' had become many, typically in opposition to each other.

The fragmentation of worldview and the development of new ways of viewing the world were also aided by cultural contact with the non-European world. Although Europeans had always had information on their neighbouring cultures, most notably the Arabic civilisations of North Africa and the Middle East, it was not until the fifteenth century that Europeans began travelling and exploring the wider world. Such voyages of exploration, which increased in number throughout the next four hundred years, and the beginning of colonialism which they encouraged, brought back to Europe new ideas, customs and practices. Such exploration also shook up long-held views of the world. For example, the discovery of different belief systems again challenged the idea of one route to the divine or the idea of one 'truth'. All these events helped to allow science to flourish without the controls it had once endured, and thus scientific methods and ways of thinking became increasingly influential by the late seventeenth and early eighteenth centuries.

Enlightenment scientists such as the English physicist Sir Isaac Newton (1642–1727) viewed the physical world as an ordered place run by set rules and believed that the job of the scientist was to uncover the rules to be able to produce an organised set of predictable laws about a given phenomenon. These rules could be uncovered through the rigorous application of empirical investigation and experimentation. The key to scientific success was the application of empiricism – that is, evidence-based theory. In order for something to be true, the scientist had to prove it to be true through the collection of valid data. Only through this process could universal 'truths' about the world be discovered. For example, Newton's Laws of Motion are organised and can be reproduced in this way.

Enlightenment philosophers, such as the Frenchman Jean-Jacques Rousseau (1712–1778), the Scots David Hume (1711–1776) and Adam Smith (1723–1790), taking inspiration from early modern science, proposed that the social world was also an organised and ordered place with rules and systems. Just as physical phenomena could be proven to exist or not exist in the world, so Enlightenment philosophers believed that social 'truths' could be proven or disproved too. The way to uncover social 'truths' was to adopt scientific empirical procedures and thus investigate society and social forms via strict testing of hypotheses. Many of these early social 'theories' with their focus on order, justice, the application of logic and the rights of the individual influenced the French and American Revolutions, with both countries formulating constitutions influenced directly by Enlightenment philosophers. However, although this shift in thinking expanded modern science greatly it did not take the study of society fully away from the philosophical.

If sociology was conceived within the Enlightenment of the eighteenth century then its birth was due to key social changes between the 1780s and the 1870s:

- *Modernisation.* The key process, a philosophical or ideological shift that was already ongoing by the time of the Enlightenment and was accelerated by the other processes listed below. Modernisation is the shift towards modern ways of viewing the world, the abandonment of traditional practices and beliefs. It marks the development of the social customs, norms and ideas, which we hold today as 'modern'.

- *Industrialisation.* The growth of industry and the shift away from an agrarian to an industrial economy. Societies based upon industrial economies are structured very differently from agrarian-based societies. Industrial societies are typically more highly stratified than agrarian economies and have greater social and economic inequalities.

- *Urbanisation.* The shift from living in the countryside in small, homogeneous communities to living in socially and culturally heterogeneous cities. This shift severed traditional social ties and customs characteristic of country living.

- *Bureaucratisation.* The application of bureaucratic forms of institutional organisation and the abandonment of traditional forms of hierarchy and patronage.

- *Societalisation.* The development of a fragmented view of identity tied not to a traditional local community but to the notion of a nation state.

- *Rise in individualism.* Enlightenment philosophers were particularly concerned with the rights and responsibilities of the individual. Most saw the development of personal liberty as crucial to the process of modernisation and promoted self-determination. Such concern for individual rights promoted and encouraged the spread of campaigns for universal suffrage and democratic values across Europe.

These processes interacted with each other and facilitated the growth of one another. They created profound social changes within a relatively short period of time – approximately four generations. Such changes to how people lived and viewed their social world demanded new ways of theorising the social world. At this point we see sociology emerging as the empirical science of society, not just based on philosophical musings but taking evidence from the social changes happening at that time. For example, Karl Marx (1818–1883) was inspired by the work of Hegel (1770–1831), a second wave Enlightenment philosopher. But Marx, unlike Hegel, actually collected evidence on which to base his theories of society. Additionally, Marx was orienting his work to actual social conditions rather than an abstract philosophical model of society. Marx's writing partner Friedrich Engels (1820–1895) visited factories and noted the terrible working and living conditions of the growing urban poor in the UK. These observations directly influenced the aims and the scope of their work. (In Chapters 4 and 5 we look in greater detail at how different social theorists interpreted and explained these dramatic social changes.)

THE SOCIOLOGICAL PERSPECTIVE

Sociology, the new 'science' of society, was empirical and sought to examine society in order to produce rules and laws concerning the operation of society. It sought to be unprejudiced and value-neutral. It did not see society as operating on commonsense lines. Society consisted of often complex social patterns which needed to be uncovered and analysed, just as a physical scientist would study a chemical compound or the laws of motion. If evidence was gathered through rigorous empirical ways then theories could be seen as true and valid.

Comfy armchairs and dirty hands

Despite the shift to an empirical approach to investigating society there remained a split between those who collected data and those who theorised from the data. If we look at a number of key early sociologists, for example Max Weber (1864–1920) and Emile Durkheim (1858–1917), we can note that the data on which their theories are based was collected not by themselves but from a variety of sources. This situation was typical for most of the nineteenth century. Data was sent back to theorists directly by commissioned collectors or more typically was collated by the theorists from a variety of sources, including missionary accounts, civil service reports, military surveys and explorer accounts. There is a problem with this situation in that the theorists could not be certain of the validity of these accounts. Was the data collected systematically? What ideological agenda did the collectors have? Did the collectors interpret their observations accurately? Evaluations of the work of most early sociologists reveal that one of the central flaws of their work is always based around uncertainties about their field data. Emile Durkheim's theory of religion expounded in *The Elementary Forms of the Religious Life* (1971, first published 1912) is based on fieldwork conducted among Australian Aborigines two decades before Durkheim wrote his book – and by fieldworkers who misinterpreted Aboriginal religious practice. This is not to completely invalidate the work of theorists such as Durkheim; there is still enough of relevance despite methodological shortcomings, but it does make some of it flawed by today's standards.

At the same time there were a small number of theorists who felt committed to conducting their own research, such as the successful businessman Charles Booth (1840–1916). Booth conducted interviews and field observations with the poor of London during the last decade of the nineteenth century, publishing his findings in the seventeen-volume work *Labour and Life of the People of London* (1902). This study is a classic example of early social research and of empirical research in general: Booth used observation, interviews and statistical analysis to produce a massive survey of poverty in late-nineteenth-century London. Theorists such as Booth had a social commitment to improving the lives of ordinary people, those most affected by social changes, and saw their research as being tools for social improvement. Booth and others were social reformers as well as researchers who wanted their work to highlight social suffering and make real changes for real people, rather than lead to esoteric theoretical debates.

After the First World War the shift towards all researchers conducting their own research was complete. It then became expected that academic theorists should play some role in the data collection process even if it was just supervisory. Receiving training in research methods and conducting some research was expected as part of the role of the professional academic sociologist. For this reason, most if not all undergraduate sociology degree courses contain research training courses within their core curriculum. More recently, however, sociology has seen a return to the division between armchair or ivory tower theorists and field researchers, particularly with the advent of postmodernity. Postmodernism's grip on sociological theory since the 1980s has led to the privileging of often-arid theories over theories generated from field data. Postmodernism has caused this by its epistemological rejection of empirical research values and its 'anything goes' approach to understanding social phenomena (Chapter 7 provides a detailed discussion of the postmodern position). The faddishness of postmodernism has led many researchers to abandon field research for 'pure' theory. It could be argued that sociology's recent inability to engage public interest in its ideas and its lack of significant participation in the policy arena can be traced to the rise in post-structuralist and postmodernist theorising. The recent government call for a 'useful' (i.e. policy-related) social science reflects this view that social research and theory have become disjointed from the 'real' world.

Influence or irrelevance?

The previous section highlighted the facts that since the beginning of sociology there have been tensions between researchers concerning the purpose of their research, and that these tensions have yet to be fully resolved. All researchers need to consider, or at some point are confronted with, the question of what is the purpose of their research and whom does it serve.

There are three main types of sociological research each with different aims and objectives. They are:

■ *Academic or 'pure' research*. Academic research is conducted by sociologists wishing to further existing knowledge or expand understanding of a specific social phenomenon. It is research being conducted with no specified policy direction, and, although it might be funded by a specific organisation, it will not be expected to directly influence wider society. Rather, academic researchers conduct their research in the hope that it will increase knowledge and understanding but do not see it as their job to change the world directly. Manuel Castells's (1994) work on information technology and globalisation and David Garland's (1990) studies on the criminal justice system fall into this category.

■ *Applied social research*. Applied social research is research funded by organisations that seek to make, change or at least influence policy decisions. Researchers will have a specific topic and range of analysis and will be expected to relate their findings to the 'real' world. This form of research dominates the fields of health, crime and education research for obvious reasons. The British Crime Survey (BCS) is an example of this type of research. Commissioned by the Home Office, it involves 40,000 respondents and has been conducted every second year since 1982. From 2001 the BCS will be conducted annually. The BCS aims to give an accurate picture of crime in the UK and is used to direct crime policy decisions.

■ *Action research*. Action research which is conducted by researchers with the intention of changing the lives of the people being studied through empowering them and making them full participants in the research process. This type of research is explicitly political and rejects the notion of the neutral and uninvolved researcher. It has been particularly promoted by feminist researchers (see Chapter 8). An example of this type of research can be seen in Ann Oakley's work on maternity care (1981).

Discussion questions

1 Consider the strengths and weaknesses of each type of research.

2 Make a list of those whom you think research should serve.

3 What possible tensions might there be in this list?

THE METHOD–THEORY RELATIONSHIP

We have highlighted the difficulty of divorcing theory from methods. A sociology completely built on theory is often too disconnected from the 'real' world or remains largely unsubstantiated due to its lack of empirical evidence. However, a sociology that is all research and no theory is purely descriptive; the data might be interesting but there is no interpretive framework on which to hang it. The fact is that theory and research are intrinsically linked; and the teaching of both typically within most sociology undergraduate curricula is evidence of this.

However, the theory–research relationship is one of delicate balance. The two are interlinked and it is often difficult to note which comes first, theory or research. There are two types of theory–data relationships of which you should be aware: deductive and inductive. A deductive approach begins with a theoretical proposition that is then investigated and shown to be either true or false via deduction. An inductive approach starts with data; the researcher notes patterns in the data, and from this induces a theory. In reality all research involves a combination of the two approaches and it is unhelpful to try to delineate them. For example, one might note that people on a bus select seats in what appears to be a rule-governed fashion. People tend to sit beside others of the same age and gender. This observation might induce the working hypothesis: 'seating patterns on buses are rule-governed'. One could then test this theory (deduction). The other approach can also be the basis for investigation. One might begin with a theoretical proposition, such as 'are seating patterns on buses rule-governed?' This proposition might be put forth based on research conducted on other forms of public transport (induction). The researcher could then test this hypothesis via deduction. However, the data might generate additional observations that induce other theories and so on. It is almost impossible to be sure what comes first, data or theory.

Karl Popper (1902–1994), a philosopher of science, highlighted this point in his works *The Logic of Scientific Discovery* (1934) and *Conjectures and Refutations* (1963). Popper notes that science portrays itself as based upon inductive theory, i.e. observations lead to theories. However, he draws attention to the fact that most observation is preceded by some sort of basic theorising; if not, how would a scientist know what to look for? Science also claims to draw universal laws and theories from empirically valid observations. Popper then highlights the fact that all observations by their nature are bounded by time and place, that is they are finite, and asks how can we draw universal and timeless laws from such essentially bounded instances? Popper views science as based upon what he calls conjectures and refutations. A theory is in essence a mere conjecture until the theorist can show it cannot be refuted, that is, a theorist should attempt to look for all those elements which might challenge a theory's validity. Popper used the now-famous example of white and black swans. We could propose the theory that all swans are white based upon countless observations of swans on a river. However, it would take the arrival of just one black swan to overthrow this theory. A new theory that explained that the majority of swans were white but which also accounted for the occurrence of black swans would be necessary. Popper termed this approach of looking for the examples that challenge the validity of research falsification.

The distinction between induction and deduction was a source of great debate in sociology during the expansion of the subject in the twentieth century, when sociologists and philosophers of science, such as Talcott Parsons, Karl Popper and Peter Winch were debating whether sociology should be viewed as a scientific discipline (a 'social science') or something closer to the humanities. Deduction was associated with those researchers trying to do research in a 'scientific' way, whereas induction was more closely allied to researchers conducting interpretive research. However, today a more pragmatic approach is taken which acknowledges the fact that the two processes are in fact interchangeable and the task of separating them a pointless one. The key point to note is that sociology cannot go forward without both theoretical work and research data.

WAYS OF KNOWING

We have been discussing the theory–data relationship and how to judge the validity of theories, but what about the data itself? How can we be sure that our data is accurate? This is an important question because if our data is not accurate we cannot be confident that our theoretical frameworks for understanding certain social phenomena are insightful. This is compounded within sociology by the fact that we attempt to explore people's experience of their social worlds. We rely on what people tell us about their world and therefore we rely on their way of viewing or understanding the world. However, how people know and understand their world can change. We noted this point earlier in the discussion about the distinction between pre-modern and modern ways of thinking about the social and natural worlds. If we look back through history or across cultures we can see variation in understanding physical and social phenomena. A simple example is that of the existence of micro-organisms, such as bacteria. Until the late nineteenth century, explanations of illness or disease based on the idea of organisms, like bacteria, that could not be seen by the naked eye were derided. Instead such illnesses were explained in a variety of ways, such as religious morality (the afflicted punished for sins) or through quasi-scientific notions ('bad air' or 'black humours'). Today we accept the idea of micro-organisms causing illness and find other explanations implausible as we now have the technology to observe such organisms. Thus how we know and understand disease and infection has radically altered within a century.

Types of knowledge

As well as appreciating the fact that how we know the world can change through time and across cultures, we should also be aware of the different sources of knowledge that exist and on which people draw to explore and understand their world. There are six basic categories of knowledge from which people draw:

- *Commonsense knowledge.* This is universally accepted; typically experiential knowledge which people assume everyone in his or her culture will know. An example would be the fact that fire burns. Every culture around the world accepts this fact, although it might have contrasting names for 'fire' and explanations of how fire works. However, all those cultures would view someone who repeatedly stuck their hand in the fire as a social misfit. This deviant status would be placed upon them as they failed to use commonsense, everyday knowledge which everyone holds true.

- *Authority-based knowledge.* This is knowledge which we hold to be true because a figure of authority, such as a parent, a teacher or a government, tells us it is true. This type of knowledge can be very persuasive but it relies upon how we view the figure of authority. For example, we may reject our parents' views of the world as we mature and rely on other sources of knowledge.

- *Experiential knowledge.* This is knowledge based upon our own personal experiences. Other forms of knowledge, for example, authority figures, commonsense and scientific, might view the use of drugs as dangerous. However, if our experiences of drug-taking have been positive and have not damaged our health, we would base our view of drugs upon our own personal experiences.

- *Traditional knowledge.* This is knowledge based upon the authority of the past and the strength of cultural symbols. People draw upon tradition to explain and justify many social phenomena, such as fox-hunting, female circumcision and ethnic conflicts. The strength of traditional knowledge relies on the position of such traditions within a given society.

- *Non-rational knowledge.* This is knowledge based on faith rather than direct observational experience or scientific testing. A typical example of this would be religious beliefs. These offer the believer a way of viewing and understanding the world but it is one based on faith and is viewed by non-believers as non-rational. This form of knowledge used to dominate European society but is now one of a number of competing forms of knowledge from which we draw. People tend to use this type of knowledge for facing up to life-altering events or in answering existential questions, such as why are we here?

- *Scientific knowledge.* This is knowledge based on rigorous empirical testing and is seen as the most valid and reliable. An example would be the laws of gravity within physics that can be shown time and again to work. This form of knowledge dominates our society.

If we take the example of the laws of gravity we can see the variation within each type of knowledge. Imagine we are confronted by a man wishing to throw himself from the top of a twenty-storey building. Using commonsense knowledge we could advise him not to do this as it would result in his death, basing this on cultural understanding of height and body mass. However, commonsense does not explain why this should be the case. We might call the police and try to use authority to force the man not to jump. But our jumper might claim that he has jumped from such a height before and survived, thus rejecting authority and relying upon his own experiential knowledge. Using non-rational knowledge we might tell him that he might survive such a fall if he has faith in God who would not let him be killed. However, there is no way of showing this would be the case unless someone actually attempted such a folly, and it relies upon our jumper's level of personal faith. Scientific knowledge, however, does offer an explanation as to why a person jumping from the top of a high building would die, due to the laws of gravity. The laws of gravity can be easily demonstrated and replicated over and over to convince our jumper not to jump.

Max Weber termed people's ways of viewing and thinking about their world a worldview. Weber characterised pre-modern worldviews as dominated by traditional and religious ways of thinking. He saw the shift towards a rational and scientific-based worldview as a key feature of modernisation. Weber saw worldview as a fixed, unitary feature. Alfred Schutz, in *The Phenomenology of the Social World* (1932), reformulated Weber's idea of worldview and presented it as a more fluid entity that could change through an individual's life as socialisation patterns and influences changed. Peter Berger and Thomas Luckmann, in *The Social Construction of Reality* (1966), developed this concept further to demonstrate that individuals maintain a multiplicity of often competing and contradictory worldviews in modern society. Thus most of us draw on all six types of knowledge in different situations, typically without noting any inherent contradictions. The researcher needs to reflect upon this fact when dealing with people's knowledge claims.

Discussion questions

1 List the different sources of knowledge that you rely upon in different situations.

2 Suggest a situaton in which you might need to use each of the six types of knowledge.

EPISTEMOLOGY

The area of philosophy that ponders questions relating to knowledge is called epistemology. This word comes from ancient Greek: *episteme* = knowledge, *logos* = study of; and so literally means 'the study of knowledge'. Philosophers interested in epistemology explore how people develop knowledge about their world and what form this knowledge takes. They are interested in how people perceive the world around them and what they base their ideas of the world upon. Social research poses epistemological questions as we are trying to construct knowledge about our and others' social world(s): how can we know something to be true and how can our data be accurate? Researchers must consider their own view of knowing the social world as this impacts directly upon their means of collecting data. Consider the example in Box 1.1.

BOX 1.1

The mermaid and the duck-billed platypus

Circuses and travelling fairs were very popular in nineteenth-century Europe. One feature of these fairs was the exhibition of freaks of nature and new alleged fantastic creatures from around the world. Along with so-called bearded ladies and wolf-boys were exhibited specimens of mythological creatures. The most famous instances of these were the popular exhibition of mermaids. These supposed mermaids were typically dead monkeys with fish tails tied to them. However, our Victorian forebears believed such mermaids to be real creatures and marvelled at such displays. We might find this funny today that people could be so easily duped by unscrupulous showmen such as P.T. Barnum, but we need to put these beliefs in the context of the age. In a world which was still being explored and classified, and to people who rarely left their own regions let alone countries and had worldviews which were in the process of change from pre-modern to modern, mythological creatures could possibly exist.

   In the nineteenth century, zoologists were still discovering and classifying new species of animals. When naturalists came across the duck-billed platypus, an animal native to Australia, they believed it to be a fake. A mammal that lays eggs, swims, has a duck's bill and webbed feet but a body like an otter did not fit into any existing understanding of mammals or zoological classificatory systems. Platypi were dissected in an attempt to show that they were fakes. We now know that platypi are indeed real animals and can explain their odd characteristics in the light of what we now know about the unique evolution of the animal life of the Australian land mass.

   It is interesting to consider why the Victorians viewed the real animal as a fake and the fake as real. Mermaids have always been a part of western mythology and so appear as part of the classificatory system of western thought. Such classificatory systems had no place for the platypus as it had no precedent, nothing to relate it to. The Victorians were aware of the fakery that surrounded fairs and circuses. In a way, the Victorians were making a fairly rational decision about what to believe and what not to believe. This decision was made in the light of their existing knowledge about the social and natural world. But this decision affected how scientists did their work – trying to prove mermaids to be real and platypi to be fakes, rather than the other way around. This is just one example of how existing knowledge about the world and how people have formulated their understanding of the world can impact upon research and theory formulation.

Source: based on Ritvo, 1997

Discussion question

List other examples of how knowledge differs both historically and culturally.

HERMENEUTICS

As well as considering knowledge, researchers also face the problem of making sense of their data, which so often consists of what people tell them in the form of completed questionnaires or through interviews. Typically our study of a social phenomenon consists of our and others' perceptions of it. On what do we base our choices of interpretation of data? Consider the example in Box 1.2.

This example is simplistic but it emphasises the issue facing all researchers: how do we interpret data in the light of competing and conflicting accounts of the same event or phenomenon? To solve the problem, researchers turn to hermeneutics. Hermeneutics is the field of philosophy concerned with interpretation. The word 'hermeneutics' comes from ancient Greek and refers to Hermes the messenger of the gods in Greek mythology. Hermes is often portrayed as having two faces, relating to his habit of muddling or losing messages, and generally trying to trick senders and receivers of his messages. It is for this reason that he gives his name to the philosophy of interpretation as a warning to all of us who try to interpret what others say or do: there are potential tricks, muddles and confusions everywhere – things might not always be what they appear to be, or what people say is not always what is 'true'. It is for this reason that researchers must consider how to develop statements of interpretation. How researchers choose to interpret their data depends partly on the researchers' epistemological choices and positions. Hermeneutical and epistemological decisions and their consideration work together and interlink to help form a researcher's methodology.

BOX 1.2

Who kissed whom?

Imagine your best friend has been dating your brother. Your brother then comes to you and tells you that he has broken up with your friend. He tells you that she was unfaithful and uncaring, citing various examples of her behaviour. Then later that same day your friend visits you and also informs you that she has ended her relationship with your brother, claiming he was unfaithful and inconsiderate, again giving you examples of his behaviour. Already you have two accounts of one relationship's end. You then receive further accounts of why the relationship ended from other friends, family, and perhaps even workmates. Imagine how many people might give you an account of the same separation, not to mention your own interpretation of events.

Discussion questions

1 Whose version are you most likely to believe? Why?

2 How would you gather evidence to decide whose version is right?

METHODOLOGY

Methodology is the overall philosophical framework of a piece of research. It involves the researcher's epistemological and hermeneutical positions, along with personal, political and ethical choices. Often, methodology is defined in a rather limited sense as the methods used to conduct a piece of research, but methodology is not just about pragmatic, instrumental choices but about deeply philosophical ones. It is a choice about how researchers view the process of knowing the social world and how they intend to orient their research within that social world. The methodological choices taken by researchers affects the entire approach of their research including the types of data collection techniques used.

There are two key types of methodological approach used within sociology:

■ the scientific methodology
■ the interpretivist methodology.

The scientific methodology

The scientific methodology is also commonly referred to as the social scientific, positive, positivist or naturalist approach. We noted earlier that sociology appeared as one of a number of new disciplines that emerged as a consequence of the Enlightenment and in reaction to sweeping social changes of the late eighteenth and early to mid-nineteenth centuries. The Enlightenment saw the scientific model as the key to investigating the natural world and to producing progress in the natural and social spheres. This model is based on a particular epistemological view of the world. The true nature of reality, in the natural world, is 'out there' to be defined, classified and measured. There is, in other words, an objective reality that can be investigated.

Enlightenment philosophers and scientists saw the universe as a logical and organised place run on rational and ordered principles. The key to understanding the universe was to uncover these principles. It was believed that this would be achievable through the application of rigorous and strict testing of hypotheses and their being proven or disproved on the basis of empirical data.

This approach also privileges objectivity and seeks to eradicate all bias that might taint results. The scientific model is one of deductive empiricism. The ultimate aim is to produce theories or laws that have been empirically tested and shown to be valid and therefore 'true'. Scientists seek out universally valid, timeless and applicable laws concerning the natural world. Validity can be further tested through the application of theories to other situations and in the fact that experiments can be repeated and still produce the same results, so-called causal laws. Such universal laws then allow us to predict results in the light of what we have already discovered and proven. For example, Newton's Laws of Motion can be applied to phenomena and situations that Newton could not have comprehended when he was first defining his theories of the motion of objects. Despite this fact, the laws are still applicable and predictive.

This methodological model states that something exists if it can be proven to exist and the reverse is also true: phenomena can be proven to not exist. An example of this might be magic. We could take a set of so-called magical spells and show through careful testing that they do not work. It would be possible to demonstrate that magic does not exist because it can be shown not to exist.

Early sociologists took this scientific model and applied it to the social world. The following quote from Durkheim encapsulates this approach: 'what it demands is that the sociologist put himself in the same state of mind as the physicist, chemist, or physiologist when he probes into a still unexplored region of the scientific domain' (1938: xiv). If the natural world was an organised, logical place so too was the social world. Society was deemed to run on sets of universal laws that could be uncovered just like the laws of physics or of chemistry. Auguste Comte (1798–1857) was the first to outline what a 'science of society' would entail. He did this in his six-volume work *Cours de philosophie positivistic* (*The Course of Positive Philosophy*) published between 1830 and 1842. Comte saw sociology as a 'social science', that is a 'science of society', that should adopt the methodological approach of the natural sciences; he labelled his method positivism (Comte's approach is examined more fully in Chapter 4).

Positivists see the social world as ordered rather than chaotic or random. If the social world, or indeed the universe in general, were not ordered then we would not be able to make predictions based on scientific laws. The fact that science can be shown to work proves that the world in general is logical, regular and timeless. This being the case, the social world can be classified, defined and shown to work on similar ordered universal laws. The job of the social scientist, then, was to uncover these laws through the same strict and rigorous testing of hypotheses in the value-free, objective style of the natural scientist. The resultant social laws would be universal, that is applicable to all societies, and timeless, that is unchanging. These universal social laws could allow social scientists to predict future social patterns and behaviours.

Positivists viewed society as 'out there', an objective reality that acted upon individuals. This was very much an Enlightenment view of society and it put forth a particular view of the individual. Individuals were self-interested rationalists who responded to social forces; and all individuals acted in essentially the same ways. This is a mechanical model of society. In a way it presents society and individuals as homogeneous entities, ignoring diversity of action and interests. People are presented as robots or machines, without free will, constantly acted upon rather than independent actors in their own right. This view of the individual can, again, be seen to originate from a model based in the natural sciences. Just as natural phenomena are acted upon by natural forces through the laws of cause and effect then so too are social phenomena. Sociologists like Auguste Comte and Herbert Spencer (1820–1903) adopted the Enlightenment view of progress via rational thinking and they hoped that the discovery of universal social laws would facilitate the progress of society.

Positivism was further refined and applied in the work of Emile Durkheim who outlined his methodological approach in *Les Règles de la méthode sociologique* (*The Rules of Sociological Method*) published in 1895. Durkheim found Comte and Spencer's work still too philosophical and not sociological enough. It is in the work of Durkheim that we see positivism being applied in its truest sense. A good example is in Durkheim's analysis of suicide, *Le Suicide: étude de sociologique* (*Suicide: A Study in Sociology*) published in 1897. Durkheim had stated that 'social facts are things and must be treated as such' (1938: 143). He wished to apply this approach to theorising suicide. He argued that suicide could be treated as a social fact rather than as a personal, psychological or theological issue. Durkheim looked at suicide rates across a number of countries, noting a great variation between nations, and proposed that variation between national rates could be accounted for in terms of social and economic disruption. In nations undergoing social or economic crises or changes there was potential for a disruption to social cohesion or harmony. Anything that threatened social harmony was likely to increase the suicide rate. In other words, economic and social forces acted upon individuals, often inducing suicides. Durkheim saw suicide as an anomic act, that is an act carried out by someone who feels disengaged and alienated from society, without a role or clear purpose within that society. On the basis of his observations, Durkheim proposed a universal law of suicide: there is a direct and causal relationship between suicide rates and social and economic changes.

An element in this law is the level of social integration: effectively integrated societies will have lower suicide rates despite social or economic forces acting upon them. He saw this law as universally applicable and also predictive, that is it could be used to predict future suicide rates in different countries. Durkheim believed sociology had the potential to explain, predict and perhaps allow us to reform the social world. Durkheim's work was hugely influential and was continued by theorists such as the American sociologist Talcott Parsons who outlined his version of positivism in *The Structure of Social Action* (1937).

The work of Durkheim and Parsons popularised the positivist or scientific approach and it became the main sociological methodology for the first half of the twentieth century. This methodology was so central to the sociological enterprise because, until the 1960s at least, sociology saw itself as a social science. The scientific methodological approach also afforded seemingly universal social laws and empirically verified data, both of which allowed sociology to play a role in social policy. The founders of sociology, such as Comte, Spencer and Durkheim, all believed that informing policy and promoting social change should be an intrinsic part of sociology. Thus the positivist or scientific approach appeared best suited to achieving the aims and objectives of classical sociology. However, by the 1960s, alternative methodologies were becoming more accepted and widely utilised. Despite challenges from other methodologies it is important to remember that the scientific approach is still typically privileged within sociology and dominates in subject areas driven by and directly linked to policy, such as health, crime and education.

The interpretivist methodology

It was shown above that the scientific methodology emerged from the Enlightenment and was seen by theorists as a means of advancing the Enlightenment 'project' of modernisation. Ironically, interpretivism also emerged from Enlightenment thought, although it took a very different epistemological direction. The beginnings of interpretivism can be traced to the work of what are known as second wave Enlightenment philosophers, such as Hegel. The second wave of the Enlightenment was not a rejection or criticism of it but an attempt to reflect and develop upon it. There was an insistence that in order to progress Enlightenment principles it would be necessary to open up the Enlightenment itself as a historical and social force for investigation. It should not be an objective, neutral, independent entity but be seen as a product of socio-cultural forces and bounded in time.

The inspiration for many second-wave philosophers was the work of Immanuel Kant (1724–1804). Kant was a lone voice among first-wave Enlightenment philosophers in that he was less interested in what he called realism, that is objective reality, and more in perception; and he departed from the scientific view of an objective world 'out there'. He believed the world to be the product of human perception and that as perceptions changed so the world changed. What is 'out there' is actually 'in' our heads and in our perceptions of others' views of the world. This theory was called idealism and it echoes the basic epistemological view of interpretivism that would be developed much later.

Hegel and other second-wave philosophers were less interested in scientific, objective investigation of the world and more preoccupied with questions regarding perceptions of culture and knowledge, and the contested nature of concepts such as knowledge, logic and truth. Hegel placed the exploration of what he called 'being' at the centre of his philosophy. In works such as *The Philosophy of Right* (1821) he sought to explore how individuals orient themselves in their world through the exploration of concepts and perceptions.

Although there are differences and disputes between the work of Kant and Hegel they do share a common epistemological root, and a unified philosophical strand can be seen to run through interpretivism. It is a view of the world as not being 'out there' in an objective sense but existing in people's perceptions of it. Everything is perception and in order to explore the world one must explore consciousness, perception or what Hegel termed 'being'. If everything is perception then there can be no such thing as an objective reality: no two people share exactly the same perception, although there might be some commonality. Without an objective reality there can be no universal causal laws as everything is affected by perception; and, as Kant noted, perceptions change with time and events. Hegel sought to explore the boundedness of culture through exploring key concepts and how they change through history and culture. This raises the question of what is possible when there are no universal laws to formulate or to apply. Both Kant and Hegel emphasise the exploration of experience and perception as our route to exploring the social world. Intrinsic in this epistemological model is the view of the individual as an active social agent. Additionally, hermeneutics becomes crucial to the success of interpretivism (see p. 17 above).

The concern with exploring reality, consciousness and perception evident in the work of Kant and Hegel was developed more fully at the end of the nineteenth century for two reasons. Firstly, such philosophical ideas mixed with Victorian Romanticism, which was an artistic movement emphasising emotion, individuality, freedom and perception over hard empiricism and rationality. Romanticism was particularly strong in Germany and many of the early proponents of interpretivism were German sociologists heavily influenced by Romanticism. Secondly, the insights of early social science subjects such as psychology and sociology allowed researchers to further explore the philosophical ideas put forward by the likes of Kant and Hegel and to attempt to align philosophy with social science 'fact'.

The two key figures in fully defining the interpretivist approach were the German sociologists Wilhelm Dilthey (1833–1911) and Max Weber.

Dilthey rejected the use of the natural science model for investigating social life. In his work *Einleitung in die Geisteswissenschaften* (*Introduction to the Human Sciences*, 1988) published in 1883, he contrasted the natural sciences, based upon *Erklärung* or abstract explanation with what he called *Geisteswissenschaften* or human sciences which he felt should be based upon *verstehen* or empathetic understanding. One could not study people using the natural science model. Dilthey instead placed interpretation at the centre of his methodology. Human science had to be an interpretive activity drawing strongly upon hermeneutics. Dilthey demanded that researchers reflect upon their and others' perceptions and experiences; the personal was key to exploring the social world. He showed his philosophical roots in a rejection of universal absolutes and an interpretation of history and culture as relative, that is changing and bounded by time rather than timeless. A final and powerful strand of Dilthey's approach was to admit that social life was so complex that it was never fully explainable and thus unanswered questions should exist. Indeed the unanswered questions were seen as an important part of the interpretive process.

Max Weber, in *The Methodology of the Social Sciences* (1949), further developed Dilthey's methodological approach by stressing the concept of *verstehen*. He saw the creation of empathetic understanding as the route into understanding or comprehending social action. Weber sought to access the worldviews of others and saw *verstehen* as the way to do this. He placed great emphasis on the analysis of individual agency: he wanted to uncover the individual's motives, feelings and perceptions. The reason for this lies in the epistemological approach Weber was taking. Interpretivism states that the world is constructed through the interaction of individuals, each with their own subjective experiences and perceptions. This mixing of subjectivities creates social worlds where commonality is created through the sharing of meaning. In focusing upon the individual's motives and actions, Weber believed he could get closer to understanding how meaning is created, imputed and shared in different social situations or in relation to different activities.

Weber's methodology focused upon what people viewed as meaningful and relevant in their social lives. However, Weber demands something more from the researcher than just observing human interaction. He contrasts two types of *verstehen*: *acktueller* and *erkländer*. The former is direct objective observation, e.g. one plus one equals two. The latter refers to a more complex form of understanding, which is about creating a situation whereby one person is able to gain a limited insight or understanding into another's life through creating an environment for empathy. In a basic way it is like being in a foreign country and listening to a joke. We might not get the full meaning of it but we understand enough to see why others are laughing. *Erkländer verstehen* demands reflection and engagement from the researcher. Only by attempting to immerse themselves within the social situation under study can researchers hope to create the right environment for empathy and thus useful interpretation.

Thus in the work of Dilthey and Weber we see the clarification of interpretivism as a methodology founded upon the epistemological view that everything is subjective perception and experience rather than an objective, 'out there' reality. Universal absolutes cannot exist in a world consisting of subjectivities and historical relativity. Society consists of individuals with agency and subjective experience. Action and meaning can be understood through the use of empathetic interpretive techniques. Research consists of a sequence of hermeneutic acts.

Interpretivism was relatively unsuccessful and unpopular in sociology until the 1960s. As was noted earlier, scientific methodological approaches dominated for a variety of reasons. Interpretivism seemed to align sociology more towards the humanities and philosophy rather than the sciences, an approach which went against the idea of a social science. Additionally, interpretivism's eschewing of objective facts meant it appeared unable to deliver policy insights – its reliability was doubted. Policy-makers typically prefer quantifiable results, and scientific approaches appear to do this better. Nevertheless, interpretivism maintained small pockets of popularity, predominantly in continental Europe, with the work of Alfred Schutz in Austria, and in the USA with the work of the Chicago School. The latter remains the best example of the sustained implementation of interpretivism. Under the direction of Robert E. Park, the Department of Sociology at the University of Chicago put Weber's methodological ideas into practice and the results can be seen in the work of, among others, G.H. Mead, W.I. Thomas and William Whyte, and in the postwar period Goffman and Becker. Most research done by the Chicago School focused upon the urban poor, socially marginalised and disenfranchised. They sought to link social research with social action and there was a strong sense of aligning research with social reform. These researchers also attempted to empower their research subjects through the research process. The work of the Chicago School offers an example of interpretivism as a possible driver of policy and reform (see Chapter 6 for a more detailed discussion of the Chicago School).

The sustained use and development of interpretivism at Chicago produced a number of different variations of interpretivism all founded on the same epistemological principles but utilising different approaches to applying these principles.

These include: phenomenology (see the work of Schutz, Peter Berger and Thomas Luckman), symbolic interactionism (see the work of Goffman), ethnography (see the work of Whyte), and ethnomethodology (see the work of Garfinkel). Interpretivism became more popular from the late 1960s onwards owing to ideological shifts both within and outside of sociology, which impacted upon theoretical positions within it.

EPISTEMOLOGICAL REVOLUTIONS OR CRISES?

The postwar emergence of neo-Marxism, feminism and post-colonialist critiques and writing caused sociologists to critique theory and practice in the light of wider social and political changes and movements. Paul Feyerband in *Against Method* (1975) noted that the history of science demonstrated that there has been no unified scientific approach and instead urged theoretical and methodological diversity: 'All methodologies have their limitations and the only "rule" that survives is "anything goes"' (1975: 296). Within sociology there emerged theoretical schools, such as structuralism, post-structuralism and feminism, which were highly critical of scientific methodologies and instead sought to apply more ethical, empathetic and possibly empowering (for research subjects) methodologies and techniques (see Chapters 7 and 8 for further discussion). Interpretivist methodologies were seen as capable of doing this and began to be popularised within sociology, particularly by feminist sociologists such as Liz Stanley, Sue Wise and Ann Oakley. However, despite advances in the use and acceptance of interpretivist sociology there remains a view that the methodology is less useful and rigorous than scientific approaches both in terms of playing a policy role and in terms of doing effective sociology.

The epistemological revolutions of the postwar era have created not only positive change but also crisis. The sense of crisis within the subject has been prompted by the extent of epistemological debate. It was noted earlier that postmodernism had emphasised theory over method. In a similar way, the impact of postmodernism has created a research crisis. Feyerband's 'anything goes' approach can lead to nihilism: if anything goes, does that also mean nothing matters? Similarly, if anything goes what does that mean for sociological research? Can we even call our research sociological? In other words, it poses the question of what is sociological research for, and for whom? In a way this returns the discipline to the debates of the nineteenth century, rather than sending it forward into the twenty-first.

However, in a more positive light, a sense of a methodological continuum now predominates, with few researchers adhering to the strict polar opposites of science versus interpretation. Although objective scientific research is still privileged by policy planners and funding organisations, interpretivism is now an accepted sociological methodology. The reality is that most researchers are aware of the limitations of each stance and take a more moderate and typically pragmatic view, often using both approaches in tandem in order to gain a fuller picture.

Science		**Interpretation**
Positivism		Phenomenology

$$\longleftarrow \!\longrightarrow$$

| Objectivity | | Subjectivity |

We can see on the diagram above the continuum of methodological choices and the two opposing epistemological poles. Most research falls away from the poles as few researchers conduct completely scientific or interpretive research. Instead most researchers would place their research part-way along the axis, moving towards the pole of influence. Chapter 2 demonstrates that practical considerations will often mean that the methodological idealism held by a researcher is compromised.

EXERCISES

1 The development of sociological research

(a) Describe the essential characteristics of sociological research.

(b) What factors influenced the development of sociological research?

(c) Consider the scientific model of research. When and how did it emerge?

(d) Consider the interpretivist model of research. When and how did it emerge?

(e) What common ground is there between the two approaches?

2 Applying the methodological models

(a) Choose a specific social phenomenon and consider how a researcher would investigate it using (i) a scientific methodology and (ii) an interpretivist methodology. (Social phenomena you might consider could include educational attainment levels of different groups; patterns of illegal drug-taking; attitudes to work and so on.)

(b) Using your chosen example, consider what each of the methodologies provides to your research which the other does not.

(c) Again using your chosen example, consider the drawbacks of each methodology. (Consider practical and theoretical problems here.)

Chapter 2

Doing social research

JULIE F. SCOTT

In this chapter the focus is on the practicalities of undertaking social research, that is the actual planning, doing and writing up of research. The research process can be sub-divided into seven key stages; each will be looked at in turn in this chapter, with particular emphasis placed on their application in actual research.

STAGE 1: CHOICE OF TOPIC

In the previous chapter the reasons behind research were discussed. It was noted that some researchers choose to do their research in order to build on existing knowledge, while others see their research as being part of an empowering process that may directly promote real change. However, before considering the reason for our research we must first step back and consider what exactly we wish to investigate: what is our research topic? We are lucky in sociology in that, technically, anything linked to society or people can be deemed worthy of sociological research. This can basically cover most social phenomena, from what might at first appear to be mundane or trivial to global social issues – for example, housework (Oakley 1974), gender and language (Tannen 1994), Hells Angels (Thompson 1985), life in prisons (Cohen and Taylor 1972), religious beliefs (Barker 1984) or racial discrimination (Back 1996).

Many researchers begin the process of topic selection based upon a broad category of sociological phenomena, for example, 'crime' or 'health'. They then narrow it down to a specific topic. You could start with the broad category of 'crime', narrow it down to 'white-collar crime' and further down to the 'victims' experience of white-collar crime'. However, there are competing factors that are at play when deciding a topic for research. Three of the most important of these factors to be considered are:

- *Professional factors.* These involve considering the context of the researcher and their research in a public sense. In the case of an academic researcher this involves questions such as: How will the research develop and aid the researcher's professional profile? Does the research fit in with the mission and profile of the researcher's 'host' institution (whether a university or a government agency)? Does the planned research fulfil grant award criteria? In the case of a student, a professional factor might be: how will this research fulfil particular assessment criteria?

- *Personal factors.* These relate to the researcher's personal interests, beliefs and often ideological positions. For example, a researcher might be a feminist who seeks to use her work to facilitate the empowerment of women. Similarly a researcher might be particularly committed to researching the low participation rates in higher education among children from low socio-economic classes due to personal experiences of struggle in getting to university due to class background.

- *Feasibility factors.* These involve considering the practical constraints and limitations placed upon the research. Such constraints might involve a shortage of time or money to fulfil an ambitious research plan. It also involves researchers considering their own limitations in terms of research skills, experience and personality. It would be foolish for a shy, inexperienced researcher, who lacked interviewing skills, to try to conduct participative research among, for example, teenage gangs. Finally, there is the consideration of whether the topic itself can be researched fully given existing research techniques and technology.

BOX 2.1

Research tip

It is always difficult to select a research topic. At first it might seem daunting simply because of the sheer amount of choice. One way of going about this might be to think about the different topics so far studied in your sociology course. Ask yourself these questions: Which ones did you enjoy and why? Which ones interested you? Which ones have you been motivated to read beyond prescribed class readings? Which ones have you already been assessed upon? Many students (and indeed researchers) select topics based on subjects which have always interested them and which they enjoy studying – it is always easier to maintain motivation during research if you enjoy and are interested in the topic. Similarly, many students prefer to stick to subjects they have already been assessed on because they can enter the research confident of their level of comprehension of the topic. Of course, many still prefer to have a complete change and pick a new topic for the sake of variety. However you choose a topic you must bear in mind the three factors listed above if you want to avoid wasting time and effort on research which is doomed to fail.

STAGE 2: REVIEW LITERATURE ON THE TOPIC

Once a topic has been chosen the researcher should embark on a thorough review of the literature available on that topic. This process can often take many months or even up to a year for postgraduate research projects or funded ones. Sometimes researchers do not have the luxury of time. However, even with time restrictions all researchers agree that it is essential to survey what has already been published on a particular subject. There are reasons for doing this:

- *To avoid repeating work already done.* Imagine spending valuable time and effort only to realise that someone else did a similar study ten years before you. Of course some researchers conduct follow-up studies that revisit the participants of an earlier study after a suitable time lapse, but such studies are not repetitive and seek to expand knowledge of the topic previously studied.

- *To try to build on existing work.* Many researchers seek to advance ideas or theories which have already been published, but feel that they can take them further. Similarly, some research benefits from being put into a new context or being updated, for example theories of gender and ethnicity have changed radically over the past 40 years.

- *To seek out the gaps in the existing literature to produce something new and original.* Researchers are always seeking to find the new angle on often old ideas/ topics or to identify completely new areas for research. For example, a growing field within sociology is the study of technology, and particularly the nature of our interaction with computers and the Internet; such topics simply did not exist previously.

- *To avoid repeating others' errors.* By reviewing the work of others we can, hopefully, follow their good practice and avoid repeating any errors they made.

Conducting a literature survey

At first a literature survey or review can seem a daunting task as most of the key areas of social life have been well studied. However, it has never been easier, thanks to electronic media. Obviously the time spent on a survey and the thoroughness of it depend on the research in question. The survey conducted for a student essay will be much shorter and less detailed than that for a dissertation or a postgraduate thesis, let alone a funded research project. Here are a few basic steps:

- *Look through general introductory textbooks on your topic and see who are the key theorists and writers.* This is a quick way to locate the important works on your subject. This can then snowball through obtaining additional names and titles through reading each book in turn.

- *Prepare keywords or phrases to use in database/catalogue searches.* You can use keywords to cast a wide search of print and electronic databases. Make a list of possible words and combinations of words. For example, if your topic was drug abuse among rural youth, potential keywords might be: 'youth', 'rural', 'drug-abuse', 'youth-drug-abuse', 'adolescent-drug-abuse' and so forth. The idea is to start general and then become more specific.

■ *Searching library catalogues.* Most libraries have online catalogues, many of which can be accessed via the Internet, so you do not even have to visit the library in question in order to check the availability of a book. As well as local university and municipal library collections, a key resource is the British Library. All books published in the UK are held there and you can order titles from them. You can use keyword searches in order to see the extent of a library's collections on a particular topic.

■ *Conduct a series of database searches.* These searches can be used to find specific titles or for more general trawling via the use of keywords. Databases have long been a resource for researchers. The earliest ones were print collections, such as the *Social Science Citation Index*. Now electronic versions are available. There is a wide range of available databases, such as *ASSIA* (lists books and journal articles within the social sciences globally) and *Global Books in Print* (lists all books published globally). Database searches provide an abstract for each book or article so you can decide which ones sound the most useful.

■ *Internet.* This is a growing resource for researchers. Most organisations, news-papers and companies have web sites, often with archives, which can be used to search for data or reports. The Internet also works on keyword searches via different search engines.

■ *Once you have a list, start to prioritise it.* Having read through abstracts, consider the order of importance of your titles and read them in this order. Remember to try to vary your reading between primary and secondary sources. The former are original works by specific authors whereas the latter provide accounts and discussion of others' works. If you rely on too many general textbooks or secondary sources you will find that your research will be superficial and general. Also, ensure that your sources are up to date. If you are researching e-commerce and your latest title was published in 1980 it is fair to say you have not searched enough.

■ *What to look for.* When reading for a literature survey you should approach each title with the following questions in mind and try and answer them:
  – What are the bibliographic details? Title, author(s)/editor(s), date of publication, name of publisher, page numbers. You will need this information when writing up your research.
  – What was the specific topic and general research question/problem?
  – What was the method used to collect data and how was it implemented?
  – What results did the research generate?
  – What conclusions did the researcher draw?
  – How would you evaluate the research?
  – Did the research cite other studies that might be useful to you?

BOX 2.2

Research tip

Familiarise yourself with your university library and its resources: most will run training sessions on database CD-Roms and other search facilities; making use of these will save valuable time. Additionally consider neighbouring libraries, university or public (major municipal libraries often have surprisingly good collections and many hold valuable archives). Finally, get to know the procedure for ordering from the British Library and learn to use its online catalogue (www.bl.uk).

Of course, researchers do not stop reading as soon as they start their research. As research continues, and as results come in, the researcher might wish to target his or her reading to specific titles or topics. As writing-up begins, the search for related materials published elsewhere continues.

STAGE 3: RESEARCH DESIGN

Once researchers have selected their topics and conducted a literature survey they begin the process of designing their research. Research design involves the researcher formulating a central research question or hypothesis and considering how this can be researched in a way that is valid and reliable.

What is a hypothesis?

The word 'hypothesis' is Greek in origin (*hypo* = under, *thesis* = placing or argument) and literally means 'under or low place'. A hypothesis is in effect an 'under' argument or underdeveloped argument, a thesis which is yet to be fully proven. All research begins with a working hypothesis. It states exactly what the research is trying to test/measure/demonstrate/prove. The exactness of a hypothesis depends on the methodological orientation of the research: the more scientifically oriented the research the more exact and rigid the hypothesis. Interpretivist research by its nature seeks to explore a topic before drawing conclusions and thus a too rigid hypothesis would stifle this process. However, all research begins with some loosely constructed central question or proposition to be investigated.

Formulating a hypothesis

A hypothesis is generated via topic selection and the literature survey – both should suggest a possible angle for study. The next task is to formulate a working hypothesis, which will be tested/explored. Consider the hypothesis '*Most students have a poorer than average diet.*' This statement is a hypothesis because it stands unproven or uncorroborated: it remains to be seen whether students have a poorer than average diet. You might think they do, but on what are you basing your assumption? How do we know it is true or false? This brings into question the related concepts of validity and reliability.

Validity

The claim above concerning the student diet is not valid. Validity concerns the veracity and accuracy of claims, it considers the grounds for claims to truth and how much they should be trusted and accepted. We make everyday claims to truth and we use a variety of means to substantiate them:

- *Casual personal observation* – something noticed in passing from which you generalise. Little thought given to the observation.
- *Unsupported assertion* – base assumptions upon your own experiences or those of others' that you know. It involves slightly more consideration than casual observations.
- *An appeal to authority* – draw upon the assumed authority of others' claims, particularly involving authority figures.
- *Scientific evidence* – based upon scientific, empirical research and therefore the most valid and reliable of all.

You will notice that each of these claims can be placed on a scale from least valid to most valid. The discussion exercise provides an opportunity for you to test your own perceptions concerning validity.

Discussion questions

For each statement below, classify it as one of the following: casual observation; unsupported assertion; appeal to authority; or scientific evidence.

1 I've never met a woman who didn't like chocolate.

2 (a) Early experience with violent films has profound effects on personality; (b) Laboratory research has found that children who had exposure to violent films for two hours a week for a six-month period had a shorter attention span and were more prone to aggressive play than those in the same study who did not receive exposure to violent films.

3 Everyone knows that coffee in moderation has therapeutic effects.

4 (a) Alcohol is dangerous to health; (b) The Chief Medical Officer warns against excessive alcohol consumption.

Our hypothesis that 'most students have a poorer than average diet' is currently an unsupported assertion and therefore not very valid. In order to make this hypothesis more valid we have to make it ready for testing. Another way of viewing a hypothesis is to see it as a series of concepts linked together, with each concept needing to be defined before the hypothesis can be tested. The key concepts in our hypothesis are: 'students', 'poorer than average', 'average diet'. These concepts are often referred to as indicators, variables or abstracts and it is these that will need to be measured and tested. To do this each must be defined or operationalised.

At the moment, 'students' is an abstract concept. There are over 1 million students in the UK ranging from 16 to 80 years old, men and women, all social classes, varying ethnicities and located in different parts of the country. We cannot include every student in our research, owing to time and cost constraints, and so must operationalise our indicators as effectively as possible: thus we could define student as '18–35 year old man or woman attending university in the north-west of the UK', or as 'all 18–35 year olds attending university in London'. Similarly, with the indicator 'average diet' we could operationalise this as 'the standard calorific intake required for an adult man', or we could define it as 'the average calorific intake of adults in the 18–35 age group for the UK as a whole'. You can see that the possibilities for operationalising indicators are endless but the researcher is trying to make them as workable as possible while also maintaining high levels of validity.

Reliability

Linked to validity is the idea of reliability. Reliability asks the question: Are your results going to be reliable given how you have operationalised your indicators? If your data is reliable then it can be seen to provide a fairly accurate answer to your hypothesis or real insight into your broad research question. For example, if we operationalised the indicator 'student' as 'all 18–35 year old men from social classes I and II attending university in London', can we be confident that our data will provide a reliable picture of student diet for the UK as a whole? In this case we could not as it excludes women (who make up more than half the UK student population), other social classes (there is already an established link between diet and class background) and also regional differences (some regions may have a concentration of particular social classes). In order to ensure that data is representative the researcher considers sampling strategies.

Testing a hypothesis

Part of testing a hypothesis involves selecting a population for study. Using the example from above our population is 'students'. It was noted that there are over one million students in the UK and so it is unlikely that we could look at each one's diet. Time and cost constraints make it necessary for us to sample this population. A sample is a way of making research more manageable through reducing the population; for example, we could reduce students to 'students aged 18–45 attending universities in the north-west of England', or even further to 'students aged 18–30 attending universities in Liverpool'. This makes the population more manageable. However, as noted above, the reliability of this sample must be evaluated, as must its representativeness.

Sampling strategies

There are two main types of sampling:

- *Probability sampling.* Every member of a population has an unknown or equal probability of selection. This is good for estimating the parameters of a population and obtaining the characteristics of a population.

- *Purposive or non-probability sampling.* Every member of a population does not have an equal probability of selection, which makes it good for more open testing of a population.

The two types are utilised in most research. If we return to our example of student diet we could use probability sampling to provide us with a set of types of students to include in our study. Purposive sampling could then be used to provide us with a range of student diet categories to be investigated. Each sampling type is associated with various methods by which a specific sample can be obtained.

Probability sampling methods

- *Random or simple sampling* – a sample is selected from a population on a purely random basis. For example drawing names out of a hat.

- *Systematic sampling* – a sample is generated from a predefined system. For example every twentieth or hundredth name on an address list.

- *Stratified sampling* – a sample is selected by a grouping of characteristics. For example gender, socio-economic status or age. The sample selected is proportional in terms of wider population demographics.

- *Cluster sampling* – a sample is defined by naturally preformed groups within a population. For example, a university could be defined as such. As a cluster the university could then be broken down into smaller clusters, for example lecturers or administrators within that university.

Purposive or non-probability sampling methods

- *Opportunity sampling* – sample members are identified purely on availability or willingness to take part. For example, gathering a sample from fellow undergraduate students found in the student union or from passers-by in the street.

- *Quota sampling* – aims to make the sample representative of the population by setting strict quotas. This is the technique used by market researchers. For example, if you wanted to research female students and you knew that 60 per cent were aged 18–25, 10 per cent 25–30, and 30 per cent 30+, you would make sure your research reflected these statistics.

- *Snowball sampling* – used where there is no adequate list from which to take a sample. This is useful for sampling deviant, small or closed populations. The researcher contacts a member of the population of interest, for example a drug pusher, and through this individual is put in contact with similar people who in turn select other people in a snowball effect. Although this is a good way of accessing often 'closed' networks it does mean that you might miss important members of a population as you are relying on your contacts and their contacts.

■ *Judgemental or purposive sampling* – the sample is selected through a purposeful or judgemental criteria that is defined by the research question. For example, if researching religious conversion, a sample might be selected with the assistance of a religious authority who knew of congregational members who had converted but who came originally from different religious backgrounds. In this example the selection judgements may inform theoretical consideration and may lead towards a comparison and contrast between sample members.

■ *Theoretical sampling* – respondents are selected progressively from a population as the research unfolds. The researcher collects, codes and analyses data, which maximises and grounds theory as it emerges or develops. Sampling stops when theoretical saturation occurs, that is, when there are no further avenues to pursue which will progress or ground theory further. For example, a researcher investigating group socialisation in a cult would stop research once every cult member had been interviewed.

Lists of potential populations for sampling are called sampling frames and researchers often draw their samples from these, particularly when conducting large-scale surveys. Potential sampling frames include the electoral register, the postcode address file, membership lists for societies and clubs, and so forth.

Pragmatic concerns

Research design is controlled by a series of pragmatic concerns that will be looked at more specifically in the next section, but these involve such questions as: How much time is there to do the research? How much money is there? Does the research require a research team? Do the researchers have the personal skills to do the research? All of these questions impact on the design of the research.

Ethics

A final facet which affects research design is the question of ethics and the ethical approach that the researcher wishes to take. The British Sociological Association (BSA) and other academic professional organisations have a strict code of ethical practice under which research should ideally be carried out. The basic tenet of this code is the principle of informed consent. This is where participants formally agree to be researched and are given clear information regarding safety, security, confidentiality, the nature of the research and the aim(s) of the research. Another aspect of this is giving the respondent the option to withdraw completely or at least agree to not answering questions he or she does not wish to. The principle behind this is to avoid harming respondents and to make them a part of the research process. Research should be open, informed and involve a dialogic relationship between the researchers and researched. Some researchers stress that informed consent is an ongoing process and that the researcher should continually reiterate and review consent throughout research. Others, particularly within feminist research, stress the need to go beyond informed consent and allow the respondents to play a participative role within the research, adding 'voice' and editing out pieces they do not want.

How open the research will be is the responsibility and choice of the researcher. Some researchers do not seek informed consent and instead choose to do covert research. This is typically used in situations where consent would be denied or where the research subjects would act differently if they were aware of the research, for example studying gangs, cults or other closed or deviant groups. Sometimes researchers begin with covert research and then switch to a more open approach and seek informed consent. It is the responsibility of researchers to justify their research approach and to protect subjects from harm. Given that sociologists work with people there is always scope for misunderstandings and harm no matter how open the research is, but most sociologists try to follow the principle of informed consent.

Discussion questions

Thinking about ethics

1 Go to the British Sociological Association's web site and read the statement of ethical practice. Which parts do you agree or disagree with?

2 Look at some of the most famous examples of covert research – Rosenhan (1973), Humphreys (1975) or Holdaway (1983) are good examples. Do you think covert research is ever justified? Give reasons for your answers.

3 What sorts of thing can be done to ensure good ethical practice in your own work in sociology?

STAGE 4: RESEARCH PLAN

After a researcher has designed a research project he or she must plan it more carefully in order to produce a clear step-by-step plan for the research. This is essential when researchers are working to a tight timetable with a controlled (or no) budget. Drawing up a research plan involves considering the following:

- *Timetable.* What is the timescale for your research? You might want to conduct an interview-based survey of the entire student population, but if you only have a month to do your research this approach is unlikely. Instead the brevity of time will require you to utilise research techniques which are fast, such as postal or telephone questionnaires. Thus timescale affects how you choose to do your research. Most researchers, once they have considered their allotted time, draw up a research timetable which enables them to view their research in an ordered way with set deadlines. These can be monthly, weekly or daily, with each set of tasks and objectives laid out on it. This can help orient the researcher through the research period.

- *Budgeting.* As with time, the amount of money available impinges on the type of research that can be conducted. For those researchers lucky enough to have funding, a research budget will be drawn up which details research expenses and costs. Researchers who receive funding will be obliged to account for all expenditure and probably have to submit a report to their funding organisation outlining all costs.

- *Personnel.* Many researchers conduct solo research because it suits them or because they do not have the budget to employ additional personnel. However, large-scale research involves a number of personnel, such as data collectors, administrative staff and computer analysts. Who you employ depends on the budget, the timescale and the type of research.

Accessing the field

The final stage of research planning involves considering access to your field of study; in other words, how do you access the sample of the population whom you hope will provide you with your data? Obviously this depends a lot on what you are researching but can typically involve negotiating with what are known as gate-keepers. These are individuals who control access to your field either because they are influential members of it (for example, a gang leader) or because of their position of authority in relation to that field (for example, a social worker). You have to negotiate entry through them and they might place conditions on your access. The conditions on your access and your research vary depending on what you are studying, but again this can place limitations on what you want to research. However, some fields require no gate-keepers. For example, if you were researching Internet relationships you have no access problems. Once the field has been accessed, researchers must consider what positions they will take within their research. There are four potential stances/roles:

- *Complete observer* – researcher is distanced from the population under study.
- *Observer-participant* (peripheral member role) – researcher operates on the edges of the population under study.
- *Participant-as-observer* (active member role) – researcher plays a role in the population under study.
- *Complete participant* (complete member role) – researcher is fully participative within the population under study.

Choice of role depends on methodological choice, ethical approach, type of research being conducted, research topic and pragmatic concerns such as time and money.

Discussion questions

Consider the pros and cons of the four researcher roles listed above in terms of: (a) access; (b) ethics; (c) data recording; and (d) validity.

What research topics and what types of research would be best suited to each of those four roles?

STAGE 5: ACTUAL RESEARCH

Having drawn up a research plan the researcher can now conduct his or her research. In this section we review the different research techniques and methods used within sociological research (and given the wide range of such techniques this section will be the most detailed of the chapter).

Methodologies and methods

It is important to note the difference between a methodology and methods. Methods refer to actual data collection techniques used in research, whereas methodology refers to the philosophical framework underpinning research. Methodological choices affect every aspect of research practice and, in particular, the choice of data collection techniques. Data collection techniques can be divided into two categories:

- *Qualitative* – techniques that measure the quality of a social phenomenon and give a sense of its tone or character.
- *Quantitative* – techniques that measure the quantity of a social phenomenon and give a sense of its extent, size, frequency and scope.

Traditionally, qualitative techniques have been associated with interpretivism and quantitative with scientific approaches. Additionally, certain types of technique have been associated within each category, thus interviewing and observational methods are deemed qualitative, and experiments and surveys are deemed quantitative. This is a rather outdated and simplistic categorisation. Different methodologies might use one category of methods or type of method to a greater extent but few researchers today would limit themselves to this strict dichotomy. Scientific researchers might overuse quantitative techniques but also find some limited utility in more qualitative forms. Similarly, interpretivist researchers will typically draw upon qualitative techniques but often use quantitative methods to add background or to measure specific social practices. Table 2.1 sets out the characteristics of the four main research methods, and each of these are examined in greater detail in the rest of this section.

Table 2.1 Characteristics of the four main research methods

	Quantitative	Qualitative	Key skills	Level of use
Social experiment	Laboratory experiment	Field experiment	■ Analytical ■ Interpreting ■ Visual awareness ■ Listening	■ Popular up to late 1960s ■ Heyday 1940s to 1960s ■ Little used now except in media and language studies
Observation	Naturalistic observation	Participant observation	■ Visual awareness ■ Listening ■ Reflecting ■ Interpreting	■ Always popular in sociology, especially in interpretivist research ■ Typically used in conjunction with other methods
Interviewing	Structured interview	Unstructured interview	■ Listening ■ Reflecting ■ Effective verbal communication ■ Interpreting	■ Always popular in sociology, especially among interpretivist research ■ Often used in conjunction with questionnaire surveys
Questionnaire survey	Postal, telephone or face-to-face surveys	Some face-to-face surveys	■ Effective written/oral communication ■ Numerical analysis ■ Good statistical ability ■ Interpreting	■ Always a key sociological method ■ Still widely used as a way to obtain large samples of the population

Human lab mice: the social experiment

History

It was noted in Chapter 1 that early sociologists sought to follow a scientific model of empirical research. This desire led many to try to mimic scientific experimental methods in the social sphere. This gave rise to the popularity of the use of experiments within sociological research. The heyday of the social experiment was between the 1920s and the late 1960s. The popularity of the experiment waned after this period due to changes in methodological approaches within sociology (such as the rise of feminist and interpretivist methodologies); wider critiques of scientific methodologies; and ethical concerns raised in reaction to a number of infamous examples of the use of the experiment, such as the work of Milgram (1974) and Zimbardo (1972). Today the experiment is not a mainstream sociological method although it has been used successfully within media studies, for example in measuring audience reactions to certain types of films, and also within language studies to quantify speech acts such as non-verbal communication.

Operation

There are two types of social experiment: the laboratory-based experiment and the field experiment. The laboratory experiment is the more quantitative of the two, following the classic hypothetico-deductive method of the physical sciences. It represents an opportunity, within the laboratory, to erase all factors that might affect results. The controlled environment of the laboratory ensures high levels of validity as well as control on the part of the research team. The researcher designs an experiment and then sets it up in a laboratory, just like a chemist or physicist might, the only real difference being that whereas a physical scientist works with chemicals or seeks to test some physical phenomenon, the sociologist is working on people and seeks to test a social phenomenon. Many of the sociologists who used experiments in the postwar years worked on issues of authority, power and punishment, seeking to try and understand how the genocidal acts of the Second World War had been allowed to occur, with typically willing accomplices in seemingly ordinary people. Probably the most famous example of a laboratory experiment within sociology is the work of Stanley Milgram (1974) – see Box 2.3.

BOX 2.3

Milgram experiment

In the 1960s Stanley Milgram conducted a series of experiments on obedience and authority. One of the most infamous of this series was his 'learning' experiment. Milgram set up a laboratory split into two rooms separated by a glass partition. In one room sat an individual named a 'learner'. The learner was strapped into a chair and hooked up to electrical equipment that would deliver an electric shock. In the other room was a large dial with electrical readings ranging from 0 to 450 volts. Milgram selected passers-by as volunteers. The volunteers were told they were participating in an experiment to see the effects of punishment on learning behaviour. The volunteers were labelled 'teachers' and were accompanied by one of Milgram's team who deliberately wore a white lab coat and carried a clipboard as symbols of scientific authority. The teacher was asked to deliver an electrical charge of increasing intensity with each question answered incorrectly by the learner in the other room. If any of the teachers hesitated, Milgram's assistant was to encourage them to go ahead and administer the shock. The learner became increasingly agitated, to the extent of screaming, and eventually went silent. What the volunteers did not know was that no electric shock was actually administered and the supposed learner was actually a member of Milgram's team who was acting as if suffering. Milgram's results were shocking: 65 per cent of all volunteers administered the maximum shock of 450 volts and none of the volunteers stopped before administering at least 300 volts.

Milgram's work vividly demonstrated how people are obedient to figures of authority even if such obedience means committing acts of violence.

Source: based on Milgram, 1974

BOX 2.4

The Rosenhan experiment

Rosenhan assembled a team of eight, predominantly drawn from healthcare professionals. Each team member was to go to a different hospital and act as if they had the classic symptoms of psychosis, such as hearing voices. Each pseudo-patient was admitted to a psychiatric ward. As soon as they were admitted, Rosenhan's team were instructed to stop acting as if they had the symptoms of psychosis and instead appear normal and sane. However, the pseudo-patients found that their supposed sanity was a sign of denial of their underlying mental health problems. Eventually the team members had to start acting as if mentally ill in order to be viewed as getting better. All the team members were released, typically after a 19 days' stay in the hospital. On release they were not diagnosed as cured but as 'in remission'. None of the hospital staff realised they were being deceived. However, a substantial number of their fellow patients realised that they were not ill. From this experiment Rosenhan concluded that the environment of the hospital is more important in influencing the diagnosis of a patient than their actual symptoms. Additionally, Rosenhan demonstrated how labelling is used against the mentally ill, often to a detrimental level.

Source: based on Rosenhan, 1973

Field experiments lack the level of control that laboratory ones have due to the fact that many factors cannot be controlled within a field environment. The researcher and his or her team select an environment and manipulate subjects within it according to the particular experimental model that they want to investigate. A famous example of this is the work of Rosenhan (1973) on mental health. Rosenhan wanted to investigate how the mentally ill are diagnosed and labelled (Box 2.4).

Evaluation

Laboratory experiments, as with scientific experiments in general, generate highly valid data and can be easily replicated. The researcher has complete control of the environment and can easily manipulate subjects. Much of this depends on how well the experiment was designed: can it generate the information required? It also depends on the interpretative powers of the team, as the experiment does not seek to interact with subjects in a dialogic manner. However, there is an issue of artificiality: would subjects act in the same manner outside of the laboratory? The field experiment is less controlled and there are perhaps too many factors that could affect data to make results completely reliable, especially if the experiment is conducted covertly so that the team must rely heavily on interpretation and there are endless variables which cannot be controlled.

Ethical issues

The biggest problem in relation to the social experiment is that of ethics. A large number of the most famous examples of the use of experiments within sociology have been conducted without the research subjects' full knowledge. Over half the volunteers in Milgram's experiment suffered long-term psychological damage. What right have sociologists to inflict harm upon research subjects? The experiment was covert and volunteers were deceived as to the real purpose of the experiment. Is it right that sociologists should deliberately mislead or deceive people? The Rosenhan case was also covert and again raises the same issues of deception and possible harm.

Even in experiments conducted overtly there is still a potential for harm as the case of Zimbardo (1972) prison experiment demonstrates. Many researchers, particularly interpretivist and feminist, object to the use of people within experiments as it goes against the very idea of interactive, equal and open research practice: people are not laboratory rats. It is for these reasons that the experiment has become a peripheral sociological technique.

Discussion questions

1 What types of social phenomenon might lend themselves to being investigated using experimental techniques? For each of these examples of social phenomena describe how you would design a social experiment in either the laboratory or the field.

2 Do you think that experiments such as those of Milgram (1974) or Zimbardo (1972) can ever be ethically justified?

3 Can there ever be ethically correct experiments in sociology?

People watching: the observation

History

Observation has been a central method of collecting data about the physical and social worlds since prehistory – we first 'knew' our world through what we saw. Classical philosophy, history, and early science and medicine depended upon observations for understanding. Many disciplines, for example zoology and astronomy, rely on observation as their main means of gathering data. Others, such as clinical medicine, rely on observation to prove theoretical work and to reformulate hypotheses. As for sociology, Auguste Comte stipulated that observation was one of the four core research methods (along with comparative studies, historical analysis and experimentation) appropriate for sociological investigation. Early social studies were survey based and relied on interviews and observations to generate data. Observation is often used as a method in its own right, but within sociological research it is usually combined with other strategies, such as interviewing and experimentation.

There are two main types of observational method: naturalistic and participant. The former is the oldest type of observational technique and has been used since classical times. It went on to become the main observational approach of the natural sciences and still dominates in many science subjects. Naturalistic observation, with its more quantitative approach and data, was more suited to scientific investigation. A modified (slightly less rigorous) version of it was soon adopted within the social sciences by the start of the twentieth century. It was popularised by sociologists, such as George Herbert Mead, Georg Simmel and Erving Goffman, who were particularly interested in the social self and with social interaction. Participant observation was developed within social anthropology as its central method of research and this approach is typically linked with interpretivist concerns. Due to interpretivism's limited impact on mainstream sociology until the 1960s – participant observation was not widely used until then, although one exception is seen in the work of the Chicago School (see Chapter 6, p. 187) – it is viewed as generating more qualitative data and so deemed less scientifically rigorous. Today both methods are widely used although participant observation is increasingly the main form of observational method used by social researchers.

Observation

Observation, like speech, relies on interpretation and so this opens up to us the possibility of multiple interpretations. Action is ambiguous and easily misread, which can make observing human actions challenging. There are different ways which the researcher can choose when observing social interaction. Although observation involves, primarily, the gathering of visual data, the other senses (smell, hearing, touch and taste) should be engaged as well by the most skilled observer. A good observer is one who is hyper-aware of the minutiae of social interaction and action and is also able to use his or her own body effectively within interaction, i.e. can 'blend in' when required. Observing, like interviewing, is a skill which can be easily practised and which develops with practice.

Naturalistic observation

Naturalistic observation is underused in contemporary sociological research, where participant observation predominates. Such observation is deemed 'pure' observation in that, unlike participant observation, the observer hides him- or herself from contact with subjects and events in the field. It can vary considerably depending on individual researchers. Researchers may intentionally choose to focus on a group in a particular location to observe behaviour and events or they may locate themselves in a particular field context and then observe what appears to happen naturally around them. The two are not mutually exclusive. Researchers interested in urban ghetto life would probably begin by locating themselves in that area and do some preliminary observations to see what sort of data was being produced. Then, as they oriented themselves in the field, they could be more selective and focus on particular events or subjects. Observers need to select a role strategy, i.e. in the field, how do they present themselves. There are many possible strategies, which have related ethical and data collection dilemmas. As was noted earlier (p. 36) there are four possible roles to assume and, of these, naturalistic observation can involve one of two strategies:

- *Complete observer* – researcher is distanced from the population under study (role 1).

- *Observer-participant* (peripheral member role) – researcher operates on the edges of the population under study (role 2).

Researchers could remain hidden within a role watching passively (role 1) or they could be open and actively assume a role within the setting but not fully participate within the setting (role 2). The practicalities of completely hiding oneself in a social setting are considerable although many researchers get around this problem by using video cameras to film events and watch from a distance via monitors. Researchers who choose to conduct covert observations but cannot be completely hidden will need a convincing guise in order to remain in the research setting. Researchers conducting open research still face the problem of subject effects – people acting differently because they know they are being watched. There is no real solution to this problem but effects can be reduced by researcher openness, long stays in the research setting and the creation of trust between researcher and researched.

Naturalistic observation requires very accurate recording of events and behaviours. It requires a rigour, which leads it to be quantitative in nature. The naturalistic observer is trying to note everything that is happening in the field and this is quite an onerous undertaking. The field setting should be mapped out and movements recorded. Participants' appearance, clothing, modes of transportation, posture, roles and interactions must all be recorded. Rituals, temporal elements, social organisations and personal interpretation should also be entered into data records. What is noted may change with the study. Most would begin with initial *descriptive observations*, which then are replaced by *focused observations* directed towards specific individual or events within the wider field setting.

Data can be collected through a variety of techniques including note-taking, use of diaries or logbooks, filming of the field setting and the use of tape recorders. The data collection strategy depends largely on what role the researcher has assumed. If they are being very open then any collection method can be used, but most often with this type of observation researchers are hiding their actual role within a disguised role and so the collection technique must tie in with that role. In settings which are anonymous, such as in a bar or a railway station, this is fairly easy; the researcher can sit anonymously within the field and make recordings. If the researcher is in a more exposed role within the field, such as a hospital waiting room or a church, then he or she must present a role which can allow for note taking or filming.

Data is collected until *theoretical saturation* is achieved, that is, the researcher is confident that he or she has all the data that is needed to satisfy his or her hypothesis. Often, to make the observations more rigorous a research team is established with each member doing their own observations of the same event. At the end of the observation period (however long this is) all the data is reviewed together to afford different 'views' of a single event or place. One famous example of a researcher utilising naturalistic observation is Laud Humphreys' (1975) study of male homosexual sex in public toilets (Box 2.5).

BOX 2.5

Observing deviant behaviour

Laud Humphreys conducted covert research in a men's public toilet situated in a public park. Humphreys assumed the observational strategy of observer-participant, adopting the role of 'watchqueen' in the public toilet, that is, an accepted role as both lookout and voyeur. After each sexual encounter occurred, Humphreys would complete a 'systematic observational sheet' recording the date, providing a description of the activity that had occurred and of the participants, and noting the location of the activity within the toilet space. Humphreys assigned different types of role-categories to the men, such as 'voyeur', 'masturbator', 'inserter' and 'insertee'. The nature and structure of interactions between the men were also recorded. Humphreys observed over one hundred men during his study. Humphreys' study allowed new insight into a form of deviant sexual behaviour which had not previously been researched. What makes this study as controversial as it became was that Humphreys would follow the men from the toilet and record their car registration numbers, which he used to trace the men. He then went to their homes and under the guise of conducting a health survey interviewed them. This way of carrying out research prompted new guidelines into appropriate research conduct.

Source: based on Humphreys, 1975

Participant observation

Participant observation as a method was pioneered within social anthropology and was not widely used within mainstream sociology until the 1960s. Among the small number of sociologists who used participant observation before then were the Chicago School. Today, participant observation is becoming more widely used as a research technique, especially among sociologists who wish to distance themselves from positivist methodologies and those engaged in 'postmodernist' or 'post-positivist' debates. An exact definition of participant observation is difficult because there are degrees of participation: observer; observer-participant; participant-as-observer; and complete participant. The researcher may be one or more of these during the course of research. Simply put, participant observation involves the observer engaging in the social world of subjects – as opposed to naturalistic observation in which the observer distances him- or herself physically, socially or mentally from subjects.

Participant observation involves immersion in the field for the researcher – he or she watches, listens, talks and participates in the daily lives of subjects. The researcher often tries to blend in and adopt the style, linguistic and social, of the locals. Often this can entail living in the field ('going native') with the associated problems of blending in and of being distanced/isolated from the researcher's own social world, which can place physical and emotional demands on the researcher. Many participant-observers reach a point when the role of observer becomes blurred with the role of participant and this can cause 'role crisis'. Thompson's (1985) study of Hell's Angels illustrates how roles can be confused by both researcher and participants. As the end of his research approached, Thompson was beaten by the biker gang when he refused to pay them for their answers to questions. Thompson was shocked by this incident as he had begun to see himself in a non-researcher role, as someone accepted by the gang. However, the beating reiterated the fact that the bikers had always seen him in the researcher role. Most participant-observers use their personal experiences as tools of research and allow experiential data and emotional responses to aid investigation – self-reflection and personal exploration are used in this type of research, but this very fact can make such research stressful for researcher and participants alike.

The collection of data from participant observation is fraught with complication. This method emphasises complete engagement with the field and so often this is not conducive to formal data collection as the researcher is trying to break down barriers between him or her and the subjects. Covert research obviously requires covert data collection – diary or note-taking is most common, typically done when the researcher is in a private or secluded area. Overt participation can involve the use of formal recording – audio, video or notes – but often this is obtrusive and many long-term fieldworkers approach data collection in an informal way. Typically, they take notes or keep diaries of the day's significant events when alone at the end of the social day. Such personal and informal note-taking is open to questions of validity in that it is highly subjective, very personalised and depends on the vagaries of memory. But the fieldworker would counter that by engaging in debates about the essential subjectiveness of such fieldwork in the first instance and the nature of authorship in the second. Eileen Barker's (1984) groundbreaking study of the Unification Church illustrates the challenges facing a researcher doing participant observation (Box 2.6).

BOX 2.6

Observing religious conversion

Barker wanted to investigate the nature of conversion to the Unification Church ('Moonies'). In the early 1970s the Moonies were portrayed as a brainwashing cult who coerced people into joining them. Barker wanted to see whether this was an accurate portrayal of the movement. After two years of contact and negotiation with the Moonies in the UK she was allowed access. Between 1976 and 1982 Barker conducted 30 in-depth interviews but during this time she also lived in a series of different Unification centres in the USA and attended workshops and seminars run by the church. Barker did not live permanently at these centres but rather stayed for short periods at different locations, moving in and out of the field. Her fellow participants knew she was not a Moonie and she did not pretend to be one at any point. However, despite such openness Barker admitted to being 'evasive' and to holding back her views and opinions on occasion, demonstrating that even the most overt research may involve some small amount of deception. Barker concluded that the Moonies were not a brainwashing cult and that they were in essence like other religious organisations. Barker's work changed perceptions of new religious organisations and aided the debunking of brainwashing theory.

Source: based on Barker, 1984

Evaluation

Naturalistic observation

The main criticism of naturalistic observation is that it is not as valid as other methods. It relies exclusively on the researcher's perceptions of field events. Therefore data is biased through the researcher's subjective interpretations and reflexive concerns. This is made harder as observers do not have quotes or interview material to reinforce what they have recorded. There is no legitimising additional data. This is probably the main reason that few sociologists would publish studies only reliant on observational data, as the Humphreys example demonstrates. However, validity can be checked through the use of multiple observers, especially if diverse in age, gender, ethnicity – then all data can be compared and cross-checked. A second criticism is that such observation lacks reliability; without statistical analysis to confirm the significance of observed patterns or trends, researchers cannot ensure that their findings are real and not merely the effects of chance. This could be improved by repeating observations systematically over varying conditions and times. One of the great strengths of this method is that it brings the researcher into the field in an unobtrusive way that does not require direct interaction with participants. This is ideal for many instances where overt and blatant methods would not work or be allowed, such as among illicit or marginalised groups or communities. Naturalistic observation also cuts down on the potential 'observer effects' as the observer is at a distance from the subjects of observation. Thirdly, this style of observation is very open and flexible – the observer can alter the questions being pursued or construct new theories. The work of Goffman (1963) demonstrates how insightful such observation can be. Lastly, naturalistic observation produces very rigorous data when combined with other methods.

Participant observation

The benefits of this approach are that the researcher engages with the field and its subjects; it stresses the personal and the 'real'. Typically, research is done over a long period and this can produce data which offers a real sense of the social setting. The data produced from participant observation allows the reader access to the field and ultimately the worldview (in a Weberian sense of *verstehen*) of field subjects. The criticisms of participant observation fall around the notion of validity – its methods, especially of data collection. It is probably the least valid of all research techniques in that it is so heavily reliant upon subjective interpretation and experiential data. Again, many researchers would combine observation with interviews as Barker did. There is also the question of reliability. Participant observation is unreliable in that each field setting and observation is unique and 'created' by the engagement of a specific researcher with a specific group of field subjects – it can hardly be replicated. However, those researchers engaged in this method would stress the need for engaging with subjectivity (and reflexivity) and that all social research is ultimately subjective. Another criticism of participant observation is that it probably raises more ethical quandaries than most other methods owing to the direct engagement within the field setting and with subjects. Often, participant observation is the proverbial ethical minefield that has to be negotiated. However, there are strategies for navigating this: openness, inclusion of subjects' voices, awareness of reflexive concerns, and so forth.

Ethical issues

Naturalistic observation

Of all sociological methods this is the least intrusive and yet this very aspect lays it open to claims of ethical abuse. This is primarily focused on invasion of privacy, whether through venturing into private spaces (without permission) or through misrepresenting oneself as a member. Subjects cannot therefore give consent or have any control over data. Often, this approach is used to study marginal or deviant groups – there is the potential for abuse of data or for misrepresentation. This dilemma is difficult to negotiate. Such work allows access to areas often stigmatised or hidden from public view, but raises the issue of whether the quest for knowledge is being done at a price. To put it another way, are the needs/rights of the subjects being subsumed within the aims of the researcher?

Participant observation

As already stated, ethics are a central consideration and problem for this method owing to its personal engagement with the field setting and subjects. Some settings require covert means, such as work among deviant or marginalised communities, and this raises tremendous ethical problems which are not easily negotiated. At the very least, the covert researcher must ensure anonymity via the use of pseudonyms and be very careful in the production of data and its dissemination. Overt researchers are far from exempt from ethical problems either. As subjective and reflexive concerns come to the fore in this type of research the researcher needs to engage in such concerns.

Discussion questions

1 The previous section included some example of observation-based research studies. List other sociological studies that have used observational techniques.

2 Was the observation participant or naturalistic?

3 What areas of social life are particularly suitable for observation? Why?

4 What areas are particularly unsuitable? Why?

Happy talking: the interview

History

The interview is both a quantitative and qualitative method of research and has been used as a means of gathering data within sociology since its beginnings in the nineteenth century. The earliest use of the interview as a qualitative method was in the social survey work of researchers like Charles Booth who combined unstructured interviews with field observation to provide rich data on the lives of Londoners at the end of the nineteenth century (see Booth's *Labour and Life of the People in London*, 1902). Other researchers of urban life in Europe, the UK and USA soon adopted Booth's work.

The use of the interview to produce qualitative data was not widely used by sociologists from the 1920s onwards as the quantitative interview became more popular. The structured interview became popular because its ability both to provide quantitative data into people's attitudes, opinions and behaviour, and to cover large populations made it an indispensable tool of the survey researcher. The qualitative interview remained common among interpretivists. The work of the Chicago School relied on a combination of participant observation with the unstructured interview, as illustrated in the work of Whyte (1943). It was not until the shift towards interpretivism from the 1960s onwards, heavily influenced by feminism, that the unstructured interview became more widely used in mainstream sociology. The interview in both its forms is still a mainstay of sociological research.

Operation

Interview types

Interviews can either be individual, involving face-to-face interaction with an individual, or group, involving face-to-face interaction with a group of subjects. It should be noted that interviews need not always be face-to-face, for example surveys (and market researchers) often rely on telephone interviews to access a wide sample of the population in a relatively quick and easy way. The problems with no face-to-face interaction are that the interviewer cannot observe the respondent's body language and that it is hard to establish trust or rapport over the telephone with a stranger.

There are three types of interview: structured, semi-structured and unstructured.

Structured and semi-structured interviews

These interview types are also known as standard or semi-standard. Structured and semi-structured interviews produce quantitative data. The stress is on uniformity through control of voice tone, gesture, and so on, so that the respondent is not being 'led' towards a particular answer. Much attention will be given to question construction and the interviewer will have planned the interview down to the last detail before conducting it. The interview is conducted according to an interview schedule (see below).

BOX 2.7

Gathering opinions

Market researchers make the most use of structured interviews. Market research is used in all walks of life: to test consumer attitudes; to measure political opinions; to survey changing patterns of behaviour; and to analyse swings in public morals. Market researchers can be seen in town centres interviewing people face-to-face but they also make wide use of telephone interviews. Opinion polls are common media fodder, particularly at events of national interest, such as elections. A number of commercial and academic survey organisations exist which are commissioned to conduct opinion polls. For example, the Gallup Organisation, which conducted its first opinion polls in 1935, has offices in 20 countries, employs over 3,000 researchers and has become one of the biggest market research companies in the world.

These interview types are seen as objective and focused on eliminating 'interviewer effects'. The semi-structured interview involves the interviewer asking most of the same questions of each subject but will often alter their sequence and, typically, follows up extra lines of enquiry, which may be subject-specific. Such interviews are more flexible (and less formal) so that subject difficulty with questions can be dealt with through alteration of wording and further information can be gained. This type is best used when interviewing groups who may have difficulty understanding the questions. The structured and semi-structured interview plays a major part in survey research.

Constructing an interview schedule
Structured interviews make use of interview schedules. The schedule is followed with each interview. A schedule is a list of every question to be asked in the exact order of asking. The interviewer takes great time in preparing the schedule and considering question type and order. Such schedules should begin with a brief introduction explaining who the interviewer is, which organisation he or she represents and the purpose of the interview. Confidentiality and anonymity should be stressed. Filter questions should be used to move between sections; questions should follow a linear and progressive order; and the interviewer needs to make sure that despite such a proscriptive schedule he or she maintains rapport with the subject – less easy to do with this type. All interview schedules should include open and closed questions. It is also advisable to try out a draft schedule before use in the field. Also to try some pilot interviews to see how the interview schedule works in the field. The full survey can then benefit from information gained from the pilot study.

Unstructured interview
The unstructured (also called non-standard or focused) interview involves the interviewer having a list of topics, which they want the respondent to talk about.

The interviewer has a freedom to phrase questions the way that he or she wants and in any order that suits. This type often becomes more like a conversation at times and is much more open. Consequently it can be harder to manage by the less experienced interviewer as it is not easy to keep the interview from going off at a tangent.

With this type the interviewer has an interview guide (see below) – this merely lists broad themes or topics to be discussed and it is not proscriptive. Such interviews are more like guided conversations and produce data which is probably more insightful than that produced by the structured approach. They are particularly useful when embarking on research which has not been covered before or when seeking a more in-depth sense of what people are thinking.

Unstructured interviews make more use of open questions and are sensitive to the general points regarding interview scheduling raised in the previous section. However, the unstructured interview requires more prompting and probing strategies from the interviewer than the structured as the questions can be more ambiguous. Also the use of hypothetical questions may be more prevalent.

Such interviews form the backbone of interpretivist research and place a great deal of reliance on the researcher to interpret the data produced. Although all interviews depend upon the interviewer's interpersonal and presentational skills, the unstructured interview places greater pressure upon the researcher to create strong rapport with interviewees.

BOX 2.8

Creating intimacy

Ann Oakley, along with many other feminist researchers, has demonstrated the importance of using unstructured interviews to create rapport with subjects, and also as a means to challenge existing power imbalances between researcher and subject. Oakley sees both issues as interlinked or, as she puts it, 'no intimacy without reciprocity'. This stance demands that the interviewer reflects upon his or her status within the interview along with sharing the experience with the subjects, even if that means sharing feelings or opinions. It also means viewing respondents as people rather than as objects of study.

Oakley used unstructured interviews to study women's experiences of both housework and maternity care. Both studies used large numbers of interviews; for example, Oakley interviewed 40 women about how much housework they did and how they and their partners organised domestic work. Both studies were aimed at raising awareness of women's experiences and of promoting policy changes – for example, Oakley called for domestic work to be recognised as 'work' and to be given an appropriate status in relation to paid employment. Similarly, her work on maternity care has led to a heightened awareness of women's experiences of becoming mothers and of the need for women to have a greater role in decision-making during their maternity care.

Source: based on Oakley, 1974, 1981

Constructing an interview guide

The interviewer selects a topic and then considers broad areas he or she wishes to explore in the interview. A few specific questions might be included but usually a guide is a list of headings or categories to discuss. Some guides might try to place topics in an order; for example, if discussing a sensitive subject such as health it makes sense to begin with less intimate questions in the interview and then increase the sensitivity of topics as the interview goes along. Guides tend to be fairly minimalist. As with the interview schedule, the guide should begin with a declaration concerning the motivation for the interview, background information on the interviewer and ethical statements. As with the structured and semi-structured interview, a pilot should be attempted and then full-scale implementation.

Question types

In constructing interview schedules and guides the researcher has to consider the types of question he or she could use. Different questions generate different types of data. There are two types of questions:

- *Open questions* – those which allow the respondents to respond in any way they wish, e.g. 'What do you enjoy most about football?' They produce fuller answers and data. These generate more data which will require more data analysis at the end of the research.

- *Closed questions* – those which offer answers for the respondent, e.g. 'Are you married?' can be answered yes or no. Such answers are easily processed and make data management less time-consuming, but are by their nature restrictive.

Most interviewers use both types of question, although structured interviews make more use of closed questions, whereas unstructured interviews typically use open questions. As well as considering question type the interviewer also has to consider how he or she words questions. There are seven key points to keep in mind in wording questions:

1 *Clarity*. Are the questions easy to understand and unambiguous? Is there any scope for the respondent to miss the point or be confused? It is important that questions be clear, as unclear questions may create a barrier between interviewer and subject, who may feel uncomfortable at not understanding the question. Also, the structured interview seeks fairly specific answers and does not need material which is ambiguous. It is always best to avoid jargon and also to consider your subjects' level of language ability.

2 *Leading questions*. These are questions which lead the subject into agreeing or disagreeing with a question, e.g. 'Would you not agree that smoking causes lung cancer?' Such questions are common in the media, but are biased in that they control the responses and so are not objective. Objective material is best sought via open-ended questions, such as, 'What do you think are the effects of smoking on health?' Of course, leading questions are often a good way of drawing out the respondent at the beginning of interviews, perhaps if they are not being

very cooperative possibly due to nerves. A certain amount of prompting and probing is needed to push any interview along and you may find yourself using leading questions just to keep the interview going.

3 *Double-barrelled questions.* These involve asking two questions in one, e.g. 'Do you watch football on a Saturday and do you enjoy the atmosphere?' Such questions can lead to confusion with a respondent who may feel bombarded by questions; they may also confuse data, through the interviewer attempting to record everything that was said.

4 *Hypothetical questions.* These are philosophical in bent and should be avoided as the respondent might give an answer which does not reflect what they would actually do in that situation, e.g. 'What would you do if your wife ran off with another man?' Of course such questions may be more useful in less structured interviews where there is more scope for exploration, but in the structured interview they are counterproductive.

5 *Secondary information.* It is advisable not to ask one respondent what they think someone else's views on a subject would be, as this is open to ambiguity. Of course, sometimes this can be a useful way of generating data in situations where the person you wish to talk to is unavailable, but you must always remember that the data is secondary.

6 *Periodicity.* When asking questions that require a time or number, e.g. 'How often do you go to the cinema?' If they say 'often', get them to be specific, such as 'weekly' or 'once a month' – 'often' is too ambiguous.

7 *Sensitivity.* It is important to be sensitive in the questions that are asked, e.g. people willingly answer questions 'truthfully' about non-controversial behaviour, such as leisure patterns, but other topics, such as health or income, might garner less honest answers.

Reflexivity

All interviews involve interaction between an interviewer and a respondent, but to greater and lesser degrees. Such interaction can involve 'interviewer effects', that is data is affected owing to the interaction between interviewer and respondent. This happens less in structured interviews owing to the proscriptive nature, but it is still a problem. The age, gender, ethnic background, social class and so forth of an interviewer can alter how the respondent views him or her. The interviewer needs to be aware of such reflexive concerns and how data could be distorted.

Body language

Linguistic research has shown that in any act of communication only 20 per cent of that communication is verbal. The remaining 80 per cent of meaning conveyed is via what linguists call paralinguistic, or non-verbal, communication. This includes body posture, voice tone and speed, body movement and so forth. Interviewers should be sensitive to their own as well as the respondent's body language and the meanings conveyed. Interviewers should also consider language and whether they share the same language as their respondents; if not the hazards of communicating across a language boundary have to be considered. Also, interviewers should consider the use of slang or dialect variations, particularly if interviewing an individual who may use slang or words unique to his or her local dialect/accent. There are also variations in use of language and body language between different groups, such as gender, ethnic groups or age groups. The interviewer must consider these variations.

Data collection

Interview data can be collected electronically or by hand. Video- and tape-recorders are often used and are useful because they produce a full account of what was said or done. However, such records, especially audio records, need to be transcribed, and this is a laborious process. Electronic recording often creates a barrier between interviewer and respondent and many subjects may feel intimated by the presence of such devices, or may alter answers. Such devices often give a sense of officialdom and this may frighten many respondents. The most popular way is to write down answers. With structured interviews there is a schedule of questions, which could be easily filled in by the interviewer. With unstructured interviews there is more data. Interviewers could write down everything but this means that they are probably not watching the interviewee and thus avoiding eye contact (which is basically rude and in extreme situations might be deemed threatening or intimidating) and are also missing body cues. Many interviewers only jot down general notes or points during interviews and then use these later to flesh out answers – this is obviously very reliant on memory and so highly subjective but it does allow the style to be more open.

Evaluation

Structured and semi-structured interviews are highly effective at generating quantitative data but do not allow the researcher to pursue interesting issues raised within the interview that go beyond the interview schedule. The unstructured interview is very effective at giving respondents a 'voice' within research and allows the generation of very broad data without limitations. However, unstructured interviews are not time- or cost-effective and can often be too ponderous and unfocused – in fact they can be too unstructured. The main drawback of all types of interview is the issue of interpretation (albeit in different degrees according to type). They rely to varying degrees on the researcher's interpretation of what is said. Additionally there is the problem of interviewer effects. Both these difficulties raise concerns regarding validity.

Ethical considerations

Most interviews are conducted openly and with informed consent. Interviewers should always seek informed consent from subjects. Particularly sensitive topics may require the researcher to constantly reassure respondents of their privacy. Covert interviews cannot guarantee such things but may be useful for certain situations.

When collected, covert research data should be *treated anonymously via the use of pseudonyms*. Whether open or covert, data should be treated carefully with consideration given to how it is to be used – use of the data may affect the lives of the subjects. Feminist interviewers raised the whole issue of ethics as part of their critique of traditional research approaches. Feminists argue that the traditional research interview replicates society's hierarchical and patriarchal structures and that interview techniques manipulate subjects. Feminists, such as Ann Oakley, push for more 'relaxed' forms of interviewing which incorporate respondent's voices. Many interviewers seek to make interviews more ethical by allowing subjects to read their transcripts and to add to them if they think anything is missing. Others would argue that this corrupts the data profoundly.

Asking the right questions: the questionnaire survey

History

It was noted in Chapter 1 that, since antiquity, peoples have been taking surveys of their own and other populations. The use of surveys as a cornerstone of social data was established during the nineteenth century when the social survey was used to produce detailed data concerning social and economic conditions. Most of the early ones were based on face-to-face interviews, as high illiteracy rates meant few could complete questionnaires. The ability of surveys to produce accurate data concerning behaviour, attitudes, conditions and opinions ensured that the survey became a central method within social science research. The relative ease with which one can administer a large-scale survey makes it a popular choice. Classical sociology was founded upon social survey work and it continues to be widely used. Most surveys can be viewed as quantitative in that they strive for validity and reliability and produce quantifiable data. Interpretivists have used smaller-scale surveys to produce more qualitative data. The ability of the survey to produce objective, quantifiable and valid data makes it the main choice for government-funded research projects into public behaviour and attitudes, and for market research and opinion polls.

Operation

The social survey relies on the administration of questionnaires. Questionnaires can be administered in three ways:

- *Postal surveys*. These involve posting self-completion questionnaires to respondents for them to complete privately. They are relatively cheap to administer and mean that researchers can cover a large population in a very cost-effective way. No interviewers are needed, and because such questionnaires tend to be very standardised and pre-coded, computers can be used to read and analyse data – also cutting costs. The disadvantage is that such surveys have a low response rate (typically less than 50 per cent) and that often when they are returned they have incomplete, illegible or incomprehensible answers. Questions must be carefully worded so that respondents understand what is asked of them, as there will be no researcher there to help them. In this context it should be noted that approximately 25 per cent of the UK population are functionally illiterate.

■ *Face-to-face interviews.* Researchers complete the questionnaire on behalf of the respondent in a structured interview setting. An *interview schedule* is constructed to direct the interview, but this allows it to be more flexible than postal surveys because question phrasing can be altered if respondents are confused. However, such surveys are expensive and time-consuming and have to employ (trained) interviewers. They rely on respondents' goodwill in taking time to participate. Add to this travel, administrative and analysis costs and it is an expensive choice.

■ *Telephone surveys.* Here *interview schedules* are again used and are filled in by the researcher. As with the face-to-face interview, telephone surveys allow for flexibility. They are also a very cheap way of surveying a population. The problems with this choice are in the fact that many sections of the population do not have access to a telephone or are not contactable by telephone all of the time (working, elderly, poor, sick) and such groups may be under-represented in the research. Also, the telephone forms a barrier between respondent and researcher and thus more sensitive questions may be difficult to ask or answer. Furthermore, interviewers must be specially trained for telephone questioning (which requires a different approach from face-to-face interviewing). Finally, such surveys require respondents to be contacted in advance so that they can agree to participate.

Constructing a questionnaire

As with constructing interview schedules and guides, time and care must be taken in devising questionnaires, in relation to question order and type (see below for information on question types and order). In constructing a questionnaire the researcher is interested in specific types of information being sought. Questions are not there to produce 'interesting for its own sake' information, however titillating that may be, but should produce data that is directly relevant to the research hypothesis. Background reading should be used to help at the draft stage. It is also important to remember that all questionnaires must be exactly the same, with the same wording and question order. This ensures validity (all interviews the same) and reliability (survey could be repeated). Surveys can obtain four main categories of information:

■ *Attributes.* These are personal and socio-economic characteristics, e.g. sex, age, marital status, occupation, religion and so forth. To gain such data you could ask a question like, 'Are you in paid employment? If the answer is yes, you can follow this by asking 'What is your occupation?'

■ *Behaviour.* This constitutes what the individual has done, is doing and may do in the future. An example might be: 'Have you ever been a member of a voluntary organisation?'

■ *Attitudes*. This refers to how people feel about a particular issue. Questions about attitudes usually use scales which the respondents choose from, as in the following example:

I think women with children should not work.

☐ Strongly agree
☐ Agree
☐ Neither agree nor disagree
☐ Disagree
☐ Strongly disagree

■ *Beliefs*. Asking respondents whether they think something is true or false can assess these. For example:

The number of single mothers in the UK has grown rapidly over the past five years.

☐ True
☐ False

Format

Questionnaires should be accompanied by an introductory letter and (if it is face-to-face) interviewer ID. Such a letter should explain the study, its purpose and who is conducting it. All questionnaires should have a contact number and address so that respondents can get in touch with the researcher (to complain or praise or seek more information) and also to reassure respondents that the survey is real and legal. There should also be a 'thank you' placed at the end of the questionnaire to show appreciation to the respondent – remember they are giving up their time, and it is common courtesy.

Questionnaires should not be too long, as this deters people from completing them, but have to be long enough to produce the data required. Ideally, questionnaires should take no more than 30–40 minutes to complete.

Question order is crucial so that people are led logically through the questions; also it is helpful to divide the questionnaire into sub-sections and use headings to break up the document. Related questions can be grouped together; and different sections should have linking phrases ('Moving on to . . .', or 'In relation to that section . . .').

Questionnaires should start with simple, straightforward questions which will lead the respondent into the questionnaire. If there are sensitive questions to ask, those questions should be placed further on. Questionnaires should not begin by asking sensitive questions, as this will be likely to dissuade the respondent from completing the survey. Also, it should be noted that the questionnaire may go to individuals who do not fit into the sample, for example it may be sampling childless couples' view of children so it should not be filled in by couples with children. In these cases the questionnaire should start by asking, 'Do you have children?' Then the interview can be stopped and this individual excluded from the survey. Such questions are called filter questions. Questions should have an individual code so that data processing and analysis is easy. For example:

Ai   What religion are you?
1. Christian
2. Jew
3. Muslim
4. Hindu
5. Sikh
6. Other
7. Atheist

So if the respondent replied 'Christian' the code would be Ai1.

The questionnaire should look professional, with good-quality paper, and a clear typeface and font size. People like dealing with things that look appealing and are more likely to complete a document that does.

Executing the survey

In implementing a questionnaire-based survey the researcher needs to consider time and cost constraints – these affect which type of survey you do (postal or face-to-face vs telephone). The researcher must think about timescale also in the sense of what is being studied. Accessibility of the sample must be considered as this will also affect how the survey is conducted; for instance sampling of working mothers may be more easily done by telephone to ensure they are at home (at night) and so as not to take up too much time. Also, the researcher must think about what is being surveyed; for instance if conducting a survey into sexual habits, postal surveys may be better as they ensure anonymity thus making it easier for people to complete them.

BOX 2.9

The British Household Census

One of the biggest examples of a questionnaire-based survey is the British Household Census held every ten years. The first census took place in 1801, prompted by concerns that the population would outstrip the country's resources. Thus the first census was seen as a way of ascertaining the needs of the population of the time. The first census reached 10.5 million people. The most recent census in 2001 was completed by 24 million. The census has run every ten years since 1801 except in 1941 owing to the Second World War. The census form is delivered to every household in the UK and people are required by law to complete the form. In 1991, 342 people faced prosecution for not completing their census forms. The census form contains 40 questions regarding age, sex, ethnicity, religion (this question appeared for the first time in the 2001 census), educational quali-fications, transport, occupation and housing details. The census is seen as a vital tool for central and local government planning as well as a means to get a 'snapshot' of the UK population. The census is a massive undertaking costing £225 million and employ-ing thousands of temporary researchers. The census is run by the Office for National Statistics. To ensure confidentiality census forms are not released into public record until a hundred years have elapsed from the time they were collected, thus the 2001 forms will not be available to public scrutiny until 2102.

Researchers always conduct a small-scale pilot study to review how well the questionnaire 'works' and what sort of data is being generated, so that questions can be changed. Once the results of the pilot have been reviewed then the full-scale survey can be implemented.

Evaluation

Surveys are cost- and time-effective and also very valid and reliable. They are easily analysed and generate highly workable statistical data. However, there are a number of drawbacks. Questionnaires are artificial and limited in what they ask and in terms of the data generated: there is no scope for exploring issues that may not have been predicted when designing the questionnaire. People might complete questionnaires differently from how they would have done had they been asked the same questions face-to-face. They might complete the questionnaire incorrectly or miss questions. Data is open to interpretation and can be manipulated in statistical analysis. This is particularly true of controversial data, such as unemployment figures or crime statistics, which are often manipulated or distorted for political reasons. Finally, the questions asked might reflect the cultural prejudices and biases of the researcher.

Ethical considerations

Even with such an objective method, and where the researcher is at a distance from the respondent, ethics are still crucial. Just because someone is in another town completing a questionnaire does not mean that ethical principles can be disregarded. Questionnaires must include ethical statements and background information regarding the survey, the researcher and contact details. Many interpretivist researchers view the survey not necessarily as unethical but as incapable of producing insightful or personal material. Researchers interested in subjectivity and reflexivity view the survey with some suspicion, and many feminist researchers have seen it as a tool of oppression used by (male) researchers to establish and maintain distance and authority of (female) subjects. There is a sense whereby the survey is impersonal but it should not be assumed that this necessarily allows a sense of ethical detachment or lack of sensitivity towards subjects.

Discussion questions

A survey on poverty was conducted by the Joseph Rowntree Foundation and published in September 2000. It found that 24 per cent of the population (15 million people) were poor and that 33 per cent of all children living in the UK (2 million) were living below the poverty line. The first such survey had been conducted in 1980 and there has been a 10 per cent rise in poverty since then. The findings of the Rowntree study were based on the following definition of poverty: 'going without at least three items regarded as necessities, such as sufficient clothing, heating and three meals a day'.

1 What are the pros and cons of using this definition of poverty as a basis for conducting a survey?

2 What other definitions of poverty might be used for such a task?

STAGE 6: ANALYSING DATA

Once data has been generated the researcher can begin to process and analyse it for key patterns, findings or trends. The process of analysing data can begin while research is continuing, particularly in large-scale projects that might seek to publish preliminary findings and then pursue certain areas for investigation. However, on small-scale projects it might be easier, with the constraints of time, to strictly delineate the different stages of research. There are different techniques for analysing different types of data and it is a good idea if you read up about it in a more specialised text such as Rose and Sullivan (1993) or Gilbert (1993). However, some basic points can be made here.

Quantitative data

Questionnaires, observations and interviews can all generate quantitative data. With the development of computers there now exist a number of different software packages which make data analysis relatively straightforward and much faster than in the past when researchers had to rely on basic coding schemes and their own statistical abilities. The aim in analysing quantitative data is to produce statistical information from which the researcher can draw patterns and trends.

- *Computer analysis*. Most researchers would make use of a computer data analysis program, the most commonly used in sociology is SPSS. These programs speed up analysis and can produce highly complex and detailed statistical analysis. Researchers require specialist training before they can use them.

- *Basic coding*. Without computers, analysis of data is still possible but requires accurate coding and good statistical ability. Basic coding involves allocating numbers or letters (or both) to categories, questions or attitudes; for example:

Religion	Code
Christian – Protestant	1a
Christian – Catholic	1b
Muslim	2
Hindu	3
Sikh	4
Jewish	5
Non-religious	6

Attitude to parental leave	Code
Strongly agree	1
Agree	2
Neither agree nor disagree	3
Disagree	4
Strongly disagree	5

- *Data matrices*. Another technique for analysing and presenting data is the use of data matrices. For example, imagine if we had continued our survey of attitudes to parental leave and how religious beliefs affect them:

	Question 1	Question 2	Question 3
Respondent A	Religion	View of parental leave	Salary range
Respondent B	Religion	View of parental leave	Salary range
Respondent C	Religion	View of parental leave	Salary range
Respondent D	Religion	View of parental leave	Salary range

A theoretical framework can be built around such data analysis through incorporating data from previous studies by others in the same field, and by utilising theoretical ideas regarding concepts studied. The use of government and other public agencies' data on gender inequality and pay for a set time period would also help provide a framework for interpretation. The more thorough the analysis and the more complete the background literature review the more useful and complete the interpretive framework will be.

■ *Statistical analysis.* Once data has been coded and is accessible then statistical calculations can be made.

■ *Avoiding errors.* It is essential that the data accurately reflects what is being measured, and time must be taken to eradicate miscalculations, wrongly defined variables and so forth.

Qualitative data

Qualitative data can also be analysed in a variety of ways. Qualitative data analysis is not concerned with generating statistics but rather in giving insight to attitudes, behaviours and beliefs. This makes it much harder to analyse and there is less to quantify; it also places much on the interpretive sensitivity of the researcher. Qualitative research typically generates a transcript that is either a written account of an interview or an observation. Analysis starts with the production of this transcript.

Producing a transcript

How you record your interview data has a great effect on what your transcript looks like. If you have used a Dictaphone and recorded everything then you have to transcribe your interview verbatim. You must ensure that you give yourself plenty of time to do this.

The format should be along the following lines. Start with a title (such as 'subject 1' or 'interview 1') followed by biographical details, date, time, setting of interview, plus duration of interview. An ethical statement and introductory comments about yourself and the purpose of the interview should follow this. Following all this the actual interview can be transcribed. The traditional way to do this is in a script format:

> *Interviewer*: How long did you work at the glass factory?
> *Alex*: ummmm, let's seee, 'bout 40 years, I guess, ermm (she pauses) maybe 38,
>   . . . (laughs) my memory's pretty bad now, love.
> *Interviewer*: Did the women there get equal pay with the men?
> *Alex*: (breaking into a smile) oh lord no! can you imagine that?

This format includes notes of body gesture, intonation, pauses and so on. If notes were taken during the interview the transcription will not be verbatim but will rely on the researcher's summary of the discussion and probably a small number of key quotes. However, it is important to try to include as much information as possible and if an interview guide was constructed to include it:

> *Subject: glass factory*
> I asked Alex about her length of service and pay at the factory. She spent about 40 years working there. She found it funny that I had assumed that the men and women received equal pay: 'Can you imagine that!'

A transcript for an observation would be similar to that from an interview except it would describe events noted – for instance a religious ritual if observing a religious group.

Analysing the data

There are different ways of analysing qualitative data.

- *Computer packages*. Although most data analysis computer packages are aimed at quantitative research, more recently there have been a number developed for analysing qualitative data. These include NUDIST and Ethnograph. Although many interpretive researchers feel such programs remove the quality of interpretation and resist their use, those trying to work through a large quantity of material may use such packages.

- *Thematic analysis*. This is the most common form of analysis of interview/observation material. The researcher begins by transcribing his or her data. Once this is complete, he or she reviews it for categories or patterns (themes). Once key themes are 'pulled', the interview data can be rearranged around these themes, with 'irrelevant' data dropped. From this an outline of themes/issues can be constructed, bringing in material/theoretical ideas from a literature review or other secondary sources. There is a need to be ruthless with material and cut out what does not appear relevant to the topic. Many researchers begin their analysis by marking out their transcripts as below:

> *Interviewer*: How long did you work at the glass factory?   *Glass factory*
> *Alex*: ummmm, let's seee, 'bout 40 years, I guess, ermm (she   *40 yrs service*
> pauses) maybe 38, . . . (laughs) my memory's pretty bad now, love.
> *Interviewer*: Did the women there get equal pay with the men?   *Equal pay?*
> *Alex*: (breaking into a smile) oh lord no! can you imagine that?   *Pay diff*

By placing keywords or summaries in the margins of transcripts it is easier to produce a quick review outline of the interview. This can be made more and more specific, and quotes can be noted; to make it easier to view, different colours/fonts might be used. With the unstructured interview data (see above) a similar summarising style could be used after key points. Some researchers utilise a more elaborate coding process, allocating specific codes for specific data elements. Key points can be coded further by placing them on file cards or on a computer file:

Alex: interview 1 12/4/99
Glass factory – manufacturing
40 years – job for life?
Gender pay differential
Equality not expected

■ *Data matrices*. Another technique for analysing and presenting data is the use of data matrices. For example, imagine if we had continued our interview of glass factory workers:

	Question 1	*Question 2*	*Question 3*	*Question 4*	*Question 5*
Wendy	Length of service at factory	View of job for life	Pay rates	Gender inequality on pay	View of equal pay
Cheryl	Length of service at factory	View of job for life	Pay rates	Gender inequality on pay	View of equal pay
Kate	Length of service at factory	View of job for life	Pay rates	Gender inequality on pay	View of equal pay
Jaclyn	Length of service at factory	View of job for life	Pay rates	Gender inequality on pay	View of equal pay

After analysis, and as with quantitative data, a theoretical framework can be constructed. And, similarly, the more thorough the analysis and the more complete the literature review, the more useful and complete the interpretive framework will be.

STAGE 7: WRITING UP RESEARCH

With research completed and data analysed what is there left to do? The final stage of most research is the production of a text of some sort. It is easy to assume that given the difficulties of the previous stages the writing up stage would be straightforward. However, writing up is often the most difficult and challenging part of the research process. The process of writing up typically refers us back to the very beginnings of our research and the motivations that led us into researching. However, the purpose of research at its inception can often seem less important at its end. The results found may even force us to confront the utility and ultimate goals of our research. One end-product of research is usually a 'text' of some sort – whether in the form of a thesis, dissertation, report, documentary film, CD-Rom, web site, book or article.

The writing process

Following research, the researcher becomes an author on entering the writing up phase of research. Throughout the process of writing, right up to and beyond actual public 'broadcast' of text (typically through publication in the case of a monograph or a journal article or submission in the case of a dissertation or a report), the author must negotiate three main realms:

- *The aesthetic.* This is further divided into (a) language use and (b) layout of text. The author must consider what style s/he wishes to use (e.g. journalistic, travel-book, serious academic, scientific, etc.), what type of language would be best and what the actual structure of the text should be. As an illustration of this, a text filled with sociological jargon says something about that author's view of him- or herself and his or her audience and research, and wider issues relating to power. Similarly the very layout of a text can inform us about that author's motivations, politics and aims. Are chapters laid out in a chronological fashion, is the personal account separated from the professional and so forth? There are also wider aesthetic issues concerning the style of writing, grammar, spelling and sentence structure.

- *The personal.* There are an array of personal concerns, principles and ideas to consider. A number of issues can affect the author's 'voice': personal goals for the research; ethical issues; political ideals; the field experiences; and ties to research subjects.

- *The professional.* This realm involves the outside world of public demands upon researchers and their research. These can include the institutional demands, publishing demands, consumer demands, commercial demands, policy demands or career demands. In the case of a student research project, there are the constraints of assessment demands.

These three realms interact and overlap with each other but they are more typically in conflict with each other. The author must try to satisfy each realm in his or her work.

The text in progress

There are three major stages of text production:

■ *Constructing the text.* Text construction begins before actual research occurs. When you decide which methodological framework to adopt you have already made an important decision about your final text. Thus, methodology and its linked concerns of epistemology, hermeneutics, politics and ethics are crucial. The actual operation of the research in the field is the next stage, which has later consequences for text – ethical choices, the demands of data collection and the reflexive capabilities of the researcher all serve to manipulate data and also shape our view of research subjects and the wider nature/aims of our research. The third stage involves analysis of data that again looks back to previous stages and looks forward to the ultimate product: what is the data for? The ultimate goal in terms of text drives the approach to analysis. The final stage in construction is the actual planning and organising of the writing process. This is a very practical stage involving consideration of time, resources and personal writing skills, as well as more directed concerns of ethical, political and methodological objectives.

■ *Producing the text.* All research produces a number of texts. The typical researcher might have field diaries, monthly/annual reports, letters, tapes, photographs and collected data – all these are 'texts' and all are different. Together they present a more complete picture of the research. Each informs the production process as the researcher 'cuts and pastes' between each – consciously and unconsciously. Data alone does not create the final research text but rather a variety of sources. In creating a text the author must make important decisions concerning format, language, style, content and so forth. These are not purely aesthetic concerns but are driven by wider political, theoretical and professional objectives/ideals. Each is reflected in the final text. If one wishes to incorporate the 'voices' of field subjects, which format would be best equipped to do this? How does the researcher incorporate personal experiences/emotions? Can we make the text open and accessible to all, avoiding replication of societal power imbalances? These are the sorts of questions asked by the author to him- or herself. Is there scope for creativity and self-expression? Many reach the question 'whose text is it anyway?' Is it the author's or does it belong to the field subjects or the commissioning organisation? Ultimately this can lead us back to questioning our very purpose in doing the research: why did we do it, was it ethical, what can it do for the subjects involved?

■ *Disseminating the text.* The final step in writing is the dissemination of the finished product whether it is book, article or dissertation. When any author writes, he or she will have an audience in mind – ultimately the test of all work is public broadcast through a variety of means, such as seminar papers, conferences, publication and actual broadcast. 'Audience' cannot be forgotten, as the public role of research texts is the crucial one. Our 'audiences' have a controlling hand in our production of text. There are different audiences: institutional (researcher's university/researcher's funder), policy (does research have an applied sense?), populist (does it have a populist agenda?), peers (is there a need for peer recognition?), personal (for career development and personal satisfaction), and finally field subjects. We may write for only one of these groups but most try to write for a number of them. Many researchers negotiate their audience by producing different texts for different audiences.

Open-endedness

The final text produced from research is not the final text concerning that research nor is it the one true version of that research. Texts are not complete nor do they end. Each text begets commentary from audiences that feed back into that text, altering how it is understood and used. Authors will add to the text, literally through revised editions, or by producing materials derived from the text or the research from whence it came. Writing and text creation is open-ended and continuous. The incompleteness of text affords audience insight to the work; one can interpret the flaws, gaps and 'loose ends' as much as the main content. The author and audience must appreciate the incompleteness and insufficiency of texts. This is particularly the view taken by interpretivist researchers who view the reflection on text construction as an important part of the research process.

BOX 2.10

Writing tips

1 Always ensure that you fully understand your assessment criteria:
- *What is being asked of you in this assignment?* In other words what are your examiners looking for? Looking through past work might help to get a sense of expectations and also layout. Seek additional guidance if you are unsure about anything to do with your written work.
- *What criteria will your work be marked by?* Get a copy of the marking criteria to guide your writing.

2 Remember good writing takes time:
- *Plan your work well ahead of the submission date.* Give yourself plenty of time to collect resources, read and then work through drafts. Rushed writing always reads 'rushed'.
- *When writing, always work through drafts.* Never submit your first attempt at a piece of work.
- *Carefully proofread drafts.* Pay attention to detail: check for spelling, grammar, sloppy structure, poor linkage and general word-processing errors. These may seem trivial but they draw the reader away from your work and focus upon your careless errors.
- *Get others to read through your work.* A writer can get so close to their own work they end up failing to see mistakes. Also, by letting others read your work you can learn from your earlier mistakes and improve your written work.

As the intention of this chapter has been to demonstrate the practice of 'doing' social research, some tips to help produce written work, and in particular for work that is to be assessed, are provided in Box 2.10 above.

Writing checklist

One way to guide your writing and to check your final draft before submission is to ask yourself a series of reflexive questions like the ones listed in Table 2.2 below. The more yes answers the more chance of your finished text being up to the assessment standard. Obviously you might want to add to the list depending on your specific assignments.

Reflecting on writing

The point has been made in this chapter that good research involves a lot of reflection on the part of the researcher. The same can be true of writing. Just as initial research experiences may be fraught with problems, drawbacks and even disasters so too can early experiences of submitting written work. Research skills and writing skills can both be improved through practice and through reflecting upon experience. When an assessed piece of written work is returned it is easy to look at the grade and then put it to one side, particularly if the grade is not what had been hoped for. However, instead of forgetting about past work it is a good idea to take some time to reflect upon it:

- *Did it get the grade I expected?* If there is a discrepancy between what you expected and what you actually got then there needs to be some reflection on why. This is especially true if the work got a low grade, but even high grades can be improved upon.

- *Read the examiner's comments.* Most markers offer comments as to what worked and what did not in students' work. Use these as a guide to avoid making the same mistakes in the future.

- *Did I get the grade I deserved?* In other words, does the grade reflect the potential of the work and of myself as the writer? If the answer is no to either or both of these questions then changes have to be made with respect to approach to writing.

- *Is my writing improving?* Is the answer is yes then what is being done right? If the answer is no then how can this be rectified?

- *Is my approach to writing correct?* Take time to think about how you write and in what conditions – could these be altered to improve your written work?

- *Who can give me guidance?* Even the best writers need reassurance at some points so do not be nervous about seeking help either from course tutors, specialist learning tutors or from the numerous guides to writing available.

Table 2.2 Writing checklist

	Yes *(Please tick)*	No *(Please tick)*
Do I fully understand what I am being asked to do?		
Do I fully understand my assessment criteria?		
Do I have a sufficient literature survey?		
Do I need to include an abstract?		
Have I included transcripts if required?		
Do I need to include a discussion of timescale and planning?		
Do I need to include a discussion of budget?		
Have I reviewed methodological issues and shown where my research fits?		
Have I discussed my choice of research techniques fully and clearly?		
Is my data presented clearly?		
Have I discussed ethics?		
Do I analyse my data sensitively and as accurately as possible?		
Do I place my research and data in the wider sociological context?		
Do I offer suggestions for improving future research?		
Do I incorporate the work of others in my data analysis?		
Do I evaluate my research in relation to the work of others?		
Do I offer a critical awareness of my research?		
Do I have a clear and well-organised structure to the text?		
Are sentences short and snappy?		
Have I used subtitles and headings to make the text clearer?		
Do sections link well together?		
Have I used the correct referencing system?		
Have I included a correctly constructed bibliography?		
Is it word-processed?		
Have I done a spell-check?		
Have I read through a draft to check grammar and spelling?		
Have I asked someone else to read through a draft to check grammar and spelling?		

EXERCISES

1 Preparing for social research

(a) The background literature review

(i) Go to your university library and familiarise yourself with its research resources. Find out if you can receive training for specific databases.

(ii) Select a topic and conduct a database search using keywords.

(iii) Aim to locate two books and two journal articles using different databases.

(iv) Use the techniques listed above to conduct a brief literature survey.

(v) Find out what other libraries in your area you can use for your research. Familiarise yourself with their facilities and what access rights you have.

(b) Planning a research project: Students and paid employment exercise

The National Union of Students (NUS) has been awarded a grant of £120,000 from the Department of Education and Skills to investigate the growing problem of student debt, stress and high drop-out rates. The timescale for the research is eight months. Building on research data collected from the Higher Education Funding Council for England listed below:

(i) Formulate a hypothesis.

(ii) Operationalise indicators.

(iii) Select a population.

(iv) Suggest possible sampling strategies.

(v) What data do you feel is missing, from the tables below, in terms of being able to produce a complete view of the student population?

(vi) Construct a research plan, including proposed methods techniques, budget, timetable.

Student population by age and sex

	Male	Female
Under 21	300,000	250,000
21–24	110,000	200,000
25+	90,000	150,000

Student population by social class

		% of student population
I	Professional	28
II	Intermediate	27
IIIN	Skilled non-manual	23
IIIM	Skilled manual	18
IV	Partially skilled	3
V	Unskilled	1

Student dropout rates by sex, age and class as a percentage of each population

	Male I %	Female I %	Male II %	Female II %	Male IIIN %	Female IIIN %	Male IIIM %	Female IIIM %	Male IV %	Female IV %	Male V %	Female V %
Under 21	1	0.6	1.5	1	11	8	45	33	78	75	83	78
21–24	0.5	0.3	2.3	1.9	15	11	51	36	79	81	85	82
25+	2	0.8	1.8	2.1	21	13	49	52	84	74	78	85

Student time use (by age) as a percentage of overall time

	Academic study %	Paid employment %	Leisure %	Family/domestic work %
Under 21	15	30	45	10
21–24	18	33	24	25
25+	16	18	14	52

Percentage of students in paid employment by age

	%
Under 21	80
21–24	92
25+	45

2 Researching social life

(a) Observation

(i) Try to conduct a naturalistic observation in a specific public social setting. Set yourself a time limit and try to log everything that occurs around you.

(ii) Try to conduct a participant observation. While participating in some personal social interaction try to take notes either during or after the event of everything that happened.

(iii) Compare and contrast the two types of observation. How would you evaluate each in terms of difficulty, data collection, ethics and observer role.

(iv) Why do you think most researchers combine observation with other techniques?

(b) Interviewing

One of the best ways of testing interview skills is to practise in front of others. This might be nerve-racking but it will still be less tense than a real interview.

(i) In a large group of 10–15, divide the group into two smaller groups. Allocate one group the task of conducting a structured interview, while the other conducts an unstructured interview. Each group should volunteer an interviewer and an interviewee. Each group will interview the other. The two groups should choose the same topic to investigate.

(ii) Each group must prepare an interview schedule or guide.

(iii) Each interview should take no more than 10 minutes and the interviewers must record responses and act as they would during a real interview. The interviewee can play any role they wish, whether it be awkward or friendly.

(iv) The whole group should compare and contrast the two interviews: what are their different pros and cons?

(v) How well are the interviewers doing? How well would you have done?

(vi) Repeat the task until everyone has had a chance to be interviewer.

(c) Surveying

Use the questions listed below to construct a face-to-face survey questionnaire. Pre-code questions and consider coding, both of questions and answers. Also reflect on question order.

(i)   What kinds of things come to mind when you think of poverty?

(ii)   Do you think any of the following are essentials for living? Car, video, microwave, mobile phone, TV, central heating, fridge, freezer, satellite TV, games console, housing, annual holiday, savings, balanced diet, new clothes.

(iii)   Which of the above would you be able to live without?

(iv)   Age

(v)   Gender

(vi)   Marital status

(vii)   Social class

(viii) Household income

(ix)   Do you ever cut back on essentials, such as food, heating, rent or clothing owing to budget?

(x)   Do you think there is 'real' poverty in the UK today?

(xi)   How would you define being poor?

(d) Analysing the data

Using the data collected from the two mock interviews above:

(i)   Construct a basic transcript.

(ii) Construct a data matrix with which to analyse the interview data.

(iii) What key themes can be extracted from the data?

(iv) What are the limitations of the data?

(v)   How might the data be improved?

Make copies of the questionnaire devised above and then administer it to a group of people. Once the questionnaires are completed:

(i)   Using the coding system, construct a data matrix.

(ii) Conduct a basic statistical analysis of the data.

(iii) What themes or patterns emerge?

(iv) How might the data be improved?

Part 2

Sociological Theory

The nature of social theory

SAM PRYKE

'Nothing like the act of eating for equalising men', continued Mr Bell. 'Dying is nothing to it. The philosopher dies sententiously – the Pharisee ostentatiously – the simple-hearted humbly – the poor idiot blindly, as the sparrow to the ground; the philosopher and idiot, publican and Pharisee, all eat after the same fashion – given an equally good digestion. There's a theory for you!'

'Indeed I have no theory', replied Mr Thornton. 'I hate all theories'.

Elizabeth Gaskell, *North and South* (1854)

The above conversation is from the mid-nineteenth-century novel *North and South* by Elizabeth Gaskell. The first speaker, Mr Bell, is an Oxford academic, given to flights of rather pretentious conjecture. The second speaker, Mr Thornton, is a hard-nosed northern factory owner who, despite making efforts to educate himself, has no time for indulging in displays of cleverness for their own sake. His approach is a straightforward, pragmatic one, taking life it as it comes. In so far as he advances any general view of society throughout the book, it is that it is ordered by the self-evident laws of free market economics to which 'there is no alternative'. This is not a theory as such, as theory, no matter how dogmatic, always leaves open the possibility of debate. Rather it is an ideological assertion. But leaving this aside, it is probably the case that many people, sociology students among them, would instinctively have rather more sympathy for the approach of Mr Thornton than Mr Bell. 'Why do we need theory?' is a question typically asked at the outset of social theory courses. The lecturer with responsibility for a social theory course may find the question irritating and, if oft repeated, demoralising. Despite this, it is not one that is much dealt with in the numerous books on social theory. Even the more recent 'student friendly' texts appear to assume that theory is a subject to be studied and then proceed to discuss the subject, usually from the 'founding fathers' (sic) onwards.

Although there has been some discussion of which social theorists should be taught to undergraduates and which of them should be given pride of place, there is generally little coverage of what social theory constitutes, what is distinctive about it and what is important in its study. Too often these questions are by-passed at the outset of social theory texts which immediately plunge into discussion of Auguste Comte, or whoever might start the roll-call of social theorists. In this introduction we take the view that questions about what social theory is, and why it matters, are important and should not be dodged. The questions raised and examined in this and subsequent chapters are academic and challenging; and we start from the assumption that the intellectual doubts that may surround social theory are genuine, important and worth considering. In the course of addressing such questions and issues we hope to indicate why it is important and stimulating to study social theory.

This introduction is not intended as a defensive exercise to, by turn, refute every criticism that might be levelled at social theory. Still less is it an attempt to 'sell' social theory to the sceptical undergraduate. If anything, it aims to celebrate the role and diversity of social theory. Starting with the question 'why do we need theory?', we introduce and work through a broadly positive set of findings about the vital role social theory occupies in understanding social phenomena. In doing this we will make certain concessions to the criticisms that can be made of social theory. This should not be considered merely an attempt to 'buy off' the critic, as we certainly would not wish to suggest that everything in the world of theory is perfect; rather it is a question of trying to achieve the right balance. Before anything else, however, it is necessary to indicate what we take social theory to be.

DEFINITIONS

There are two differing, if interrelated, ways of approaching the vexed issue of definition. One is to try to point to the core assumptions in the corpus of work known as social theory – its major concerns and what it actually does, for instance. This approach is taken by Alex Callinicos in a recent book that sketches chronologically the development of social theory from the eighteenth-century Enlightenment onwards. He argues that social theory has three identifying features: a concern with society as distinct from political institutions; an ability to distinguish between different kinds of society; and a preoccupation with the analysis of modernity (Callinicos 1999: 1–2). This may serve as one means to locate and follow the rise of social theory, but trying to bring together a common set of assumptions and purposes from a vast and diffuse body of work in this fashion is problematic. A definition such as Callinicos's may be valid for holistic, structural social theory of the type favoured by Marx and Durkheim. Even here, though, the first given feature – society as distinct from politics – is not necessarily evidenced in the work of Marx. More obviously, however, it does not encapsulate the nature and intent of the kinds of social theory that are concerned with micro forms of social behaviour. Ethnomethodology, which has had some influence in academic sociology since the 1970s, is not much concerned with macro comparisons between societies, but chiefly with the process of how rules are established in the course of everyday life. Thus attempts to delineate the parameters down which social theory proceeds – for example, its aims and objectives, what it is concerned with and what sorts of things it wants to say – are all but impossible to establish. This is partly a product of the plurality of approaches to social theory and, indeed, it may be more appropriate to talk of theor*ies* rather than a single theory.

A second and, we feel, more profitable approach in constructing a useful definition, is to try to identify the procedure inherent in the thinking that characterises social theory. To pursue this line would not involve identifying what a social theory is concerned with as a whole, but rather the commonalties in the construction of a social theory. It would involve trying to discern whether there are common means by which the various 'houses' of social theory are constructed, rather than considering the extent to which they share any general resemblance. As the focus shifts away from the intent to the nature of social theory, so the exercise becomes more concerned with the 'what is a theory?' rather than 'what is "social" theory?' This may seem a more difficult means to try to arrive at a useful definition, and indeed it does take us into the province of the philosophical construction of thought. However, philosophy, if used sensibly, is above all a means of clarification and, in an initial sense, that is what a definition is concerned with. Ultimately a definition of social theory derived in such a fashion would have to proceed by careful examination of the various theoretical schools of thought on offer. Although that is neither possible nor desirable here, some initial points can be made about theory in general.

A theory is a set of linked, interrelated propositions that attempt to explain the origin, motivation and purpose of a particular phenomenon, such as religious practice or patterns of employment. Prefixing the word 'theory' with the term 'social' simply indicates what type of theory it is; there are theories of genetic development, quantum physics and so on. The validity of a social theory can be assessed by how accurately it explains the social phenomena it is concerned with. Therefore, it must be in some way testable. A theory that might appear appealing because of its sophistication but is ultimately unknowable belongs not so much to sociology as to a branch of philosophy known as metaphysics. However, as a theory is about the nature of social life it cannot be simply 'knocked down' and discounted by individual instances of social life that would appear to contradict it. In this sense a theory is necessarily an abstract body of knowledge. This being the case, it can and should be assessed by its internal logical coherence, and its logic in comparison to other social theories.

This rather general definition of what a social theory is, we would suggest, unavoidable. However, the following sections attempt to substantiate it through looking at some of the typical criticisms of social theory and responding to them.

Discussion questions

Look at extracts a, b, c and d. Which of the following descriptions most closely fits each extract: social theory; unsubstantiated assertion; religious/metaphysical belief; moral principle. Provide a brief explanation for your answer.

(a) A polygamous lifestyle on earth will ensure that one is elected to a heavenly kingdom after death. Every male will be given a world of his own to people with his extended family; a woman's selection will depend on the number of children she produces.

(b) The achievement of social life among people, the existence of social order and social solidarity, is ensured by collective standards of behaviour and values. Without the regulation of society, individuals would attempt to satisfy their own desires and wishes. For a working society, individuals need to accept a set of values.

(c) The right way for people to live is to treat other people's property with respect and never to take it without their agreement.

(d) It is clear that red-haired people will always work harder than those with blonde or dark hair.

RESPONDING TO CRITICISMS OF SOCIAL THEORY

As mentioned earlier, a consideration of some of the questions and criticisms raised about social theory will, we feel, help provide an understanding of the nature of such theory and its importance as an area of study in its own right. In the rest of this section we examine a number of these common criticisms under the following headings: social theory is simply unnecessary; social theory is obscure and self-obsessed; and social theory is dead, white and male.

Social theory is simply unnecessary

This was touched on above: theory is an unnecessary exercise as we do not really require a general understanding(s) of social phenomena. This sort of charge comes in part from other academic disciplines. Historians, for instance, sometimes complain that sociology substitutes theoretical musings for an actual knowledge of facts. More widely, the continuing hostility of sections of British and North American academia for the type of theory called post-structuralism is that its original French exponents were given to abstract theoretical speculation that factual Anglo-Saxons are not prone to. This kind of objection to social theory is even found in the discipline of sociology. It is occasionally claimed that theory is dispensable as it is possible 'to just do' sociology by the collection of facts alone. This approach is sometimes referred to as empiricism. And it is fair to say that even among sociologists who do see theory as being important and worthwhile there are occasional misgivings over the fact that, with one or two honourable exceptions, the subject's most eminent figures are theorists who have rarely done any first-hand research. While we can perhaps leave aside some of the more petty and nationalist criticisms of social theory, the latter point is rather more important.

In order to respond to the objection that social theory is unnecessary we need to consider two things: (a) the role and importance of theoretical thinking and (b) the relationship of theory to research.

In relation to (a), the initial point that needs to be made about the role and importance of theoretical thinking is that it is not a mental process that is quite separate from everyday life. It is impossible to state in general what proportion of our thought on a day-to-day basis might be described as deploying 'theory' in some rudimentary way. Obviously, much of our immediate knowledge and use of it does not depend on anything that might reasonably be called theory. We do not need to utilise what could be called 'theoretical thinking' in trying to explain, for example, why our one-year-old is crying if we know for a fact that she did not sleep this afternoon and is tired and irritable; and we do not need a theoretical knowledge to know what to do about it – feed her, bath her and put her to bed. However, other kinds of explanation do involve theoretical explanation. It is fairly common in everyday conversation to hear somebody say, 'I have a theory about . . .'. This could be a seemingly intelligent preamble to pure speculation about something, or it could be something rather more than that. For instance, we might hear somebody say something like, 'I have a theory why Dave and Margaret's marriage broke up. It was when Dave started working away from home about three years ago that things started to go downhill.' The person saying this does not, presumably, know the full story with all the details. Rather, he or she would be relating the beginning of a downward spiral of a relationship in response to the strain produced by one of the parties being away from home for long periods. He or she does not know for sure that it was the isolation and loneliness, the pressures of bringing up children single-handedly and/or the temptation to be unfaithful that contributed to the breakdown of a relationship. However, he or she does know that these things are more likely to arise when a couple are away from one another. The knowledge may come from personal experience, previous instances and from a wider perception – in itself acquired in various ways – of the mechanics of relationships: what sustains them, what makes for their disintegration and so on. What the speaker has done is really very simple: he or she has used his or her general understanding and applied it to the particular instance. Of course, the speaker may be quite wrong in his or her 'theoretical interpretation'; nonetheless this form of thinking should be distinguished from pure guesswork where there is neither a precedent nor a larger pattern that might be used to explain an event.

Of course, there is a lot more to a fully developed social theory than this. The point is that theoretical thinking is not the obscure and esoteric exercise that people sometimes imagine it to be. And, moreover, while the 'step up' into social theory requires both intellectual knowledge and rigour, it is not such a quantum leap from the everyday ways in which we interpret the world around us. To continue with our example of marital break-up, aspects of Durkheimian social theory, in particular, might explain the context of the break-up of a relationship in relation to, for instance, the anomie of advanced contemporary societies in which relationships suffer dislocations and disruption. In order for this to be a convincing theoretical explanation it would be necessary to establish, firstly, that the incidence of separation and divorce among couples where one of the parties worked away from the family was greater than average and, secondly, that there was a wider economic and social context for such patterns of working which makes for a generalised tension within marital relationships. This sort of analysis is hardly likely to have been done by the imagined speaker quoted above, as it would require financial and professional resources. A sociologist might be able to.

This takes us to (b) the issue of the relationship of theory to research, the second of the two things that need to be considered. As indicated above, the eminence of some theoretical sociologists seems in a perverse kind of way to derive from the fact that they have never conducted any empirical research. For instance, the famous contemporary sociologist Anthony Giddens has rarely engaged in the processes of research, such as interviewing people, organising questionnaires and so on. Rather, he has been content to gather together the findings and arguments of others in the compilation of his numerous books. Indeed, it can sometimes appear that there is a sort of division of labour in academic sociology between those who collect the data and those who spin the data into theory and win the academic plaudits. Having said that, Giddens does actually draw upon empirical research in his writing. In the 1970s, a group of British social theorists (such as Paul Hirst and Barry Hindess) emerged who, deriving their 'inspiration' from the thought of a French philosopher, Louis Althusser, rejected empirical investigation almost entirely, to the extent of labelling it vulgar. More recently, the theoretical musings of the German sociologist Ulrich Beck have attracted much attention. While it would be inaccurate to say that Beck has nothing interesting to say about, among other things, the nature of risk in contemporary society, it is difficult to find evidence of how research figures in his thinking. His books rather give the impression that he has simply sat down and written about society through the medium of pre-existing theory (Beck 1992) – a criticism that has also been levelled at Goffman (see Chapter 6).

All of this is to suggest that there is no necessary and automatic connection between systematic research and theory. Perhaps the matter is captured most accurately and tellingly by the French sociologist Pierre Bourdieu who is likely to have at least as great a legacy within the subject as either of the thinkers mentioned above: 'Research without theory is blind, and theory without research is empty – it doesn't even merit the name theory' (Bourdieu 1992: 162). In line with this position, we would argue that research is vital to a theory. A theory by its very nature must be testable in order to convince – it should be able to produce evidence that its postulates are correct. People may accept a set of assertions because they are thought intuitively or aesthetically appealing. Alternatively, people may believe in a set of postulates because they are taken on faith as they concur with a general outlook, of perhaps a political or religious type. However, such a body of thought does not constitute a social theory. While we are inevitably swayed by a number of subjective factors in formulating or assessing a theory, to be meaningful such assessment must be based on more than subjectivity.

Why, then, is theory necessary to research? There are a number of possible reasons we might give. The first and the most important is that theory informs and organises the type of research we undertake, as the particular theoretical approach adopted will influence both the questions and issues examined and the particular type of research method adopted. This is because of the integral relationship of a theory to a research method. It is not the case that theory A will inevitably insist upon research method A, or that theory B will automatically lend itself to methodology B. The relationship is more complicated than that. Nevertheless, there are certain dispositions of theories to research methods. For instance, the general concern of symbolic interactionists with the search for meaning and order within the micro encounters of individuals and small-scale groups, means that they are unlikely to be concerned with statistical data on the socio-economic characteristics of broad social groups. Rather they have tended to favour observation of interaction by the researcher. It is not necessarily the case that they will dismiss the use of statistics altogether – although this might be so and they will probably have criticisms to make about the compilation of statistics. It is much more likely that as their gaze is directed at small-scale processes of behaviour, then their research will inevitably focus there. Conversely, Marxists' concentration upon the larger picture of capitalism with a strong historical emphasis has meant that they have favoured data and findings that apply to societies as a whole, or indeed to world capitalism. It is important to stress that this is only a tendency; although Marxism is concerned with the totality, its application in sociology has often rested upon one particular aspect of society (for instance, in the case of Beynon's research, a car factory; Beynon 1973).

Leaving aside the issue of the degree of fit between a particular theoretical approach and a particular research method, it would appear from the discussion thus far that theory very much drives methodology. Therefore the sociologist will select his or her method on the basis of the theoretical approach first adopted. In general terms it is probably the case that theory comes before the methodology rather than the other way around. However, it may well be that dissatisfaction with a method in the course of using it – the collection of statistics for instance – will lead to a modification or even wholesale change of the sociologist's theoretical stance. This is to say that the relationship between theory and method is often more complex and bound up with the experience of fieldwork than is sometimes assumed. This does not alter the fact that theory acts as the background to the nature and direction of data collection. Put simply, what view we take of the world informs how we try to find out about it.

Secondly, theory informs how we interpret the data collected. This is not simply a case of arriving at particular conclusions, but also refers to the type of theoretical scrutiny we apply to the data. For instance, a symbolic interactionist may examine organised gambling for the shared terms and conventions that enable the practice to take place, while a more structurally oriented sociologist may simply be concerned with the class and gender of people who participate in gambling.

Thirdly, theory can act as a stimulus to pursue particular research topics and questions. Thus sociologists may seek to verify or refute certain theoretical arguments that they have encountered in the work of others, and which perhaps strike a chord with them or with which they disagree. Similarly, sociologists may be stimulated to return to earlier findings in the light of more recent theoretical thinking. This suggests a split between those in sociology who compose the theory and those who do the 'donkey work'. It is not one that we would support, but there is no doubt that it exists. It does not, however, affect the vital relationship between theory and research.

Discussion questions

1 List the sorts of research question that some of the theorists you have come across – for example feminists, Marxists, interpretivists and postmodernists – might ask in investigating juvenile crime; church membership; use of mass media.

Fill in the matrix below with your suggestions

	Juvenile crime	Church membership	Mass media
Feminist			
Marxist			
Interpretivist			
Postmodernist			

2 What methods might each theorist use to answer those questions?

Social theory is obscure and self-obsessed

In the previous section we have suggested not only that social theory can be necessary to organise and interpret research, but also that, broadly speaking, theory involves a shift from the general to the particular, and that that is not in itself a wholly new kind of thinking. However, there is a second and, in a way, more basic criticism of social theory: it is contrived (intentionally difficult), jargon-ridden, internally oriented and of unnecessarily numerous hues and persuasions. In our view there is rather more to this point than the claim that social theory is simply unnecessary. In essence, the objection that we will consider can be summarised as the claim that (a) social theory is poorly written and (b) it is really about itself rather than being about anything else.

The criticism that social theory has a tendency to disguise the commonplace in complexity and explain itself in convoluted, jargon-ridden prose has been made at least as much from within the discipline as from outside. Perhaps most famously, American sociologist C. Wright Mills ridiculed the arch-functionalist sociologist Talcott Parsons for his tendency to take three pages to say something fairly straightforward that could be put in a single sentence (Mills 1959).

BOX 3.1

Mills' translation of Parsons' 'grand theory'

In his renowned introduction to sociology, *The Sociological Imagination* (1970) C. Wright Mills criticises the structural functionalist theorist Talcott Parsons for his unnecessarily obscure and wordy style. The extract below is taken from this criticism, in which he claims that Parsons' book *The Social System* can be translated and reduced from 550 pages to 150.

Grand Theory

Let us begin with a sample of grand theory, taken from Talcott Parsons's *The Social System* – widely regarded as a most important book by a most eminent representative of the style.

   An element of a shared symbolic system which serves as a criterion or standard for selection among the alternatives of orientation which are intrinsically open in a situation may be called a value . . . But from this motivational orientation aspect of the totality of action it is, in view of the role of symbolic systems, necessary to distinguish a 'value-orientation' aspect. This aspect concerns, not the meaning of the expressed state of affairs to the actor in terms of his gratification–deprivation balance but the content of the selective standards themselves. The concept of value-orientations in this sense is thus the logical device for formulating one central aspect of the articulation of cultural traditions into the action system.

   It follows from the derivations of normative orientation and the role of values in action as stated above, that all values involve what may be called a social reference . . . It is inherent in an action system that action is, to use one phrase, 'normatively oriented'. This follows, as was shown, from the concept of expectations and its place in action theory, especially in the 'active' phase in which the actor pursues goals. Expectations then, in combination with the 'double contingency' of the process of interaction as it has been called, create a crucially imperative problem of order. Two aspects of this problem of order may in turn be distinguished, order in the symbolic systems which make communication possible, and order in the mutuality of motivational orientation to the normative aspect of expectations, the Hobbesian problem of order.

   The problem of order, and thus of the nature of the integration of stable systems of social interaction, that is, of social structure, thus focuses on the integration of the motivation of actors with the normative cultural standards which integrate the action system, in our context inter-personality. These concepts are, in the terms used in the preceding chapter, patterns of value-orientation, and as such are a particularly crucial part of the cultural tradition of the social system . . .

To translate: people often share standards and expect one another to stick to them. In so far as they do, their society may be orderly. (End of translation)

Source: Mills, 1970, pp. 32–6

   The charge applies to other sociologists besides Parsons. Pierre Bourdieu is widely regarded as among the most important of contemporary social theorists, but both his critics and enthusiasts have complained of his tendency – partially corrected in more recent writings – to make everything he discusses seem highly complex (Jenkins 1992; Fowler 1997). Postmodern social theory claims to have freed itself from the elitism of traditional social theory by extending its remit to include groups and issues that were hitherto excluded. Again, however, both those who have welcomed and rejected postmodernism have noted that it frequently adopts a convoluted style that actually seems intent upon reinforcing the traditional barriers of academic access through intimidating the reader. It is perhaps unfortunate that there are few if any contemporary sociologists who have the ability to express complex ideas with the panache and clarity of the leading biology writers (and bestsellers) like Stephen J. Gould and Stephen Dawkins. More generally, some have cited sociology's seeming inability to express itself well as an important reason for the decline in its public profile and importance since the mid-1970s (Halsey 1996).

However, we would argue that there is only *some* truth in the accusation. There are a number of issues to distinguish here. In the first place, the charge that the subject is practised by intellectual charlatans who have somehow fooled the rest of us into believing they have something important to say, is likely to be made by those who are almost entirely ignorant of sociology and seem to have some kind of grudge against the subject in particular and academics more generally. Secondly, it is important to note that the issues addressed by social theory are, by their very nature, complex. So, while clarity of expression should be valued, the fact that something is not immediately comprehensible does not mean that the writer is incapable of explaining him or herself clearly. It could be that simplifying something – or to use the contemporary expression, 'dumbing down' – will result in a caricature. Indeed, we would argue strongly that when reading social theory it is essential to develop the ability to distinguish what is really rather obvious but poorly put from that which is complex but important – and therefore worth persevering with.

Thirdly, sociological terms – the word 'jargon' has a pejorative connotation – are vital to the ability of sociologists to express themselves with precision. In this respect, sociology is no different from any other discipline. It is not simply the case that professionals think up unfamiliar terms that are not generally used in everyday life so as to keep out the uninitiated. Nor, relatedly, that learning to do sociology involves learning to use such terms 'in the right way'. Rather they can be considered tools that should be used for appropriate purposes in the craft of sociology. For instance, the terms 'sex' and 'gender' have important distinctions in that they allow sociologists to specify meaning. Sex refers to biological differences (and to a sexual relationship of some type), while gender refers to the social roles and expectations associated with masculinity and femininity which cannot be reduced to biology. In a perverse way, the 'problem' with terms is not their unfamiliarity but their contested and multiple meanings. Some sociologists, for instance, would argue that gender is wholly socially constructed. Others would wish to incorporate the importance of a genetic influence into gender difference. But this does not weaken the importance of the distinction between sex and gender.

Fourthly, it is not the case that reading social theory is necessarily an instrumental procedure required to exact information from the lifeless prose of the book or journal. Some of the 'great sociologists' were indeed master stylists. Emile Durkheim's *Elementary Forms of Religious Life*, for instance, is written with tremendous poise and self-confidence; and some of Marx's writing has the qualities of great journalism. However, we do not use the word 'master' unwittingly: there is a definite tendency for Durkheim to laud his enormous intelligence and knowledge over us – although, as it happens, in this book and others he made some blatant errors (Lukes 1973). Today, few contemporary sociologists write with Durkheim's authoritative sweep. The general point is that in studying social theory you should develop an ability to read texts to discern whether or not the writer attempts to engage their arguments with you, rather than simply trying to dazzle or coerce you into agreeing with them. This is not, moreover, simply to see whether 'you like' a theorist or not, as the plausibility of the argument is, in part, contained in the mode and the clarity of its expression. In short, to gain an understanding of social theory requires an ability to read critically. On occasions you may come to the judgement that the text is convoluted rubbish. However, a blanket condemnation of this type should not be used as an easy option to condemn all social theory.

The second aspect of this criticism is that social theory is an academic form of navel-gazing as social theorists only ever talk about social theory. Indeed, there is an introverted aspect to much contemporary social theory. Too often it appears to have shifted from a general body of knowledge and methodological procedure designed to map an understanding of the social world to a form of academic self-address in which one sociologist takes issue with another's theory, or more usually aspects of it. At worst, then, theory can seem a form of scholastic nit-picking. Relatedly, some people become frustrated by sociologists' apparent inability to agree about anything. For instance, many introductory sociology textbooks, especially at A-level, present the subject as a set of basically incompatible theoretical interpretations – the functionalist view, the Marxist view and so on – of any given topic: the family, work, deviance. While there is little point in trying to fend off all of these charges, there are at least two valid responses that we would like to make.

Firstly, as indicated above in the discussion of definitions (p. 74), part of the way of assessing the validity of a social theory – or indeed any theory – is to examine its internal logic and coherence. Therefore the process of theoretical scrutiny is an important one. In part this is done through comparing the claims of one theoretical position with those of another (as well as by assessing how well a theory stands up empirically). Secondly, it is simply inconceivable to hope to locate one, 'ultimate' sociological theory. Several sociologists have attempted to devise a single theoretical edifice. Most famously, Talcott Parsons argued in the late 1940s that 'there is every prospect that the current diversity of theories will converge in the development of a single theoretical structure' (Parsons 1948). His contention was that, in order for sociology to be taken seriously as a full and mature science, it had to rid itself of internal disagreement and unite around a single theoretical pole. In the following decade, the 1950s, there developed at least the semblance of unity within North American sociology through structural functionalism and an integrated empirical research agenda, as exemplified by the work of Lazarsfeld *et al.* (1944). Even during this period, however, there were those like Robert Merton who, while sharing much in common with Parsons, were unconvinced by the quest for intellectual consensus, and others, such as the various members of the Chicago School, whose research orientation was rather different (Merton 1948). In the period since the 1950s differing theoretical approaches have experienced periods of influence. The major change since the mid-1980s has been the almost total effacement of Marxism by different varieties of postmodernism. However, despite this sea-change it is still possible to speak of a diversity of theories, rather than one sociological theory. Moreover, there is no good reason to think, or even hope, that there will be one single, overarching approach in the future.

There are various reasons for this, some of which are dealt with elsewhere in this book when different theoretical positions are examined. It is sufficient to mention here that it is a mistake to equate an absence of debate with scientific strength. There is certainly greater theoretical agreement in a subject like physics than in sociology, but it is not the case that all natural scientific disciplines are characterised by a single theoretical understanding. Evolutionary and genetic biologists disagree, for instance, about the most fundamental issues. Within the social sciences it is true that there appears to be a higher degree of internal disagreement in sociology than in other subjects. In a small and politically conservative subject like international relations, the realist perspective has been largely dominant, while debate in economics is not generally marked by wholesale theoretical differences. However, given the very wide range in the interests of sociologists, given the subject's uneven development across nations and continents, given the tangled web of philosophical antecedents and influences that one finds in social theory, it is inevitable that the subject is one of theor*ies*, rather than a theory. However, even while this is the case, it is also true that sociology is not beset by incessant disagreement. It is not the case that if you put two sociologists in a room three positions will emerge – as has been said about rabbis and theological interpretations. Two of the most important figures in contemporary sociology, Pierre Bourdieu and Anthony Giddens, have devoted a fair amount of their time to trying to synthesise the work of others into a distinctive approach that overcomes the alleged pitfall of a division of structure and agency in social theory (Giddens 1984; Bourdieu 1990). How far they have succeeded is not at issue here; the point is that rather than simply dishing out criticism of others, their intent has been to critically draw upon existing traditions to formulate an original sociology. In sum, while the lack of agreement can be frustrating and can prevent a useful exchange of views, the diversity of theoretical understandings in sociology is inevitable but should not be exaggerated. While some postmodernists suggest that a diverse sociology is in line with the fragmented times in which we live (Calhoun 1995), as with most other things that they claim are distinctly new, there are in fact precedents for this position. Robert Merton, for instance, certainly not somebody who would generally be considered a postmodernist – in fact, often bracketed with Parsons as the archetypal postwar functionalist – made this claim in the 1970s (Merton 1976).

Social theory as dead, white and male

So far we have argued that the criticisms of social theory as unnecessary, contrived and locked in internal disagreement might contain important elements of truth but do not undermine the importance of studying it. The same applies to the third criticism. The claim in itself is relatively straightforward: social theory is the product of dead, white, bourgeois men. Sometimes heterosexual is added to the checklist of privilege to complete the picture of social and economic power and exclusivity. The work of the majority of what are seen as the 'classic' social theorists, both in terms of its remit and underlying assumptions, reflects, it is argued, their geographical, class and gender position. Therefore, while the social theory of Marx, Durkheim and Weber, to take the obvious and principal examples, might not be overtly sexist, Eurocentric and heterosexist, occasionally what they say in these respects is tainted by their background. Their social theory is, moreover, somewhat anachronistic as the societies in which they lived and which they examined are almost unrecognisable to us today. By default, therefore, they can tell us very little about such subjects as sexuality, identity and ethnicity, which attract so much attention today (Parker 1997). This sort of critique broadens into the assertion that what we chiefly do when studying an arts or social science subject at university is study an institutionalised canon of 'great' thinkers – Shakespeare, Chaucer, Dickens, Elliot in literature for instance; Marx, Weber and Durkheim in sociology. This critique reflects the rise of postmodernism, identity politics and, more specifically, some feminist analyses of epistemology.

Is this critique of social theory valid? It is self-evidently a gross oversimplification to imply that the only thing social theory is concerned with is 'the classics'. Nevertheless, Marx, Weber and Durkheim do occupy space within the books and courses on the subject and, more generally, many of their concerns have been taken up by subsequent social theorists. Is it not, then, finally time to ditch Durkheim and co, declare an end to social theory as it has hitherto been conceived and practised and throw open the subject to a range of influences and concerns that have previously been overlooked as a result of the blinkered gaze of its practitioners (Genosko 1998)? In responding to this question, there are numerous issues at stake, some of which are complex and cannot be dealt with in any detail. Nevertheless, the following points can be made and go some way to discounting this critique.

The first point concerns the social background of social theorists. It is obviously true that the majority of social theorists are European men from relatively affluent backgrounds. However, until fairly recently (and arguably to some extent to this day), the ability to devote time and energy to intellectual thought and writing was the privilege of a small minority of middle-class men. There were no women or sons of street sweepers at the German or French universities in the late nineteenth century because they were excluded by formal rules or prohibitive costs. Thereafter, universities have been for the most part male-dominated and middle-class institutions. However, one should be careful about blanket descriptions of privilege as not all the social theorists were born into wealthy families. Pierre Bourdieu, for instance, unlike the majority of high-ranking French academics, is not from the Parisian intelligentsia, but is the son of a minor civil servant in south-west France. His feelings of being an outsider in the higher echelons of the French university world have influenced his research and theorising. Moreover, while earlier social theorists may have had private incomes that facilitated their academic careers, they were not necessarily free of discrimination. This was nearly always true of Jewish academics. Durkheim was born into a Jewish family, Georg Simmel was never awarded a university chair in Germany because he was Jewish, while Norbert Elias, together with a whole generation of intellectuals, including the Frankfurt School theorists such as Horkheimer, Marcuse and Adorno, had to flee the Nazis in 1933. In recent years the cumulative impact of feminism on social theory has been far reaching. Much of it is, of course, written by women. While it is still possible to find social theory books that proceed as if feminism had never happened, they are rare. On the contrary, feminism is now central to social theory, though principally through the way in which it has problematised the assumptions of classical sociology, rather than through its substantive contributions to social theory. In much the same way, it is possible that in future the influence of queer theory, much of it written by gay scholars, will influence the assumptions and direction of social theory. In sum, to argue that social theory *simply* consists of the privileged gazing down upon the oppressed is a caricature.

However, even if it were the case that every single social theorist did fit this privileged stereotype, there is a more fundamental objection to this line of argument. This is that it is illegitimate to discount an individual's contribution to any field of endeavour – intellectual, artistic or sporting – simply because of 'who' they are. At its crudest, this type of reasoning rests on the assumption that an individual social theorist is simply a cipher for their social position – that they will reproduce parrot fashion the assumptions of their class and gender. Sociology in this sense simply becomes a crude form of ideology or, and this is now a far more popular argument, a transcript of individual biography. The trouble with this sort of argument is that it is very difficult to square with any actual reading of the work of writers like Marx and Weber. Although both men were solidly middle-class, nineteenth-century Germans, their work was concerned, in differing ways, to pick apart the cosy assumptions of the nineteenth-century bourgeois world which they inhabited. Moreover, it would make little sense to see major studies such as *Das Kapital* and *The Protestant Ethic* as slices of autobiography. In fact, we are not really dealing with a credible argument here but an assertion. It is not something that can lead anywhere productive as it seeks at best to explain and at worst to discredit what somebody has to say simply because of who they are. It can become, therefore, a form of intellectual censorship, hardly any better than the nineteenth-century racist assertions that what somebody had to say was necessarily illegitimate if they were black or female.

A closely related and slightly more sophisticated variant of this case is that of 'epistemic privilege', or perhaps better put 'oppression stacking' (Harding 1987). Here the argument is not so much about the replication of privilege in social theory by white, middle-class males, but how the insight of social investigation is aided by the real-life experience of discrimination that the researcher has been sub-jected to. Therefore it follows that, for instance, research on racism will have greater analytical depth and sensitivity if the researcher is black and has probably experi-enced racism in some form. However, it is not automatically the case that some-body who suffers in a particular way will empathise with others in a similar plight. In certain instances the very opposite may be true. Indeed, a danger with this line of argument is that it can logically be carried to absurd lengths, whereby the more forms of oppression an individual is subject to the greater the insight of their obser-vation. Thus in British society in 2000 a disabled, female Romanian gypsy asylum seeker, who is a lesbian single mother, would perhaps come out on top, or rather at the bottom, in the 'seer' stakes.

All of this is certainly not to suggest that the background and biography of a social theorist – or any other kind of intellectual – is not important, as it certainly is. This is true of both intellectual style and substantive assumptions. For instance, Weber's style of argument and, at times, difficult prose is indicative of the periodic psychological distress he experienced and a methodology that always tried to incorporate the full range of causes of any given occurrence. Substantively, a strong argument can be made for a single consistent thread of German nationalism run-ning throughout Weber's work, something which can at least in part be attributed to his background and, quite obviously, his nationality (Anderson 1992). How-ever, this does not mean that one should moralistically attempt to discredit his thought on the vast variety of things he wrote about, including nationalism. It is legitimate to argue that one should be aware of and take account of the various influences and antecedents in intellectual thought. This is part and parcel of studying social theory. But it is small-minded and ultimately dangerous to discount – or equally to laud – somebody's ideas on the basis of who they are or what they may have been through.

Another element of this critique is that social theory is Eurocentric not just in terms of the geographical origin of those who wrote it, but also in its focus and frame of reference. This means that while social theory might purport to be about social development, structure and interaction throughout the modern world, in reality it is based on the experience and observation of western societies. Some-times it does not even trouble itself with the claim of a universal application, but seems to assume that what is true in a particular European society is true elsewhere. Famously, Sigmund Freud has thus been criticised for assuming that his psycho-analytic findings have a universal application although they were drawn from a small number of case studies of bourgeois Viennese women at the turn of the twentieth century (Fromm 1980). Moreover, so the argument proceeds, even when classical social theorists foraged outside of this particular part of the globe they continued to gaze through a Eurocentric lens. Thus Marx spoke about the peculiarities of the 'Asiatic' mode of production, regarding Europe as the norm. Simultaneously, the very title of one of Durkheim's most famous books about Australian Aboriginal society, *The Elementary Forms of the Religious Life*, indicates a judgement that non-western belief systems are less advanced than European ones. Arguably, therefore, social theory is loaded with cultural assumptions which can merge into outright prejudices. The background to this is, of course, European imperial domination from the fifteenth century of the continents to its west and east, and the subsequent attempt from the eighteenth century to impose European institutions and civilisation upon most of the non-European world. Integral to this was the assumption that South American, African, Arab and Asian cultures were intrinsically inferior to that of Europe, and were simultaneously somehow exotic (Said 1980). If such cultures and societies were to be examined at all, they were judged by a European grand narrative of progress and civilisation. Social theory thus can be charged with being a form of cultural imperialism.

Now this criticism is an important one, even though the argument that social theory is a form of cultural imperialism might apply much less to sociology than to other disciplines, such as anthropology whose development was embroiled in the nineteenth-century attempt to classify non-western peoples as uncivilised and racially inferior (Jenkins 1997: ch. 1). However, it is certainly a fair comment that while much social theory (and indeed sociology more generally) purports to be concerned with global affairs, it is really about advanced capitalist societies. For instance, despite claims to the contrary, the recent writings of European social theorists like Anthony Giddens and Ulrich Beck are really about dealing with problems such as welfare and crime in liberal parliamentary democracies such as Britain, Germany and the USA (Beck 1997; Giddens 1998). In similar vein, the current interest among sociologists in globalisation has tended to assume that there is a far more even distribution of resources (especially information technology) across the planet than is in fact the case. In short, the problem of Eurocentrism in social theory is not just an historical one; it is still evident.

However, there are a number of points that can be made that should prevent us from simply dismissing social theory as something that applies only to societies such as Britain. The very term 'Eurocentric' tends to assume a greater unity of societies, cultures and outlooks than has ever been the case (Ahmad 1992). Within social theory it is clearly not the case that there has ever been one, overriding tradition. Although the subject does have something of a 'classical heritage' in Marx, Weber and Durkheim, we saw above that a major feature of social theory is its lack of consensus rather than its uniformity. Furthermore, it is not necessarily the case that a form of theorising about one part of the world is necessarily invalid elsewhere. Humanity and societies are not split off into totally different sub-sections. It is quite possible to make observations about difference and similarity between societies within an overarching theoretical schema. As suggested above, theory is concerned with drawing from the diversity of specific instances into a logical set of generalities. For instance, particular problems have been highlighted with Durkheim's study of religion, some of which may derive from a Eurocentric perspective, but the attempt to discern common social functions in religious practice in different societies is entirely legitimate. In general, while one should be aware of the criticism of Eurocentrism, and approach social theory with it in mind, it is perhaps more productive to use this criticism to broaden and sharpen the analytic potential of social theory, not deny its legitimacy.

There is a final issue that needs to be dealt with in this section that has been mentioned several times already: the relevance of the 'classics'. This book does not primarily concentrate on these 'founding writers', it is not part of the flourishing trade in evaluating and re-evaluating their work in terms of what they 'really' said, or at any rate should have said. However, since much contemporary social theorising has developed as a response to the work of the founding theorists, and since we have already noted that these early theorists have been described as being anachronistic (among other faults), it is a good idea to indicate briefly why we think that the classics are of enduring importance. We will suggest two major reasons here. Firstly, the writings of Marx, Durkheim and Weber provide the discipline with concepts and terms that, while not immediately familiar, are of continuing relevance. Take, for instance, Marx's concept of alienation. Marx discussed alienation in relation to the lack of control over their labour experienced by nineteenth-century workers and, more specifically, to the separation of the workers from the results or products of the time and effort they invested in them. Marx argued that work was simply being reduced to a cash nexus under capitalism. More than one hundred and fifty years after this analysis there are few people who have worked in, say, a fast-food outlet or a telephone call centre who would deny the contemporary relevance of alienation. Secondly, the coherence, analytical power and imaginative potential of the conceptual frameworks that Marx, Durkheim and Weber provided sociology with are still unsurpassed. For instance, Durkheim's understanding of the effects of integration and anomie upon individual and community are possibly of greater relevance at the turn of the twenty-first century than they were at the turn of the twentieth. Similarly, Weber's thesis of the Protestant ethic and the spirit of capitalism – in essence a study of the importance of ideas in shaping history – continues to generate debate. Meanwhile a good case can be made for Marx as the first great theorist of globalisation, as his writings on the integration of global capitalism through a single world market have proved remarkably prescient. All of this is not to say that everything these thinkers said is as important and valid now as it ever was – assuming of course it was correct in the first place. Rather it is to suggest that the work of Marx, Weber and Durkheim present sociology with a treasure trove that has by no means been emptied (Mouzelis 1997). And it is not the case that the classical thinkers had nothing to say about the things that preoccupy contemporary sociology. Durkheim's understanding of identity is arguably a more integrated and compelling one than that of the postmodernists who talk endlessly about it (Warde 1994).

SUMMARY

In this chapter we have made the case for the role and importance of social theory in the face of some of the common criticisms it encounters. Social theory was defined as a set of linked propositions about the social world that attempt to explain social phenomena as a whole or a particular aspect of it.

■ We have seen that thinking theoretically is not an esoteric academic process but is actually used far more frequently than we might think. Within the discipline of sociology it is a crucial means to direct, structure and then interpret research, as social theory organises and informs our conception of the social world.

■ Also, while social theory is too often written in an obscure and over-complicated style, this is by no means always the case. It is vital that sociological terms and concepts are expressed with clarity and a necessary degree of detail, and it is clear that some of the subject matter is not, by its very nature, immediately straight-forward. The related criticism that social theory is hopelessly internally divided can be rather overstated. In so far as it is true, such divisions are both inevitable and something that should be welcomed.

■ The idea that social theory is just the product of dead, white males is an unfair overgeneralisation that does not do justice to the range of sociological theoris-ing. The claim that it applies only to the relatively privileged part of the world referred to as the West should be taken seriously. However, it is not the case that social theory, even in its classical form, is of relevance only to Europe and North America. In short, social theory is indispensable to sociology and thereby to a coherent understanding of the social world.

EXERCISE

Commonsense and sociological interpretations

Consider the following extracts.

Relocation of Refugees 'should not be rushed' – Lucy Ward

The government should allow more time to prepare local communities for the arrival of groups of asylum seekers to prevent a repetition of clashes such as those in Glasgow, according to a local government chief.

As Downing Street denied that a Home Office review of the controversial asylum dispersal sys-tem meant that government asylum policy had failed, the chief executive of the Local Government Association warned that support services had to be in place before large groups of refugees could be housed in 'clusters', often in deprived inner city neighbourhoods.

Time was also required to explain to local residents the circumstances under which asylum seekers were coming and to make clear the kind of help they were receiving, said the LGA chief executive, Brian Briscoe.

His warning follows concern among authorities that the government's desire to do speedy and low cost deals with private landlords to get refugees placed quickly was backfiring because there was no time to prepare local communities or establish services such as education, health care and legal support.

Misplaced resentment among the community at alleged privileges granted to refugees on Sighthill in Glasgow, where Kurdish asylum seeker, Firsat Dag, was stabbed to death last week, has been blamed for angry protests against the placements.

Source: The *Guardian*, 14 August 2001

Virgin in $1bn deal with SingTel – Chris Ayres

Sir Richard Branson's Virgin Group yesterday announced a massive global expansion of its mobile phone interests with a $1 billion (£625 million) joint venture with Singapore Telecom (SingTel).

The new company to be called Virgin Mobile Asia, follows Sir Richard's Virgin Mobile joint venture with Deutsche Telekom's One 2 One subsidiary in the UK. Virgin Mobile is thought to have attracted some 250,000 subscribers.

Under the terms of Sir Richard's deal with SingTel, the Asian telecoms group will invest $500 million in return for a 50 per cent stake in Virgin Mobile Asia. Virgin, meanwhile, will invest just $50 million, and share half of all profits. 'They are investing more money than we are and in return what they are getting is the brand and marketing skills of Virgin. We feel it is equitable', Sir Richard said.

Source: *The Times*, 20 May 2000

Blair is facing exodus of his women MPs – Roland Watson

Tony Blair was told yesterday that he faces an exodus of women MPs unless the House of Commons adopts more family-friendly hours.

As one Labour MP, Tess Kingham, announced that she would be standing down at the next election to spend more time with her three children, a colleague said that others may follow her example.

The Labour leadership had been anxious to capitalise at the next election on the party's record 101 women returned to Parliament in 1997. However, the decision of Ms Kingham, 36, MP for Gloucester – whose partner, Mark, is acting as househusband – highlights a widespread feeling among Labour MPs, both men and women, that the party has failed to modernise the Commons.

Many women MPs in particular are as disillusioned with what they regard as Labour's lukewarm approach to reforming parliamentary working hours as with the regular late nights themselves. Anne Campbell, who organised a petition signed by 210 MPs calling for a reformed regime, said that Ms Kingham's decision could discourage other women from becoming MPs.

Ms Campbell, MP for Cambridge, said: 'It sends out the message that Parliament is out of touch and is so bound up in the traditions designed for an earlier age that it cannot reform itself to be a modern and efficient working environment.

Source: *The Times*, 20 May 2000

(a) Suggest a 'commonsense' interpretation of each of the extracts.

(b) How do sociological interpretations differ from 'commonsense' ones?

(c) How might different social theorists (that you have come across so far) explain each of the extracts?

Chapter 4

The origins of classic social theory

SAM PRYKE

In the previous chapter we saw that social theory is integral to any coherent analysis of social life. Moreover, in so far as 'doing theory' requires a particular form of thinking, it should not be seen as a specialised form of activity that is removed from everyday mental life. The kind of theoretical thinking involved in academic social theory is certainly a more sustained and difficult enterprise, but it is not wholly different. In this chapter, we consider where social theory came from, examining in particular the intellectual origins of social theory in the eighteenth-century Enlightenment and some of the classical nineteenth-century social theorists, including Comte, Spencer, Durkheim, Marx and Weber. This is such an enormous task that it has the danger of reducing the complexities of the subject to hazy overgeneralisation and caricature. To try to avoid this, only the headline themes of the work of the Enlightenment and only certain aspects of the work of particular theorists are covered.

THE ENLIGHTENMENT

It is something of a convention in sociology textbooks to make some initial and general remarks about the importance of the Enlightenment to the subject, before beginning with the major social theorists of nineteenth century. However, in a sense, studying Marx, Weber, Durkheim and co. cannot be divorced from studying the Enlightenment, as the work of these great thinkers was a debate with the issues of this movement. Nowadays, many, if not all, sociologists position their attempts to understand the social world in relation to Marx, Weber and Durkheim, so there is a refracted influence. Even contemporary postmodernist accounts of social life generally take as their point of departure a rejection of the claims of the Enlightenment, particularly in relation to the disavowal of the meta-narratives of early social theorists. Therefore in approaching the study of social theory, from a purely practical point of view, it is useful to take things back another step to the origins of social thought in the eighteenth-century Enlightenment. So we will begin this examination of the classic social theorists by considering the origins and major themes of the Enlightenment – not because it makes the format of this book a little different from most others, but because it is hoped that it will provide context and understanding to the subject matter and nature of social theory. Moreover, and as indicated, the themes of nineteenth-century social theory are to be found within the ferment of the Enlightenment: rationality and science, the social and historical context of human thought and behaviour and historical progress.

The initial question that arises is what is meant by the term 'Enlightenment'. Probably many an undergraduate student has seen the word repeatedly used in books and articles without being quite sure what it refers to, beyond perhaps its literal meaning. In fact this is a good starting point, as its eighteenth-century advocates conceived it as the spreading of the light of knowledge and rational understanding in order to break through the gloom of tradition and superstition. In such a way it was thought that humanity as a whole could raise itself up economically and morally from the poverty and ignorance that had hitherto characterised life. Its philosophy was, according to one of its most eloquent spokesman, Antoine de Condorcet, hated by all those who owed their existence to prejudice. A recurrent theme in eighteenth-century definitions of Enlightenment is that it is the realisation of humanity's potential – the self-emancipation of humanity. Immanuel Kant declared in 1784: 'Enlightenment is mankind's exit from self incurred immaturity . . . Have the courage to use your own understanding! is thus the motto of the enlightenment.' A year later his fellow German, Karl Reinhold, stated more prosaically: 'I think that Enlightenment means, in general, the making of rational men who are capable of rationality.' Subsequent understandings and emphases of the Enlightenment are strongly influenced by what view the writer has on its objectives and legacy. The great intellectual historian of the period, Peter Gay, states that it is reducible to two words: 'knowledge and power' (Gay 1966: xiii). For Gay it was a fantastic development whose ongoing achievements are to be applauded. A contemporary of Gay, George Mosse, argued by contrast that it ushered in 'a preoccupation with a rational universe, nature and aesthetics' that acted as the cradle of modern racism. For Mosse the processes of categorisation, differentiation and exclusion at the heart of the Enlightenment led inexorably to the Nazi holocaust of the twentieth century (Mosse 1978: 3).

Disagreement about what the Enlightenment was and what it gave rise to are so fundamental that there is little point in trying to reconcile them by providing a catch-all definition. Rather we can perhaps proceed by asking 'who' the Enlightenment was. As the above quotes from the the German philosophers would indicate, it was a highly self-conscious movement of European writers, artists and scientists – grouped under the word philosophers or *philosphes* – who sought to further the cause of rationality and progress. Most of them were male and from bourgeois or aristocratic backgrounds. Generally they were not attached to universities but, in so far as they were part of institutions, to academies and societies. Many were able to devote their life to learning through the independent financial means of their families. Though some found rural locations to think and write, Enlightenment *philosophes* were drawn to certain fast-expanding European centres of commerce and intellect, including Paris, Berlin, Glasgow and Edinburgh. There is continuing dispute about the extent to which the Enlightenment reached, or indeed attempted to reach, beyond fairly small literate circles in the most advanced European countries. There are, moreover, issues over the extent of agreement among its proponents. However, leaving aside such matters concerning its unevenness and internal contradictions, the Enlightenment represented an impressive movement of European scholars, many of them quite brilliant, from a range of subject backgrounds, who were intent upon the rational transformation of the world. From it, social theory emerged.

The Enlightenment did not just happen spontaneously. How, then, are we to explain this novel intellectual and political movement? There are number of trends and developments that acted as the context and sometimes the direct impetus, for the writings of its proponents.

Firstly, the rise of capitalism. Under the heading of capitalism we should include the commercialisation of agriculture, the rise of manufacture and the expansion of trade between European states. Crucial to the latter was the opening up of the natural resources of the Americas to European exploitation at the end of the fifteenth century. This depended upon the transatlantic slave trade. The rise in international trade of commodities stimulated the growth of manufacturing industry and financial services from the seventeenth century. Enlightenment *philosophes* were, with few exceptions, admirers of the productive energy and capacity of capitalism. At least this is true of free-market capitalism. Adam Smith, the most famous representative of the Scottish Enlightenment, saw the theoretical workings of the market, as opposed to all the characteristics of the emerging capitalist class, as of unqualified benefit to everybody involved. Economic monopoly and slavery were generally condemned by Enlightenment *philosophes* as aspects of the conservative order, resting as they did upon restriction and violence. Condorcet, in the context of a call for greater equality within and between nations, thought that free market trade in sugar would in itself lead to the end of slave trade.

Secondly, the Enlightenment rested upon and in fact contributed to the transformation of knowledge in the sixteenth, seventeenth and eighteenth centuries. This consisted of the advances in scientific method associated with Francis Bacon, René Descartes, Isaac Newton and John Locke. They rejected metaphysical understandings of nature derived from ancient texts and speculation for an emphasis on the pursuit of truth through observation, experience, calculation and analysis. Discovery in this field was not something simply of interest to and celebrated by scientists. As the poet Alexander Pope put it somewhat later but clearly illustrating the excitement and philosophical synthesis of the age:

Nature and Nature's laws lay hid in night
God said, let Newton be! And all was light.

Closely linked to developments in scientific method were breakthroughs in geometry, calculus and algebra, anticipated, as Enlightenment *philosophes* acknowledged, by Arab mathematics. Contemporaneous to this were the advances in astronomy, navigation and industrial production.

Thirdly, the Enlightenment reflected the emergence of a reading middle class: a bourgeois public, receptive to the ideas of the *philosophes*. This educated, self-confident and increasingly articulate stratum organised itself and thereby created a *civil society* through academies of learning, professional bodies, voluntary, charitable and economic societies and, most famously, the Freemasons. The ideas of the age were circulated by periodicals, newspapers and a massive expansion in the publication and sale of books (Hof 1997: pt IV). Condorcet lauded the invention of print in freeing 'the education of the people from the all political and religious shackles' (1955: 102).

These socio-economic trends were to culminate in the late eighteenth century in what the historian Eric Hobsbawm refers to as the dual revolutions: the overturning of the French monarchy and the astonishing acceleration in productive output brought about by the industrial revolution (Hobsbawm 1989).

If these changes in economy and society acted as context to the Enlightenment, we have yet to indicate beyond generalities what it was concerned with. In doing this the reader should be conscious that a number of texts and thinkers are being grouped together, as our concern is with the major orientation of the eighteenth-century movement and not, for the most part, its internal disagreements. This said, it is the case that most of the people associated with the Enlightenment would not have dissented with the broad overview that follows. Firstly, as indicated, it was a movement that championed rationality and critical enquiry. The explanation of phenomena, be they natural, biological, economic or social, was to be deduced from investigation of their internal workings and relationships, rather than in relation to any great train of being or purpose. Quite quickly, reason became reified, in other words it came to be treated as an object or transcendent category that had a 'thing-like' existence and was to be pursued in itself. However, this was a subsequent development within philosophy once the pursuit of reason had entered its discourse. The emphasis of rationality set the Enlightenment against the superstition of the village life and the pulpit – in so far as a difference between the two was recognised. Voltaire famously fumed against the Catholic Church as a bastion of reaction. However, it is only correct to argue that the Enlightenment was secular in so far as it challenged the authority and power of established religion to pronounce upon truth and insist a Christian was duty-bound to accept its dogma as an act of faith. This challenge was itself revolutionary but it is important to point out that few Enlightenment figures went so far as to declare themselves outright atheists. Most welcomed the progressive role of Reformation reform within Christianity.

The natural sciences, above all the experimental physics of Newton, were thought to be at the cutting edge of the rational; but eighteenth-century thinkers did not recognise the disciplinary boundaries between subjects in the way that they are conceived today. Rather it was thought that the developments in one branch of learning had immediate consequences and benefits for another. Condorcet thought that the advances in numerical calculation and the vibration of resonating bodies in mathematics were being directly incorporated in the composition of music and art. Similarly, the discoveries of physical sciences could be incorporated into law and history (Condorcet 1955: 165, 190). A concern for rationality extended to a distaste for eighteenth-century politics, be it manoeuvrings and pronouncements of absolute monarchs or the petty intrigues of palace and court. Progress had occurred despite the machinations of rulers, not because of them.

Secondly, the Enlightenment thinkers generally had a positive view of human nature. They rejected the notion that improvement in the common condition was impossible because of some innate weakness, selfishness or lust for power rooted in the human condition. Acceptance of this view would mean that that there would be little point in attempting to effect reform or revolution to improve the general good, as human nature would provide an insurmountable obstacle. If one conceives human nature to be essentially unchanging then purposive attempts to alter it will be futile or even dangerous. What change may occur will be gradual and through its own volition. Even in the wake of the French Revolution, the event which all Enlightenment thinkers had anticipated and welcomed but were much disappointed by, Saint-Simon could optimistically maintain, 'Men are not as bad as they think they are: they are more severe on themselves than they deserve' (1952: 77). The *philosophes* tended to equate typical forms of behaviour and dominant forms of personality by reference to the conditions of the wider society. The first modern thinker to make this claim central to a philosophy of history was the eighteenth-century Neapolitan Giambattista Vico. He denied human nature was 'static or unalterable or indeed that it contained even a kernel or essence', and argued that it was continuously transformed as man adapted to changes in the world (Berlin 1976: xvi). David Hume, in an essay rightly notorious for a racist aside, claimed that the character of a national people was not due, as was commonly thought, to climate or natural geography. This notion, associated with Montesquieu and Herder, was something that 'men of judgement condemn'. With the possible exception of sexuality and a propensity for alcohol which were widely held to be influenced by temperature, national character was attributable to the 'morals' of the particular society. By 'morals' Hume meant the social and political constitution of a society. Adam Smith famously claimed that the sure march of the wealth of nations was due to a human propensity to 'truck, barter and exchange one thing with another'. However, he denied there was any great difference in natural talents between individuals. Rather their observable differences were a product of their particular occupations in the division of labour:

> The difference between the natural talents in different men is, in reality, much less than we are aware of; and the very different genius which appears to distinguish men of

different professions, when grown up to maturity, is not on many occasions so much the cause as the effect of the division of labour. The difference between the most dissimilar characters, between a philosopher and a common street porter, for example, seems to arise not so much from nature as from habit, custom and education. When they came into the world, and for the first six or seven years of their existence they were perhaps very much alike, and neither their parents nor their play fellows could perceive any remarkable difference.

(Smith 1986: 117, 120)

Thirdly, as indicated, Enlightenment thinking included a conviction of the progressive nature of history. Hobsbawm refers to this as the most important achievement of the Enlightenment, although it is has probably been questioned more than any other aspect of the Enlightenment. There are two interrelated aspects to consider here. A conception of historical time being linear rather than cyclical and a notion that societies move at different speeds in a single, unfolding direction, rather than being essentially unchanging or predetermined to repeat certain phases and episodes – at their most dramatic, wars or invasions – within an inescapable treadmill of human existence. This cyclical view had dominated conceptions of history from antiquity, through Ibn Khaldun, the great Islamic thinker of the medieval era, to Machiavelli, the sixteenth-century political iconoclast (Callinicos 1999: 11). In the context of the rise of nation states, European colonisation of the Americas and increasing forays into Africa and Asia, eighteenth-century Enlightenment *philosophes* such as Montesquieu characterised societies as moving forward into uncharted territories. It was for historians to discern the particular spirit of every age. The work of Scottish Enlightenment historians, above all Adam Ferguson in his *An Essay on the History of Civil Society* (1767), added a greater factual dimension to this dramatically revised conception of historical time. A thinker like Condorcet subsequently insisted that the history of all societies had ascended to different levels up a ladder of ten stages of progress, from tribal to Enlightenment society. He acknowledged that only a minority of people within a few societies had reached this tenth stage of Enlightenment. Moreover, the movement of history (if not the human mind) was not irreversible as the civil liberties and freedoms individuals had acquired might be taken from them by their rulers. Earlier, Voltaire had ridiculed those who thought that societies might never experience setbacks through some form of calamity. In similar vein, Condorcet thought that certain societies might become stuck at certain levels, unable to progress, owing to their lethargy. However, the general flow of historical change was most definitely in a positive and upward direction. There was, moreover, no limit upon progress within Condorcet's tenth stage; as the human mind was capable of infinite perfection, so was society. It was the particular responsibility of intellectuals, i.e. of those already enlightened, to ensure progress to perfection through the application of science. Saint-Simon sums up the Enlightenment's perception of the orientation in history: 'The Golden age of the human is not behind us but before us; it lies in the perfection of the social order. Our ancestors never saw it; our children will one day arrive there; it is for us to clear the way' (1952: 68).

Explicit within a progressive view of history was a conception of civilised and savage peoples and societies. It is not difficult to see why people have suggested that there is a direct link between the Enlightenment and European imperialism of the nineteenth century. The expansion of European powers across Africa and Asia was, after all, conducted in the name of civilisation.

If rationality, a contextualised conception of human nature and progress are the major themes of the Enlightenment, it remains to indicate more specifically what it was in the eighteenth-century Enlightenment that prompted the emergence of social theory. Again it is possible only to draw out strands of influence from a mass of antecedents and influences. Among other things, we might point to the following:

- A rejection of an essayist, literary style of writing common to aristocratic dandies and dilettantes of the saloons and clubs of, in particular, mid-eighteenth-century Paris, in which the writer attempted to impress the reader with their command of language rather than their ideas and analysis, in favour of greater *intellectual rigour*. Enlightenment writers generally wrote for the expanding middle-class audience mentioned above and therefore they generally expressed themselves well and clearly. However, this in itself was not the aim of the enterprise. As their concern was with the rational, the prose of the books and articles of the *philosophes* was more rigorous than rhetorical. Though overstated and polemical claims were often made, there was invariably at least an attempt to substantiate them with argument and fact. This tendency was furthered in France by the increasing differentiation of disciplines, with their more particular and specialised institutions and audiences, after the revolution of 1789. As regards sociology, the intent of social theorists is rarely to engage and interest the reader through a flamboyant style of writing. The classic nineteenth-century texts that can be considered as social theory and that were written with panache and flair, for instance Marx's *Communist Manifesto*, were not aimed at a specialised academic audience but a general one. While Durkheim was a hugely talented writer, the brilliance of his texts is not in their style so much as their analysis. So it could be argued that the sober, not to say boring, tone of most academic sociology is a product of the Enlightenment, or more specifically the latter Enlightenment period.

- Social theory subsequently took as its starting point, even if it was to directly or indirectly disagree with it, the Enlightenment contention that *society is composed of individuals*. The context of this was a reaction against the absolutist belief that society was but an outgrowth of the monarch who was the representative of God. 'Sovereign power resides in my person alone', as Louis XV put it (Hume 1966: 477).

- Social theory drew from Enlightenment moral philosophy in its attempt to extend the *rational analysis of individual behaviour*. The approach of Adam Smith is a good example of this; the quote above (pp. 96–7) attempts to show how different talents and character are unintentionally but functionally formed through pursuing rational self-interests, derived from the propensity to brook, barter and trade in the market economy. It is the *habitus* of the division of labour (the nature of particular occupations), and the immediate history to it through education and so on, that gives rise to personality differences involving contrasting customs and habits. However, through the market's ability to resolve competing economic objectives – in the simplest scenario the interest of the seller meets with the interests of the buyer so that they both go home happy – in a way that all parties achieve what they want, society is ultimately strengthened. Thus different talents, produced by the division of labour as humans fulfil their propensity to 'brook, barter and trade', enter a common stock from which there is mutual and general benefit. Whatever one thinks about the social cohesion produced by market economies, the point is that in Smith's estimation this was not produced by prior consultation and agreement, or by innate personality, but rather by the *unforeseen consequences of action*. The insight (anticipated by earlier thinkers) has subsequently been used by social theorists. Its general influence has been on the way social theory has concerned itself with the self-ordering, regulation and internally unfolding nature of social life, without the conscious intervention of political actors.

■ Social theory derived from the Enlightenment, again principally from the moral philosophy of Montesquieu and Rousseau, highlighted a concern with *social interconnectedness* – with the ways and means of sustaining civil society (the space between the state and private life) as it expanded through clubs, associations and so on in the eighteenth century.

■ This fused with the *rational and juridical understandings of the state* derived from politico-legal Enlightenment philosophy. This produced a concern for rational and liberal administration, alongside a concern for the self-regulation of the social and a distaste for the arbitrary actions of governments.

■ Social theory took from Enlightenment *philosophes* a concern with the *categorisation and typology* of societies, historical periods, economic systems, types of behaviour, beliefs and so on. The great quest of the French Enlightenment, illustrated by the 28 volumes of the Paris *Encyclopaedia* written by numerous contributors, was to separate and order all known aspects of human knowledge.

Taken together, then, social theory took from the Enlightenment intellectual rigour, a conception of society composed of individuals, an attempt to rationally understand their behaviour, a concern with social interconnection, a rational approach to the state and a stress on classification and typology. These specific points should be added to the general themes and orientations of the eighteenth century that were highlighted earlier. Without wishing to overstretch the point, it could be said that when sociologists attempt to assess the historical development of a particular social practice, or draw up a method to classify related but different sorts of behaviour, they are acting in the tradition of the Enlightenment (even if they probably would not generally conceive of things in such grandiose terms).

In order to understand the more explicit social theorising within the emerging discipline of sociology in the nineteenth century we need to refer briefly to the aftermath of the French Revolution, the self-proclaimed highpoint of the Enlightenment. The political atmosphere within France and wider Europe had changed somewhat by the time Auguste Comte – often called the first sociologist by the simple fact that he was the first person to use the name sociology – made his major contributions to social thought in the 1830s. The promise of universal liberation of the French Revolution that had occurred 40 years earlier was initially greeted with widespread enthusiasm across Europe. In so far as it was still hailed as a great achievement some 40 years later, it did so despite rather than because of its achievements. The initial period after 1789, when the English poet Wordsworth could declare 'dawn was it bliss to be alive', had been followed by the Jacobean Reign of Terror, 1793–1794. In the subsequent period Napoleon began his rise to power by dint of war and conquest, alienating many non-French supporters of the revolution. This culminated in his proclamation as emperor in 1804. After his fall in 1815, France reverted to monarchy until 1830, and then the Orleanist regime of Louis Philippe until the revolution of 1848.

None of this acted as a brake upon the development of learning; far from it. In the midst of industrialisation, urbanisation and imperial expansion, universities, academies and societies of learning were established across metropolitan and provincial Europe. Similarly, journals and serious newspapers were founded, and book publishing increased and diversified. Disciplines were formally founded and advances declared across most fields of learning (see Hobsbawm 1989: 15). Paris acted as the centre of all this in relation to both the natural and social sciences. The impact of the revolution there had led to the founding of government academies intended to apply the natural sciences to the social world. This led to heightened exposure and circulation of the terms of social theory – society, social physics, social science – but simultaneously the national closure of debate. In spite of the occasional chauvinisms of Enlightenment scholars, they had perceived themselves as participating in a Europe-wide philosophical debate. With the formalising of distinctly national French academies in the early nineteenth century, together with the general rise in nationalism, social science became somewhat more parochial in tone and agenda (Heilbron 1995: 169–73). At the same time, academia became more difficult to enter as qualification requirements and formal initiation were introduced to establish elite reputations.

As academia became more hierarchical in the early nineteenth century, so the unity of social theory was influenced by opposing currents of intellectual and political thought. Three distinct trends are observable. Firstly, Romanticism, especially prevalent in Germany and associated with figures like the poet Goethe, which involved a disavowal of the overly cold and mechanistic nature of Enlightenment philosophy and an emphasis on emotion, sentiment and intuition in art and life. Secondly, and similarly involving a distaste for science, political conservatism, associated with Edmund Burke in Britain and de Maistre in France, with a rejection of purposive social engineering in favour of an emphasis on gradual and piecemeal change within a conception of a stable and orderly society. Thirdly, as a response to the growing inequalities of industrial capitalism, the rise of socialism as both a critique of capitalism and a political practice. We saw above how Enlightenment thinkers like Adam Smith had confidently predicted that the free market would make everybody rich. In the midst of the industrial revolution in Britain, Belgium and France, the poverty and squalor of the emerging working classes, squashed into the slums of the expanding towns and cities, indicated that this was obviously not the case.

Interestingly, both these developments – the specialisation of the university system and the cross-currents of intellectual thought – are observable in the life and work of Auguste Comte. Despite his best efforts, Comte was never able to secure himself a permanent position within the academic world. And, despite the fact that he is above all associated with positivism – the replication of the procedure of the natural sciences in the social sciences – both Romanticism and conservatism, if not socialism, are observable in his work. Comte (along with Spencer, Durkheim, Marx and Weber) is one of the early 'classic' social theorists whose work and influence is examined here.

Discussion question

Enlightenment thinkers were not as naively optimistic about the future of humanity as they are sometimes portrayed. Not all of them thought that progress would inevitably and inexorably occur. Nevertheless, there is no doubt that eighteenth-century *philosophes* profoundly believed that the impact of science and education would be of unqualified benefit to everyone. Over two hundred years later the Enlightenment's banner of universal happiness and improvement seems, to say the least, a little ragged. Consider the confidence of one prominent thinker, Antoine-Nicolas de Condorcet in his *Sketch for a Historical Picture of the Progress of the Human Mind* written shortly before he took his own life in 1795. Among other things, he thought that progress would result in:

■ The replacement of superstition and prejudice by science and rationality.

■ The increase in general happiness.

■ The ever greater perfection of the human mind.

■ Greater equality within and between nations.

■ Longer life expectancy with greater quality of mind and body in old age.

1 If one was to draw up a balance sheet two hundred years later, what assessment would be made of Condorcet's predictions? (In particular, you might consider the extent to which science has been an unqualified benefit to humanity.)

2 Think of examples of the way in which progress is used as an ideology, i.e. something that cannot be counteracted, something that only 'little people' who don't understand don't accept. What interests are usually served by this use of progress?

3 To what extent do you think that the original aims of the Enlightenment are ideals that should command some support in contemporary society?

AUGUSTE COMTE

The influence of Romanticism came towards the end of Auguste Comte's life and, when it did, it is likely that it was as much to do with his personal life as any direct influence of the movement's advocates. In his later years, as a result of academic disappointment and social isolation, Comte increasingly came to extol love, feeling and the supremacy of the heart in the quest for knowledge and fulfilment (Comte 1858: 355). Perhaps in this period he found some happiness in an otherwise turbulent life. Born into a conservative and strongly Catholic family in Montpellier in 1798, Auguste Comte left the elite Ecole Polytechnique in 1816 when the school was closed by the government following student protests. Shortly afterwards, he began a period of intense collaboration with the half-mad aristocrat Saint-Simon. Over the next eight years Comte, together with Saint-Simon, formulated many of his most important and influential ideas. Having grown tired of Saint-Simon's assumption that the young provincial should act as an obedient pupil to the master, Comte publicly broke with him in 1824. The immediate cause was a petty publishing matter, but there were intellectual aspects to the dispute that we will touch on a little later. The following year Comte began in appropriately stormy circumstances a marriage to Caroline Massim, a Parisian bookshop keeper and former prostitute (Giddens 1996). The marriage was to last nineteen years until Caroline finally left her husband for good. During that time she had to cope with Comte's mental breakdowns, depression, social withdrawal and physical violence. The two of them struggled with intermittent poverty as Comte never secured the permanent academic position at his old institution, the Ecole Polytechnique, that he desperately desired for his reputation and income. Despite several minor positions – which he subsequently lost – he was never able to acquire a full-time appointment at the school. Instead, the couple lived on the proceeds of his tutoring and journalism. This in itself became intermittent as Comte quarrelled with most of his friends and supporters. In part this was because of Comte's irascible personality, but it was also because his general social theory – sociology as he termed it after he had given up social physics – was increasingly scorned for its general pretensions in an age which was becoming increasingly specialised and professional. He did, for a period in the late 1820s and early 1830s, enjoy critical acclaim and an impressive audience for his books and public lectures. Moreover, during the 1830s he produced his greatest work, *The Course of Postive Philosophy*. However, his reputation suffered from a growing detachment from developments in learning as he increasingly came to regard reading as a form of mental pollution.

Two years after the break-up of his marriage in 1844, Comte developed an infatuation for Clothide de Vaux, a woman much younger than himself who had been abandoned by her husband shortly before. Clothide died a few months later of consumption, her affair with Comte having been purely platonic. Comte continued to cherish her memory as the essence of love until his death in 1857. As suggested above, it was in this period that he increasingly advocated a quasi-mystical religion of humanity. By this stage of his career he had lost all credible academic support, as he gathered around himself a small number of disciples. We are not concerned here with his ideas in this period, but with the principal ones he outlined earlier in *Postive Philosophy*.

The tone of his writings in the 1830s is certainly far from mystical. While rather vague and abstract, it was also restrained and measured. Whatever turbulence Comte was experiencing in his life at the time, it does not surface in his writings (Giddens 1996: 155). His prose is not as open and accessible as that of the earlier Enlightenment thinkers or most nineteenth-century social theorists. Aside from any difficulty Comte might have had in expressing himself well, this was because his intent was to construct a measured theory of society, rather than to strive for a political objective. This intent was the part cause of his dispute with Saint-Simon. Comte wanted his work to further the Enlightenment goal of progress by jettison-ing tradition and superstition in social explanation. In that way he hoped ultimately to make society a more moral and sociable place. However, in line with the con-servative reaction to the revolution, which he described as an 'evil', he opposed the pursuit of happiness and perfectibility as an illusion (Comte 1853: 59). Rather in a laborious style he set himself the ambitious task of drawing up a general social theory of humanity in order to further 'a homogeneous rationality' (1853: 42). In line with the approach of his one-time mentor Saint-Simon, Comte thought that this was the job of intellectual elites, a sort of secular priesthood. Here we examine two central and interrelated aspects of it: positivism and historical method.

Comte's name is synonymous with the term 'positivism'. Positivism refers to the application of the methods of the natural sciences in social enquiry to produce a 'social science'. Comte initially favoured the term 'social physics', making his inten-tions for social theory unequivocally clear. In his view, the discipline had arrived late in the development of knowledge, being possible now only because of the growth in knowledge. The complexity this involves does not make the claims of sociology and the laws it discerns any less trustworthy or less scientific than other subjects according to Comte. On the contrary, its late arrival enhances its scientific status. It must use the techniques of science – experiment, observation and comparison – across its particular field of study, that of history, to ascertain the existence of social laws. The aim is not simply an exercise for its own ends: 'For it is only by know-ing the laws of phenomena, and thus being able to foresee them [that it is possible to] modify one or another for our advantage' (Comte 1853: 20).

One can very easily question the scientific credibility of Comte's approach, as there is very little in *Positive Philosophy* on how empirical evidence might be generated in order to produce or subsequently verify a social law. In fact, in his view science should in any case move in the opposite direction. Rather than the construction of a social law moving from particular findings to general laws – that might then be able to the explain particular phenomenon – the sociologist should start with the general and then move to the specific. This he thought was the essence of the scientific approach: 'There can be no science of society unless society is studied as a whole, not split into parts' (1853: 81). This was not a methodological procedure that should be adopted for convenience, but reflected the fact that society was an interconnected whole. As he argued: 'Science comes to the whole human race and regards it as one social whole' (1853: 95). Therefore sociologists should not waste their time by accumulating knowledge that pertains to only one segment of it. Such disparate accumulation would be contrary to scientific method and the nature of society. Sociology is concerned with general laws; it should study the totality of society because society is a totality.

A problem with Comte's dogmatic insistence that social enquiry should always move from the general to the specific is that it tends to rely upon abstractions about the nature of society. It is difficult to conduct research on society *per se*. All one can do is compose generalisations of greater or lesser plausibility. However, it is important to note that in some respects Comte's social theory is analytical in its focus, in as much as he explicitly rejected the possibility of social laws being valid across time and space. In other words, he rejected the notion that there are universal laws of human behaviour that apply to all historical societies. As he put it: 'the search for social laws is a relative enterprise as opposed to the absolutes of the ancients' (1853: 70). This claim represents an extension of the Enlightenment contention that nothing is fixed and permanent in social life because there is no innate human nature. Relatedly, Comte denied that there are philosophical absolutes that span all disciplines. There should, according to Comte, be no a priori assumption that evolution follows the same path and conforms to the same laws in both the natural and the human world. Sociology should not, therefore, necessarily adopt the same laws as biology. This point is reinforced by his belief that humanity is unique.

Comte devotes much time in *Positive Philosophy* to discussing how the relative advances of knowledge between and within the different disciplines effect a general movement across the board; in other words, to what extent do developments in one discipline give rise to those in others and add to the general sum of human knowledge? This emphasis on knowledge – the positive spirit – being the driving force of history is, similarly, within the tradition of the Enlightenment. He also speculates about how change in one part of society affects other parts and alters the whole.

Two things emerge out of this issue, both of which Comte anticipated. On the hand there is a direct link to organic conceptions of society found, to varying extents, in what has developed as structural functionalism. Comte speaks at one point about a need 'for a spontaneous harmony between the whole and the parts of the social body' if change is to occur; and considers how the 'political regime must correspond to wider universal consensus of the social body' (1853: 78). On the other hand, there is the closely related issue of *uneven and combined development* that Comte speculated on, although he claimed that the principle had yet to be established in sociology. The issue here is how there can be profound contrasts in the pace of change of different aspects of a given society. For instance, in the space of three or four generations formerly poor, backward third world economies in the Persian Gulf have become rich as they have accumulated all the consumer durables and information technology of the West. At the same time they have maintained the strongly conservative interpretations of Islam that have existed for 1,400 years. This raises the question of whether there will inevitably be some catch-up whereby religion adapts or declines, or whether apparent contrasts will continue. Because Comte's focus was upon the general nature of society and therefore the general change experienced, there is reason for thinking that he would have some difficulty in accounting for this kind of situation. Either a society and all the parts within it progress as a whole or remain constant as a whole. He attempted to deal with contradiction by introducing yet another concept of enduring importance in social theory, that of the dialectic. Although he did not use the word 'dialectic', his thinking about how the resolution of two opposites can lead to progress is in this tradition. As he puts it when discussing the tension between the forces of political centralisation and devolution: 'This miserable oscillation of our social life must proceed until a real doctrine as truly organic as progressive shall reconcile for us the two aspects of the great political problem' (1853: 22). This conflict was part of a wider struggle between order and progress. The fact that Comte posed this problem indicates the dual influences of the Enlightenment and the conservative reaction to the revolution. The dialectic is an attempt to accommodate and cope with the two traditions.

Although change might occur through contraction, it does so, as it were, 'at its own pace' in an unfolding fashion. As noted, Comte thought it wrong and dangerous to try to force the pace by revolution. When a revolution did occur it did so through an accumulation of pressure that could be resolved only by a violent and sudden change. Human agency is therefore limited in an evolutionary march of progress; politics must conform to gradual changes in society. The shifts have been general in history as human societies have moved from theological, to metaphysical, to scientific states of affairs. The job of the sociologist is to discover in a scientific fashion the social laws of a particular era, by placing historical facts within their evolutionary context. The enterprise will enable us to empathise and thus acquire respect for our ancestors. More generally, Comte repeatedly returned to the evolving nature of order in society. He was critical of accounts that thought that order was an artificial imposition upon humanity to compensate for its selfish and violent nature. Rather, order was a natural state of affairs. However, he was simultaneously opposed to accounts of human life that seemed to overlook the importance of the state in maintaining order. For instance, he pointed out that classical economists, such as Adam Smith, ignored the importance of discipline in industrial production. In the factory and elsewhere, discipline had to be maintained among workers in order for goods to be produced. As the positive social doctrine advanced so did humanity's ability to regulate itself.

Comte's social theory is closely related to the eighteenth-century Enlightenment. His most important works clearly champion the rational and evidence an historical if vague and general approach to social laws and knowledge. The issue of society and social interconnection are key throughout. His analyses are written in a careful style with much attention to the separation of different kinds of phenomena, especially knowledge. However, they reveal the strains and disappointments of post-revolutionary France and register the conflicting responses to 1789. Comte certainly did not reject progress and science, but in common with conservative opinion he disavowed revolutionary change, and, indeed, downplayed the importance of politics and human agency in general, favouring a more gradual, piecemeal approach to social change. Within his social outlook, the pursuit of the perfection of the mind and ever greater happiness are illusions. Moreover, the family, not the individual and his rights, was, according to Comte, the building block of society. The conservative orientation of Auguste Comte was taken a stage further by the next nineteenth-century social theorist that we consider, Herbert Spencer.

Discussion question

Comte emphasises how the different parts of society are interconnected – how change in one part affects other parts and the whole. Applying this to contemporary society, consider how changes in the family in British society in the past fifty years have been influenced by shifts in religious practice and belief. Then consider the impact of changes in family life and religious belief on other areas of contemporary society.

HERBERT SPENCER

The life and times of Herbert Spencer were rather less colourful than those of August Comte. Spencer never married or, as far as is known, had a sexual relationship of any kind. He did not pursue public quarrels and controversy or found a movement dedicated to spreading his own ideas. Spencer's London of the latter half of the nineteenth century was a more orderly and restrained city than Paris of Comte's heyday in the 1820s and 1830s. Certainly this is true of the conservative and largely male circles of the gentlemen's club and private library in which Spencer moved. He was a thoroughly unflamboyant character, so introverted that he found it increasingly difficult to speak in public. While Comte craved academic recognition, Spencer refused the honorary degrees offered to him. As with all thinkers who have anything interesting to say, there are significant differences of interpretation and emphasis in his work. However, there are not the radical differences that can be found in the work of Comte.

Despite such differences, there are more than superficial similarities between the two early sociologists. Both were, it seems safe to say, rather lonely and isolated figures who never gained formal university positions. Spencer, like Comte, came from a modest background, his father being a Derby schoolmaster. The Spencer family's nonconformist dissent made them politically sympathetic to the radical cause of the Chartists of the 1840s, but the key traits Spencer seems to have had ingrained in his upbringing were hard work and self-denial. Spencer did not attend university after finishing school and instead initially worked as a draftsman and engineer in the railway industry for some years while writing for various nonconformist newspapers. Journalism became a full-time job and led Spencer to move to London in 1848 to become deputy editor of *The Economist*. He gave up the position five years later in order to devote himself full-time to his own writing. Following the

completion of *Principles of Psychology* in 1855, Spencer experienced a bout of neurotic disorder as a result of the book's poor reception. For the rest of his life he
experienced periodic insomnia and an inability to concentrate for long periods.
Nevertheless, he produced numerous books and regular journal articles over the next
two decades. He enjoyed critical acclaim and high sales in both Britain and the USA
during the 1860s and 1870s. However, as the *laissez-faire* social and economic
climate of mid-nineteenth-century Britain began to change with the colonial expansion and state growth and regulation of the 1880s and 1890s, Spencer increasingly
seemed to be a dated figure. He continued to enjoy success in the USA, but was a
somewhat forgotten figure by the time he died in 1903. Therefore the rhetorical
question that has been repeatedly put since Spencer's death, 'Who reads him now?',
was actually relevant during his life (Peel 1971: 29–32). Despite this it was customary at least until recently to refer to him as 'Britain's greatest sociologist'. Perhaps
this was because of the volume of Spencer's output as much as the weight of his
ideas. We should approach Spencer with a view to understanding the development
of social theory in a British post-Enlightenment phase, as much as seeking to apply
his ideas to the globe in the early twenty-first century. However, as Spencer wrote
for a general public audience, as opposed to a specialist academic niche, his books
are not only much more readable than most of those written by professional social
theorists today, but contain important and enduring ideas. As indicated, Spencer
published numerous books on various subjects. We are concerned here only with
his thoughts about sociology's scientific status and his view of social evolution.

For Herbert Spencer, sociology is concerned with imparting sufficient scientific
rationality in order to dispel everyday misconceptions about the world. He was
obviously troubled by humanity's inability to comprehend the true nature and
significance of current economic and social developments. Moreover, he disliked
instinctive public reactions to events. One of his most famous works, *The Study of
Sociology* starts with a description of public hysteria – a nineteenth-century moral
panic – surrounding an outbreak of foot and mouth disease. Other more journalistic books like *Man v. State* (a collected set of magazine articles) are less than subtle attempts to make his reading public accept that the laws of the free market are
incontrovertible, and attempts to contradict them are therefore dangerous. For Spencer,
sociology should not, as Saint-Simon thought, set itself the task of bringing about
rational governance. Nor was it accurate to see it, as Comte did, as a guiding social
doctrine, the culmination and highest form of scientific activity. Spencer's conception of the subject was less ambitious, as he thought that it should delimit human
activity rather than channel it in a positive direction. In so undertaking this objective, which combined both radicalism and conservatism, he thought he could aid
the march of progress. However, he was rather gloomy about its likely impact. Given
that Spencer thought that sociology is a science, it follows that sociologists must
strive for objectivity in their observations. Above all, sociology must avoid national
or class bias and an admiration for overt forms of power. Interestingly, he thought
that in order for this to happen, researchers must try to attain an empathy with
their subjects.

We saw above that Comte held that sociology was a science. However, he did not think that its laws were akin to those of the natural sciences. It might be possible to draw exact parallels between the social and the natural world, but there was no prior reason for thinking that this would be the case. Sociology was the highest science but this was because it had arisen as a result of the progressive development of knowledge, not because it extended the essential findings of biology, chemistry and so on into the social world. In this respect, Comte was less dogmatic about the replication of the natural sciences in the social world than certain eighteenth-century Enlightenment thinkers and certainly less so than Herbert Spencer. Comte did not think that the subject matter of sociology, society, was less likely to deliver consistent and therefore verifiable results when experimented upon and observed. Rather, he rejected the possibility of an overarching set of laws, a general science, derived in the first instance from the natural sciences. Spencer, by contrast, was adamant that the way sociology should establish itself was by basing its analysis upon the laws of the biological sciences. It was not that biology could provide a blueprint for sociology, but that the workings of the biological organism and social collective were essentially the same. Usually he referred to this as an analogy – as a direct correspondence. And as it existed in his view, 'there can be no rational apprehension of the truths of sociology until there has been reached a rational apprehension of the truths of biology' (Spencer 1880: 330). It was not only the case that biology prepared the mind for the kind of applied thinking required by sociology – although this certainly was the case and therefore the sociologist should study biology (and psychology) as a preparation for sociology – it was more that by learning about the evolution and functioning of the organism, the student of sociology was indirectly but definitely learning about the evolution and functioning of society. Notwithstanding Spencer's occasional concessions that there are social processes that have no biological equivalent, and the odd suggestion that he felt the social and the biological should not be thought of as identical, he considered the relationship 'not a figurative resemblance, but a fundamental parallelism' (1880: 325).

Before proceeding it is worth pointing out that his account was not a crude attempt to co-opt Darwin's theory of evolution into sociology. Although the two men were familiar with each other's work, Spencer had formulated the major aspects of his social evolutionism prior to the publication of Darwin's *Origin of the Species* in 1859. When he read the book he claimed that it merely confirmed his findings (Coser 1977). Nevertheless, it is certainly true that Spencer was the key figure in the stream of social thought known as social Darwinism. In any event, it is important to consider why Spencer thought that society is analogous to the biological organism.

Spencer thought that the laws of evolution he uncovered were universal to humanity – they were the same in every society. However, in a somewhat contradictory vein, he denied that there is one scale of humanity: 'human groups, like individual organisms, do not form a series, but are classifiable only in divergent and re-divergent groups' (Spencer 1880: 325). Elsewhere he does talk about civil-isation in general terms, and in relation to a single universal scale. Whatever size societies and organisms eventually reach they all begin from the smallest beginnings: 'Societies like bodies, begin as germs – originate from masses which are extremely minute in comparison with the masses some of them eventually reach' (cited in Coser 1977: 91). Spencer gives a number of processes that characterise growth in both the biological organism and society. The most important are differentiation, sub-division, acquisition of other organisms (which retain their sub-divisions) into the whole, specialisation and regulation. Like organisms, societies are initially simple and homogeneous in their make-up. Subsequently, tribes and small-scale groups evolve basic leadership structures and begin a process of internal differentiation and specialisation according to function. This social change is brought about within the context of growth but is not spontaneous. Rather it occurs because of adaptation to externalities; because of the influence of and struggle with the external environment. In Spencer's view adaptation is 'the greatest and underlying social and biological truth' (Spencer 1880: 342). War is the primary challenge to which societies must adapt as it necessitates leadership and organisation in order to resist the enemy, and it furthers the natural tendency to cooperation of a people when faced with a common threat and the need to cope with the scarcity of resources that conflict entails. The cooperation that war necessarily involves is, in the first instance, of a coercive type – people enforce certain procedures, forms of interaction and activity in response to the war threat – but the important point is that it occurs at all.

To what extent Spencer thought differentiation continues to occur because of war, and to what extent it acquires its own momentum with the growth of a society, is not entirely clear. What is true is that he sees societies prior to that of his own in the nineteenth century as warlike or, as he put it, 'militant societies'. And it is true that intermittent war was the norm in all parts of the world until a partial pause in hostilities in a small part of Europe in the nineteenth century. However, it is also simultaneously true that the total war – society against society – that Spencer sees as typical of militant society, in which the people are an extension of the army, did not really take place until the full onset of nationalism shortly after his death. Prior to that, certainly before the wars following the French Revolution, most armies of European states were composed of foreign mercenaries, and wars were of gen-eral indifference to the peasant mass of the population. Leaving these issues aside (which do question Spencer's understanding of history), the key point is that as soci-eties develop, so, like organisms, they separate internally. As they do so, regulatory agencies evolve to oversee the relationship between two or more parts of the wider whole. According to Spencer, such regulatory agencies, or as we might term them social institutions, are not merely instrumental to that relationship, but in time develop their own characteristics and functions – an instance of the unintended consequences of action.

It is not difficult to apply Spencer's thoughts about structural differentiation to society, and to the development of particular institutions within it. For instance, in the course of, say, the rise of a family-run grocers to a multinational supermarket chain, there will have been many differentiations of personnel and departments both within and between parts of the company. Sections of the company will monitor the performance of others and regulate the relationship between two or more parts within it in order to further the coherence, and thereby the performance, of the supermarket as a whole. What is more difficult to see is why Spencer thought war was of such central importance in driving social evolution. What one has to bear in mind is that Spencer was concerned with the most general evolutionary drift across history. He thought that, in general terms, war made for differentiation and regulation. In any event, he thought that although war played the central role in evolution, progress consisted of the movement from militant, warlike, societies to industrial, peaceful and cooperative ones. Industrial societies live in relative harmony with their neighbours and are characterised by greater internal complexity and integration. The kind of society Spencer had in mind was the early Victorian one in which he lived. It was one of increasing heterogeneity as differentiation – especially in relation to work through the division of labour – multiplied; but simultaneously he thought it exhibited greater functional integration. Rather than industrial societies becoming ragged, fragmented and disorganised with progress, the multiplicity of roles and occupations that exist serve to knit the social fabric ever more tightly together. Militant societies were, according to Spencer, loose assemblies that coalesced only through the demands of war. Industrial societies were based upon the voluntary cooperation and self-regulation as humans were able to strike a compromise or contract between their contradictory extremes of altruism and egoism, enmity and amity. The external regulators Spencer talks of in relation to militant society are less relevant in his view to industrial society. The law and the bodies given to enforcing it – the judiciary and the police – are, after all, unnecessary if people recognise that if they sink their individual differences they will further their own mutual interests and happiness. The cancellation of enmity and amity, altruism and egoism, assumes a market model of social interaction and exchange, drawn from Adam Smith, in which the rational pursuit of individual ends benefits all and thereby strengthens the social whole. This is the basis of the sanctity of individual freedom and liberty in industrial society.

Implicit in all of this was the self-conscious perception of the modern, industrial citizen. Spencer described the movement thus: 'If you compare savage with civilised or compare successive stages of civilisation with one another, you find deception and credulity decreasing together; until you reach the modern scientific man, who is at once exact in his statements and critical respecting proofs' (1880: 115). Spencer's thoughts here about the peaceful orientation of industrial society prefigure the emergence in the post-1945 era of the so-called industrial convergence thesis. It argued, not altogether successfully, that global industrialisation would reduce enmity between states as they became, in essential respects, identical. His thoughts about greater differentiation giving rise to greater integration is a key aspect of the structural functionalist perspective.

In Spencer's view, the historical trend was towards the industrial society, but progress was not inevitable. He lamented that colonial war in the context of later Victorian British imperial expansion was giving rise, inadvertently, to an enlarged and coercive state. It is interesting to note that Spencer thought that the instability of racially hybrid societies would necessitate greater authority to hold them together. Any direct attempt to regulate and interfere in society was directly contrary to the voluntary restraint of industrial society. Spencer considered all forms of socialism to be types of slavery. Moreover, change in the social structure was a gradual process that could not be artificially accelerated through political intervention: 'As between infancy and maturity there is no short cut by which the tedious process and development may be avoided; so there is no way from the forms of social life to the higher but one passing through successive modifications' (Spencer 1880: 397).

At every stage of his argument Spencer tried to make analogies between biology and social process. Sometimes the comparison does seem to have at least some plausibility. For example, he claimed that the rise of government in human societies is akin to the development of the central nervous system in organisms. Less persuasively he claimed that the competition of body parts for oxygenated blood gives rise to cycles of sleep and is equivalent to economic competition producing periods of boom and slump. His claim that the formation and functioning of the of the Birmingham canal system matches the alimentary canal in the human body is bizarre (Spencer 1969: 61). Spencer acknowledged that while the parts of an organism are directly connected with one another, the parts of a society are separate. But he argued that language played a role analogous to nerves and arteries and therefore developed to bridge the gaps between different parts of society. Our ability to talk and write and communicate with ever greater speed and ease across space compensates for the fact that society is 'discreet instead of concrete', and makes 'the social aggregate a living whole'. In fairness to Spencer, he did make allowance for social processes that in his view have no biological equivalent. However, where this was the case, as with immigration, he considered it so insignificant that the general social–biological analogy was not troubled.

Spencer attempted to reconcile this stress upon the social whole, whose functional integration and coherence was like an organism, with the insistence that society is composed of individuals. There is no ambiguity in his thinking in this respect: 'Nothing comes out of society but what originates in the motive of an individual' (Spencer 1880: 378). Society does not have an existence independent of its constituent parts. Rather it is created, as it were, from the individual up and is the sum of its parts. The individual, as the society, as the organism, must adapt to changing externalities. This takes us to Spencer's notorious phrase – though it is normally attributed to Darwin – 'the survival of the fittest' (Spencer 1885: 68). The consequence of failing to adapt in the struggle for existence was annihilation. In the struggle for survival between tribes, races and individuals, the least fit perish. Occasionally Spencer voiced some liberal misgivings about the suffering that this process entailed. More usually, however, he was convinced that, as this was an aspect of progress, it was both inevitable and sure to contribute to the long-term general good: 'Severe and bloody as this process is, the extirpation of inferior races and individuals, leaves a balance of benefit to mankind' (Spencer 1880: 195). His arguments about the survival of the fittest became at times quite ridiculous, as when he claimed that the type of women that survived militant society were those who had acquired the characteristics best able to cope with the egoistic, wild men who had then predominated. Social policy and general philanthropy, designed to mitigate the effects of life's harsh competition for survival, were contrary to the laws of sociology and biology and in his view therefore 'pure evils' (Spencer 1885: 68). We thus return to Spencer's intention that sociology should open our eyes to the realities of social evolution. It is, however, doubtful that many people were fully convinced by this particular claim, even during his heyday.

The social theory of Herbert Spencer appears in some respects to be far removed from the Enlightenment optimism. Certainly it has all the traits we listed above as being indicative of social theory. It is rigorous rather than literary; insists that society is composed of individuals; is concerned above all else and in a very strong form with social interconnection and concentrates upon the unfolding nature and regulation of social life below the level of the state and politics. However, his intent seems to be to make his readers accept that there is little that we can do but to accept prevailing social conditions as inevitable. External economic forces appear as 'iron laws' from which there is no escape. The invisible hand of the market takes on a quasi-supernatural status in Spencer's social outlook – it just is, or 'you can't buck the market' in modern parlance. There is no place for human agency – the ability of society as a whole or certain parts of it – to consciously act to change or even to influence the course of events. Social change has its own pace and direction, and attempts at social engineering, even the mildest social reform, are wrong and dangerous. In this respect and most others, Spencer's social theory exhibited a particularly Victorian and, to use a now discredited adjective, 'bourgeois' take on the tradition of Enlightenment and social theory, not a rejection.

Spencer was nothing if not an advocate of the rational. Indeed, given the strength of the biological analogy one might reasonably object that his scientific approach takes no account of such things as emotions and desires in human life; or rather he treats them as irrelevant to progress. It is probably true that Spencer took a less positive view of human nature than most Enlightenment writers, but he did not impute any innate mental traits that would in themselves prevent progress. When he seems to do so in discussion of enmity and egoism in human affairs, he simultaneously suggests that amity and altruism cancel them out. Finally, and most importantly, Spencer was not pessimistic about the trend of human history. The whole orientation of his historical outlook was that society – all societies and therefore humanity – is progressing towards an industrial age of peace and cooperation in which the regulations which do exist are voluntary ones. This vision places Spencer much nearer to the hopes of Enlightenment thinkers than the next social theorist we consider, Emile Durkheim.

1 Spencer argued that as societies develop so they differentiate internally, i.e. they divide into parts, such parts acquire increasingly specialised functions, others arise in order to regulate the relationship of two or more parts.

   Suggest reasons for the growth of differentiation and specialisation as societies develop.

2 Spencer thought that it is possible that society can function through the free market in which people check and control motivations like enmity and philanthropy in the course of an exchange that benefits both parties. In this way society becomes a less coercive and a more cooperative place.

   Can you think of any situations in which this is the case? What else is needed in order to ensure that exchange between two or more parties can take place?

EMILE DURKHEIM

In a certain sense, Durkheim is the first 'proper' sociologist as well as social theorist we have considered, in as much as he had a university position in the subject. In acquiring one in 1887, amidst some bitter opposition from sections of the French university establishment who considered sociology a *gauche* upstart, Durkheim went to considerable lengths to combine social theory and research practice. Although he drew upon Spencer, and considered his work to be in the French tradition of Saint-Simon and Comte, the whole orientation of his work was away from the grand and abstract systems-building of these theorists, towards an empirically grounded and theoretically informed sociology. He is the first sociologist who would probably have understood the claim of the contemporary French sociologist Pierre Bourdieu: 'research without theory is blind, and theory without research is empty' (Bourdieu 1990). According to Johan Heilbron,

> Emile Durkheim was the first to transform Comte's idea of social science as a relatively autonomous field in to a workable research programme. Durkheim succeeded in effecting what Comte had made feasible, and he did it in a way that earned him academic recognition. Sociology in France had become conceivable with Auguste Comte, but it was not until Durkheim that it became practicable as well.
>
> (Heilbron 1995: 265–6)

Durkheim's professional and political determination to establish sociology as a recognised academic subject in French education, both at university and at school level, together with the bold clarity of his style of expression, make his work particularly comprehensible. However, as for the most part he was concerned with building a body of empirical informed work, rather than constructing theoretical schemes, it is less easy to capture his general conception about how society functions. Durkheim is the first sociologist in whom one can readily identify an understanding of religion, a perspective on crime and so on. Below we first briefly consider the life of Durkheim before looking in a little more detail at how he approached sociology, his theoretical method and finally his understanding of order and integration. The reader should be aware that once again we will not, for the most part, be concerned with the internal differences of interpretation and emphases in his substantial body of work. It may be that there are Durkheims rather than Durkheim, as one intellectual biographer puts it, but below there is basically only the one sociologist (Lukes 1973: 2–3).

It is perhaps fitting that, as Emile Durkheim did more than anyone else to bring sociology from the outside into the university curricula, he should come from outside the bourgeois academic world of nineteenth-century France in several senses. He was born in 1858 into a Jewish family in Espial in the province of Lorraine in eastern France. His father was the town rabbi and early in his life Emile decided to follow in the family tradition and become a rabbi too. However, at a young age he experienced a slightly mysterious crisis of religious faith while under the tutorship of a Catholic governess. From then on he became an agnostic and headed for a secular career. Durkheim was a brilliant student and, admittedly after several unsuccessful attempts, entered the Ecole normale supérieure in 1879, graduating successfully three years later. He subsequently taught at lycées in the Paris area for five years before gaining an initial university position teaching sociology and education to undergraduates and trainee teachers at Bordeaux University. He was to remain at Bordeaux for fifteen years. About this time Durkheim married Louise Dreyfus. Little is known about his family life beyond the fact that the couple had two children, and that Louise devoted herself to the home, while her husband pursued his career. His own domestic life probably mirrored his belief that women are 'fundamentally traditionalists by nature, they govern their conduct by fixed beliefs and have no great intellectual needs' (Durkheim 1963: 166). The 1890s were certainly an extraordinarily productive period. Between 1893 and 1897 Durkheim published three of his most famous works, *The Division of Labour in Society* (1893), *Rules of Sociological Method* (1895) and *Suicide* (1897). Moreover, in 1898 he founded the journal *L'Année Sociologique* that drew together Durkheim's growing band of intellectual supporters and acted as a lever to establish sociology in French academic life. The family moved to Paris in 1902 when he was given a position at the Sorbonne, the appointment being made a full professorship five years later, the first in sociology in France. His work on religion and belief culminated in the publication of *Elementary Forms of Religious Life* in 1912. Durkheim died in 1917; possibly his grief over the death of his son in the First World War in 1915 shortened his life. One can only speculate about whether or not Durkheim carried alongside such a successful career insecurities from his provincial Jewish background. There is no indication that he was treated differently, certainly none that he was discriminated against at any stage of his career. However, there can be no question that he was aware that he was something of an outsider.

As indicated, Durkheim was never drawn to the grand theoretical edifice of Comte. He considered his three stages of humanity – the metaphysical, the philosophical, the scientific – to be of minor interest. His vision of sociology was at once more limited and more ambitious than that of Comte or Spencer. More limited because he wanted to confine his pronouncements to matters he could substantiate with research. More ambitious because he wanted to harness sociology to systematic social diagnosis that could 'test the social order against a conception of normality, or health' (Lukes 1973: 76). Moreover, it could aid the efforts of humanity to understand the world in an increasingly secular age by 'extending scientific rationalism to human behaviour' (Durkheim 1938: xxxix). However, before sociology could act as an instrument of social reform, it would first have to establish its status as both a science and a specialised discipline within French academia. This achieved, its practical potential might help ensure the wider stability of the society in which Durkheim lived, the French Third Republic. It is an exaggeration to suggest that Durkheim's concern for social order – in common with *fin de siècle* social theory – was his principal one, as is the related claim that he was above all a conservative (Nisbet 1965). However, it is the case that Durkheim was a strong but critical supporter of the regime that had been established after France's defeat by Germany in 1870. The Third Republic was the eighth regime, founded on the fourteenth constitution, since the Revolution of 1789. Durkheim thought that it had 'stimulated and reawakened men's minds' after the lethargy of the years of Napoleon that had preceded it. His political support for the society was, however, tempered by his assessment of the tasks facing sociology. Through articles and lectures he took up and debated issues of the day, and was close to figures in and around government in the 1890s. Therefore one can hardly say that Durkheim was an aloof intellectual; although he considered it more productive to work to include sociology in the school and university curricula than to enter directly into politics.

It is also true that Durkheim's determination to establish sociology as a 'proper' academic subject influenced his forthright, often polemical style. His blunt admonishment to 'treat social facts as if they are things' at the beginning of *Rules of Sociological Method* must be among the best known, if most disputed, tenet in academic sociology (Lukes 1973: 34). Although Durkheim never summed up so succinctly his closely related claim that a social fact must be analysed through its constituent parts, it is probably as well known and equally contentious. The claim that social facts – crime, divorce, industrial accidents, etc. – have the same status as actual physical objects, and should be considered outside the mass of individual instances which make up a type of social phenomenon, was clearly designed to advance the scientific and general importance of sociology. Actually, Durkheim agreed with Comte that sociology was not reducible to the methods and procedure of the natural sciences. However, the claim that when studying something like crime or divorce the subject should be treated as a real and definable thing, that is out there and observable, having a real, general cause and trend, falls within the approach of the natural sciences. If we assume that, say, divorce is only the collective term for hundreds of different instances of marital breakdown, then it is difficult, if not impossible, to give general reasons for a change in the divorce rate. If we treat it as a clear phenomenon and leave aside the motivations of the numerous couples to end marriage, then we are in a stronger position to assess the general factors as to why the divorce rate has gone up or down. This is precisely what Durkheim did with varying suicide rates for different groups. Using statistics, he analysed the reasons why some groups, religious and occupational, are more likely to commit suicide than others. For him the particular paths of individuals to suicide were irrelevant, as were their given motivations as revealed in suicide notes. He did not claim that a person who killed himself for a given reason lied or deluded him- or herself, and that really there was a general social cause that they were unaware of that made them take their own life. Rather he was concerned with the wider presence of or lack of restraint surrounding suicide of the group, religious or familial, to which an individual belonged: 'Suicide varies inversely with the degree of integration of the social group of which the individual forms part'. As an example of this, he argued that the degree of social integration of Catholics and Jews into their groups, meant they were less likely to commit suicide than were Protestants. For good reason, *Suicide* should be considered as much a methodological demonstration of sociology's scientific status as an account of its subject matter.

It follows from such an approach that we should treat society itself as well as particular social facts, such as crime, as observable and analysable 'things'. Again Durkheim was quite explicit on this point: society is beyond the individual (*sui generis* as he usually put it), it is not merely the sum of the individuals who compose it. He did not mean that one can put on a coat and hat and go out and find an object called society. This may be the case with totems that symbolise a religion that represents a society to itself, even if in reality it is only a wooden or stone effigy. What he meant was that it exists in the collective consciousness of the group. Collective consciousness has a reality that differs from the individual parts of which it is composed. In order to try to understand these points we have to consider the problem of order in Durkheim's sociology.

Durkheim's first book, *The Division of Labour in Society* (1893), was a reworking of his doctorate and a summation of numerous lectures and articles produced in the preceding years. The issue at the heart of the book is how individuals are integrated into modern, industrial societies with their myriad of occupations and levels. The issue was not a new one but had been central to Herbert Spencer and relates to Tönnies' concepts of *Gemeinschaft* and *Gesellschaft* dealt with elsewhere in this book (pp. 147–51). Durkheim argued that in primitive societies, when individuals had been bound together because they were essentially the same, *mechanical solidarity* functioned. However, when individuals increasingly had particular occupations and locations, clearly they were not alike. The question thus arose of what tied individual to individual to make up the collective whole. Herbert Spencer, through an elaboration of Adam Smith, had argued that men enter into a market system of exchange in which amity and enmity cancel one another out. He thought, as we saw above, that the result would be a more cooperative society in which order would stem from the perception of the benefits it would bring, not from a moral order independent of exchange or from coercion. Durkheim disagreed with this. As he argued:

> But if the division of labour produces solidarity, it is not because it makes each individual an *exchangist*, as the economists say: it is because it creates amongst men an entire system of rights and duties which link them together in a durable way . . . the division of labour gives rise to rules which assure pacific and regular concourse of divided functions.
>
> (Durkheim 1933: 406)

It should be pointed out that this conception of *organic solidarity* does not suggest a morality that exists independent of the division of labour, but it does suggest that it gives rise to a wider and deeper morality that is not just a realisation of personal, individual benefit. This raises the question of what exactly is morality for Durkheim.

The word implies good and bad in character. Durkheim intended it to have these meanings, but only in respect to the fact that its absence would have damaging implications for the well-being of society. His conception of morality is of the sum of the ties that bind an individual into society:

> In general, the characteristic of moral rules is that they enunciate the fundamental conditions of social solidarity. Law and morality are the totality of ties which bind us to society, which make us a unitary aggregate of the mass of individuals. Everything which is a source of solidarity is moral, everything which forces him to regulate his conduct through something other than the striving of his ego is moral and morality is as solid as these ties are numerous and strong . . . Morality consists in being in solidarity with a group.
>
> (Durkheim 1933: 396–8)

So although individuals have highly particular and specialised roles in the division of labour, society's moral hold over the individual is that much greater now than in the past. The niches and identities one may have as worker with a particular role in an organisation, as mother and so on, all make for a web of moral ties that bind us into the wider society. Society is actually strengthened through the division of labour as organic solidarity exists.

This notion that the division of labour in itself spontaneously strengthens the social morality is not particularly plausible. We might have particular obligations and duties, but the argument that somehow society as a whole benefits out of the sum seems doubtful. It might be argued that society is weakened by narrow personal commitments. In any event, in Durkheim's later works organic solidarity is far less important to the question of how and why society exists. Lukes suggests that Durkheim was having doubts about organic solidarity even when he came to write *The Division of Labour*. In *Suicide* and *Elementary Forms of Religious Life* the role of 'collective conscious', society as instilled in the minds of individuals, is given greater weight. Once again Durkheim makes matters clear: 'For society can exist only if it penetrates the consciousness of individuals and fashions it in its image and resemblance'. Society, as suggested above, exists externally to individuals and it projects itself into our minds. In this way, morals and beliefs are internalised: 'The influence of society is what has aroused in us the sentiments of sympathy and solidarity drawing us toward others; it is society which, fashioning us in its image, fills us with religious, political and moral beliefs that control our action' (Durkheim 1963: 211–12).

This quote brings us to the issue raised above of the way in which the collective consciousness differs from the sum of its individual parts. A collective has, in fact, 'its own ways of thinking and feeling to which its members bend but which are different from those they would create if they were left to their devices'. He argues, persuasively enough: 'An individual would never create gods, myths and dogmas, moral duty, discipline if left to his own devices' (Bellah 1973: 16–17). Only the collective can take on and perpetuate these states. But the collective does not appear only as corrective to the wayward individual. On the contrary, Durkheim argues that through the collective consciousness as expressed through religion the individual can realise and express him or herself.

A basic and familiar criticism of Durkheim is that he did not consider issues of power, ideology and inequality. It is certainly true that such issues are not to the fore for Durkheim to the extent they are for Marx. However, issues of social and economic justice do enter his theoretical conception of order. He argues that discipline can exist only if people consider it just. A moral order underpins the distribution of income. If one section becomes excessively rich, discipline is threatened. A social breakdown – anomie – is a subject upon which Durkheim had definite points to make: points that are still relevant nearly a hundred years after they were written. In the passage below he speaks of the way individuals are unable to cope with disappointments and are thus more prone to anomic suicide.

> Such is the source of excitement predominating in this part of society, and which has extended to other parts. There is a state of crisis and anomie is constant and, so to speak, normal. From top to bottom of the ladder, greed is aroused without knowing where to find ultimate foothold. Nothing can calm it, since its goal is far beyond all it can attain. Reality seems valueless by comparison with the dreams of fevered imaginations; reality is therefore abandoned, but so too is the possibility abandoned when it becomes a reality. A thirst arises for novelties, unfamiliar pleasures, nameless sensations, all of which lose their savour once known. Henceforth one has no strength to endure the least reverse. The whole fever subsides and the sterility of all the tumult is apparent, and it is seen that all these new sensations in their infinite quantity cannot form a solid foundation of happiness to support one during days of trial.
>
> (Durkheim 1963: 256)

For this reason he was opposed to the unchecked extension of the market economy. It frees industry from moral restraint and, as we have seen, morals are the ties that bind and integrate the individual into society.

Whatever one thinks of Durkheim's sociology there is no denying its coherence and consistency. What is less clear-cut is his relationship to the Enlightenment. On the one hand his sociology is very much in the tradition of rational understanding and reform in order to further progress. In order to strengthen this he adopted a mild, reformist socialism to try to stabilise but improve the society in which he lived, the French Third Republic. He thought this worthwhile because, despite its faults, it had the potential to strengthen the moral order through science and education. In this respect he was closer to those eighteenth-century figures who thought that knowledge would lead to greater happiness than the austere scholasticism of Comte or the severe 'hands off' warnings of Spencer. Simultaneously, it shifted the theoretical orientation of sociology away from the individual towards society. We saw above how Comte, under the influence of Catholic conservatives who hated the revolution, claimed that the family, not the individual, is the hub of society, and, more importantly, made the individual part explicable in relation to the social whole. Spencer claimed that the individual and their motives are the starting-point of analysis. However, in the former case it is questionable how much impact this had upon Comte's sociology, while in the latter it is difficult to square Spencer's methodological individualism with the organic analogy. Therefore, before Durkheim, the legacy of the Enlightenment contention that we should start with the individual was a confused one. With Durkheim there is no ambiguity: the society exists outside of the individual through a collective conscious that fills our minds with its political, moral (social) and religious beliefs. Its nature is not the sum of the individual parts that constitute it, but it is distinct in itself – it has its own character. In order to understand society, to further the science of sociology, we must approach the thing-like social facts within it, from the point of view of the totality. Therefore the question is always, how does a social action relate to the wider social context?

Durkheim's viewpoint on the Enlightenment tradition was the source of lasting disagreements. Some people claimed his supposed contempt for the individual made him an intellectual precursor of the rise of fascism over the next 40 years (Catlin in Introduction to Durkheim 1933). Others have portrayed him as a rather naive, middle-class socialist (Lukes 1973). More important for our purposes is that his partial endorsement of the Enlightenment – rationality and progress but society, not the individual, as the focus of sociology – makes his contribution to social theory an ambiguous one. On the one hand, some features of social theory outlined above can be found in Durkheim's work in an exemplary form. Central to his theoretical approach are intellectual rigour – something he thought was a moral imperative in itself – a concern with social interconnection and the importance of classifications and typologies. At the latter he was quite masterful, though whether or not he was always right – as with his breakdown of the merits of different definitions and approaches of religion – is another matter. However, as Durkheim relegated the importance of the individual, there is less sense of the unfolding nature of social life. If we are programmed by society to act in a certain way then there is less chance and contingency in our individual interactions and actions. Sociology has the task of uncovering the nature of the external social environment of individuals and their place within it, but there is little place for the unintended consequences of action. Social action is determined by the society.

KARL MARX

Karl Marx would perhaps have enjoyed the irony that in our global times when his ideas are, at least at one level, never more relevant, sociology, the academic discipline that allegedly provides an explanation of society, often treats him as irrelevant. Marxism does find occasional support from unlikely sources outside the academic establishment. A wealthy Wall Street investment banker wrote in the October 1997 edition of the *New Yorker* that, 'The longer I spend on Wall Street, the more I am convinced that Marx was right. I am absolutely convinced that Marx's way is the best way to look at capitalism' (cited in Wheen 2000: 5). He was referring to political corruption, monopolisation, alienation, inequality and global markets, not socialism. This is not the place to debate the contemporary relevance or irrelevance of Marx but to provide an overview of the principal points of his theoretical approach to understanding society. We begin with a brief account of his life and work before examining Marx's basic analysis of the nature of humanity and his understanding of historical change, of social class, of knowledge and of alienation.

Marx's life and times

Karl Marx was born in Trier in the German Rhineland in 1818. His father was from a long line of rabbis, but as a child of the Enlightenment he was not himself a religious man. His conversion from Judaism the year before his son was born was for more practical than religious reasons. Despite partial Jewish emancipation following invasion of the German states by the Napoleonic armies, anti-Semitism remained strong across the provinces of Germany and it hindered Marx's otherwise successful career as a lawyer. Marx's mother, from what we can gather, seems not to have been a strong influence on her son's development. But through his father, together with a neighbour, Frier Ludwig von Westphalen, the young Karl Marx imbibed the influence of Kant and Rousseau, Goethe and Hegel. Having finished his school education, Marx first enrolled at Bonn University before transferring to Berlin. There he famously became a 'Young Hegelian', Wilhelm Hegel having being professor of philosophy at the university. Hegel's spirit apparently dominated the university despite the fact that he had been dead for five years by the time Marx enrolled in 1836 (Coser 1977: 59). Although a talented student, Marx frequently fell foul of the highly conservative university and Prussian authorities. He had hoped to become an academic, but whatever chances he still had were extinguished in 1841 when his dissertation was submitted to the University of Jena. Its radical tone and interpretation of otherwise standard philosophical material – 'On the differences between the natural philosophy of Democritus and Epicurus' – did, however, enhance his growing reputation as a rather flamboyant radical. Having burnt his bridges with the university hierarchy, Marx worked for a short time as a journalist for an anti-establishment newspaper in Cologne. However, attacks penned by Marx on the Prussian state and then the Russian tsar Nicholas I led to the newspaper's suppression. Despite an uncertain income and future, Marx married his childhood sweetheart Jenny von Westaphalen in April 1843. She was from a respectable and well-to-do family that rather looked down upon Karl Marx and thought him a thoroughly unsuitable choice for their daughter.

Realising that his prospects were poor in Germany, Marx emigrated with his young wife to Paris in late 1843. It was to be a key moment in his political development. In Paris, Marx became aware of socialism for the first time through the writings of figures like Saint-Simon and Parisian (and exiled German) working-class activists. There he met Friedrich Engels and began a friendship that was to be both politically and financially crucial to him and his family for the rest of his life. While in Paris he read the British political economists like Mill and Ricardo, adding a third and crucial influence to that of German philosophy and French socialism. Although both politically and socially Paris was an exciting place for Marx and his wife, they were compelled to leave France for Belgium in 1845 following an article by Marx in a socialist newspaper attacking, on this occasion, the Prussian monarchy. In Brussels, Marx, buoyed by the revolutionary currents that culminated in the revolutions of 1848, wrote the most famous of his early works, the *Communist Manifesto*. With expectations of imminent revolutionary success he travelled back to Germany in 1848 and then briefly to Paris. As the prospect of revolution receded, Marx and his wife embarked for London in 1849. Marx thought that London would be a temporary resting place before returning to the thick of political activity on the continent of Europe. However, apart from occasional trips, he and his family were to spend the rest of their lives there.

The subsequent years were difficult ones for Marx and his family. The severe poverty they at times experienced contributed to the death of their son. Despite this, they maintained a semblance of a middle-class lifestyle – including servants, a personal secretary and trips to the continent – largely through the money provided by the wealthy Engels (Wheen 2000: ch. 8). The political downturn of the 1850s presented Marx with the opportunity to devote himself to the study of political economy which he pursued among the holdings of the British Library. His studies in this period were ultimately to culminate in the publication of *Capital* in 1867. Marx was involved in the formation of the First International Working Men's Federation in 1863, an attempt to bring together socialists of various persuasions from Europe, America and elsewhere. The movement lasted only thirteen years but recurrently took up a good deal of Marx's time and energy. The International split, following the Paris Commune of 1871, as a result of disagreement over the issue of whether or not it is legitimate to use violence in the pursuit of social change. The final years of Marx's life were relatively prosperous ones for his family, but his writing output slowed. Jenny Marx died in 1881, Karl two years later.

Marx's wide-ranging influences and interests included an admiration for the Enlightenment, the German idealist philosophy, especially that of Hegel, a commitment to socialism and a knowledge of classical British political economy. To this we should add a love of poetry and literature, especially evident in the flow and style of some of his texts. Therefore Marx did not create an entirely new social theory. His originality lay in his ability to work from established sources to produce quite new and distinctive results. Once again the writings of a great thinker can be seen to spread across more than one theoretical position, although the differences between the young and the old Marx were probably not as great as some have argued. And once again we are not chiefly concerned with teasing out the nuances. However, in contrast to other social theorists considered in this chapter who were independent scholars or academics, Marx was not so concerned to establish a particular method within a binding framework. As 'above all else a revolutionist' – as Engels put it in his speech at Marx's funeral – Marx was concerned to explain society in order to enable change.

Marx's work – starting points

Marx rejected any notion that humans have an innate essence or inherent tendency to act in certain ways. He rejected, too, the contention of Hegel that there is any universal flow of a historical spiritual or idealist type. His starting point was always the circumstances and conditions in which people find themselves and the way in which they survive and reproduce. The issue of what distinguishes men from animals did not particularly interest him: 'Men can be distinguished from animals by consciousness, by religion or by anything else you like'. However, he continues: 'They themselves begin to distinguish themselves from animals as soon as they begin to produce their means of subsistence' (Marx and Engels 1963: 7). This then is crucial: the point at which and the way in which men produce their means of subsistence; as prior to that they were indistinguishable from animals. The way or the method of the production – in the first instance simply in order to survive – is referred to by Marx as the *mode of production*.

The mode of production is based upon a certain level of knowledge and its practical application through technology – the means of production – and a particular set of social relationships among individuals. The sum of the social relationships of individuals makes society. Therefore the individual does not stand alone, he is not analytically discreet. Rather he is to be explained by the sum of social relationships in which he is intertwined. 'The real nature of man is the totality of social relations' (cited in Bottomore and Rubel 1963: 83). The nature of these social relations (which correspond to the level of production) determine social being. Reversing Hegel, Marx famously put it thus: 'It is not the consciousness of men that determines their being, but, on the contrary, their social being that determines their consciousness' (Marx 1963: 67). What people think is determined by the wider social conditions of any given society. There is no set human nature, and 'being' is explicable only in relation to society. 'Society' is not a constant that stands outside of time in some way, but is historically relative.

Marx did not just think that the everyday thoughts of individuals and groups were reflective of their social conditions. The state, the law, the prevailing morals, the leading religious ideas, the dominant philosophy are all products of a particular society, itself a product of a particular age. They may be 'false' in the sense that they are ideological constructions – they reflect and serve certain interests – but they are part and parcel of that historical society. 'The same men who establish social relations in conformity with their material power of production also produce principles, laws and categories in conformity with their social relations. Thus, these ideas, these categories, are no more eternal than the relations which they express. They are *historical and transient products*' (cited in Bottomore and Rubel 1963: 108–9). Therefore although we are presented with certain rules and obligations that appear timeless – for example, religious principles or certain morals or familial norms – they are in fact features of the period and of the mode of production that produced them. As an age changes and disappears, so, *at some point thereafter*, will those rules and obligations. Marx summarises the whole process succinctly:

> In the social production which men carry on they enter into definite relations that are indispensable and independent of their will; these relations of production correspond to a definite state of development of their material powers of production. The totality of these relations of production constitutes the economic structure of society – the real foundations on which the legal and political superstructures arise and to which definite forms of social consciousness correspond. The mode of production of material life determines the general character of the social, political and spiritual processes of the life.
>
> (cited in Bottomore and Rubel 1963: 156)

Historical change

Marx distinguished a number of modes of production: ancient, Asiatic, feudal and capitalist. Each society has a dominant form of class relationship and struggle, based on a particular form of exploitation. This raises the question of what Marx meant by the terms 'class', 'class struggle' and 'exploitation'. Class for Marx was not primarily a matter of the distribution of income – of wealth and poverty – although inequality was certainly a consequence of it. It was rather something determined in the first instance by the relationship of aggregates of people to one another in production. It is an oversimplification to suggest that Marx supposed that there are only two classes in any given society, but he did think that there are dominant classes and therefore dominant class relationships. The famous oppositions are given at the beginning of the *Communist Manifesto*: freeman and slave, patrician and plebeian, lord and serf, guildmaster and journeyman. In each case the oppressing group owns and controls the means of production and extracts a surplus from the oppressed group – the slave, the worker and so on. This is the nature of exploitation: the ability of a minority to live from the labour of the majority over which it exercises varying degrees of coercion. In slavery, characteristic of the ancient mode of production, the slave is physically compelled to work for the master. In capitalism, workers are notionally free to sell their labour power, but have to do so in order to survive. Exploitation necessarily entails class antagonism as the minority and majority confront each other in production. Contrary to the usual claims of employers, unions and government, Marx thought that far from the interests of labour and capital being the same, they are diametrically opposed. With every ascending mode of production the exploitation of the majority is heightened as more surplus value (roughly speaking, profit) is extracted from them. Class rule is thus sharpened and becomes more transparent and as a result the class struggle intensifies.

How, though, do different kinds of society, based on different modes of production, come to replace one another? In other words, what did Marx see as the dynamic of history? There are two interrelating but differing explanations to be found in Marx's work. In the *Communist Manifesto*, a pamphlet intended by Marx and Engels to ferment the revolutionary brew of the mid-nineteenth century, the message is clear: 'the history of all hitherto existing societies is the history of class struggle'. Class struggle results either in the 'revolutionary re-constitution of society, or in the common ruin of the contending classes'. So the antagonism which exists between different classes, between 'oppressor and oppressed', is 'uninterrupted' and reflected in a fight that is 'now hidden now open' and which drives history from society to society (Marx and Engels 1959: 45–6). The emphasis found here on human agency, on the ability of people to consciously transform their lives through transforming the conditions in which they live, is rather different from the more mechanistic account of historical development found in *Preface to the Critique of Political Economy* written some twelve years later when revolution seemed less imminent. Here the stress is upon progress through the removal of obstacles that stand in the way of the forces of production:

> At a certain stage of their development, the material productive forces of society come into conflict with the existing relations of production, or – what is a legal expression of the same thing – with the property relations within which they have been at work hitherto. From forms of development of the productive forces these relations become fetters. There then begins a period of social revolution. With the change in the economic foundation the entire immense superstructure is more or less rapidly transformed.
>
> (cited in Bottomore and Rubel 1963: 156)

Marx continues to speak of how the nature and dimensions of the change cannot be assessed by the participants themselves, in the same way as our opinion of an individual is not based on what he thinks of himself. The objective assessment we can make is one of the economic scale of change.

Perhaps both these considerations – the will and power of a class to change society and the importance of the conditions which give rise to the inclination, in terms of both structure and agency – are conveyed in one of Marx's greatest lines. At the beginning of *The Eighteenth Brumaire of Louis Bonaparte* he captures the constraints of historical change (though admittedly here he is concerned as much with the psychological baggage that people carry as with the structural limitations): 'Men make their own history, but they do not make it just as they please; they do not make it under circumstances chosen by themselves, but under circumstances directly found, given and transmitted from the past' (Marx 1958: 10).

The preoccupation of Marx's vision and explanation of history relates to the period in and system under which he lived: capitalism. Capitalism is the highest form of class society, but the one that provides the possibility of a revolutionary transformation into a classless society by dint of the way in which it heightens out of all recognition the productive capacity of the economy, but simultaneously creates its own gravedigger, the working class. Precisely for this reason Marx was tremendously impressed by the productive energy of capitalism and welcomed its spread across the world. In it a growing class of proletarians exist and are in conflict with the owners of capital, the bourgeoisie. The working class is nominally free but it is forced for subsistence to sell its labour power. The worker receives back a fraction of the labour time he or she expends in the form of a wage. The greater part of the worker's time is given over to the capitalist in the production of commodities. This process of production is therefore the most exploitative of all class societies. Workers might be considerably better off working in factories and offices in capitalism than they had been before, but for Marx this is not the point. Exploitation is defined by the level of surplus extracted, not the relative level of poverty.

As capitalism is the most exploitative society, so it is the most alienating society. For Marx, alienation consists not of the individual worker experiencing social isolation – anomie – from society as a whole; rather it arises from the experience of his labour and from the products of his labour being removed from him and existing as objects with which he or she has no integral relationship. 'The alienation of the worker in his product means not only that his labour becomes an object, takes on its own existence, but that it exists outside him, and that it stands opposed to him as an autonomous product' (Marx 1959: 83).

The exploitation and alienation of capitalism are increasingly evident to the working class. The social bonds and forms of ideological camouflage that partially masked the class struggle in previously existing modes of production, are progressively lowered in capitalism by its very dynamism. Capitalism has no respect for tradition, religion or nationality as it seeks new markets to make greater profits. In one passage in the *Communist Manifesto* Marx memorably compares capitalism to the sorcerer's apprentice: once summoned up, its activity cannot be restrained. Its inherent instability – together with the historical tendency of profit to fall – gives rise to successively deeper booms and slumps. In them, the intermediate groups in the class system, the petite bourgeoisie and so on, increasingly fall into the ranks of working class, while those at the top of the hierarchy reap greater profits from mergers and acquisitions. The crisis that capitalism experiences, together with an increasingly class conscious and organised proletariat, aware of their exploitation and oppression and determined to end it, gives rise to polarisation and ever more antagonistic class struggle. Marx confidently expected a socialist revolution to arise out of this, after which the working class would hold power. Socialism would in turn be superseded by the first classless society: communism. An issue for social theory is that well over a hundred years after Marx's death his basic prediction has self-evidently not occurred.

Summary

It is particularly difficult, and not really appropriate, to try to divorce Marx's theory of society from his attempt to change it. However, the fact that Marxism has apparently 'failed' does not mean that it should be discarded. As suggested, important aspects of Marxism are now more apparent than ever as global capitalism embraces the world, while simultaneously stretching out vast disparities of wealth and poverty. In examining Marxism and its fate we are, in fact, looking at a particular interpretation and development of Enlightenment thinking. Marx drew upon the Enlightenment emphasis on historical progress and purposive political action to achieve freedom. However, his work also bears the influence of British classical political economics and the notion of the unfolding nature of economic change which forms a structural basis that mediates and constrains the intentions of human beings. In addition, Marx drew upon the distinctly German idealist philosophical traditions which saw social change as occurring through conflict and contradiction. Marx brought these disparate influences to bear in developing a social theory that presents a stark and unrelenting analysis and critique of capitalism.

Discussion questions

1 List conflicts between groups of people that have occurred or are occurring in different parts of the world. Look at media coverage of some of these conflicts. To what extent has class played a role in the conflict? What other factors have played a significant part?

2 Consider Marx's notion of alienation. Provide some examples of alienation in modern society. Apart from work, where else does alienation occur?

MAX WEBER

Because of the political impact of Karl Marx's thought – or at least political uses thereof – more has been written about him than any other social theorist discussed in this book. However, within the academic discipline of sociology, Max Weber has arguably been the single most influential figure. There are several reasons for this. The range and erudition of his writings means that they are of relevance across a number of academic fields. Unlike most scholars both in Weber's time and in our own, he did not confine his attention to a particular topic or, indeed, discipline. He only came to sociology in the formal sense of accepting a professorship in the subject late in life and then did so with reluctance, claiming that it was only to rid the discipline from its collectivist tendencies (Runciman 1978: 3). Prior to that he had held university positions in political economy and economic history. Substantively, his intellectual interests include the comparative analysis of religions, types of political power and administration, law, the stratification of societies, the development of capitalism, and the rise of rationality and science. He did not confine his studies to any particular historical period, giving the impression that he considered himself as competent and as entitled to discuss events in the ancient world as he was to discuss events that were taking place in his day. Methodologically, he attempted to combine macro concerns for both economic and spiritual development with the meanings and motivations of individual actions. So although (or perhaps because) his writings are diffuse, replete with multitudinous qualifications to the claims he makes and, on occasions, contradictory, there is a lot in Weber.

A second reason for the influence of and interest in Max Weber is that although there are consistent themes in his work – broadly speaking, the nature of domination in human society, the role of ideas in history, the impact of the industrial capitalism first on Europe and then on the world, and the scope and limitations of the social sciences – it is possible to evaluate it and re-evaluate it in terms of its contemporary sociological relevance. The major shift in academic sociology since the mid-1970s in this respect has been from the use of Weber as a counterpoint to the materialism of Marx, to an interest in Weber as a theorist of modernity. The move coincides with the decline of support for Marxism within university social science departments and the rise of postmodernism. Anthony Giddens, in his advocacy of 'late modernity' in particular, has recently moved away from treating Weber as a theorist of capitalism to Weber as a theorist of modernity (Giddens 1990: 68–9). A recent highly popular use of Weber has been the 'McDonaldisation' thesis of George Ritzer (1993). Therefore, while it was noted above that there are 'Durkheims' and 'Marxs', a plurality of interpretations is even more marked in the case of Max Weber. Once again, however, our concern here is not, for the most part, to try to identify the differing emphases within a single theorist's work, but to present an overview of Weber's social theory. Again a brief sketch of his life helps to set the context for a consideration of his analysis of social action, the rise of capitalism and rationalisation.

Weber's life and times

Max Weber was born into a well-to-do Prussian family in 1864, the beginning of the seven-year period that would see the unification of Germany. His childhood in Berlin was an unhappy stage of a generally troubled life. His father, Max Senior, a National Liberal politician and lawyer, was by all accounts a domineering figure who bullied both Max and his wife and Max's mother, Helene. Helene bore his regular attempts to humiliate her with a grim devotion to her husband and family, fortified by a strong religious faith. Fred Pampel (2000: 87–9) suggests that this created a lasting ambivalence in Weber between a determined sense of duty, derived from his mother, and a certain admiration for authority and power drawn from his father. In any event, it certainly made for a tense and threatening atmosphere within the family home. Weber found refuge in books throughout his early life. He was stimulated too by the writers and intellectuals who visited the Weber family home. A brilliant student, Weber studied law at the universities of Heidelberg, Berlin and Gottingham. He rarely socialised during these years, something he thought a frivolous and tedious waste of time, and was equally contemptuous of the student drinking and duelling fraternities that dominated college life. Throughout his life he rarely took physical exercise and only went outdoors when he had to.

Despite his austere and anti-social persona, Weber married his second cousin Marianne at the age of 29. Those who knew the couple described the Webers as 'close', but this was only in respect to companionship and intellectual engagement, as the evidence suggests the marriage was sexless. It would be wrong to draw a caricature of Weber's attitude towards sex from the puritan figures, who renounced sexual pleasure for earthly gain and self-consciously channelled their lusts into their work, he examined in his most famous book *The Protestant Ethic and the Spirit of Capitalism*, published in 1902. However, the comparison is, perhaps, not wholly inappropriate. Certainly Weber's work routine intensified in the early years of marriage, as he managed to undertake three jobs simultaneously. This was to bring career rewards as, at the age of just 32, he was awarded a full professorship at the prestigious Heidelberg University. However, the following year he had a nervous breakdown from which he never completely recovered. The immediate cause was his father's death which he blamed upon himself. Weber had argued with his father while he was visiting his son and daughter-in-law together with his wife Helene. Feeling sufficiently confident to challenge his father's bullying manner as a result of his hard-achieved academic position, he ordered him from the house following a row. Max Weber Senior died alone a few weeks later. The cumulative cause was his persistent overwork, faltering health and determined self-denial.

Max Weber spent much of the next six years listlessly travelling in Switzerland and southern Europe supported, paradoxically, by money from his father's inheritance. During this period he was unable to find the mental energy to read or write for more than a few minutes at a time. As he had lived for his work he was lost without it. In 1903 he was forced to give up his university position, but did return to private academic work the following year and even gave several lectures in America. He did not formally hold a university position again until 1919, when he became professor of sociology at Munich University. Max Weber died the following year at the age of 56.

To the strains within Weber's personal life we should also touch on those within the wider society in which he lived (Coser 1977: 253–6). Germany became within this period the world's second largest industrial economy with a wealthy and acquisitive bourgeoisie. However, it did so without significant political change as the emperor retained enormous autocratic power. Parliamentary democracy only partially existed and much of the state remained somewhat feudal. The emergent mass working-class socialist party, the Social Democrat Party, was subject to clumsy repression.

The constraint and repression of Wilhelm German society pre-1914 led to various social and political tensions that are observable within Weber's work: on the one hand a concern with democratisation, on the other an interest in how power can be wielded by subjective resources like charisma; an understanding of the historical demand for greater equality but a conservatism that made him fearful of revolution; an intense dislike of militarism yet a consistent pride in the historical achievements of the German nation; an understanding of the essential role of bureaucratic rationality within modern states but a grim foreboding that society was increasingly coming to resemble an 'iron cage'; and, relatedly, an appreciation of the role of the intellectual in modernity but a hatred for intellectuals. To this should be added a methodological attempt to combine a concentration on objective social facts in the manner of Durkheim, with a concern for the subjective inner feelings of humans in the tradition of German idealist philosophy since Kant. We explore this issue further in the following discussion of Weber's approach to sociology.

Weber the social theorist

As a German, it was hardly surprising that Weber's approach to the social sciences is to be located within nineteenth-century German debates about the nature and procedure of the social sciences. To understand them fully we need a major detour into the *Methodenstreit* (dispute about method) between economists and historians of the 1880s. In fact, the details of the debate need not concern us here. The principal issue was whether or not it is legitimate to posit regular laws of human behaviour across history, and whether or not it is possible to develop frames of reference to understand the world independent of the values we bring to the process. Weber's position, as it emerged in the course of engagement with intellectuals such as Menger, Rickert, Schmoller and Dilthey, is that there is no qualitative difference in the methods and aims of the social and natural science (Ray 1999: 165–8). Both always proceed by abstraction and generalisation and intend to identify cause and effect. He rejected the idea that only isolated fragments of understanding are possible, but not that 'facts' are somewhat irrelevant compared with totalising theories. Both facts and the abstraction from them are necessary in science. The values of the researcher enter the process because, given the infinite diversity of reality in formulating research methodologies and theories, and in selecting a particular subject matter, the researcher will inevitably pick out those aspects that reflect our values at some level (Callinicos 1999: 162). Therefore values orientate the subject matter of research and affect what is and what is not included within it. They do not, or at least for Weber should not, influence the actual conduct of research once begun. Put simply, values will influence what is researched but should not influence how it is done. The whole point of Weber's approach to social science is to demonstrate its objectivity despite the imposition of the values we bring to it.

However, Weber did not think that the procedure of the social sciences was akin to that of the natural sciences – physics and so on. We saw above how Durkheim dismissed the final thoughts and stated motivations of people who commit suicide. As his starting point was the social whole, he explained action in terms of how it related to the whole. Therefore at the aggregate level, the level at which Durkheim thought sociology should operate, the differential suicide levels among, say, different occupations was to be analysed by the general pressures, insecurities and so on that the occupational group experiences within the wider economy and society. Weber did not reject the existence of objective external social forces. Large tracts of his writing analyse the objective aspects of economic development, but he did consider it both possible and necessary for the social sciences to go beyond the natural sciences in this respect:

> In the case of the social collectivities, precisely as distinguished from organisms, we are in a position to go beyond merely demonstrating functional relationships and uniformities. We can accomplish something which is never attainable in the natural sciences, namely, the subjective understanding of the action of the component individuals.
>
> (Weber 1968: 15)

Therefore meaning, subjective understanding, is what makes the social sciences unique. They are not any more or less 'scientific', simply different. The obvious consequence of this stress on the meaning of action is that sociology should concern itself with phenomena of a social character. Events in society that are entirely unintended – such as a road accident – fall outside the remit of sociology as by the very definition of an accident the participants did not intend the event to happen. However, what the participants of a road accident subsequently do have is a social character: 'their attempt to avoid hitting each other, or whatever insults, blows, or friendly discussion might follow the collision, would constitute "social action"' (1968: 23).

Having made social action central to his sociology Weber then proceeded to produce a typology of its nature that he graded in terms of rationality, the first type being the most rational, the fourth being the least rational (Ray 1999: 168–9).

1 *Instrumental rational.* This is the type of action that involves an individual or group in identifying a goal and then assessing what type of action, given the particular social context, is required in order to realise it.

2 *Value-rational.* This refers to the kind of action that is designed to further a value because that value has intrinsic worth. The action is carried out independent of the prospects for the success of the value.

3 *Affectual.* This categorises the social action that corresponds to a particular feeling or state of mind. It is what we do because it coincides with the wider sense of how we feel.

4 *Traditional.* This action stems from ingrained habit: we do it because we have always done it.

1 Using Weber's four-point typology, assess what category you think the following actions fall into:

(a) Somebody crossing themselves.

(b) Throwing a punch during an argument.

(c) Taking hold of somebody while dancing with them.

(d) Investing money in a share option.

(e) Walking into the awning of a shop.

(f) Supporting a football team through attending matches.

(g) Taking part in a demonstration against the closure of factory.

(h) Taking part in an annual Remembrance Day parade.

2 In the light of your attempt to categorise social action, how useful do you think Weber's typology is?

3 Can you think of any other categories that you would wish to add?

This discussion of social action takes us to the issue of the 'agency' in social change, which we will consider by looking firstly at Weber's analysis of the Protestant ethic and then his notion of rationalisation.

The Protestant ethic

Weber's Protestant ethic thesis is sometimes presented as the mirror image of Marx's materialist stance on the rise of capitalism. The argument goes roughly as follows. Marx thought that capitalism was caused by material, or more strictly economic, factors. The religious ideas of the emergent capitalist class, the bourgeoisie, that advocated in some way economic actions likely to give rise to capitalism, were simply a political reflection of their material interests. Religious ideas do not have any force and impetus of their own, but as part of the superstructure of society are determined by the economic base. By contrast, Weber thought that ideas were of key importance in the advent of an economic system. Capitalism arose first in northern Europe because the ideas of a major religious group, broadly the Protestants, motivated the kinds of activity – hard work, thrift and reinvestment – that resulted in capitalism. Therefore ideas should be seen not just as the justifications people arrive at for their real material motivations, but also as having an existence and historical power in their own right. There are passages in Marx and Weber that would support this kind of interpretation. However, this contrast is something of an exaggeration and, indeed, almost a caricature. Marx most certainly did have a materialist interpretation of history, but his conception of social change is not a wholly cold and mechanistic one. Weber did wish to give greater weight to the role of ideas over economic motives, but he did not replace an exclusive concentration on one for an exclusive concentration on the other. For instance, Weber's greatest scholarly work, *Economy and Society*, is a study of economic development. His most famous book, *The Protestant Ethic and the Spirit of Capitalism*, is as much as anything a methodological exercise. In it, Weber wanted to test the proposition that certain forms of religious belief are, unconsciously, more conducive to the development of capitalism than others. It is therefore a study of the unintended consequences of action. He does not deny that ideas are in themselves in part motivated and then shaped by economic development and class interest. Rather, he wanted to demonstrate a certain relationship, 'an elective affinity', to prove that some belief systems are more conducive to certain forms of economic activity than others.

The background to this endeavour was twofold. On the one hand, he pointed to the emergence of industrial capitalism in largely Protestant countries – notably Britain, Germany and the USA. On the other, Weber observed that Protestants had tended to be more economically successful than Catholics within countries where there were sizeable numbers of both Christian denominations (Pampel 2000: 98). Weber was fully aware that great civilisations had existed prior to the advent of industrial capitalism. In fact, he probably knew as much as anybody about ancient societies and empires. Like Marx, he pointed to their inability to reproduce themselves; despite an accumulation of riches and learning, such societies lacked the dynamism of modern capitalism with its ceaseless quest to reproduce itself through the acquisition of new markets and the investment and reinvestment of profit. The development of capitalism in China had been handicapped by objective conditions, but also by 'lack of spiritual conditions'. 'Above all it has been handicapped by the attitude rooted in the Chinese "ethos" and peculiar to a class of officials and aspirants to office'. Similarly in India 'Hinduism and the karma doctrine made it impossible to shatter traditionalism . . . and to rationalise the economy' (Weber 1983: 84, 108). The golden age of Spain only lasted approximately 150 years as the merchants and adventurers quickly squandered the fortunes they had plundered from the Americas in economically wasteful private acquisitions such as houses and estates. This for Weber was one aspect of Catholicism: a licence to hedonism that could be redeemed by confession and repentance to God through his earthly mediary of the clergy. The other, by contrast, was a religious veneration of figures that were able to physically and spiritually isolate themselves from and renounce earthly pleasures. Such a belief system was ill-suited to the development of capitalism.

Protestantism by contrast, certainly in the forms of Puritanism and Calvinism, was far more conducive to the early entrepreneur or industrialist for several reasons. In discerning this, Weber was aware that his case was rather abstract. He used the diaries of a figure like Benjamin Franklin who hated waste and urged his fellow Americans to work hard above all else in life. And he refers to the sermons of the founder of English Methodism, Charles Wesley, with their clear message that labour was key to God's calling upon earth and personal happiness. Thus he relied upon certain 'ideal types': individual illustrators of a general state of affairs, bearers of wider arguments and projections. The methodological enterprise involves making a particular instance indicative of a given general state of affairs.

What was it in Weber's view that made Protestantism propitious to capitalism? Five central reasons can be identified. Firstly, the stress placed upon thrift and saving.

Secondly, a tendency to reinvest capital into further economic activity. Third, a belief that it was divine will that the individual Christian should serve his God through hard work. To answer God's calling was to devote one's energies to patient and methodical industry. Shirking hard work was in itself a sin or at any rate likely to give rise to it: 'the Devil will find work for idle hands to do', as the saying has it. Fourth, the rewards accrued from work – the happiness of the individual and family – were commensurate to the effort expended. 'What you shall sow you shall reap' partly captures this belief. One can see here a tendency to rationality as the approach is one of the calculation of return, certainly not the 'happy-go-lucky', 'take life as it comes', 'take a chance', 'in for a penny in for a pound' homespun sort of philosophy. Fifth, the conscious renunciation of indulgence, excess and above all sexual pleasure not through a holy abstinence (often followed by sinful excess), but by channelling desire into work. The link to Weber's sexless, but academically productive, life is apparent here.

In this way Weber built up an intricate and powerful analysis of the capitalist orientation inherent within the Protestant ethic. The are a number of historical criticisms – capitalism pre-dated Calvinism; early Calvinists were as much early socialists as capitalists – that can be levelled at the Protestant ethic (Ray 1999: 180). Moreover, as Weber in part intended the book to be a methodological exercise to demonstrate that ideas have an independent role in social change, an important criticism is that he seems to undo his own caution by the end of the book. He starts by saying that he is not trying to prove the exact opposite of Marx, i.e. that it is ideas that determine historical development, rather than ideas being a reflection of class interest. However, by the end he seems so convinced by the case he has made – that Protestantism gives rise to capitalism – that he does seem to say this. As noted above, internal tension is one of the characteristics of Weber's sociology.

Rationalisation

There are several reasons for thinking that rationalisation is the single most important issue in the work of Max Weber. On the one hand it is the process that brings together the impact of a number of the things that concerned him, especially capitalism, bureaucracy, power and religion. On the other, it is key to his general pessimism about modernity. The first issue is a sociological matter; the second matter took him away towards more abstract, theoretical speculation on the future of modernity. We examine each of these aspects of rationalisation in turn.

By the term 'rationalisation' Weber was not principally interested in the discoveries that the Enlightenment *philosphes* championed, although he saw the eighteenth century as being of major importance. Rather he was concerned with how the instrumental action mentioned above, pursued through the imposition of sets of codified rules and procedures – bureaucracy – was being felt cumulatively across society. As Turner puts it, 'As a social process, rationalisation includes the systematic application of scientific reason to the everyday world and the intellectualisation of routine activities through the application of systematic knowledge to practice' (Turner 1996: xix). The major way in which rationalisation occurs in this sense is through the systematic imposition of bureaucracy; the administrative means for ensuring that given rules are adhered to by personnel whose job responsibility it is to insist upon certain procedures. As Weber explains:

> Experience tends to show us that the purely bureaucratic type of administrative organization – that is, the monocratic variety of bureaucracy – is, from a purely technical point of view, capable of attaining the highest degree of efficiency and is in this sense formally the most rational known means of carrying out the imperative control of human beings.
>
> (Weber 1947: 357)

For Weber, the principal player in installing bureaucracy has been capitalism:

> Though by no means alone, the capitalist system has undeniably played a major role in the development of bureaucracy. Indeed, without it capitalistic production could not continue and a rational type of socialism would have simply to take it over. Its development, largely under capitalistic auspices, has created an urgent need for stable, strict, intensive and calculable administration. It is this need which gives bureaucracy a crucial role in our society as the central element in any kind of large-scale administration. Only by reversion in every field – political, religious, economic and so on – to small-scale organisation would it be possible to escape its influence to any considerable extent.
>
> (Weber 1947: 331)

In other words, only by turning back to a peasant society is it possible to escape the necessity for rationality which is achieved by bureaucracy. This is not just an institutional affair that takes place above the concerns of the individual. Rationalisation in everyday life refers to the way in which institutions and norms become progressively further removed from the individual. The church thus loses its authority for the congregation member. Deductive and universal frameworks about which the individual has little understanding replace legally ad hoc judicial processes. Politically, rationalisation entails the decline of traditional and charismatic forms of leadership for the faceless career politician who acts as a mere servant of the bureaucratic government administrative structure that surrounds him or her. In education the rise of the exam system based on a universal curriculum is a symptom of the need for the expert with a certificated, specialised knowledge that can be formally used to exclude others for positions of importance. The rise of the exam is key to the replacement of the 'older type of cultivated man' by the specialist (Gerth and Mills 1948: 240, 243). Elsewhere Weber referred to the specialist as the intellectual and the specialisation of intellectualisation. By this he meant that process which divides life into separate and incompatible spheres of value, draining meaning from it as a whole. Western societies now had, according to Weber, an 'absolute and complete dependence of its whole existence, of the political, technical and economic conditions of its life, on specially trained officials' (Weber 1983: 23). Besides trained officials, Weber also included under the term 'intellectuals' religious prophets and teachers, sages and philosophers, jurists and finally empirical scientists. However, as Perry Anderson comments: 'However much he disliked it, Weber never formulated an alternative to intellectualisation. In part, that was certainly because he regarded specialisation as the unalterable condition of modernity, whatever its cultural by-products' (Anderson 1992: 188).

It should be pointed out that Weber was not wholly pessimistic about rationality. In as much as it is synonymous with coherency and consistency in individuals and society it is possible to identify a more positive approach to rationality in his writings. However, his general theoretical interpretation of its consequences was far from cheerful. In this the key philosophical influence was that of Nietzsche (see Chapter 5, pp. 160–6 for a fuller discussion of Nietzsche's influence). For Nietzsche, as Turner comments:

> the values and practices of everyday life, which were centred on reciprocity and emotion, were being transformed by the rationalistic cultures of a technological civilisation driven by industrial needs . . . The life world was being destroyed and rendered inauthentic by the new rationalistic culture of the state as the values and morals of the private world were colonised by rationalistic culture of the public arena.
>
> (Turner 1996: xiii)

It is this projection, together with the idea of the 'disenchantment of reality' derived from Schiller, that acted as the background to Weber's gloomy thoughts about modernity as being characterised by, 'Specialists without spirit, sensualists without heart; this nullity imagines that it has attained a level of civilization never before achieved' (Weber 1947: 182). Though memorable, such phrases reflected Weber's confusion. For one thing the contempt for the specialist and intellectual they evidence clashed with his given commitment to objectivity in the research process. So he immediately corrects himself thus, 'but this brings us to the world of judgements of value and faith, with which this purely historical discussion need not be burdened' (Weber 1947: 182). On the other hand, Weber was wary of delivering Enlightenment-like judgements upon the forward, unilinear trend of history. On one occasion he indicates that it is wrong to include capitalism in a wider movement towards rationalisation because rationalisation is itself a highly uneven process both within and between societies. Taking Weber's work as a whole we can find passages that indicate that he thought that there was indeed a dominant movement in history towards rationality – for instance, on one occasion he talks about how the fact that exams are being spread across the world is indicative of the international rise of the expert – as well as passages that indicate that the historical process is subject to blockages and circular movement.

Summary

Weber's sociology occupies an intermediate position in the history of social theory. It has a classical heritage, but is simultaneously contemporary. Therefore one finds within it both a concern for society as an interconnected whole and a presumption of what individuals mean and understand by their own actions. There is an insistence that the social sciences should be objective, but an acknowledgement that values inevitably frame the research process. Weber sought to amend the materialist understanding of social change of Marxism by incorporating the independent power of ideas while rejecting a purely idealist account of history. He recognised the importance of rationality and bureaucracy to the efficiency of society, but deplored the way in which it was crushing the creativity and meaning from contemporary existence. He thought rationality a clear trend, but shied away from the projection of it as a master narrative. Ultimately, Weber was far enough removed from the Enlightenment, both theoretically and timewise, to be able to look back upon its optimism in progress as rather naive. As he puts it at the end of *The Protestant Ethic*: 'Victorious capitalism, since it rests on mechanical foundations, needs its support no longer. The rosy blush of its laughing heir, the Enlightenment, seems also to be irretrievably fading, and the idea of duty in one's calling prowls around like the ghost of dead religious beliefs' (Weber 1947: 182). Given the history of the twentieth century, not least the First World War that Weber lived to see, it is not difficult to see why sociologists see his work as of continuing relevance as we enter the twenty-first.

EXERCISE

Below are listed key themes associated with the social theorising of different classic sociologists. Consider the sections in the chapter on each of these four social theorists and answer the questions.

Herbert Spencer – the notion that society is like a living organism – it evolves and functions in the same way.

Emile Durkheim – the notion that social order is based on shared values – that there is a 'collective conscience' of a society.

Karl Marx – the history of society is driven and determined by (a) antagonism between classes and (b) the structural conditions that face economic systems.

Max Weber – as societies evolve they become ever more rationalised.

1 Provide examples for each of the themes listed above.

2 How relevant do you think each of these themes is to contemporary society?

Chapter 5

The nature of the sociological enterprise and the strains of modernity

TONY FINNEGAN

A key task of the emerging discipline of sociology in the late nineteenth and early twentieth centuries was to understand the complexity of new social structures, social relations and social formations that had developed during the previous 100 to 150 years. The landscape of Europe, for sociology in its beginnings was mostly European, had transformed from small-scale, complex systems of competing petty kingdoms to large-scale industrialised nation states. At the beginning of this process such societies had been centrally dependent upon an agrarian economic base that had changed little in the preceding one thousand years. Within this picture of a static and fixed Europe, islands of urbanism and industrialism had existed, but for the majority of the population of such societies these mattered little. The bulk of the population lived and worked on the land in semi-isolated communities, just as their forefathers had done for generations before. Life and labour had, it appeared, a natural order and permanence. Where economic and social contact took place it was limited to the sale of agricultural goods between rural centres or to the slowly but steadily growing numbers of towns and cities. Individuality was subsumed within the collectivity and collective forms of organisation and solidarity. There was much more that was common between individuals than there was that was different.

With the onset of both the industrial and intellectual revolutions that swept through much of Europe from the middle of the eighteenth century, rapid developments in every sphere of life took place. Difference between individuals became increasingly apparent. New forms of transport such as the railways emerged and, as a result, new economic and social opportunities were presented to individuals. These new technologies helped to break down the barriers between the rural and the urban. Previously close-knit communities that had been the life-blood of many of the small nation states and societies now gave way to large urban and industrial centres in which the possibility of new and more complex forms of social interchange grew. At this time, and concomitant with the economic and technological changes, there were changes in the very concept of national identity. Unions of countries (such as those of the German Federation) led to the forging of new economic, political and industrial bonds and unities that shaped a new map of Europe. Unified nation states such as Britain became increasingly dominant – economically as well as politically and militarily.

In many ways there are parallels between the development of early sociology and contemporary social thought in modern global society. Just as today much of the sociological literature attempts to deal with, or come to terms with, the nature of the new globalised and increasingly sophisticated and interlinked world, so too did the early attempts at sociological theorising. And in similar vein to our own attempts to grasp the complex problems of postmodern and post-industrial society, sociology in the late nineteenth and early twentieth centuries attempted to deal with large-scale social change, albeit restricted to the continent of Europe. Just as the social, industrial and economic changes of the eighteenth and nineteenth centuries allowed the creation of new and clearly defined nation states, so too, for instance, might the contemporary forces of globalisation create new supranational forms of identity for the individual.

However, one significant difference between the two periods is the way in which sociological theory has been transformed from the grand or 'meta-theories' of the late nineteenth century, to the widely diverse and eclectic approaches of today. Classical sociology as it developed in the mid to late nineteenth century and early twentieth century could be seen to be highly progressive, infused with a clear sense of social optimism, a sense that society was developing in a particular direction – this is apparent in the work of Marx, Durkheim and Weber. Moreover, the sociological enterprise as a distinct branch of social science, can be said to have developed in response to the growth of modernity. Yet, as Krishan Kumar (1993) points out, modernity is itself a problematical concept and one which perhaps needs a clear definition.

> Modernity carries the hallmarks of western society since the eighteenth century. It was industrial and scientific. Its political form was the nation state, legitimated by some species of popular sovereignty. It gave an unprecedented role to the economy and economic growth. Its working philosophies were rationalism and utilitarianism. In all these ways it rejected not just its own past but all other cultures that did not measure up to its self-understanding. It is wrong to say that Modernity denies history, as the contrast with the past – a

constantly changing entity – remains a necessary point of reference. But it is true that
Modernity feels that the past has no lessons for it; its pull is constantly towards the future.
(Kumar 1993: 392)

In essence, modernity is a key concept derived from within the Enlightenment project that swept Europe during the eighteenth century. The Enlightenment period
was, in its later phase, one in which political and revolutionary ideas took hold and
for the most part changed the social, political and, to a certain extent, even the economic landscape for ever. The Enlightenment itself had emerged out of revolutionary
changes unleashed in the development of industrialism and from the intellectual
critique of established order as personified by the French Revolution. The French
Revolution of 1789 did not produce the Enlightenment as an intellectual project;
this had been in train much earlier, as writers such as Alexis de Tocqueville (1955)
had pointed out. It was in reality a heterogeneous set of ideas which cannot be said
to correspond to one particular form of philosophical reasoning, or indeed to any
one philosopher. The very name 'Enlightenment' given to this period of European
history demonstrates that, as a force, it would illuminate the minds of men. At its
heart, the Enlightenment, in all of its various branches – philosophy, natural science, literature or metaphysics, for instance – was, Kumar argues, 'anti-traditional'.

However, there is another side to modernity as it emerged from the Enlightenment that needs to be considered, and which is the focus of this chapter: the strains
that modernity brought about. The predictions of rational and ordered societies,
ones in which democratic discourse and the pursuit of happiness and freedom would
hold sway, gave way in the late nineteenth and early twentieth centuries to numerous instances of repression, dictatorship and conflict. Through examining the ideas
of four theorists, Tönnies, Simmel, Nietzsche and Freud, we shall see that the project of modernity was not an unproblematical or automatically accepted philosophy.
Each of the four writers identified here – and it would be stretching a point to
call them all sociologists – provides us with a valuable critique of the project of
modernity. One central link between them is their concern for the 'human condition'.
Each saw the optimism of the Enlightenment and the growth of modernity as a promise
unfulfilled. Each had as their central focus the effects of change on the individual
or small-scale group. Theirs is not, then, an attempt to see the transformation of
society as some sort of impersonal force in which social agents are secondary to
social structure, but rather an attempt to chart the effects of modernity on the
individual and at the level of the individual.

For Tönnies the individual is, in crude terms, deprived of their bonds of community, of the intimacy that previous social structures and social relations had provided. Modernity represents a loss of belonging and a feeling of isolation for the
individual. For Simmel, the emphasis is on the transformation in the nature of the
individual consciousness brought about by an increasingly formal and rational urban
life that leads in turn to the objectification of the human condition. For Nietzsche,
modern society as it has emerged from the Enlightenment brought with it the corruption of the human soul, new social formations and ways of thinking and acting

which are increasingly repressive of the innate spirit of the individual mind. Civilisation is for him a sham, a complex force for restraint rather than liberation. For Freud, similarly with Nietzsche, there is a focus on the ways in which modern society seeks to sublimate and repress many of our natural, even basic, instincts. While radically departing from Nietzsche in seeing modern society as the pinnacle of civilisation and development, Freud appears to agree with him in recognising that beneath the veneer of modern urban life, forces of disharmony and discontent lurk. So for each of these writers modernity was less the triumph of reason and more a sort of Faustian bargain in which we sell our souls for the price of civilisation.

This chapter examines these different attempts to understand and explain how individuals come to terms with modern society, and how in turn such society had changed beyond the initial promise offered by the Enlightenment. It will be argued that reappraising the ideas of Tönnies, Simmel, Nietzsche and Freud can help provide a better understanding of the strains existing in contemporary society. Indeed, many of our current concerns with the fragmentation of social relations, the isolation of the individual and the growth of impersonal and bureaucratic forces on our lives clearly relate to those described by Tönnies, Simmel, Nietzsche and Freud.

> **Discussion questions**
>
> We all feel that we live in a modern world, that our society is a modern society.
>
> **1** Try to define what is and is not modern.
>
> **2** What sorts of things do you think best illustrate modernity?
>
> **3** What things do you feel define a pre-modern form of existence?

THE REVOLUTION IN IDEAS

Robert Bierstedt (1979) believes that the French Revolution allowed the coalescing of intellectual ideas of tremendous force into a radical and physical movement for change at every level that would create what we now regard as modernity.

> No one can do justice to the ideas of the Enlightenment, and no summary can suffice. But four propositions, perhaps, can capture the temper of the times better than others. There was first the replacement of the supernatural with the natural, of religion by science, of divine degree by natural law, and priests by philosophers. Second was the exaltation of reason guided by experience, as the instrument that would solve all problems, whether social, political, or even religious. Third was the belief in the perfectibility of man and society, and accordingly, the belief in the progress of the human race. And finally there was the humane and humanitarian regard for the rights of man, especially the right to be free from oppression and corruption of governments – a right claimed in blood in the French revolution.
>
> (Bierstedt 1979: 5)

Thus, modernity is a relatively recent phenomenon which emphasised the power of ideas to shape the economic, political and social world in which we live. This heritage of radical ideas can be best seen in the work of Thomas Paine. Paine's *The Rights of Man*, as Aldridge (1974) points out, expressed in the boldest possible terms the need for social and political change, the need for what Paine regarded as freedom from 'corrupt governments'. In fact it was this very search for freedom that made Paine an émigré to America in 1774 and subsequently led him to write his now famous *Rights of Man*, which was published in 1791. This milestone in social and political philosophy was produced as a response to the injustice Paine saw all around him, both in his native Britain but also in the colonies of the New World; such is the power of ideas that the *Rights of Man* was seen by some as a defence of both the American Revolution of 1776 and French Revolution of 1789. Furthermore, to those who read and subscribed to its radicalism, it was seen as a mechanism for the scrutiny of and explanation for the reasons for discontent in European society of the period. In essence it charted the progress of one social, economic and political system to another. It argued that certain remedies were available for the removal of the evils of arbitrary government, of the injustice of poverty, illiteracy, unemployment, and war. Such rights have been continually reaffirmed in more recent times, most notably through the United Nations' Declaration of Human Rights and the European Charter on Human Rights. Nowadays these seem normal and natural modes of thought and part of our basic democratic rights. However, to the European ruling class of the day, Paine's increasingly popular ideas clearly spelled the possibility of an end to a way of life and a fixed social order that had existed for millennia. Moreover it held the threat of violent revolution. As a result, most European governments ordered the book to be banned; and in Britain it led to a demand for the imprisonment of the publishers. It is interesting to note that nearly sixteen years after the American Revolution, alarm bells still rang out in Britain about the *Rights of Man*; indeed Paine, then still regarded as a subject of the British Crown, was tried in absentia and found guilty of both treason and seditious libel.

Yet, as with so many acts of state repression, it was too late: the genie was out of the bottle and the forces of revolution, in part precipitated by Paine, took hold. The French Revolution eulogised Paine's central premise that man must become the author of his own destiny. It graphically demonstrated an old establishment being violently overthrown by radical forces of social change, within which the concept of democracy was a significant element. Paine, then, could be said to represent a new form of intellectual, an individual whose ideas and visions transcended national boundaries. Enlightenment writers, as Nisbet (1973) points out, saw themselves as pan-European. However, as Nisbet acknowledges, this revolution of the intellect was not the only revolution taking place; there were two revolutions taking place simultaneously, one intellectual and the other industrial. To understand modernity we must also start to understand the physical as well as intellectual changes taking place.

THE INDUSTRIAL REVOLUTION AND SOCIAL CHANGE

The reasons for the industrial revolution, as with the Enlightenment itself, were many and complex. We can roughly define the industrial revolution, which had its earliest and most pronounced effects in Britain, as taking place from the last two decades of the eighteenth century to the middle of the nineteenth century. As with the Enlightenment the forces behind the industrial revolution had been in train much earlier, perhaps over a period spanning several hundred years. Yet it was in the late eighteenth century that the visible effects of this revolutionary process become explicit and widespread. Fundamental to the industrial revolution was the expansion of capitalism; indeed the two developments are intertwined. Capitalism, the creation and expansion of markets for new mass manufactured goods, such as cotton, was at heart the driving philosophy of industrialism. Yet the base of the industrial revolution was the simple idea of applying machinery and technology to the widespread process of production. Production, whether on the land, in agriculture, or indeed in the creation of goods, such as textiles, no longer needed to be small scale, localised, intensive and craft based. It became large scale, speeded up and deskilled through the process of mechanisation; in essence manufactured by machines, rather than produced by hands.

Capitalism did not create industrialism and had existed prior to the industrial revolution; rather it facilitated its dramatic expansion. As with the revolution in ideas marked by the Enlightenment, the industrial revolution brought sweeping new social, political and, importantly, economic forces into play. It changed the ideological landscape and also the physical geography of Europe at that time. Coupled with the Enlightenment, the industrial revolution in effect created what we now regard as modernity. A simple example of this comes from France and the marrying together of Enlightenment thinking and the new technologies of the industrial revolution in the form of the guillotine as the tool of executioners during the French Revolution. This was seen as the epitome of Enlightenment thinking, a device designed on the scientific principles of modernity, quick and sure, replacing what was then regarded as the previous barbaric practice of executions by the Ancien Régime. As a new technology, Madame Guillotine, as it became known, was applied during the Terror to cleanse France of the old establishment, the backwardness and barbarity of the past, just as the new philosophies of the Enlightenment would do.

One of the key features of modernity is the way it allowed for and encouraged the expansion of urbanism. While urbanism had clearly existed prior to the industrial revolution, the scale developed during this period had never been seen before. Villages and small towns which had for centuries led a relatively static existence, now, due to the proximity of natural resources, including labour power, expanded rapidly. In the period 1750 to 1850 the population of Europe grew from 140 million to 266 million, a rise of over 90 per cent in the space of 100 years (Wood 1975). Such was the pace of change that places like Manchester, which had previously been little more than a small town at the head of the River Mersey, faced dramatic transformations. Manchester had one cotton mill in 1780, but by 1830 had over 99. Following the broader trend of European population growth, the population of Manchester went from little more than 10,000 in the middle of the eighteenth century to 70,000 in 1801 and 250,000 by the late nineteenth century. Such was the importance of its industrial growth, and the appalling conditions in which its workers lived, that the German social philosopher and collaborator with Karl Marx, Friedrich Engels, based his influential book *The Condition of the Working Class in England* (Engels 1971) on observations made there. The conditions of labour in these new industrial centres were trans-formed. There may be an argument that for many workers their movement to the industrial town and cities of the early nineteenth century reflected a real and significant improvement in living conditions. Why, after all, did so many choose to move to places such as Manchester, or Düsseldorf in the Ruhr region of Germany? However, to a significant number of social commentators, writers and philosophers, such as Engels or Emile Zola writing of the plight of French coalminers in 1885, such conditions seemed worse and more soul-destroying than those they replaced. For such writers, these towns and cities were seen as wrenching expanding num-bers of workers from the protective conditions of family, parish, village and guild life. These new centres of industry were characterised by their slums, with most workers and their families living in common squalor and wretchedness. As Engels remarks:

> Masses of refuse, offal and sickening filth lie among standing pools in all directions; the atmosphere is poisoned by the effluvia from these, and laden darkened by the smoke of a dozen tall factory chimneys. A horde of ragged women and children swarm here, as filthy as the swine that thrive upon the garbage heaps and in the puddles. In short, the whole rookery furnishes such a hateful and repulsive spectacle as can hardly be equaled in the worst court of Irk. The race that lives in these ruinous cottages, behind broken windows, mended with oilskin, sprung doors, rotten doorposts, or in dark wet cellars, in measure-less filth and stench, in this atmosphere penned in as if with a purpose, this race must really have reached the lowest stage of humanity.
>
> (Engels 1845, cited in Wheen 2000: 81)

The level of urban expansion, population growth and the wretched conditions under which many lived could also be seen across much of northern Europe. The relentless pace of urban industrial growth sucked into it ever growing num-bers of workers. A vast new social experiment was taking place in which the con-ventions, rules, mores and authority of the past no longer held sway. As we noted above, early classical sociology aimed to provide a way of scientifically understand-ing the growth of modernity from the Enlightenment. In portraying sociology as the queen of sciences, Comte demonstrates the link between the Enlightenment and the *raison d'être* of sociology itself, the need to illuminate all aspects of the social.

The conditions described above demonstrate progressive change, but also show a negative or dark side to such change: the movement of population into densely packed towns and cities in which crime, deprivation and child labour were all common experiences. Consider how the conditions described here of nineteenth-century Europe may be applied today to many third world or newly industrialising countries such as Brazil, Mexico or India.

1 What, if any, are the parallels between these societies and those of Europe in the nineteenth century?

2 To what extent is there a common process that all societies must go through to become modern?

WHAT WAS MODERNITY?

As with the great European philosophers of the Enlightenment, such as Montesquieu, Rousseau, Voltaire and Paine, the combining forces of the industrial revolution and Enlightenment produced their own evangelical voices in Britain, most notably Ferguson, Smith and Hume. David Hume can be said to be the father of the new European moral philosophy that emerged from the Enlightenment: his vision helped to shift European thought away from its emphasis on the prescriptive. Ferguson, Hume and Smith created a new philosophy which was a more empirical moral philosophy than their European equivalents. This was illustrated in Adam Smith's *Wealth of Nations*, published in 1776, which set out to both explain and justify new forms of social organisation and the absolute necessity for the 'division of labour', which was so much a hallmark of the new industrialism. The division of labour was a defining process that had implications for wider social, economic and political organisation within society. As can be seen throughout this book, the division of labour is a recurring focus of analysis across the spectrum of sociological analysis. It was the combination of the two forces of change to the division of labour and the new intellectual radicalism that would produce modernity; and the intellectual requirement for its comprehension led to what we now know as sociology.

It was in this period of European social thought that ideas of scientific progress, rationality and the triumph of human agency over nature became key concepts for an understanding of the social world. Enlightenment philosophy and the consequent advent of modernity indicated a rejection of the mysticism of religious thought and the affirmation of humankind's control over its destiny. Despite what we now regard as the barbarity of the French Revolution, the whole Enlightenment process can be seen as one in which there was a sense of great optimism in the triumph of man over nature, at both the material level and the level of human consciousness. This sense of progress and direction in which human development was evolutionary and revolutionary, taking humanity to greater, more advanced and more highly sophisticated forms of social organisation, is apparent in the work of the founding theorists of sociology.

These founding writers attempted to chart the development of industrial society. Comte, for instance, was a true son of the Enlightenment, infused with its optimism and faith in the conquest of nature. His positivist approach pointed the direction which successive writers would take. The works of Marx, Durkheim and, to some degree, Weber all share the Enlightenment optimism of Comte, positing the progressive development of European civilisation from primitive to modern, from backward to developed. For such writers there appeared to be in train an evolutionary process in which the only path is upwards or forward, continually refining, developing and progressing. Marx assesses the nature of each successive mode of production as superior – technically, if not morally – to the one that went before. For Marx, modernity in the shape of capitalism brings with it new class structures and new revolutionary process for change, for him there is a:

Constant revolutionizing of production . . . distinguish the bourgeois epoch from all earlier ones. All fixed, fast-frozen relations, with their train of ancient and venerable prejudices are swept away, all new-formed ones become antiquated before they can ossify. All that is solid melts into air, all that is holy is profaned, and man is at last compelled to face with sober senses, his real conditions of life, and his relations with his kind.

(Marx and Engels 1959: sct. 1)

Within this Marxist model there is a vision of a radically changed society from that which went before; a society, which in the broad terms of dialectical materialism, is also a result of social evolution, a product of historical inevitability. While we would not wish simply to equate the progressive ideas of individual writers such as Durkheim, Weber and Marx, it is clear that there is within each a sense of progress and evolution of the human condition, within which the structures, ideas and philosophies of pre-industrial societies can find no place. Yet while many sociologists of the mid to late nineteenth century saw modernity as an historical inevitability or, for Marx, simply a staging-post on the road to a new society, there does tend to be agreement about the negative aspects of urban industrial life. In all the social theories of the nineteenth century we see to a greater or lesser extent some questioning of modernity and modern social life and a critique of the pressures of urbanised, industrial and fast-paced life.

Today it is quite popular to talk about the pressure and strains of modern life, of the increasingly hectic existence we all appear to suffer from. This can be illustrated by Prince Charles railing against modern architecture, or modern farming practices – a critique often infused with a rejection of many aspects of modern living. This accords with stories of business executives giving up their fast-paced lifestyles and abandoning their material wealth in favour of alternative, rural lifestyles. The concept of 'individual downsizing', abandoning the hurly-burly of city life in favour of an existence less materially rewarding but more intrinsically and spiritually satisfying, is a popular contemporary image. Moreover, and not just as demonstrated via television advertisements, the popularity of such alternative lifestyles appears to be growing with each decade, as does a radical, even revolutionary rejection of modernity. Luddites in the early part of the nineteenth century attempted to hold back the forces of mechanisation of the textile industry. Today such a violent rejection of modernity can be found in the forces of eco-protest, animal liberation movements or protests against global capitalism. Such recent popular movements for the rejection of many aspects of modern society accord well with the Luddites of early nineteenth-century Britain. Such movements, then and now, start to question and reject the modern forces of social change.

What, then, was particular about the nature of such change in the mid-nineteenth century? As we shall see, the four writers examined in this chapter spanned a period in which the promise of modernity seemed flawed. From the middle of the nineteenth to the early decades of the twentieth century, modernity came to full fruition, the social, political, economic and even physical landscape of most of Europe and North America changed dramatically. Many despotic and undemocratic regimes, some which had existed for a thousand years as monarchical dictatorships, as in the case of France, quickly gave way in the face of violent and bloody revolution. In Britain, the transition to full democracy was largely peaceful and progressive, but the conditions under which the mass of the population lived, as pointed to by Engels, were very onerous. In other societies, most notably Germany, existing and rigid regimes used the tools of science and technology to transform themselves from backward agrarian economies into modern industrial giants. Yet despite a wave of European revolutions in Italy, France, Austria and Germany in 1848, the further advance of democratic reform held open by the Enlightenment ended more-or-less in failure. The autocratic regimes of Germany and Austria repressed, often by violent counter-revolutions, movements to liberty, equality and fraternity while the new and increasingly machine-based world that was being created allowed for the transformation of the means of production, distribution and consumption. It also allowed for the mechanisation of warfare and death. Perhaps the most glaring example of modernity put to its worst use was during the First World War, with the killing of millions by the new progressive weaponry.

As we have seen above, a central feature of modernity was that of population growth and urbanism. Urbanism brought with it problems of noise, pollution, poverty, moral decline and criminality. It is often argued today that a central legacy of industrial society has been the reshaping of the urban environment in which we live. While perhaps qualitatively better than the back-to-back terrace counterparts of the nineteenth century, 1960s tower blocks appeared to recreate many of the alienating elements of urban life first experienced in the nineteenth century. Modern reactions against our urban industrial society have a resonance that echoes back over the years. During the period of industrial and urban expansion, and often in response to the failure of Enlightenment ideals of freedom and democracy for the masses, new radical social movements started to emerge. The period spanned by our four writers was one in which the rise of modern popular political ideologies became most visible. However, the nature of the working-class consciousness was arguably more marked by its passivity and seeming willingness to accept wage slavery and the consumerist society that had been created. Ironically, and as we shall see in a little more depth later, it could be argued that writers such as Simmel, while understanding that economic factors shaped the trajectory of individual social actions, recognised that economics alone did not solely determine them. While the expansion of the working class, the development of universal education and popular democracy were seen by writers such as Durkheim as hallmarks of the advancement of urban civilisation, for some cultural critics, such as Matthew Arnold (1960), the expansion of the working class itself held a threat, one in which there appeared to be a general levelling down, a process of proletarianisation of society and culture.

All in all we can perhaps see that there was a mixed response to the growth of modernity. While there was a general acceptance of it by some, such as Marx, Durkheim and to some extent even Weber, for others there was either a rejection, or at least a questioning, of modernity itself. It is both this disenchantment with, and attempt to understand the process of, change that these four writers focused on. Each of them in their own way offers both an insight into the process of creation of modernity and a critique of it.

Discussion questions

A key measure of modernity as it emerged out of the Enlightenment has been the expansion of the 'rights of man' through the process of the growth of democracy and the legalisation of human rights. However, such rights are often not wisely used. The German nation voted into office the Nazi Party in 1933, with consequent and dramatic effect on the human rights of millions in Europe. The Nazi Party were able, as an elected government, to utilise the pseudo-science of eugenics as justification for their barbarity.

Suggest some other examples of how 'Enlightenment freedoms' (such as free speech, the vote and so on) can lead to different (and less positive) ends than those envisaged.

FERDINAND TÖNNIES

Tönnies' intellectual career spanned a period of enormous social change and upheaval in German society from the expansion of the German empire in the Franco-Prussian war of 1870 to the First World War of 1914–18, the great depression of the 1920s and the subsequent rise of fascism in the early 1930s. He was able to witness first-hand the breakdown of what he saw as the very fabric of German society and its restructuring in rational and impersonal terms. In many respects Tönnies' work can be seen to reflect the crisis in social theory that started to emerge prior to the First World War. Indeed it has been argued that German sociology at the turn of the twentieth century had itself originated from a crisis of consciousness among its major practitioners – Tönnies, Simmel and Weber (Falk 2000). They all attempted, according to Falk, to understand the mechanisms that had created German society from disparate, complex and often competing component forces. Central to this process of understanding, for Tönnies, is the concept of 'will' as something which changes as social formation changes. As with Simmel, Tönnies

BOX 5.1

Ferdinand Tönnies

Ferdinand Julius Tönnies was born on 26 July 1855 in the small agricultural community of Oldenswort, Schleswig, in the northern part of Germany that borders Denmark. He was the son of a well-to-do farming family tied both to locality and to the wider world. His brother was a merchant who traded with Britain and Tönnies learned much of the world outside Oldenswort from him. Tönnies studied at the University of Tubigen and gained his doctorate at the young age of 21. He taught sociology at the University of Kiel from 1881 until 1933, when he was dismissed in a Nazi purge of German academics. Tönnies had considerable disdain for the Nazis, recognising them as a corrupting force. He died while in self-imposed internal exile on 9 April 1936 in Kiel, Germany. His best known and seminal work *Gemeinschaft und Gesellschaft* (Tönnies 1955) was published as a draft in his first year of lecturing at Kiel University in 1881. However, he is also as well known in British academic circles for his contribution to our understanding of the seventeenth-century English philosopher Thomas Hobbes.

attempts to understand social action at a basic, sort of quasi-psychological level. Such an approach is a deliberate move away from the more openly macro-sociological ideas of writers such as Marx, Durkheim and Weber. Indeed, Loomis (1955: xviii) believes that Tönnies' work is an attempt to locate the nature of the individual by means of a synthesis of rationalism, romanticism, idealism, materialism, realism and nominalism. This is reflected in the range of influences on Tönnies, including the German philosophical tradition from Hobbes and Spinoza right through to Marx. For Tönnies the concept of voluntarism, as previously defined by Hobbes, was central in understanding social action. It is this link between the psychological basis of choice and social basis of social action which, for Tönnies, allows us to define the trajectory of human interaction.

Tönnies and ideal types of 'will'

For Tönnies the 'project of modernity' is fundamentally associated with the rise of urbanism and an urban way of life and a conceptual mechanism for understanding this transition from traditional to modern society is through the use of ideal types. Whereas Weber used ideal types in understanding different types of action, at the core of Tönnies' sociology is the notion of ideal types of 'will' by which individuals both judge and act. He categorised two forms of will. Firstly, *Wesenwille* or natural will, in which the individual makes a judgement of the intrinsic value of an act, rather than its so-called practicality. *Wesenwille* operates within varying degrees of rationality. As its name suggests, *Wesenwille* is akin to the normal, innate condition within all of us. This approach, then, demonstrates a rejection of the more materialist sociology of writers such as Marx:

Every individual natural will arrives at its complete and mature existence in the same way as the organism which it represents, by gradual growth developing from the embryo or tender bud which contains the (psychic as well as physical) form as it has been predetermined and originated by the union of cells derived from its procreators. According to this origin, natural will has to be understood as inborn and inherited.

(Tönnies 1955: 121)

Tönnies, as with Durkheim and later Parsons, drew a biological analogy of the human condition. In doing this he posits a unique purity which he feels becomes lost as society develops. It is clear that in adopting this 'ideal type of will' Tönnies juxtaposes the naturalness of *Wesenwille* against another form of will which is less directly shaped or determined by the individual. The second type of will Tönnies called *Kürwille* or rational will.

Tönnies' rational will is similar to Weber's concept of rational social action and can be seen as a means of marking off modern capitalist society as a distinct social formation. As with Weber, *Kürwille* appears to involve a conscious choice of a given means to a specific end. It involves choice on the part of the individual social actor; but choice can only come under certain conditions, whereby individuals are themselves free to makes choices. *Wesenwille* is manifested in what Tönnies defined as *Gemeinschaft* (community) type societies. As we shall see, these are societies in which order and social cohesion are maintained by traditional rules and a universal sense of solidarity, which in turn fits the organic model of social union. *Kürwille* is found in *Gesellschaft* (association) type societies; these societies maintain their social cohesion by purely rational-based self-interest. This is not to deny that aspects of *Wesenwille* no longer exist, rather *Kürwille* is the stronger element in such societies. Thus *Gesellschaft*-based societies tend to be held together by purposely formulated requirements – in effect a social contract between the individual and society. Yet in practice, as Tönnies readily admits, all societies show elements of both kinds of will, because man's conduct is neither wholly instinctive nor wholly reasoned. In other words, they are end-points of a continuum.

These ideas are articulated in what we now regard as Tönnies most important work *Gemeinschaft und Gesellschaft* ('*Community and Association*'), which was completed in 1887. This only became widely available to an audience outside Germany after it was translated into English in the first decade of the twentieth century. From that point on it had an important impact on the growing academic discipline of sociology both in Germany and in the wider world. For Tönnies, modernity implied loss, and in particular the loss of community. As such, modern urban society is regarded as a break with, rather than an evolution from, the past. Moreover, modern urban social relations represented something quite unique, quite different and quite alien. In essence, he argues that society had moved from pre-industrial and pre-Enlightenment social relations based upon the centrality of *Gemeinschaft*-type social interaction and values to modern society in which post-Enlightenment and industrially based social relations of *Gesellschaft*-type values and interaction dominate.

For Tönnies, *Gemeinschaft* relations are a far more natural condition, where life is relatively immobile and fixed, both geographically and socially. Here, the life of the individual is ascribed at birth. The individual, in possession of *Wesenwille*, exists in a condition where habit, tradition and pleasure form the motivating elements of individual physical and social existence. There is a commonality of being that appears unshakeable and immovable. In such societies, the home is the centre of the world, the family and immediate social relations around the small community are the key focus of life. Loomis (1955) suggests that Tönnies work presents us with a halcyon portrayal of a lost world, a world in which there is a natural truth and a natural morality based around shared struggle and shared pleasure. While, culturally, *Gemeinschaft* societies were largely homogeneous, with rigid moral enforcement by so-called cultural custodians (church and family), such morality and the power of moral guardians was accepted as natural. Authority was imposed on individuals in a paternal, munificent way, without malice or intent, as a means to preserve peace and social solidarity. For Tönnies this authority can take three forms which often overlap with each other: authority of age, authority of wisdom and authority of force. Tönnies contends that a combination of these three types of authority brings into existence a combined form of authority or beneficence. This type of society promotes a deep sense of belonging, a sentimental attachment to *place*; the feeling of belonging to one location and set of values. This intense emotional identification is the core of the notion of *Wesenwille*.

> The will and spirit of kinship is not confined within the walls of the house or bound up with physical proximity; but where it is strong and alive in the closest most intimate relationship, it can live on itself, thrive on memory alone, and overcome any distance by its feeling and its imagination of nearness and common activity.
>
> (Tönnies 1955: 49)

We can expect, Tönnies argues, that in such societies a deep sense of social cohesion and social solidarity will pervade. Moreover, in such situations and locations there is no sense of democratic public opinion, or indeed any attempt to measure the views of the community. It is a simple, peaceful and ordered life. *Gemeinschaft* society, then, is characterised by an overwhelming sense of community.

In *Gesellschaft*-type societies, social relations would be based upon association rather than community. For Tönnies, *Gesellschaft* society was everything that was not *Gemeinschaft*. Society is artificial, the organic connections of *Gemeinschaft* society are replaced by the quite brutal, forced relations of individual survival – an 'every man and woman for themselves' form of social organisation. Unlike the system of self-sufficient economics that existed at the village level, a complex system of exchange is required in the urban environment within which the 'rational value' of everything must be known for successful exchange to take place in an impersonal world. This is a theme that is taken up and developed by Simmel (see below). In Tönnies' vision of modernity there is an increase in scale and impersonality of social relations which become legally enforced, rather than enforced through social custom or social mores. Such a society dissolves the bonds that had hitherto existed. Competition is increasingly favoured over cooperation; the role of the market and exchange value over use value and the latent functions of village commerce. In taking this approach Tönnies appears to pessimistically predict the growth of capitalist globalisation.

> In the synthesis of city and capital, the highest form of this kind is achieved: the metropolis. It is the essence of a national *Gesellschaft*, but contains representatives from a whole group of nations, i.e., of the world. In the metropolis money and capital are unlimited and almighty. It is able to produce and supply goods and science for the entire earth as well as laws and public option for all nations. It represents the world market and world traffic; in it world industries are concentrated. Its newspapers are world newspapers, its people come from all corners of the earth, being curious and hungry for money and pleasure.
> (Tönnies 1955: 266)

In *Gesellschaft*-type society, public opinion is important and indeed measured (i.e. the democratic franchise is extended to many sections of society). In effect, *Gesellschaft*-type society is a more rational, achievement-oriented structure. In such societies, relationships are much more mobile and fluid, both geographically and socially. Tönnies predicted a wave of change sweeping across Europe with the rise of capitalism and the ever-increasing spread of modernity, not in relation to specific societies as such but rather in generalised terms. In Tönnies' eyes society had moved from the personal, intimate, small-scale, emotional and traditional to the impersonal, un-intimate, large-scale, rational and contractual. The implication of such changes was to be a sense of loss of dignity, at both the personal and the social level. As said, particular societies are not completely one or other type and Tönnies recognised that even within urban industrial and *Gesellschaft*-type societies it would be possible for there to exist *Gemeinschaft*-types of relations within specific areas that had been less touched by modernity.

In setting up the typology of community versus association, Tönnies offers a distinct psychological underpinning of his model of societal evolution (Freund 1979). To recap, Tönnies conceives 'community' as 'natural' or 'organic will' (*Wesenwille*), while 'association' is conceived as 'rational will' or *Kürwille*, with one juxtaposed against the other. Natural or organic will is seen as genuine or authentic, as it is part of the fundamental structure of the human condition. Rational will, on the other hand, is man's rational imposition of structure on the world, the conscious psychological action to change the world. It follows for Tönnies that it is the nature of this consciousness that conditions the very creation of the two types of social structure: association and community. Tönnies paints a pessimistic picture of the inevitable growth of *Gesellschaft*-types of social relationship. In many ways his work could be seen to have had a direct bearing and influence on the work of Simmel. His theme of the disharmony of modern urban life is one which clearly has a resonance in the work of Simmel (and also Weber).

It is increasingly popular to appear to reject some aspects of modern society, for instance the desire to escape the 'rat race' even for a weekend, or to abandon the materialism that seems to dominate modern life. Often modern life is felt to be impersonal, artificial and unnatural. When we are served at a burger bar, do we really believe them when they say 'have a nice day'?

1 What possible ways of rejecting modernity can you think of? How successful are they?

2 To what extent can religion help us to cope with modern life? (Think of different religions and belief systems.)

GEORG SIMMEL

Urbanism

As we have seen, the development of urbanism was dependent upon the growth of industrialism from the late eighteenth century through to the twentieth century. It is this process of change from rural to urban that most concerned Simmel. While it is true to say there had always been a process of movement from the rural areas

---

BOX 5.2

Georg Simmel

Born into a lower-middle-class Jewish family in Berlin on 1 March 1858, Simmel suffered much of the anti-Semitism evident in Germany of that period. While he enjoyed the opportunities offered to the middle class to study at university, his later career did not follow the path of other non-Jewish intellectuals of his day. He studied both as an undergraduate and as a postgraduate at the University of Berlin, receiving his doctorate in 1881. He was a contemporary of Max Weber, with whom he established both a professional and personal association. Throughout his life Simmel engaged in detailed correspondence with both Weber and, in particular, Weber's wife. Simmel, probably as a result of his Jewish background, did not enjoy the widespread fame and success of his intellectual and academic contemporaries such as Weber. And while he did teach at the University of Berlin from 1885 until the outbreak of the First World War, this was in a capacity as a contract lecturer (*Privatdozent*), providing public lectures to fee-paying students, his income dependent upon these fees. It is perhaps a mark of his abilities as a speaker and communicator of ideas that Simmel's lectures were always popular and very well attended. His second teaching post at Strasbourg from 1914 to 1918 was far more secure, yet away from the intellectual centre of German life; Strasbourg at that time being regarded as a provincial outpost of German intellectual life. Simmel wrote very widely, ranging from short essays, the most well known being *The Metropolis and Mental Life* (1903), to large texts such as *The Philosophy of Money* (1907).

to the towns, what industrialism brought was the process of large-scale mass migration. New agricultural techniques, brought about by the development and application of science to agriculture, meant that the productivity of the land increased dramatically. From the sixteenth century onwards an agricultural revolution had taken place, and this revolution displaced large numbers of agricultural workers at the very time that the development of industrialism started to occur. Thus large numbers of workers were displaced at the very time they were needed in the new urban industrial environment. However, as Simmel demonstrates, this was not necessarily such a neat and harmonious process. The rapid expansion of many cities meant that they were not ready or equipped to take in the vast influx of workers from the land. Pollution, overcrowding, noise, crime, the decline of the importance of religion, and civil and industrial unrest became the common experience of the newly created urban working class. It is the nature of this new common experience, in particular its effects at the level of the individual, that Simmel focused on and analysed.

In his early intellectual career Simmel was deeply influenced by the work of positivist sociologists such as Auguste Comte and Herbert Spencer. In their work the individual is reduced to a product of society; however, Simmel evolved a sociology that was much more fluid, eclectic and open to the idea of interaction between individuals and society. By the end of his intellectual career he had moved to a position which, it has been argued (Ørnstrup 2000), brought him into opposition to positivism. In many respects Georg Simmel continued and developed a number of the core themes of Tönnies work. Although it has often been argued that much of German sociology of this age was developed in response to Marxist theory (for instance, the image of Weber debating with the ghost of Marx), such a view might be somewhat fallacious, as much of Marx's work only became available in Germany after Weber's death, and was certainly not fully available to Simmel until quite late in his career. However, Ritzer does argue that Simmel had

> An immediate and profound effect on the development of American sociological theory, whereas Marx and Weber were largely ignored for many years. Simmel's work helped to shape the development of one of the early centres of American sociology – the University of Chicago – and its major theory, symbolic interactionism.
>
> (Ritzer 1996: 28)

Such influence is, Ritzer argues, due to the fact that, unlike Weber and Marx, Simmel was more concerned with the small scale, the individual and in particular the nature of individual action itself. Moreover, as both Ritzer and Ørnstrup point out, Simmel's work was diverse, ranging from very large studies of a similar scope to those of Weber and Marx, to short accessible essays covering a wider range of subjects and issues than did either of these writers. This helps to explain Simmel's influence on early American sociology. And equally important for American sociology was the fact that some of the emerging academic giants of sociology there (Robert Park and Albion Small, for example) had been students of Simmel in Germany in the late nineteenth century.

Psychology and consciousness

Simmel's influence on Small and Park can be said to have helped shape the emergent field of symbolic interactionism within early American sociology. This perspective emphasised how individuals in effect continually create and recreate their own society. According to Bottomore and Frisby (1978), Simmel appeared to operate with a multifaceted concept of the individual and society which accords well with such an approach, and his theoretical model was imbued with a need to understand the psychology of the individual. Throughout Simmel's work there is the notion that the social emerges from the psychological nature of interaction. There is an interplay of two elements, which in turn provides the key to understanding some significant aspects of Simmel's sociology. This can be seen through the process of socialisation whereby people have to recognise and accept the existence of social structures and social conventions for them to have any meaning. This developing sociological approach is very close to what would become the symbolic interactionist idea of the social construction of reality in which a dialectical process takes place: individual action creates the conditions under which social action is produced and this in turn acts upon and shapes further individual and social interaction. For Simmel, 'interaction' or rather 'association' is the basic foundation of a society.

In social life, a vast range of forms of action are created which the individual has to come to terms with by imposing order and coherence on them. It is the continual interplay of the individual to the social via the process of socialisation which is so important here. So the process of socialisation is never static, but rather continually in a state of flux, as it is interpreted and reinterpreted by the individual; and it is this process of flux that gives society its dynamic nature. We are made by reference to others both as individuals and members of social groups. In turn, we are, according to Simmel, in competition with others, and as members of a group we learn who we are, both at the individual level and also at the societal level. Different levels of socialisation hold individuals within different groups, and to different degrees. An individual may be aware of their position with the group by means of understanding both the boundaries and the threats to that group. In this way the psychology of the individual and the development of individual consciousness is tied up with the process of socialisation itself. For Simmel, everything in society, at every level, even the microscopic, interacts with everything else and through this changes. Society is in a state of continuous flux and development. But how do we move from the individual to the group and from that to society? This is best expressed by the way Simmel employs the concepts *dyad* and *triad* (Ritzer 1996: 273).

Social interaction between three people can be, and often is for Simmel, radically different from that between two. The dyad is simply the combination of and interaction between two individuals; the triad is far more complex, it is a group. As such it is 'social' in a more meaningful sense in terms of the possibilities of social action open to the members of the triad. Within a triad, new social roles and new social relationships become possible; a system of power and authority is more openly possible in a triad than in a dyad. As society becomes larger – a scaling up from the triad – the possibilities for individuality to express itself also becomes greater. This is perhaps the crux of his sociology of emergent urbanism and something that serves as a link between the work of Simmel and Tönnies. In small-scale societies the potential and the actual level of social control of the individual is far greater than in larger-scale societies.

As society's physical size develops so too does the level of complexity, a complexity that the individual has to continually adjust to. Many classical sociologists struggled with this dilemma. For Tönnies, this complexity was represented by a movement from *Gemeinschaft* to *Gesellschaft* social relations. For Marx, Durkheim and others, the increasing complexity involved in the division of labour produced its own effects: for Marx the subordination of the individual into the collective; for Durkheim new forms of social solidarity and the development of the collective consciousness. How, then, can an individual be an individual, preserving their own autonomy, yet at the same time belonging to the social? In many senses this is the fundamental dilemma of modernity: how are we to make sense of our world; how are we to prioritise meaning and experience?

Simmel's most famous work *Metropolis and Mental Life* attempts to understand this process of transformation from small-scale and relatively unsophisticated societies to large-scale, urban and highly complex modern societies. However, he does not focus simply on the structural level of change, but rather on the need to understand how the individual deals with and comes to terms with this process of transformation. As we have seen, Simmel argues that all social life is experienced at a deeply psychological level which gives it meaning. In urban life the tempo of existence is far higher, the demands on the mental capacity of the individual far greater and more complex than those previously encountered in a rural existence:

> Here the rhythm of life and sensory mental imagery flows more slowly, more habitually and more evenly. Precisely in this connection the sophisticated character of the metropolitan psychic life becomes understandable – as over against small town life which rests more upon deeply felt and emotional relationships. These latter are rooted in the more unconscious layers of the psychic and grow most readily in the steady rhythm of uninterrupted habituation's.
>
> (Simmel 1903, cited in Frisby and Featherstone 1997: 175)

Simmel is not saying that there is only one form, or at least one dominant form, of urban consciousness, but rather that at the individual level urban consciousness can take a variety of forms. Indeed, the very individuality of manners, dress and intellect itself provides us with evidence of such variation. Metropolitan life can bring out the best in the individual, who can be stimulated in ways not previously encountered via the rural existence. The power of the individual personality is seen to respond to the continued stream of stimuli offered to it. Moreover, if the individual is able to meet the psychological challenge of existence within the complex urban milieu, the individual has indeed triumphed. As with many other classical sociologists, Simmel is positing a process of struggle and negotiation of modern life at the individual level. As Watier (1998) argues, Simmel's work attempts to explain how the individual will survive in modern society. However, he appears to go much further than this: it is also the struggle of the educated bourgeoisie against what he saw as the growing proletarianisation of spiritual and material life within society. This process of proletarianisation was a direct consequence of the development of modern society, modern technology, modern conditions of living (in particular urbanism) and mass communication.

In the rural environment the economic aspect of life is small scale, with the individual knowing at an intimate level those with whom he (for it usually was a he) conducted his business; his sphere of economic interchange is limited, and for the most part fixed by custom and tradition. Production would be largely for immediate consumption, or, where a surplus is generated, exchanged for the goods produced by those living close by. This system of exchange encouraged intimate dependency and reliability, based upon trust and tradition. The market as it existed was limited, localised, intimate and known. This is not to deny that the urban environment and markets existed, but rather that they did not dominate in the ways they would under modernity. The very scale of urban development, of mechanisation and industrialism unleashed by the two revolutions, is at the core of Simmel's project.

In the *Philosophy of Money* (1907), Simmel doesn't simply take money as his final objective of analysis, but uses it as a mechanism through which we can start to understand other dimensions of social interaction and social phenomena. As with Marx, and to different degrees Durkheim and Weber, Simmel focused on the inherent problems associated with capitalism. However, for Marx, capitalism is superseded and the money economy transformed under socialism into a utopian society which meets the complete needs of the individual; for Simmel, capitalism is permanent. In many respects his view of the permanence of capitalism shares a resonance and pessimism with the work of Weber (1947) and later writers of the Frankfurt School such as Herbert Marcuse (1964). Yet as with Marx, Simmel believes that modern capitalism is coercive of the individual who has to work to find the money to buy the objects that he or she desires. Like Marx and Weber, it is the market that sets the value, and thus the amount of money, that is required to meet the desires of the individual. For Marx (1976: Vol. 1, chs 1, 6) this would result in the process of commodity fetishism and for Weber the increasing disenchantment of the individual.

Within capitalism there is for Simmel simply a shift from the qualitative to the quantitative nature of social existence via the growth of the money What modern capitalism and a money economy have done is depersonalise social relations; we are deemed to be a person not on the basis of subjective judgements of who we are, but on measurable and seemingly objective criteria, which often carry some monetary value. In this respect Simmel appears to be prefacing ideas later developed within structural functionalism and the work of Davis and Moore (1945). Thus a lawyer or a doctor is deemed to be more valued, and thus more highly rewarded in money terms, than a postal worker or teacher. We are, according to Simmel, relativising life; everything has a value which can be measured and calculated. For Simmel, this contrasts sharply with agrarian and small-scale societies. Moreover, there is a logic of modern urban society that cannot be denied. In modern urban society, production has to be for the market rather than the individual, but such markets exist at a higher order, at a far wider and more impersonal level, than that of the rural community. As Marx, Durkheim, Weber, Tönnies and others considered, urban life is also one in which the role of the market and, most importantly, the role of money are central. It may seem self-evident to say that money is the common currency of urban life, as our modern lives would not be possible without the fuel of cash and monetary exchange. For classical sociologists, especially Simmel, but also Marx, it is also the role that the cash economy fulfils in creating exchange value which is so important here.

We have, then, argued Simmel, developed within modern urbanised capitalist society a situation where exchange value is more important than use value. Money is the mechanism by which exchange value is conveyed and measured at both the social and individual level. The market becomes the rational mechanism by which large areas of social interaction take place and are regulated:

> Money is concerned only with what is common to all; it asks for the exchange value, it reduces all quality and individuality to the question: How much? All intimate emotional relations between persons are founded in their individuality, whereas in rational relations man is reckoned with like number, like an element which is itself indifferent . . . Money with all its colourlessness and indifference becomes the common denominator of all values; irreparably it hollows out the core of all things, their individuality, their specific value and their incomparability.
>
> (Simmel 1903, cited in Frisby and Featherstone 1997: 176–8)

The money economy of the modern urban environment demands from the individual a new form of interdependence, less and less the face-to-face contact of rural existence, and more one of trust in the impersonal forces of the monetary economy and exchange value. Here there is a degree of overlap between Simmel and Weber (1930), both see the market as the most rational and highly efficient mechanism for the distribution, allocation and exchange of scarce resources. A good example of this is provided when he talks about the way our concept of time is regulated and coordinated. Thus for an efficient market to work, clocks must be synchronised within a given market. Goods and services, the movement of people and products will all take place against a given standard of time. Clearly this was especially true in the nineteenth century and driven for the most part by the expansion of the railways. In Britain and most other European countries, prior to the development of a national rail network, different cities and parts of the country would operate according to 'different clocks', that is to say immediate localised concepts of time. Each region would have its own natural rhythm. But the expansion of markets at a national level demands that this change, that some form of coordination exist.

The development of capitalism demands standardisation and coordination. If such a localised system of telling the time prevailed it would be near impossible to regulate and plan the distribution of goods and services across boundaries, hence the need for some wider applied standard. Imagine for a moment how difficult it would be to travel between Liverpool and London if both operated at different and uncoordinated time zones? It would be impossible to develop a timetable for the trains or to calculate journey times.

In what other ways might our society be driven into chaos by such lack of rational systems of organisation? (Think about the disruption caused by the failure of the information technology network at college or university, or a failure of the local cashpoint system.)

This process of standardisation impacts at the level of individual psychology for Simmel. The urban individual is governed by impersonal rules that would not be found in the rural milieu. Simmel argues that we take for granted such aspects of modern urban life; and we have become blasé. This attitude conditions us not to respond to the stimulus of our environment.

> An incapacity thus emerges to react to new sensations with appropriate energy. This constitutes that blasé attitude which, in fact, every metropolitan child shows when compared with children of quieter and less changeable milieus . . . The large cities, the main seats of money exchange bring the purchasability of things to the fore much more impressively than do the smaller localities. That is why cities are also the genuine locale of the blasé attitude. In the blasé attitude the concentration of men and things stimulate the nervous system of the individual to its highest achievement, so that it attains its peak.
>
> (Simmel 1903, cited in Frisby and Featherstone 1997: 178–9)

For Simmel this move to an urban existence may be materially enriching, but juxtaposed against this is the increased blasé attitude of the individual member of society to such material abundance. In essence the quantity of urban life does not result in the individual perceiving any great growth in the quality of life, we become indifferent. In many respects we seek solace in our own individuality, the urbanised individual, is Simmel believes, a much more reserved person. Family and close friends become more the locus for the individual; the space is created in which such individuality is shared among the known and trusted members of the circle. So while providing the possibility of an abundance of material freedoms, modern urbanism at the same time forces greater introspection and self-reliance on the individual than would ever have been encountered in a rural setting. As Simmel observes:

> It is obviously only the obverse of this freedom if, in certain circumstances, one nowhere feels as lonely and lost as in the metropolitan crowd. For here as elsewhere it is by no means necessary that the freedom of man be reflected in his emotional life as comfort.
>
> (Simmel 1903, cited in Frisby and Featherstone 1997: 181)

An additional and quite significant effect of the urban metropolitan existence is the range of opportunities it affords the individual. The reach of the individual extends beyond his or her own physical limitations. Modern forms of technology, communication and the division of labour result in a situation in which an individual can have influence, if not power, over a far greater spatial and temporal arena than would be possible in rural conditions. Perhaps a modern example of this might be the Internet or World Wide Web – forms of technology that can be used for good or ill, where one might find much valuable information, but equally, also, racist and sexist ideas and opinions of the basest form.

Simmel would understand such developments as logical outcomes of the need of the individuals to express their individuality, for there is a real and continuing process in which the subjective personality is forced to bend to objective and impersonal social forces. There is in essence a continual struggle, in which the individual has to define their very individuality by raising their voice. Thus metropolitan life produces conditions in which ever new excesses and excessive actions are seen as the vehicle by which the individual will stamp their individuality on the metropolitan world. Simmel pointed to the irony that the division of labour and the complexity of the market itself objects to such excesses but also transforms them into normal elements of metropolitan life. Once again perhaps this might be best illustrated by a more modern example. Hebdige (1983), saw the 'punk revolution' of the late 1970s as a struggle against the establishment.

> Punk claimed to speak for the neglected constituency of white lumpen youth, but it did so typically in the stilted language of glam and glitter rock . . . Punk rock's gutter-snipe rhetoric, its obsession with class and relevance were expressly designed to undercut the intellectual posturing of the previous generation of rock musicians.
>
> (Hebdige 1983: 63)

Punk fashion, music and style might be regarded in Simmel's terms as an attempt to stress individuality. However, with hindsight we can see how such a sub-culture was eventually subsumed and exploited by the music and fashion industries of the mid-1980s onwards. Thus the Enlightenment and the emergence of modernity, or for Simmel the metropolis, have brought both opportunities and perils. As individuals we might be freer than at any time in our history, we have more in the way of material choice open to us, but at the same time we are constrained within impersonal, yet highly rational, processes which threaten to subsume our very individuality. Interestingly, Simmel argues that individuals such as Ruskin and Nietzsche hated metropolitan life because of the regulation it imposed on man, for the ways in which the rational came to dominate seemingly irrational basic instincts within man. In many respects these are themes readily visible in the work of our next critic of modernity, Friedrich Nietzsche.

In modern metropolitan society the voice of the individual is difficult to hear over the cacophony of other voices. As such the individual must find some way to 'raise their voice' to demonstrate their individualism.

1 Suggest some ways in which such expressive individualism is evident today, around you and in the wider world.

Simmel also believed that with the growth of the market everything had a material price. Recently we have seen American multi-billionaire Denis Tito become the first space tourist. In the week of 21–27 May 2001 a record number of people climbed Mount Everest, the oldest being 67, the youngest just 16. It is now possible to take a guided holiday to the top of this mountain for £15,000. Simmel indicated that through the common availability of such opportunities we may increasingly become blasé.

2 Suggest some other examples which reflect the desire of the individual to demonstrate their individuality.

FRIEDRICH NIETZSCHE

As with other social theorists and social philosophers, Nietzsche was backward looking in so far as he attempted to find some form of historical justification for his ideas. However, his historicism can be said to take a genealogical approach in which he appears to trace surface developments, combinations of minor shifts, rather than portray some grand, overall explanation for historical change. As such it may be argued that there are no evolutionary laws according to Nietzsche in the way that can perhaps be found in other classical social theorists such as Marx, Durkheim, Weber and, as we have seen above, Simmel and Tönnies. In taking this approach Nietzsche felt he was able to show that morals have a particular history. As Mahon (1992) observes, it is this genealogical approach to the history of moral development that so influenced the later work of Michel Foucault. Magee (1987) argues that it was not until the final years of his life that Nietzsche attempted to build a systematic, all-encompassing and systematic philosophical model of any kind. Yet in his final four years he sought to bring together his main themes into a central and panoramic work, *The Will To Power*, published in 1901. While Nietzsche is quite well known within English-speaking philosophy, critics have suggested that he is not held in the same regard as other European philosophers. Schacht (1983) believes that it may be the case that while English-speaking philosophy accepted the importance of the Nietzschian contribution to expanding the parameters of philosophy, it has done so under some sort of sufferance:

> Outside of what used to be called the Continentally-inspired underworld, he [Nietzsche] for the most part has either been ignored altogether, or accorded only minor significance as a forerunner of existentialism, or else crudely caricatured, vilified, and cavalierly dismissed.
>
> (Schacht 1983: ix)

BOX 5.3

Friedrich Nietzsche

Friedrich Nietzsche was born on 15 October 1844 in the small village of Röcken, in the deeply religious and nationalistic province of Saxony in Prussia. His early family life was dominated by his father's deeply held Lutheran religious beliefs; indeed, at the time of Nietzsche's birth his father was pastor to King Friedrich Wilhelm IV of Prussia, after whom Nietzsche was named. Moreover, Lutheran Protestantism can be seen to have infused Nietzsche's wider family, as demonstrated by the fact that his paternal grandfather had previously written several books defending Protestantism, while his maternal grand-father was a village pastor of the Lutheran Church. In 1858, Nietzsche won a place at Schulpforta, at the time one of Germany's leading Protestant boarding schools, from which he graduated in 1864, and moved to the University of Bonn where he studied philology and theology. After two years at Bonn, he transferred to the University of Leipzig. During compulsory military service in 1867 Nietzsche suffered a serious chest injury and was allowed to leave the military and return to study at the University of Leipzig in 1868. Nietzsche's early academic career was deeply influenced by the ideas of Schopenhauer and the German operatic giant Richard Wagner. Wagner was to become a close friend of Nietzsche up until 1878, when Nietzsche started to reject the more virulent anti-Semitism of Wagner. Nietzsche was an exceptionally gifted student and was awarded his doctorate in 1869, without having to write a dissertation or take an exam, as was customary at that time at the University of Leipzig. In the same year he was appointed professor of philology at the University of Basle, Switzerland. Despite the fact that Nietzsche had pre-viously been invalided out of the German military, he returned and served as a volunteer medical orderly during the Franco-Prussian war of 1870. Yet once again, ill health forced him to return to a career in academia in 1871. From this period onward, Nietzsche was plagued by ill health, so much so that in 1871 he was required to take a year's sick leave from his position at Basle. This became permanent early retirement the following year. Between 1879 and 1889, while seriously ill, he lived a rather isolated, if productive, life, moving between Switzerland and the gentler climate of the French and Italian Riviera. It is during this period that Nietzsche produced perhaps his best known work, *Also Sprach Zarathustra* ('*Thus Spake Zarathustra*'). Following a mental collapse in Turin, Italy, in 1889, Nietzsche returned to Basle and then to Naumberg, Germany, where he died in 1900.

However, his work has, according to Magee, had deeper cultural influences in Britain, in particular through the work of great literary figures such as George Bernard Shaw, W.B. Yeats and D.H. Lawrence. In the works of all three writers we see a rejection of the moral constraints of contemporary society, and above all an engagement with the concept of power and authority.

As with both Simmel and Tönnies, Nietzsche can be said to have emerged out of the German idealist tradition. The role of Nietzsche in attacking modernity as it emerged from the Enlightenment is central to late nineteenth and early twentieth century thinking and Nietzsche can certainly be placed alongside the other social theorists examined in this chapter. Importantly, Nietzsche, along with Marx, was one of the first modern philosophers to openly challenge the idea of a supernatural realm of existence. If one phrase is associated with Nietzsche, it is 'God is dead' (quoted in Schacht 1983: 110). As with Marx's notion of religion as the opium of the people, with its purpose to oppress and subjugate the masses, for Nietzsche religion and the supernatural realm provided an equally important and sinister, if somewhat different, role. Nietzsche argued that society creates a situation in which values are manmade, rather than god-given. Such morals and values are relative rather than absolute; social products rather than natural or spiritual in any real sense at all. While Marx justified the denial of god as breaking the chains of one part of capitalist ideology, for Nietzsche it was not so simple. At one level his denial of the spiritual, of God, is not so unusual, but at another level, it begs the question, what replaces God? For Marx a denial of God was a necessary condition for advancement towards a classless society. For Nietzsche, in modern society we are increasingly slaves to convention, to habit and routine, and God has become a central part of that routine and those conventions, so much so that a belief in the supernatural, in God, provides a central underpinning of western civilisation (Marx and Engels 1963).

To understand what Nietzsche is driving towards, we need to understand that his philosophy is an attack on what he defines as the four central traditions within western society and civilisation. These traditions have ancient roots, but since the Enlightenment period have become more firmly embedded in western society and the general western psyche. Firstly, he aimed to challenge Christian values and morality. At the core of modern Christianity is a basic concept of morality, a key component of which is compassion. For Nietzsche, compassion is the key weakness at the core of Christianity. As Solomon (1985) points out, Nietzsche wishes to personify Jewish ethics as a 'slave morality', something that he regards as structured on envy. The Christian ethics which emerged from the Judaic tradition and which made a virtue of meekness, poverty and humility were seen by Nietzsche as even worse. The instruction to turn the other cheek, to accept oppression and assault, rather than to struggle against it, are described as the ethics of the weak, of those who hate and fear strength, pride and self-affirmation. Such ethics, he feels, undermine and weaken the human drives that have led to the greatest and most noble human achievements. Thus, all the central values and positive elements of Christianity, such as brotherly love, passivity, self discipline, but above all compassion, are rejected by Nietzsche because, quite simply, these values appear to favour the weak, the underdog. Moreover, for Nietzsche, the very concept of compassion is a double-edged sword; it creates conditions in which compassion itself is expected, but more importantly demeans and weakens the individual who provides such compassion. For Nietzsche, life should be lived to the full, and compassion acts as a brake on such a process, constantly forcing the individual to check their actions against such morals and values.

The second tradition that Nietzsche attacks is that of 'secular morality' as defined by the work of certain moral philosophers. As pointed out earlier in this chapter, the ideas of Ferguson, Hume and Smith played a crucial role in allowing the full force of Enlightenment thinking and modernity to take shape. Theirs was a philosophy in which the principle of 'the greatest good for the greatest number' became a ruling idea, a social compass and new morality. For these writers there was both an inescapable rational and moral requirement for new social structures and forms of social organisation that involved the acceptance of democratic processes and the acknowledgement of the growth of public opinion. For Nietzsche this approach had widespread common appeal because it pandered to a new form of secular morality, to a lowest common denominator, akin to the rules of the common herd. It replaced religious morality which had been found wanting by Enlightenment ideas with what he regards as little of substance. In other words, he is rejecting the secular morality of democratic values and laws.

> Let us not be deceived! Time marches forward; we'd like to believe that everything that is in it also marches forward -that the development is one that moves forward. The most level headed are led astray by this illusion . . . 'Mankind' does not advance, it does not even exist. The overall aspect is that of a tremendous experimental laboratory in which a few successes are scored. Scattered through the ages, while there are untold failures, and all order, logic, union and obligingness are lacking. How can we fail to recognize that the ascent of Christianity is a movement of decadence . . . That the [French] Revolution destroyed the instinct for a grand organization of society. Man represents no progress over the animal; the civilized tenderfoot is an abortion compared to the Arab and Corsican.
>
> (Nietzsche 1968: 55)

The third, and in some ways even more insidious tradition for Nietzsche, related to the everyday morality of the masses. As with the idea of secular morality, Nietzsche questions everyday morality as being 'base', something inferior and weakening of the individual spirit. What we have seen with the emergence of civilisation is the increasing imposition of laws and the widening of the rule of law. Moreover, modernity brings with it a new urgency to the rule of law; property rights are increasingly strengthened with the development of capitalism, protection of the individual under law becomes increasingly important. However, for Nietzsche, laws are there simply to make things easy for the weak. This was in essence part of the Socratic tradition of western civilisation. To Nietzsche, Socrates was part and parcel of formulating a rational approach to rule and to law. With Socrates, reason starts to triumph, replacing the more instinctive tradition that had applied up to that point. From here onwards a new realm of experience took over and the Christian tradition emerged, blending with the Judaic traditions of ancient civilisation. In turn, and as with Christian morality and secular morality, society governed by a system of laws is inimical to the central spirit of the individual. A society increasingly regulated by law is one in which all, including the powerful, are constrained. Leadership in such a society must have a consensual and legal basis. However, for Nietzsche a true leader is not a democratic leader but a hero, a law unto himself. He both makes and applies the morality of the age, the laws and the values. He is not constrained by common morality or the mundane rules and regulations that apply to mere mortals.

Yet our society and civilisation had indeed constrained and repressed the individual, the Enlightenment and modernity had sought to control through formal sanction and law these inbuilt impulses and the 'will to power'. Nietzsche's criticism of the Enlightenment project is illustrated by his attack on Voltaire and Rousseau:

> The state of nature is terrible, man is the beast of prey; our civilization represents a tremendous triumph over this beast of prey nature: thus argued Voltaire. He felt the mitigation, the subtleties, the spiritual joys of the civilized state; he despised narrow-mindedness, also in the form of virtue, and the lack of delicatesse, also among ascetics and monks . . . The moral reprehensibility of man seemed to preoccupy Rousseau; with the words 'unjust' and 'cruel' one can best stir up the instincts of the oppressed who otherwise smart under the banner of the vetitum and disfavor, so their conscience advises them against rebellious cravings. Such emancipators see one thing above all: to give their part the grand accents and poses of the higher nature.
>
> (Nietzsche 1968: 62)

In many regards, Nietzsche, like Marx, believed that the quality of the product, of the mind, is dependent upon the nature and quality of its origins, and it is possible that Freud obtained this key to his ideas on the unconscious mind from Nietzsche. In essence, we create our values to meet our needs dependent upon our circumstances (origins). Thus for Nietzsche, in every civilisation and in every epoch of history, values are social and psychological products. As Stern argues, in many respects Nietzsche was a major precursor of Freud:

> He places a great deal of emphasis on the unconscious. For instance; Nietzsche's criticism of German idealism hinges on his view that it fails to take into account the unconscious drives which determine our actions, that German idealism simply takes over from Christianity a wholly negative attitude towards the unconscious drives in us and builds a civilization on their suppression – again, you can see how close this is to the Freud of *Civilization and its Discontents*.
>
> (cited in Magee 1987: 239)

In some respects it would appear that Nietzsche is taking a relativist and subjective approach to morality and values, that different moralities and values are right for different people. But where does this put western civilisation and western culture? Quite simply, we must live life to the full and any social system which is created will be quite arbitrary, dependent upon the will of the powerful. Life is the only value, the living of that life to the full is the only goal of that life, or of existence in general. What constitutes truth is that which serves life. Nietzsche saw human nature as composed of two interlinked and contrasting sides: a 'Dionysian' element, so called for the Greek god of wine and pleasure, and an 'Apollonian' element named after the Greek Sun god or god of beauty. The Dionysian element of human nature was that of instinctive, impulsive and undisciplined human nature. For Nietzsche, in the post-Enlightenment world the Apollonian element had triumphed – we now lived in a world in which there was order, discipline, control and acceptance. Individuals as social animals had become meek, compliant, undemanding and dependent.

The triumph of the Apollonian element, however, led to a sterility within society, real human capacity was held back, restrained and controlled. The only way that society could really fulfil itself and recognise full human capacity would be if individuals were allowed to find the Dionysian element of their nature. For Nietzsche, earlier civilisations all had Dionysian heroes at their centre, historical figures who challenged the status quo, and released the full potential of human society. Our culture in Apollonian society is far too restrained and civilised, failing to acknowledge in culture or literature the vital role of our Dionysian heritage. Moreover, in failing to recognise that there can be a Dionysian element to human nature, the very objectivity of modern rational society is itself questioned. How can so-called rationalism be the basis of human progress, Nietzsche argues, if that progress fails to acknowledge the key role played by the dark side of human nature in the triumph of man over nature?

Given this notion that democratic civilisation and western culture serve to shackle the powerful in favour of the humble, the unintelligent and the weak, it is perhaps not surprising that Nietzsche has been associated with the rise of Nazi ideology. As Nietzsche himself observed:

> I know my fate. One day there will be associated with my name the recollection of something frightful – of a crisis like no other before on earth, of the profoundest collision of conscience, of a decision evoked against everything that until then had been believed in, demanded, sanctified. I am not a man I am dynamite.
>
> (Nietzsche 1908, cited in Stern 1977)

The idea of 'the will to power' and the ideal of the *Ubermensch* or 'superman', an individual with the essence of 'the will to power', the man whose natural instincts are not repressed, do accord with the qualities which Hitler and the Nazi regime advocated. However, it is unfair to tar Nietzsche with a Nazi brush. Unlike many of his contemporaries he was not anti-Semitic, or indeed totalitarian, in any real sense. For Nietzsche, the superman will also be a generous man, a self-controlled man, a man continually struggling as much with himself as with the wider world. In this context, the use of the concepts 'will to power' and 'superman' by Nazi ideology reflect a bastardisation of Nietzsche. What we can take from Nietzsche is his depth of understanding of the human condition; and writing just a little earlier than Freud, and from within philosophy, rather than psychology or psychiatry, some of his ideas have a deep resonance with those of Freud. As with other theorists, he felt that western culture and civilisation, based as it was upon the key idea of rationality, would lead in an opposite direction to that advocated and hoped for by Enlightenment thinkers. Modern western society and civilisation can be characterised by the continual repression of individuals rather than their liberation. As regards social theory, we may conclude that Nietzsche's philosophy favours much more the nature of social agency, rather than social structure, in the process of social change. His concepts of power, his rejection of rationalism and above all his idea of the relative nature of ideas have deeply influenced European social thought. Sociologically, the impact of his ideas have been most strongly felt in the development of post-structuralism and in particular the work of Michel Foucault (1977) for whom social life is to a large extent determined by repression and suppression, the use of power and the interplay of the seemingly irrational elements of human nature. In many respects the core of Nietzsche's critique of modernity is its failure of the individual, but within his work the true nature of what it is to be an individual is never fully explored or elaborated, other than in terms of failure of power and the corrupting effects of modern civilisation. It is Freud who is arguably the first modern social theorist to come to grips with the nature and consequences of individuality in a modern society.

Discussion questions

Nietzsche appears to articulate a deep frustration with society. Indeed, as pointed out here, the Nazi Party was seemingly able to tap into such frustrations and personify them as the decadence of democratic society. The Nazis' solution was to end democracy. But this is precisely what Nietzsche both prophesied and rejected as a solution. For him the solution would be as bad as the problem.

1 In what ways might Nietzsche be articulating real concerns, real frustrations?

2 How might these be manifested in contemporary society?

SIGMUND FREUD

The importance of Freud to the questioning of modernity is immense. His work questioned the supposedly rational and logical idea of human nature so firmly held by the Enlightenment and scientific reasoning. In the writings of Marx, Durkheim and Weber there are the implicit and clearly positivist assumption that individuals are created from within society, that society imposes itself, directs and largely determines what it is to be an individual. While Simmel attempts to 'relativize scientific reason', Freud goes beyond this to place it in the individual or subject, something which Nietzsche had already started to do. In this respect, as indicated earlier, there are some striking parallels between the work of Nietzsche and that of Freud. Both question the 'autonomy of the subject', focusing on the forces at work in the constitution of the individual. Both refer to the sublimation of sexual desires of the individual and feel that modern culture has transformed these basic and even animal instincts into cultural energy. In their work there is a sense that individuals and the society of which they are part are simply passively awaiting the voice of the hypnotic leader.

It is Freud who really starts to provide us with a theory of the human mind, a method by which we can start to question the autonomy of the subject. As such, Freud's theories attempt to balance the effects of agency by illuminating how individual personality is created. The individual personality is composed of three interlinked elements or structures: id, ego and super-ego (Freud 1963a). The id –

BOX 5.4

Sigmund Freud

Sigmund Freud was born into a middle-class wool merchant's family on 6 May 1856, in Freiberg, Moravia, which was at the time part of the Austrian Habsburg empire, but is now known as Príbor and is in the Czech Republic. Freud's father Jakob was a rather remote and authoritarian figure. In contrast, Freud's mother is believed to have been a key focus of his early life, to whom he was deeply emotionally attached. In 1859, due to economic problems, the Freud family was forced to move to Leipzig in Germany and then the following year to Vienna where they would remain until the Nazi annexation of Austria in 1938. Along with many other Jewish residents Freud had to face the anti-Semitism that was a part of daily life in Austria of this period. After graduating from the Sperl Gymnasium in 1873, Freud decided to study medicine at the University of Vienna, where he was a pupil of Ernest Von Brücke, one of the leading physiologists of his day. In 1882 Freud gained a post as a clinical assistant at the General Hospital in Vienna. Here he trained with the psychiatrist Theodor Meynert and the professor of internal medicine Hermann Nothnagel; both were to prove formative influences on his later career. Three years later Freud was appointed lecturer in neuropathology, and started to develop an interest in médical and clinical uses of cocaine; an interest that would later haunt his career. In late 1885 Freud studied for a period under the tutelage of Jean-Martin Charcot at the Salpêtrière clinic in Paris and it was here that Freud was introduced to patients classified as hysterics. This opened up to Freud the possibility that psychological disorders might have their source in the mind rather than the brain.

In 1886 Freud married Martha Bernays, the daughter of a prominent Jewish family. They were to have six children, including Anna who became a highly influential psycho-analyst in her own right. Returning, inspired, from France, Freud started to practise neuropsychology at an office in central Vienna that he was to occupy for nearly 50 years. It was here that Freud was to successfully treat his most famous patient 'Anna O' who suffered from a wide variety of hysterical conditions, and who would later serve as a touch-stone for his academic work. Owing to pressure from the Nazis, Freud was forced to leave Vienna in 1938, when he was 82. He moved to London, where he continued to work for a year until his death in 1939. He is buried in the same cemetery as Karl Marx, Highgate, London.

---

the unconscious aspect of our personality which is made up of instinctual energy 'Eros and Thanatos' – is largely impervious to moral standards. In this context the id is a basic level of the personality. Id processes involve biological functions and needs, including the need for pleasure. The ego is part of the conscious representation of personality. Its main function is the repression and control of the id. Ego processes are, in the main, mechanisms for dealing with the real world, including perception, memory and learning. Without the ego, social disorder would prevail as the basic drives of the id would take a dominant role in determining the actions of the individual. As such, without the ego civilisation would not be possible. The super-ego is what we might think of as the conscience of the individual, the moral stop on actions that direct and facilitate our everyday social interactions. The super-ego is conditioned via the process of association and role identification, i.e. 'we learn to become'. Super-ego processes are, in the main, those of internalisation by the individual; here morality is a key element.

For Freud, the influence of the unconscious mind on social actions can be seen to operate at two levels or 'component instincts': the level of bodily pleasure, our basic 'sexual instincts'; and instincts directed towards 'death and destruction'. These concepts are personified as the Eros and Thanatos instincts. The Eros instinct promotes a tendency for disharmony within civilisation, due to the tension between the urge for individual sexual gratification and the sublimated wider love for society and mankind in general. Our innate aggression is an expression of Thanatos, the death instinct expressed outwardly. We must constantly struggle to control such instincts, for our own self-preservation and for the preservation of civilisation itself. Becoming 'social' requires that the individual represses both of these instincts. Moreover, Freud believes, because Eros and Thanatos are themselves at odds with each other, conflict and guilt is engendered and is virtually inevitable. Civilisation will inevitably seek to thwart man's instinctual drives; such is the price we pay for civilisation itself. The best we can hope for, he believes, is that the balance between our inner drives and the controls imposed on us by society are in balance. What is unique about modern society is the need to repress these instincts even further than in previous social formations. Here we clearly have echoes of the work of both Tönnies and Simmel: greater individuality and freedom, itself a product of Enlightenment thinking, has at one level liberated the individual, without constraining their component instincts.

> **Discussion question**
>
> In Freud's work *Civilization and Its Discontents* (Freud 1963b) we get the impression that civilisation is but a veneer on a highly tormented human psyche. This implies that concepts such as good and evil are at best relative, and at worst irrelevant.
> What are the potential dangers to civilisation from this approach? (Think of how it might give a free hand to human actions of the cruelest nature.)

It is, Freud believes, the repression of the unconscious mind that is a universal phenomenon and in this he goes some way to providing an understanding of the location of the individual within society. There is a universal process of personality formation in and between every culture. This is clearly demonstrated by the universal nature of social taboos that exist in all cultures and societies and are designed to repress, or as Nietzsche puts it, sublimate, some of the basic psychological instincts of individuals. We find such taboo repression in every society in every historical period.

Freud's book *Civilization and Its Discontents*, first published in 1930, provides the clearest exposition of his ideas. This study is in similar vein to Simmel's

Metropolis and Mental Life and Tönnies' *Community and Association* in that it offers a critique of modern life, of urban culture and urban civilisation. As such, it builds on a very long tradition of the critique of urban life and modern civilisation. Freud provides a lucid understanding of how aggressive instincts operate within society. Indeed, *Civilization and Its Discontents* must be read as a reaction to the horrors of the First World War, which Freud himself had witnessed and dealt with in the form of soldiers returning from war suffering all kinds of neuroses, psychoses and psychological disorders. As Jacobs observes:

> He argued that modern man denied the reality of death and had developed ways of soft-ening the impact of the death of others. The Great War had cracked open the veneer of civilization and exposed the degree of aggression buried beneath the surface.
>
> (Jacobs 1992: 19)

The First World War had a profound impact on Freud: it held open the wounds of society at the level of the mental stability of the masses. Moreover, it is not just in war that this increased pressure to mental neurosis can be found. It is part and parcel of the very nature of western capitalism. Freud comes close to Simmel in his estimation of the measure of human discontent when he talks about the loss of satisfaction and growing hostility to civilisation; indeed, there are also echoes of Marx's notion of alienation, Weber's of disenchantment or even Durkheim's of anomie:

> It arose when people came to know about the mechanism of the neurosis, which threatens to undermine the modicum of happiness enjoyed by civilized men. It was discovered that a person becomes neurotic because he cannot tolerate the amount of frustration which society imposes on him in the service of its cultural ideals, and it was inferred from this that the abolition or reduction of those demands would result in a return to possibilities of happiness.
>
> (Freud 1963b: 25)

For Freud, one mechanism that society itself had developed to ensure the cohesiveness (and even the fragility) of modern civilisation is the development of the modern family form. Rearing within the family form allows individuals to be trained to restrict their unconscious impulsive desires. It is the family in which the super-ego component of personality operates; it is through the examples of others that one can internalise standards and morality to oneself. The family is then the major site of social morality, it is essentially the internalisation of parental com-mands. Self-denial of the individual within the family is rewarded by acceptance within the family and society in general.

As Callinicos (1999) observes, Freud's writing on family structure suggests that gender differences are not simply and solely biologically determined, but are also socially constructed. The argument that socially constructed roles prepared women for their future place in society has, of course, been widely debated within the social sciences. Freud's insights into the creation of the individual personality allow a considerable degree of understanding of how socialisation occurs, and how role conformity occurs. Clearly Freud's work openly challenged what had to that point been the central orthodoxy of society – an orthodoxy that had been given support by the Darwinian idea of natural selection and evolution. In challenging gender roles in such a way, Freud could be seen as opening up the rational scientific orthodoxy to scrutiny. However, it is also apparent to many feminists that Freudian theory contains a form of blatant sexism, which Freud himself never disavowed.

Yet Freud's work also emphasises a complexity to the human subject that goes beyond the simple deterministic assumptions previously made within philosophy and early sociology. Freud questioned the rational and progressive nature of the Enlightenment project, by pointing to the hidden and irrational desires that form the basis of the subject. Indeed, there is something of an irony in that Freud saw his own work as the very extension of the Enlightenment project itself; a means of providing the scientific tools by which the individual and society could thus be transformed (Brandell 1979). Through knowing oneself, one is able to master oneself and thus transform society:

> Freud summed up his position in a letter written in January 1927; in it he shows himself to be a loyal disciple of Comte: 'In secret – one cannot say such things aloud – I believe that one day metaphysics will be condemned as a nuisance, as an abuse of thinking, as a survival from the period of religious *Weltanschauung*.' The orthodoxy of his positivism is underlined in its formulation; it is not merely Christianity, not even mere religion but metaphysics in general that Freud rejects.
>
> (Brandell 1979: 18)

The tool for this re-embracing of the Enlightenment project was, for Freud, psychoanalysis. His ideas on psychoanalysis start to provide us with an understanding how human behaviour that was previously seen as irrational can be understood in rational terms. Through psychoanalysis we may come to understand that all individuals are at one and the same time both rational conscious beings with ordered minds, and also beings with unconscious and disordered minds within which very basic and profound emotional struggles are taking place. Psychoanalysis would penetrate the defences of the individual, peering in at the unconscious, the very key of our being, and in turn would allow a 'coming to terms' with who we are. In many senses, psychoanalysis was a process of self or individual enlightenment, just as earlier the European Enlightenment had shone a new light of understanding on society

The importance of Freud to social thought is profound. His work attempts to place the concept of the individual back at the heart of understanding society. Freud's is a model of understanding which sociologically we must regard as one which significantly favours the role of social agency in the development of society. As Bocock (1976) notes, his work has in many respects rivalled that of Marx in its impact and popularity. It not only created a distinct branch of psychology, but also helped to shape sociology not only in its influence on the Frankfurt School, the work of Talcott Parsons and structural functionalism, but also in its impact on modern post-structuralist theory.

The growth of modern psychiatry and psychology (at least in the USA) demonstrates the impact of Freud's ideas on western society. However, both psychiatry and psychoanalysis are not without their critics. It is often argued that we have become too reliant upon the tools of modern psychiatry, and that quite often our mental disorders are more imagined than real.

1 Provide some examples of how psychiatry has medicalised conditions previously considered normal and natural.

2 Why have fields of medicine such as psychiatry and psychoanalysis failed to make an impact in non-western-based societies?

SUMMARY

The four writers highlighted in this chapter were living at a time of the assumed triumph of industrial capitalism and had in common severe doubts and uncertainties about the process of modernity as it arose from the European Enlightenment.

For Tönnies, modernity had brought about a transformation in the lives of every individual which he felt could not be regarded in positive terms. The naturalness and deep intimacy of individual and social existence that had been the hallmark of pre-industrial society had given way to the impersonal and largely dehumanising forces of urban industrial capitalism. In its simplest terms, modernity was about the loss of community. While life in pre-industrial *Gemeinschaft*-type society had been for the most part, homogeneous, fixed, immobile and socially limiting, it was nonetheless secure. The cultural custodians of church, family and community provided points of reference for the individual, allowing for a deep sense of place and belonging. In the move towards *Gesellschaft*-type industrial and urban society, we reach a condition somewhat akin to Durkheim's concept of anomie – cut adrift from all that we know and value and at the whim of the capitalist urban economy. These themes are taken up and expanded by Simmel.

Simmel highlighted the transformation in the fortunes of the individual in urban industrial and capitalist society. Modernity and the metropolis brought an ever-changing social panorama in which an abundance of choice appeared to operate. A maze of social actions and interactions had been created in the new urban environment in which human potential was undiminished. The possibility for new forms of social interaction and association appeared endless, but so too did the potential overload on the individual. It is difficult, Simmel believed, for a single individual to grasp the complexity of modern society, and while modernity and metropolitan life can bring out the best in the individual, it can also bring out the worst. Simmel believed that modernity can be coercive to the individual; and it is here that his analysis comes close to Marx's concept of commodity fetishism. We are driven by the very abundance of modern society to seek to proclaim our individuality through excess, be it in the consumption of goods or services or in acts of individual ostentation. Furthermore, we are levelled down by the money economy and the cash nexus; able to afford to indulge our senses through our economic position in society we become increasingly blasé to such material wealth and seek ever-greater stimulation or thrills. On the other hand, those faced by economic impoverishment are left behind, increasingly alienated and disenchanted. For both Tönnies and Simmel there appears to be no middle ground. Modernity had brought about a transformation in society which now unleashed tremendous productive forces through the expansion of capitalism, yet the cost to the individual psyche could not be fully measured or understood.

In the work of Nietzsche, there is an unconscious drive to the 'will to power', a process of true inner realisation of the potential emergence of the 'superman' qualities of the individual. A denial of the Enlightenment is clearly identified by Nietzsche:

> When one speaks of humanity, there lies behind it the idea that humanity is that which separates and distinguishes mankind from nature. But in reality there is no such separation; the 'natural' qualities and those called specifically 'human' are inextricably entwined together. Man is in his highest and noblest powers entirely natural and bears in him nature's uncanny dual character. Those capacities which are dreadful and accounted inhuman are, indeed, perhaps the fruitful soil out of which alone all humanity in impulse, act and deed can grow.
>
> (Nietzsche 1872, cited in Hollingdale 1973: 100)

This prophecy of doom was realised in Europe under the Nazi regime. In setting up the concept of superman, Nietzsche appears not to be inverting moral judgements but rather to challenge ideas of what constitutes good and evil in the first place, to reformulate these morals (Hollingdale 1973). Nietzsche suggests that modernity has subverted the true nature of humanity and the individual, producing a moribund civilisation in which the virtues of the herd predominate and the cost to the individual are incalculable.

> For some time now the whole of European culture has been moving towards a catastrophe, ceaselessly, violently, like a river that wants to reach the end.
>
> (Nietzsche 1968: 460)

For Freud, modernity and Enlightenment thinking had, in similar vein to Nietzsche, simply masked the inner turmoil within the individual. The complex and seething forces of the unconscious were at one and the same time repressed and held in check by the veneer of civilisation, but they were prone to exposure at times and with devastating consequences. Freud's view of the First World War was one in which the cracks had widened enough to allow the dark forces of the unconscious to emerge:

> It stripped us of our later cultural superimposition's, and has let the primeval man within us into the light . . . We recall the old proverb *Si vis pacem, para bellum*. If you want to preserve peace, arm for war. It would be timely to paraphrase it: *Si vis vitam, para mortem*. If you want to endure life, prepare yourself for death.
>
> (Freud 1973: Vol 12)

Thus while all four theorists lived during a period of the supposed triumph of European civilisation and of increasingly intertwined global history and profound and remarkable change, they were concerned about the consequences. In many respects, the values that underlay western civilisations were nothing more than mirages; and the supposed high-water mark of western civilisation had increasingly been taken over by a spiritual and cultural crisis of the deepest nature. These writers all share an interest in the human condition and its relationship to society, but all share a questioning of the progressive nature of such change and entertained serious doubts as to the direction that modern society was taking. All note the frailty of such progress and, most importantly, all share an understanding of the costs that every individual had to pay for the price of such progress.

EXERCISES

1

Below are brief passages from each of the four theorists discussed in this chapter. Read each of these and consider the questions that follow them.

1 Tönnies

In this passage Tönnies defines the nature of human will, making a comparison between *Wesenwille* or natural will and *Kürwille*, rational will. He believes that an understanding of the differing nature of the two types of will provides us with a more fundamental explanation of the nature of social action.

> Natural will is the psychological equivalent of the human body, or the principle of the unity of life, supposing that life is conceived under that form of reality to which thinking itself belongs (*quatenus sub attributo cogitationis concipitur*). Natural will involves thinking in the same way as the organism contains those cells of the cerebrum which, if stimulated, cause the psychological activities which are to be regarded as equivalent to thinking (and in which the center of speech is undoubtedly a participator). Rational will is a product of thinking itself and consequently possesses reality only with reference to its author, the thinking individual, although this reality can be recognized and acknowledged as such by others. These two different concepts of will have in common the fact that they are conceived as the causes for or tendencies toward action. Their very existence and nature allow, therefore, an inference from them as to whether certain behavior of the individual is probable, or, under specific conditions, is necessary. Natural will derives from and can be explained only in terms of the past, just as the future in turn evolves from the past. Rational will can be understood only from the future developments with which it is concerned. Natural will contains the future in embryo or emergent form; rational will contains it as an image.
>
> (Tönnies 1955: 119–20)

(a) Give examples of how (i) natural will and (ii) rational will influence your own actions.

(b) Tönnies assumes that *Kürwille* or rational will is always a product of modern urban society. What problems are associated in making such an assumption?

(c) Why do you think that Tönnies employs the biological analogy to help understand psychological processes?

2 Simmel

In this passage Simmel focuses on the ways in which the individual is stimulated into action and the way that action will differ as a consequence of the stimulation it receives. In this he appears to suggest that the stimulation obtained by the individual in an urban metropolitan setting will differ radically from that experienced in a rural setting.

> The psychological basis of the metropolitan type of individuality consists of the *intensification of nervous stimulation* which results from the swift and uninterrupted change of the outer and inner stimuli. Man is a differentiating creature. His mind is stimulated by the difference between a momentary impression and the one which preceded it. Lasting impressions, impressions which differ only slightly from one another, impressions which take a regular habitual course and show regular habitual contrasts – all these use up, so to speak, less consciousness than does the rapid crowding of changing images, the sharp discontinuity in the grasp of a single glance, and the unexpectedness of onrushing impressions. These are the psychological conditions which the metropolis creates. With each crossing of the street the tempo and multiplicity of economic, occupational and social life, the city sets up a deep contrast with the small town and rural life with reference to the sensory foundations of psychic life. The metropolis exacts from man as a discriminating creature a different amount of consciousness than does rural life.
>
> (Simmel 1903, cited in Frisby and Featherstone 1997: 175)

(a) In your own words describe what you think Simmel means by the psychological basis of metropolitan life.

(b) Give examples of how the tempo of life in the metropolis is greater than that experienced elsewhere.

(c) Why does Simmel believe that man is a discriminating creature? How might this be demonstrated?

(d) To what extent do you think that the differences between the rural and the urban are more or less in contemporary western society than when Simmel was writing?

3 Nietzsche

A major concern of Nietzsche was to trace the impact of the Judaeo-Christian tradition on modern life. In doing so he is highly critical of what he feels is the weakening of the human spirit. In this extract Nietzsche defines the Judaeo-Christian tradition as both arrogant and corrupting.

> Read the New Testament as a book of seduction: virtue is appropriated in the instinct that with it one can capture public opinion – and indeed the most modest virtue, which recognizes the ideal sheep and nothing further (including the shepherd): a little, sweet, well-meaning, helpful, and enthusiastically cheerful kind of virtue that expects absolutely nothing from the outside – that sets itself altogether apart from 'the world.' The most absurd arrogance, as if on one hand the common unity represented all that is right, and on the other the world all that is false, eternally reprehensible, and rejected, and as if the destiny of mankind revolved about this fact. The most absurd hatred toward everything in power: but without touching it! A kind of inner detachment that outwardly leaves everything as it was (servitude and slavery; to know how to turn *everything* into a means of serving God and virtue). Christianity is possible as the most private form of existence; it presupposes a narrow, remote, completely un-political society – it belongs in the conventicle. A 'Christian state,' 'Christian politics,' on the other hand, are a piece of impudence, a lie, like for instance a Christian leadership of an army, which finally treats the 'God of Hosts' as if he were chief of staff. The papacy,

too, has never been in a position to carry on Christian politics; and when reformers indulge in politics, as Luther did, one sees that they are just as much followers of Machiavelli as any immoralist or tyrant of the impudent dogmas that have adorned themselves with its name: it requires neither the doctrine of a personal God, nor that of sin, nor that of immortality, nor that of redemption, nor that of faith; it has absolutely no need of metaphysics, and even less of asceticism, even less of a Christian 'natural science.' Christianity is a *way of life*, not a system of beliefs. It tells us how to act, not what we ought to believe. Whoever says today: 'I will not be a soldier,' 'I care nothing for the courts,' 'I shall not claim the services of the police,' 'I will do nothing that may disturb the peace within me: and if I must suffer on that account, nothing will serve better to maintain my peace than suffering' – he would be a Christian.

(Nietzsche 1968: 124–5)

(a) What are the virtues of Christianity that Nietzsche so rejects?

(b) Do you agree with his position?

(c) In what ways does Nietzsche imply that the growth and popularity of Christianity has shaped western culture?

(d) Why do you think that Nietzsche rejects the Christian concept of love for fellow man and the idea that the meek shall inherit the earth?

4 Freud

This extract demonstrates the way in which Freud believed that modern science, firstly through the work of Copernicus and then Darwin, serves to dethrone humanity from its privileged place in creation.

The second blow fell when biological research destroyed man's supposedly privileged place in creation and proved his descent from the animal kingdom and his ineradicable animal nature. This revaluation has been accomplished in our own days by Darwin, Wallace and their predecessors, though not without the most violent contemporary opposition. But human megalomania will have suffered its third and most wounding blow from the psychological research of the present time which seems to prove to the ego that it is not even master in its own house, but must content itself with scanty information: information of what is going on unconsciously in its mind. Hence arises the general revolt against our science, the disregard of all considerations of academic civility and the releasing of the opposition from every restraint of impartial logic.

(Freud in Brandell 1979: 58)

(a) Why does Freud appear to argue that scientific knowledge is now ascendant knowledge?

(b) Freud's ideas and his reference to the work of Darwin imply a biological reductionism. How might a sociological approach criticise such ideas?

2

All four theorists examined here came from the comfortable middle- or upper-class intellectual tradition of Germany and Europe. While all attempt to understand and analyse the nature of society, the role of the individual within society, the social forces that act on and shape individual action and the complexity of social interaction, they did so from a relatively privileged position of economic security, free from many of the more mundane concerns of life. As such their ability to minutely analyse, dissect and scrutinise the complex and changing world in which they lived was not shared by the majority of the population in Europe at the time.

Yet this produces a dilemma – such writers can be considered DWEMs (dead, white European males) and sociology and social science in general is dominated by such characters.

(a) Try to find examples from the passages above or the discussion in the chapter which highlight how the background of the four theorists influenced their ideas.

(b) How might the contributions of feminist and postmodern theories provide alternative ways of looking at the world? (You can use the knowledge you already have of these theories or look at Chapters 7 and 8).

Chapter 6

American sociology and the interactive self

MIKE KEATING

Would anyone notice if you suddenly disappeared in a puff of smoke? Who would be most affected by your spontaneous departure and how long would you be cherished in their memory? If your grandad had died before he met your grandma, or your mum had not shown up for the date with the man who became your dad or even if they had met but used a contraceptive on the day you were conceived, you would not be here, now, reading this. On a grander scale, if Hitler had died of his injuries in the First World War would the Second World War have broken out in 1939 and would England have won the World Cup in 1966 if Jimmy Greaves had played instead of Geoff Hurst?

Whether we are playing the game of 'what if?' in regard to personal biography or historical consequences, the general issue is the same; do individuals make a difference? Do they make decisions which have an impact on themselves and others and do they have a significant part to play in the drama of social life? Conventionally, sociology has had little time for perspectives which allocate much attention to individual action; what individual people say, think and do are largely irrelevant to a discipline which emphasises social structures and processes. As Tom Burns reminds us: 'Sociology began as virtually a resistance movement against the trend towards individualism which set in near the very end of the eighteenth century' (Burns 1992: 20).

The attention of social researchers may have shifted to include the 'attitudes, opinions, beliefs, and behaviour of individuals', but the underlying difference between a sociological perspective and a psychological one is that the former places individual perception and action within the context of social history rather than emphasising differences of personality. According to the more deterministic European theories of Marx and Durkheim, individuals are part of some great historical project of modernity; a grand plan in which their ideas and activities as individuals are of little account. More recently, structuralist writers have celebrated the 'death of the subject' altogether and dismissed interest in the personal as a form of 'psychological reductionism' inspired by an ideological obsession with individualism.

In America, however, the roots of sociology are firmly embedded in a fascination with individual behaviour. Not only are individuals the active ingredients at the point of social interaction but society is seen as 'emergent' from this interaction between individuals as they go about the business of their everyday lives. The perspectives of symbolic interactionism and ethnomethodology have given American sociology a distinctly individualistic flavour which contrasts sharply with the dominant traditions in European sociology and with the structural functionalism of Talcott Parsons. With the rekindling of interest in social action theories in the 1960s, Alan Dawe argued that the guiding principles and focus of these ideas are so different in nature from those which characterise the traditional obsession with social system, order and function that social action theories must be seen as a distinctly different type of sociology altogether. In an article challengingly entitled 'The Two Sociologies' he summarises the position clearly:

> There are then, two sociologies: a sociology of social system and a sociology of social action. They are grounded in the diametrically opposed concerns with two central problems, those of order and control. And, at every level, they are in conflict. They posit antithetical views of human nature, of society and of the relationship between the social and the individual. The first asserts the paramount necessity, for the societal and individual well-being, of external constraint; hence the notion of a social system ontologically and methodologically prior to its participants. The notion of the second is that of autonomous man, able to realise his full potential and to create a truly human social order only when freed from external constraint. Society is thus the creation of its members; the product of their construction of meaning, and of the action and relationships through which they attempt to impose that meaning on their historical situations.
>
> (Alan Dawe 1970)

It often seems as though this shift of sociological attention towards what Middleton has called 'the preoccupation with identity' (1997: 111) is a recent phenomenon in social theory which takes its impetus from the limitations of structural and deterministic ideas and the 'oversocialised concept of self' found within them. Despite the impression given by sociology textbooks which conventionally promote this view, in American sociology at least, the reverse is true; the dominant early tradition, as exemplified by the Chicago School, was rooted in an approach which was fundamentally individualistic in outlook. Even though it is called a school, the sociology department at Chicago was not founded upon a unified body of knowledge but was in essence a collection of individuals brought together by a shared interest in research and the theoretical ideas of George Simmel. There were other schools such as the more empiricist Iowa School founded by Manford Khun, and there were writers such as Charles Cooley at Michigan who contributed to the social action approach, but it is primarily the contributions of Chicagoans from Robert Park to Erving Goffman who provide the backdrop to the interactionist approach. Because of the diversity of interests of those involved and the lack of a unifying methodology or theory, Rock (1979) has described symbolic interactionism as 'peculiarly resistant to thematic summary' because those writers who are categorised as social action theorists or symbolic interactionists are more concerned with 'the difficulties which are involved in describing human affairs' than the task of producing some overarching theory of society. Their tradition is an odd one which 'shunned the major etiquette of academic writing' and represents a 'denial of the philosophical traditions which gave birth to . . . sociology'. This closeness to the everyday world and the injunction to students to get their hands dirty by observing it produced an eclectic array of insights into the lives of the poor, the deviant and the underprivileged. However, this popular and accessible quality has led to its neglect in an academic environment in which sociology attempts to prove its academic worth as a discipline through its representation of itself as 'a form of high mystery' accessible to the initiated only. By rejecting the idea that analytical social theory can reveal the ultimate workings of society hidden from the blinkered gaze of the ordinary individual, the social interactionists' emphasis upon 'the limited sections of visible social life' open them up to the charge that they are not social theorists at all:

> [Symbolic interactionism] pretends neither to absolute truth nor to an exhaustive interpretation of society. It is unusual in its acceptance of uncertainty and modest scope. Instead of constructing great edifices of formal thought, it has produced a mosaic of minor ethnographic studies. Instead of treating the world as a resource for theory, theory has been made subordinate to particular and concrete problems. Interactionism does not offer a definitive ontology, but merely stresses the difficulties which are involved in describing human affairs.
>
> (Rock 1979: 2)

To make matters worse, the social action approach derives its intellectual stimulation from a range of theoretical and methodological approaches which are confusing and contradictory; the formalism of Simmel, the pragmatism of Dewey, the behaviourism of Watson and the ethnographic methods of anthropology are mangled together in a paradigm which should tear itself apart. For theoretical purists and examination-driven students alike, the refusal of social action theory to conform to the neat pigeon-holes of sociological classification causes problems but it does not permit us to ignore what is being said. Rock agrees that the 'discontinuities and erratic shifts of style and content' merely give symbolic interactionism the appearance of 'a chain of loosely connected sociologies which have straggled together over time', but the implications of these ideas for social theory have been significant even if the perspective is considered by some to be antitheoretical, incoherent or even hopelessly psychological in nature.

Consequently, despite the historical perception that it has been treated as 'peripheral to the main sociological enterprise', symbolic interactionism is not only fundamental to the foundation of American sociology but over time has seen its oral tradition and hands-on approach to everyday life formalised and transplanted into the mainstream, where it is taught in sociology classes, written about in theory books and assessed in examinations. In particular areas of study such as deviance, medicine and education it has achieved a 'colonialist role'; for instance, no social worker, nurse or teacher can be unleashed upon the world today without some grasp of labelling theory and its impact upon 'the self'.

In this chapter we examine the ideas from philosophy, sociology and psychology which had a direct influence on the development of symbolic interactionism in America at the beginning of the twentieth century. In this early period, 'the story of the founding of the Chicago School is to a large extent the story of the beginnings of sociology in the United States' (Ritzer 1994: 67).

THE FORMALISM OF GEORG SIMMEL

Despite being one of the most popular public lecturers in Berlin, a prolific writer and a close friend of Max Weber, George Simmel was the most neglected of the early European sociologists on his own soil but enjoys the reputation of being the founding father of American sociology where his unsystematic and varied style is not only well suited to the fragmented approach of the early social action theorists but also influenced the functionalist Robert Merton and the conflict theorist Lewis Coser. Although Simmel's work was examined in the previous chapter (pp. 152–9), it is useful here to look at this work in relation to the development of American sociology and, specifically, symbolic interactionism.

Simmel was influenced by Kant's philosophical attack on the metaphysical notion that the essential nature of the real world could be grasped through the use of reason, and his conclusion that our knowledge of the world around us was in essence uncertain owing to the gap which existed between the objective world as it is and our subjective attempts to make sense of it. Dating back to the early days of Greek philosophy, the idea had prevailed that there was an ultimate order to the universe which could be ascertained through rational enquiry. Later, Galileo claimed that it was possible to 'mathematise nature', and Newton unearthed the laws which made the physical world tick. The Enlightenment encouraged this optimistic belief that reason and science would reveal the true order of the real world and bring Nature to heel (see Chapter 4 for a more detailed discussion of the influence of the Enlightenment).

In this way the division between reality and our knowledge of it would be resolved; reality becomes 'knowable' and what is known becomes no less than the world as it is. Kant rejected this view of our relationship to the world and suggested that what is knowable is always a step away from ultimate reality, and what is known is not reality in its essence but an impression of it gained through experience. Reality may be constructed of 'things in themselves' (*noumena*) which relate to other things in such a way as to provide unified order, but our experience of these things and their relationships with one another are no more than subjective impressions of them (*phenomena*). The empirical basis of science which gives it its objective status relies at the end of the day in an appeal to the senses which we experience subjectively as sensations. The world we sense through sight, smell or touch is not the world as it is but an approximation of it. If you place your hand in a bowl of warm water (noumenon) you will experience the warmth of the water (phenomenon) and deduce that they are one and the same thing. But if you run your left hand under the hot tap and your right under the cold and then immerse them both in the same bowl your hands will give you two different experiences of the same thing – clearly there is a difference between the world as it is (noumenon) and our experience of it (phenomenon). In this sense, Kant argues that our experience of the world is 'synthetic' and that factual knowledge is not identical to reality but an impression of it.

The problem with such a view is that it reduces all empirical experience to a form of subjectivism and renders scientific knowledge uncertain if not impossible. Kant attempted to avoid this by arguing that our knowledge of the world was more than a series of invalid and unrelated impressions. The objects of knowledge may be 'synthetic' phenomena but the way we organise and understand these experiences is rational according to basic rules which are universal facets of the human mind – this type of knowledge he called 'analytic' and, because it did not rely upon facts (empirical experience) it is referred to as 'a priori knowledge' (i.e. before the fact). If the external world can be envisaged as an infinite range of potential experiences, we can identify these external events as the content of knowledge which must be distinguished from the sense which the mind makes of it according to the a priori or analytic knowledge which it brings to these experiences – this knowledge imposes form upon the content of raw experience. The manner in which we perceive, conceive and understand events is not determined by the external events themselves but by conceptual forms such as space, time, quantity, causality and so on.

The impact of such ideas upon sociology can be seen in the emergence of phenomenology and the work of writers such as Weber and Schutz who resisted the positivist tendencies of Comte, Durkheim and Marx and their attempts to contain social reality within grand theoretical schemes. Rock links this general argument to the symbolic interactionist perspective:

> So vast and intricate is social life that it dwarfs any attempt to encompass it . . . No sociological understanding can attain a state of finality and closure. Because the real can never be wholly known, there is a most profound difference between a description and what is described. All that may be accomplished is a cautious reconstruction by means of

intellectual categories that enhance understanding. Those categories are constrained or remain part of an imaginative contrivance only; they are not the same as the entities they purport to examine; neither do they enjoy an existence outside the mind of the employer. The assembling of a system of concepts may reinforce a sociologist's grasp, but it neither reflects nor encapsulates the real world . . . The lack of fit between model and the modelled cannot be repaired by tinkering; no amount of attention, embellishment or elaboration can transform the description into its object . . . [Kant's argument] came to be seen as the most formidable and destructive barrier to any scheme for the total comprehension of life. The entire development of sociology may be presented as a prolonged response to the questions set by Kant's depiction of the connection between matter and mind. Symbolic interactionism can become intelligible only within the environment of uncertainties that was created by Kant.

(Rock 1979: 30–2)

This connection between Kant's critique of scientific reason and sociology is nowhere more obvious than in the work of Georg Simmel who argued that despite its appearance as an objective and external structure, social reality is an artificial creation with no more substance to it than that which we lend it through our thoughts and actions.

There is no solid social order, no hidden hand shaping it and no set of social laws holding it together. In what can be seen as a direct attack upon Durkheim's notion of 'social facts' and Marx's theory of 'historical materialism', Simmel argued that social phenomena (groups, institutions, structures) are, in Rock's terms, 'synthetic creations' and have no more substance than that which we give them; society exists only so long as we breathe life into it. If there is such a thing as society, it exists in our consciousness of it and hangs together as an orderly structure only so long as people share this consciousness and act upon assumptions implicit in it. This view and its implications for mainstream sociology are made clear in Rock's summary of Simmel's position:

All phenomena are artificial and, in the sense that they could be otherwise, they are also arbitrary. They are neither invented nor discovered, but produced. Society and its components are ongoing accomplishments, they are in a state of continual production as their members actively impose order on the world. They have no reality outside that accomplishment. Society is made possible by a process of consciousness which bestows structure on otherwise incoherent happenings and things. That consciousness exists in the individuals who make up society, it is the prerequisite of social life . . . Men produce society in their interactions with each other. Such production flows out of conflict, intimacy, co-operation, struggle and competition. It is an endlessly fluid process which cannot be portrayed as a structure or a simple system. It consists of the myriad exchanges between men, not the fixed, autonomous supra personal entities which some sociologists have claimed are ontologically superior to men.

(Rock 1979: 37)

It is Simmel's rejection of macro-sociological and deterministic explanations which attracted American sociologists, and particularly his emphasis upon the role of the active individual in the creation of society. This alternative to the schemes of Marx and Durkheim is not atomised chaos but an emergent social order which is constructed out of the 'routine social encounters' of people engaged in the interactions (Simmel called them 'associations') of everyday life. As McHugh points out, this is simply another view of social reality rather than a rejection of it; by providing answers 'from the ground up rather than from the top down' (McHugh 1968: 8), we see social interaction as 'a pulsating web of relations whose interplay produces order and change' (Rock 1979: 38). The object of study remains the same but the instrument of study is a microscope rather than a telescope.

If we consider the range of associations and events open to any member of society as the 'incoherent happenings and things' referred to above, these are best thought of as the content of social life upon which people have to impose form in order to make sense of the world. In other words, the opportunities for association available to people throughout their lives are vast and occur in a range of social settings (such as peer group, family, school, politics, work, crime and warfare), but these very different types of association are characterised by a limited number of forms which emerge in all aspects of social life across all societies. As Ritzer (1992) points out, Simmel was concerned 'to allow these forms to flow from social reality' and to avoid 'the ramification of a theoretical scheme' which is found in functionalism. In this way Simmel hoped to 'impose some order on the bewildering world of social reality'. Whether we are concerned with the worlds of business or crime, religion or schooling or the activities of individuals in small groups, we will notice that certain types of social character emerge (the poor, the miser, the stranger, the aristocrat, for instance) but the associations between these characters reveal the range of social forms which permeate all social life. These forms include superordination/subordination, cooperation/conflict, intimacy and secrecy and it is the task of the sociologist to map these general forms on to the potential chaos of social activity to show how people go about the business of making sense of everyday life. Running a business is not the same as being a mafia boss or the headteacher of a comprehensive school, but many of the social forms identified by Simmel could be seen to emerge in these different enterprises; the content may be unique but the strategies for dealing with it are limited.

Discussion question

Under each social form give an example of how each actor might engage in that form of association.

	Domination	Subordination	Cooperation	Conflict	Secrecy
Mafia boss					
Entrepreneur					
Headteacher					

Although Rock has argued that 'the exact scope and nature of Simmel's influence is highly problematic', it is clear that Simmel had a significant impact in the development of American sociology. The focus on individual interaction, the rejection of reified models of social structure and an emphasis on the importance of individual consciousness in the construction of social reality find echoes in the work of Park, Blumer and Goffman, while his work on social forms bears a similarity with Weber's work on ideal types, which also has a bearing on the development of American sociology.

THE PRAGMATISM OF WILLIAM JAMES AND JOHN DEWEY

While Simmel placed much emphasis upon the means by which the conscious subject and the sociologist make sense of the world by imposing intellectual form upon it, this was taken further by American pragmatists who argued that social reality is nothing more than our consciousness of it and the social consequences of decisions made upon this consciousness. In this sense, the distinction between the objective 'world out there' and our subjective attempts to understand it disappears; the starting point becomes reality as we perceive it and the way in which this reality is shaped and changed by such perceptions.

Unfortunately for the grand theorists who seek to reveal the 'high mysteries' of social life, the answers are not to be found in abstract models of society but in the rational actions of ordinary people. In pragmatism the emphasis shifts to everyday experience and the instrumental means by which social actors turn situations and resources to their own advantage through a rational comparison of means, ends and possible consequences. This focus upon the point of view of the actor as the starting point for understanding social behaviour represents another assault upon the positivist belief in an external social reality and replaces the idea of a fixed social structure with a fluid notion of society as the active creation of individuals as they interact with one another in pursuit of survival and success.

To many, this utilitarian approach to human nature and social action hardly counts as philosophy at all. The major questions of truth, beauty, reason and morality are important only in so far as they can be used to achieve the ends which individuals define as relevant to their chances of success. Truth is not some holy grail to be quested after by crusty academics but a quality which is relative to the needs and perceptions of ordinary people in the struggle to survive. This position was summarised in Charles Pierce's 'pragmatic rule' where he suggested that truth can be reduced to the meaning something has for an individual in so far as it is useful. The attraction of such a practical and instrumental approach to social life in a new and rapidly changing America at the turn of the twentieth century is easy to imagine but it is also not surprising that it was dismissed as 'the philosophy of the business man' (Martindale 1960: 297). Although a crucial influence in early American sociology, the two figures most associated with its development were a psychologist and an educational philosopher.

William James (1842–1910) turned to philosophy following the publication of his *Principles of Psychology* in 1890 in which he had argued that intelligence was an instrument used by people in the evolutionary struggle for survival. From this he developed the pragmatist position that ideas and actions derive their meaning from their consequences; no hypothesis can be rejected 'if consequences useful to life flow from it' and the usefulness of something (and therefore its meaning) is determined by the goals of the individuals concerned. This instrumentalist approach to knowledge and truth can be applied to economics ('What is good is what is good for business') and to Machiavellian notions of politics, but it can also be seen in the sociological work of Goffman whose view of social action stressed the successful management of impressions for the survival of the self.

James's exploration of the existence of consciousness also led him to discuss notions of the self and self-consciousness in a manner which clearly anticipates later developments in social psychology or symbolic interaction. In this discussion James distinguished between 'pure ego' (the 'I') and the 'empirical self' (the 'me') which is further divided into the 'material self', the 'spiritual self' and the 'social self'. In this system of classification his description of the 'social self' shows how closely his ideas prepared the ground for the later work of Cooley, Mead and Goffman:

> We are not only gregarious animals, liking to be in sight of our fellows, but we have an innate propensity to get ourselves noticed, and noticed favourably, by our kind . . . Properly speaking, a man has as many social selves as there are individuals who recognise him and carry an image of him in their mind. To wound any one of these his images is to wound him. But as the individuals who carry the images fall naturally into classes, we may practically say that he has as many different social selves as there are distinct groups of persons about whose opinion he cares. He generally shows a different side of himself to each of these different groups. Many a youth who is demure enough before his parents and teachers, swears and swaggers like a pirate among his 'tough' young friends. We do not show ourselves to our children as to our club companions, to our customers as to the labourers we employ, to our own masters and employers as to our intimate friends. From this there results what practically is a division of the man into several selves, and this may be a discordant splitting, as where one is afraid to let one set of his acquaintances know him as he is elsewhere, or it may be a perfectly harmonious division of labour, as where one tender to his children is stern to the soldiers or prisoners under his command.
>
> (James 1890, in Lemert 1993: 173)

John Dewey (1859–1952) was a philosopher primarily remembered for his contribution to educational theory and practice whose ideas influenced educational reforms at home and abroad. He was based for some time at the University of Chicago and plays an important part in our story because he recruited George Herbert Mead to the department of philosophy in 1894 where his courses in social psychology were to have such an impact on the development of American sociology in the next century. Strongly influenced by the ideas of Hegel and James, Dewey pursued the idea that the distinctions between subjective mind and objective matter were unhelpful and that instead of being alienated from the objective world, the individual was actively involved in creating it; individual and society evolve together as part of an ongoing dialectical process of social regeneration. Individual actions are not the automatic outcomes of biological instinct or social conditioning (see next section) but are best seen as 'problem-solving processes' which transform the world about us. Once again the unified structure of reality and our certainties about it become replaced by a fluid and changing set of processes in which knowledge is uncertain and contingent upon action:

> Practical experience and action become a multifaceted entity, synonymous with existence, the objects of knowledge and nature itself. Knowledge as an experiential process had radically different implications from knowledge imagined to be a mirroring of some independent reality or an incision into an unchanging universe . . . Reality shifts as men build it up in their transactions with nature and with one another. It shifts as their problems and vantage points change. Indeed, there is no one reality but a pluralistic universe in which perspectives jar or become amassed. The result is an indeterminacy, an abandonment of the quest for the phantom of certainty and its usurpation by an acknowledgement of openness.
>
> (Rock 1979: 70)

The ability of individuals to interpret the world, their freedom to define it and the power to shape it through praxis are strong themes in Dewey's work. The mind is not simply a mechanistic device for the production of responses; it is a self-conscious and reflexive process capable of classification, imagination and judgement. This ability to reflect and transform refers not only to the world around us but, again, to our notion of self. The identity of the individual is not fixed but fluid; like thought itself, the individual's self is best conceived of as a process. There are strong links here with Hughes's idea of moral career and Mead's view of the social self which we look at later. Indeed, Dewey's significance for American sociology may be more important than his contribution to the philosophy of education, and some writers have argued that he was more influential in the development of symbolic interactionism than Mead himself (see Ritzer 1992: 328).

BEHAVIOURISM

Behaviourism is primarily a branch of psychology which takes the individual as the unit of analysis and treats human and animal behaviour in much the same way. Heavily influenced by positivism, it argues that the only knowledge is empirical knowledge and that the only behaviour we can speak about scientifically is that which can be observed and measured. Behaviour is seen as a conditioned response to external stimuli as exemplified in Pavlov's work with dogs, Skinner's experiments with rats and Watson's attempt to transfer these insights to the techniques of child-rearing. At first glance there seems to be no point of contact between this mechanistic view of human behaviour and the introspective descriptions of consciousness referred to earlier; however, the behaviourists were interested in social interaction (in social situations one individual acts as the stimulus for another's response) and how particular interactive responses appear to be automatic and predictable. As American sociologists are drawn to examine the microscopic aspects of social life it is easy to see how their empirical interest in patterns, games and rituals could produce a descriptive account of social behaviour which ran the risk of losing sight of consciousness altogether.

While interactionists such as Blumer clearly resist this tendency, Mead (who taught Watson at Chicago) actually preferred to be known as a 'social behaviourist'. Although he rejected the 'radical behaviourism' of Watson because it treated human beings as passive objects rather than as active subjects, there is a strong tendency in Mead which assumes that social behaviour is shaped by social factors. The behaviourist tendency was not shared by other members of the Chicago School; writers such as Blumer were keen to resist reductionist and determinist influences wherever they came from:

> Blumer clearly saw symbolic interactionism as embattled on two fronts. On the one side were the behaviourists, who saw human behaviour as caused by external stimuli. On the other side were those who adopted a sociologistic perspective and saw behaviour as caused by the larger culture and the structure of society. Blumer was troubled by both perspectives largely because they saw action as mechanistically caused by external factors rather than as being created by people.
>
> (Ritzer 1994: 100)

THE CHICAGO SCHOOL

As the nineteenth century drew to a close, American society found itself undergoing continual change. Not only was it rapidly transforming itself into an industrial and urban giant, it was also characterised by immigration from Europe and migration from within, as people left rural communities in search of fortune in the new cities of the north. Among these migrants were 'provincial intellectuals' attracted to the posts being offered at the new city universities and by the new questions being posed by the rapid transformation of society, including the problem of national unity for a fledgling democracy forged out of the melting pot of American history.

> There was little precedence for building a highly industrialised and urbanised nation state on the basis of mass, heterogeneous immigration. There was even less precedence for building national unity on such a base through democratic means. The historical precedents for democratically directed change were neither numerous nor, from the standpoint of many American intellectuals, very encouraging. The great influx of peasants into the United States aroused, among both the well-off and the educated, much fear of social (if not class) war and mob rule . . . From the standpoint of progressive reformers, the great problem was the growth of what they saw as special interests; how national cohesion could be developed in the face of increasingly powerful and monopolistic business interests, a growing and sometimes militant labour movement, and the increasing size and organisation of immigrant, ethnic groups.
>
> (Fisher and Straus 1979: 461–2)

Cities like Chicago were seen as naturally evolving laboratories for the incubation of such problems, and those who sponsored the new university there believed that part of its function was to provide answers to these questions and to recruit and train the national and regional elites who would manage the solutions. This practical relationship between the academic and the political worlds provides the impetus for the philosophical pragmatism which we have already identified as one of the intellectual strands to influence Chicago-based sociology.

The founding of the first graduate sociology department in the world by Albion Small in 1892 was to have a dramatic impact on the development of American sociology. Small used his position as the first head of the first graduate school in sociology to shape the discipline. He co-authored the first sociology textbook in 1894 and founded the *American Journal of Sociology* the following year which he used as a vehicle for his numerous translations of Simmel. In 1904 he was instrumental in persuading Weber to visit America, and in 1905 co-founded the American Sociological Society. Under his chairmanship the department at Chicago attracted and trained the first graduates in sociology (some of whom went on to establish sociology at other universities) and recruited members of staff such as W.I. Thomas and Robert Park (a student of Simmel's). While Thomas was forced out of the university under a cloud of scandal, Park continued the administrative work of Small in keeping Chicago at the forefront of American sociology.

Fisher and Straus (1979) distinguish two trends at the Chicago department of sociology in the first half of the twentieth century: the 'Median interactionism' which influenced theoretical developments in social psychology, and the 'Chicago-style sociology' of researchers like Thomas and Park. Although these two had some influence on theoretical ideas, they are more closely associated with the empirical research techniques which would reveal the social perspectives of their subjects. In his study of Polish immigrants (Thomas and Znaniecki 1927), Thomas preferred a life history approach using letters and diaries as his data. Park, on the other hand, was a trained journalist who favoured a form of participant observation he called 'scientific reporting'. This ethnographic tradition is closely associated with the Chicago School, and students who trained there were far more likely to spend their time making observations on the streets of Chicago than writing essays in the university library.

For a variety of reasons the stranglehold of the Chicago School on American sociology began to weaken from the 1930s onwards. The 'early giants' (Small, Park, Thomas and Mead) passed on (expired, retired or fired) at a time when sociology was undergoing a shift towards more statistical research methods and theoretical models which emphasised the structure and functions of social institutions. Rival university departments of the East Coast, particularly at Harvard, began to challenge the dominance of the Chicago School both intellectually and politically. They founded their own professional body (the Eastern Sociological Society) in 1930, ousted the Chicagoan secretary of the American Sociology Society five years later and insisted that an independent journal (the *American Sociological Review*) become its official mouthpiece. In 1937, Parsons published *The Structure of Social Action* and the paradigm shift in American social theory was well under way (see Ritzer 1994: 79–85 and Coser 1979: 311–18).

For the next twenty years American sociology is closely associated with the number-crunching of researchers, such as Lazarsfeld, and the structural function-alism of Parsons – derided by C.W. Mills (1970) as 'abstracted empiricism' and 'grand theory' respectively (see p. 81 above). During that period the ethnographic research methods and philosophical pragmatism of the Chicago School were kept alive by Everett Hughes and Herbert Blumer and, in what some have referred to as the Second Chicago School, there was a postwar revival which is best represented by the work of two promising graduates: Erving Goffman and Howard Becker. By 1952, however, both Blumer and Goffman had moved to Berkeley (symbolic of yet another paradigm shift; this time to the universities of the West Coast) and Becker had taken a post at Northwestern University. The second coming of Chicago soci-ology had fizzled out.

For a perspective in sociological theory which is dutifully covered in all modern textbooks as a theory it is interesting to note that its founders were not sociologists and that what they were founding was not a theoretical school. Most of the early writers in this tradition were a combination of philosophers, psychologists and anthropologists with the head during its most significant period a trained journ-alist. If anything, the Chicago School is acknowledged more for its contribution to research than to theory. For a perspective so popularly regarded as a social theory it is remarkably non-sociological and atheoretical. As Craib has remarked: 'Symbolic interactionism . . . is a theory of persons, of social action, which in its most distinct form does not attempt to become also a theory of society' (1984: 79).

In order to help get some grasp on this disparate 'theory of persons', we turn our attention to the key contributors, some of whom have been referred to in passing in this brief history of the Chicago School.

W.I. THOMAS (1863–1947)

Thomas's research interests led him to examine the interplay between the con-sciousness of the individual and the objective conditions of culture and social life. Whether he is analysing the impact of disorganisation upon the personality of the Polish immigrant (1927) or the problems of adjustment facing delinquent girls (1923), his research is inspired by the theoretical proposition that there is 'always a rivalry between the spontaneous definitions of the situation made by the member of an organised society and the definitions which his society has provided for him' (quoted in Martindale 1960: 348). Despite his important contributions to socio-logical research Thomas is remembered primarily for his assertion that 'If men define situations as real they are real in their consequences'.

When Thomas made this famous remark he did not intend it to mean that life is simply what people imagine it to be or even that we can transform our lives through willpower. If he had, it would be quite easy to point to the fact that making the statement that 'pigs can fly' does not empower them with flight any more than the belief that the world is flat led anyone who believed it to fall off the edge the first time they set sail. Rather he is asking us to be aware of the largely unintended consequences of putting our beliefs into action and the impact that these actions will have upon our relationships with others and the social construction of reality.

If the assertion that pigs can indeed fly became widely believed then farmers and airline pilots would alter their work routines dramatically, but this belief in itself would not create one authentic case of aerial porker power. It would lead, however, to changes in our relationships with pigs, the sky and one another. In a more serious vein, the persecution of 'witches' in the sixteenth and seventeenth centuries and the genocide practised by Nazis in the pursuit of the Final Solution in the twentieth century are no less real simply because the ideologies on which they were founded are regarded by most of us as absurd. If enough people are prepared to put into effect the promptings of such ideas, they create and sustain a reality which fulfils the deranged prophesies of the original belief system.

In ethnographic research and symbolic interactionism, the importance of the individual's definition of the situation cannot be overestimated. By insisting on the primacy of the subjective orientation of the actor it emphasises the significance of the individual within social action. Individual actors may have roles to play and a script to follow but they also bring to bear upon social interaction their own preconceptions of what the social situation is all about. In this sense social action is more than a predictable response scripted by the normative order which has programmed us all; rather it is a conscious reaction to circumstances which involve the attempts by individuals to determine their own agendas and impose their definitions on others. Such a view undermines mechanical views of social action and problematises aspects of social behaviour which are rarely questioned:

> Men-on-the-street create their own versions of their affairs, and these versions exert influence; because they are problematic, we cannot take them for granted in accounting for social action.
>
> (McHugh 1968: 132)

This understanding is echoed in Schutz's idea of 'multiple realities' and the need to examine the 'taken for granted' assumptions which people use to construct their version of events. It is also closely related to Becker's view that deviant behaviour is created by our definition of it as such. Both of these ideas are mentioned later in this chapter.

In this jumble of 'multiple realities', social order is still possible although it may not be as orderly as we would like. We all have our own ideas about how we define situations, but so does everyone else; consequently the outcome is never certain. The results of our attempts to define situations as real may turn out very differently from our expectations but they are no less real all the same.

The idea that intended actions may have objective consequences which are unexpected was developed by Merton in his work on manifest and latent functions. Although known as a functionalist, Merton refers directly to Thomas and Znaniecki's research into Polish cooperatives to support his thesis that 'categories of subjective disposition' such as intention have 'generally unrecognized but objective functional consequences' (Merton 1967, quoted in Lemert 1993: 329).

CHARLES COOLEY (1864–1929)

When we look at the story of social action theory and its almost synonymous development alongside the Chicago School, the name of Charles Cooley is always mentioned. One of the few key writers in this tradition not based at Chicago University, Charles Cooley overshadows W.I. Thomas in the introduction of the insights of social psychology into sociological discourse. Cooley was an academic theorist who did not get his hands dirty with the kind of social research popular at Chicago; instead he worked with Mead before he left Michigan to team up with Dewey at Chicago, and his writings show a similar interest in theorising the self. Instead of talking in deterministic terms about social forces shaping individuals, Cooley was more interested to explore the ways in which conscious individuals interact with self and others to build up a picture of society and their place within it. In order to do this, Cooley argued we had to take a psychological stance, but he rejected the teachings of behaviourist psychology which emphasised stimulus–response models of human behaviour. To Cooley, the complex behaviour of the individual could not be reduced to the physiological principles of conditioning theory; the salivation patterns of dogs in response to the ringing of bells may be appropriate to the training of a dog but Cooley believed that human consciousness was more than the sum of pleasant and painful experiences. The individual being developed a consciousness which was capable of reflection, introspection and imagination, and the key to any individual's personal development was the concept of the looking-glass self. By this Cooley meant that we construct our view of who we are through a continuous process of interaction with others in which we see ourselves reflected in their responses:

> As we see our face, figure and dress in the glass, and are interested in them because they are ours, and pleased or otherwise with them according as they do or do not answer to what we should like them to be; so in the imagination we perceive in another's mind some thought of our appearance, manners, aims, deeds, character, friends, and so on, and are variously affected by it.
>
> (Cooley 1902, quoted in Lemert 1993: 204–5)

Cooley's looking-glass analogy has been criticised for suggesting a rather rigid and automated view of the self as a mere reflection of the reactions of others, but this misses the role of the imagination in the operation of the looking glass self. Just as we can never know what it is like to be someone else so it is not possible either to know how we appear to others. The limits to such self-knowledge are alluded to in Bob Dylan's song *Positively 4th Street* which is an attack on two-faced friendship practised by pragmatists who 'just want to be on the side that's winning'. In the closing verses Dylan points to the impossibility of knowing how we appear to others and the shock that such a revelation might hold:

> I wish that for just one time
> You could stand inside my shoes
> And just for that one moment
> I could be you
>
> Yes I wish that for just one time
> You could stand inside my shoes
> You'd know what a drag it is
> To see you
>
> (Bob Dylan 1964)

Cooley resolved this problem by insisting that the closest we can come to knowing ourselves through social interaction is by interpreting the clues of expression and body language which our friends, enemies and acquaintances give out in response to our presence. As Goffman was later to point out, this is more than simply one-way traffic; it is a dynamic process in which the presentation of the self involves impression management and the prospect of manipulating the perceptions and responses of others (see pp. 200–2).

In addressing the issue of social expectation, Cooley is really getting at the way in which society achieves integration of its members through the processes of socialisation but from an individualistic perspective. In this he distinguished between the face-to-face or personal aspects of socialisation which occur within primary groups such as family or friends and those which take place on a broader stage where secondary groups like teachers and workmates indicate the general rules to follow and bring us into contact with wider social expectations. A century after first developing these concepts we still find them useful in helping us to understand the different levels on which social integration takes place and the importance of interpersonal interaction in the formal processes of social conformity.

Discussion questions

List the primary and secondary groups that you are or have been a part of.

1 At which stages in your life have the particular groups been most important?

2 Which have the biggest influence on your behaviour now?

GEORGE HERBERT MEAD (1863–1931)

Mead is a pivotal figure in the development of American sociology in terms of both his ideas and his personal contact with other thinkers in the pragmatic tradition. After breaking away from the narrow-minded ideas of his strongly puritanical family, Mead pursued his studies at Harvard where he met William James. While James turned away from psychology to study philosophy, Mead moved in an opposite direction and went to Germany in 1888 to study psychology. At the University of Berlin he was influenced by Dilthey's emphasis on interpretive methods and Wundt's ideas on the significance of 'gesture'. On his return to America, Mead taught at Michigan where he met Cooley and Dewey; and when the latter was made head of philosophy at Chicago he insisted that Mead join him as an assistant professor. The chance to become actively involved in social ideas and reform appealed to Mead and he remained at Chicago for the next 40 years. A brilliant lecturer who found difficulty in putting pen to paper, Mead's ideas only achieved a wider audience when his students' lecture notes were published after his death. One of his best known students was Herbert Blumer, who coined the term 'symbolic interactionism'.

Mead's influence is widespread and he is associated with the development of social behaviourism, phenomenology and a sociology of knowledge grounded in social psychology. He is best known, though, for his theorising of the self within the context of symbolic communication between individuals and for the impact of these ideas on symbolic interactionism. While animals instinctively express themselves through gestures and automatically react to such gestures with programmed responses, human beings are a conscious species with a highly developed ability to interpret and communicate meaning. In Mead's view, the ability of humans to communicate meaning through symbolic gestures and especially through language is what distinguishes the species from other animals and renders the study of human behaviour so rich and problematic. As they interact with others, human beings are involved in a process of giving and responding to gestures which convey meaning. Their interpretation of these meanings for the self and others forms the basis of action in the sense that individuals make conscious decisions over appropriate action which take into account their own orientation, the gestures of others and the situations within which they find themselves.

Discussion questions

A dogfight is the predictable outcome following a serial display of aggressive gestures (sniffing, growling, snarling and so on); and as Mead says 'the act of each dog becomes the stimulus to the other dog for his response'. The fight usually ends when one of the dogs signifies submission (running away, rolling on its back, yelping). Humans also engage in ritual gestures which may or may not end in violence but the outcome depends upon an assessment of others' gestures and the context within which such posturing takes place.

1 If you were on the receiving end of an aggressive gesture (verbal or physical), how would your response be influenced by:
   (a) your own orientation,
   (b) the nature of the gesture,
   (c) your interpretation of the gesture,
   (d) the situational factors involved?

2 What responses on your part would escalate the situation?

3 What might help to avoid a fight?

By highlighting the role of significant symbols in the communication of meaning and the reflexive nature of the conscious individual in decision-making, Mead distances himself from the crude behaviourism of his day which focused exclusively on observable behaviour and denied the subjective aspects of social action. He points us towards a more creative and proactive model of behaviour which celebrates the hidden activity of the mind and its power to shape social life. This indication of an inner reality operates on the conscious level only; Mead had no time for Freudian ideas of the power of the unconscious. Instead he shared with Cooley the idea that our notions of identity and social reality are socially constructed out of interaction with others.

However, Mead rejected Cooley's 'excessively mentalistic and introspective views of the social nature of the self' (Coser 1979: 308). While Cooley's subjectivism could lead to a psychologistical position in which mind and self become trapped within the individual's subjective experience, Mead's social behaviourism stressed the social factors implicit in identity formation. Despite the fact that individuals have different experiences and perceptions of the world and develop different definitions of their situation, their 'multiple realities' are linked by shared meaning and significant gestures which act as a bridge. Verbal language is the most powerful form of significant gesture and in his view formed the basis of self, social interaction and culture. While gestures of animals and sometimes humans are simply involuntary expressions of emotion, language is the conscious communication of meaning via gestures which are intended to elicit a response. Language has the power to transform events through the giving and taking of meaning. Mead may have called himself a social behaviourist but this emphasis on language clearly indicates a world in which conscious individuals make choices and in which options have consequences which have to be taken into account.

Drawing on his ideas of a creative and conscious self and the previous theories of self put forward by James and Cooley, Mead developed his own theory of the self which incorporated biological fact, psychological constructs and social experience. The biological core of the self depends on the physiological apparatus (such as the brain and central nervous system) to apprehend the world through the senses. However, we develop an awareness of self which is both personal and social. In this development, the ability of the mind to distinguish between two aspects of self is crucial because, Mead argues, the human mind not only distinguishes between the psychological self and the physiological aspects of the body but also is able to treat the self as if it were an external object too. Hence we talk about our self as if it were someone else; we reflect upon its performance and even engage it in conversation – talking to yourself is not a symptom of mental disorder, it is an essentially human characteristic which we call 'thinking'. As we develop this self-reflective ability we become aware of a distinction between the subjective, spontaneous and creative 'I' and the external, objective and social 'me'. At the risk of oversimplifying the distinction, the 'I' represents that aspect of the mind which does the reflecting while the 'me' is the object of that knowledge. This constant process of self-reflection is not an hermetically sealed form of mental ping-pong; it takes place within a social environment in which the social self (the 'me') engages also in interactive exchanges of meaning with others. The development of the social self involves both the response of others and the critical assessment of the 'I':

> The 'I' is the response of the organism to the attitudes of the others; the 'me' is the organised set of attitudes of others which one himself arouses. The attitudes of the others constitute the organized 'me', and the one reacts towards that as an 'I'.
>
> (Mead 1934: 175)

In the establishment and maintenance of our identity we become aware that the social self is shaped by the expectations and reactions of those around us. In this process the self is shaped by those who are close to us (the 'significant others') and those who represent the values of the community (the 'generalised other'), but in this process Mead never lets us forget that the reflexive self has a role to play in the interpretation and negotiation of these influences and as such the 'self' is never fixed but always open to transformation and adaptation:

> The individual is continually adjusting himself in advance to the situation to which he belongs and reacting back upon it. The self is not something that exists first and then enters into a relationship with others, but is, so to speak, an eddy in the social current and so still a small part of the current.
>
> (Mead 1934: 182)

There is some disagreement over the contribution of Mead to American sociology (he was, after all, a member of Chicago University's philosophy department who gave lectures in social psychology) but he has come to be regarded as a key figure in the development of sociological thought and the growing interest in the self. Mead, then, emphasised the meaningful nature of social life and the importance of language in the processes of thinking, expression, communication and learning as well as the social construction of the self. Our everyday behaviour and the gradual formation of a recognisable identity are not expressions of a fixed personality but fluid and flexible responses to the dynamic processes of social interaction. This recognition of the influence of social phenomena on individual consciousness marks Mead out as a 'social realist' who may be distinguished from the mentalist and nominalist tendencies of Cooley and Blumer.

HERBERT BLUMER (1900–1986)

A student and follower of Mead at Chicago, Blumer coined the phrase 'symbolic interactionism' to describe the way in which individual behaviour is seen to develop through our interaction with others rather than being a mechanical response to external stimuli. Blumer went on to become president of the American Sociological Association and, although not as well known as Mead, probably played a greater part in popularising the ideas behind interpretive sociology. He had little time for grand theorising and encouraged his students to study everyday life, as it was through their ongoing interactions with one another that individuals recreate society. According to Cuff *et al.*, society may have the appearance of some huge machine, but, for Blumer, is 'nothing other than the patterns of individuals going about their lives' (1998: 132).

Sometimes these patterns are enduring and support social convention (going to church at Christmas), but on other occasions they are transient (fashion) and at other moments may challenge social order itself (riot). Rather than being fixed by social structure, individual behaviour is related to interpretation of meaning and therefore unpredictable. This idea that to some extent we are making up social life as we go along is called 'emergent action'.

> A gratuitous acceptance of the concepts of norms, values, social rules and the like should not blind the social scientist to the fact that any one of them is subtended by a process of social interaction – a process that is necessary not only for their change but equally well for their retention in a fixed form. It is the social process in group life that creates and upholds the rules, not the rules that create and uphold group life.
>
> (Blumer 1969, in Cuff *et al.* 1998: 136)

While Blumer was clearly influenced by his mentor Mead in the development of his own position, he reacts against social behaviourism and the 'realist' tendency to suggest that social order shapes consciousness. According to Ritzer, Blumer is best appreciated as a 'nominalist' who:

> conceives of the individuals themselves as existentially free agents who accept, reject, modify or otherwise define the communities norms, roles, beliefs and so forth, according to their own personal interests and the plan of the moment.
>
> (Ritzer 1992: 328)

Central to this nominalist position and Blumer's development of symbolic inter-actionism is the meaningful nature of social action. While other approaches linked behaviour to internal or external influences which could be said to determine them, Blumer insisted that people act in accordance with the meaning that objects and symbols have for them, that meanings emerge from the learning processes to be found in social interaction, and that in this process meaning is open to interpretation and therefore may be transformed. In this sense, Blumer had no time for the deterministic tendencies of psychoanalysis, behaviourist psychology or social pathology: 'these approaches grossly ignore the fact that social interaction is a formative process in its own right . . . [which involves people in] directing, checking, bending and transforming their lines of action in the light of what they encounter in the action of others' (Rock 1979: 186).

Blumer's theoretical contribution to the development of symbolic interactionism is important. However, he had little time for theorising as such, and, true to the Chicago tradition, Blumer believed that the key task for sociology was empirical research: he was a champion of participant observation as a means for getting close to the meaningful acts of those under study. To him, sociology based on the natural science model was doomed to failure because it drew a statistical veil over social action and substituted facts for first-hand knowledge. For a theorist who prioritised the meaningfulness of action it is not surprising that Blumer highlighted the importance of employing research methods which were designed to get close to the subject and to understand action from the subject's point of view. Blumer defended his preference for participant observation by attacking those who criticised it as a 'soft' option in social research:

> [Getting close to the empirical social world] is a tough job requiring a high order of careful and honest probing, creative yet disciplined imagination, resourcefulness and flexibility in study, pondering over what one is finding, and a constant readiness to test and recast one's views and images of the area . . . It is not 'soft' study merely because it does not use quantitative procedures or follow a pre-mapped scientific protocol.
>
> (Blumer, quoted in Ritzer 1994: 94)

ERVING GOFFMAN (1922–1982)

Probably the best known and most successful American sociologist, Goffman was a bestselling author in his day and his texts continue to be regarded as classics within sociology. Regarded as something of a maverick, Goffman does not fit easily into the pigeon-holes reserved for social theorists and his research is often attacked for its eclectic and unsystematic nature. However, he remains one of the few sociologists that you can read for pleasure.

Born into a Ukrainian Jewish family in Canada in 1922, Goffman dropped out of university in favour of a career with the National Film Board of Canada. There he met Denis Wrong (who was later to write a classic condemnation of deterministic sociology) and they both returned to Toronto to complete their studies. Goffman switched from chemistry to sociology and this led to the graduate school at Chicago where he studied, conducted his early research and eventually taught. At Chicago he could not avoid the influences of social anthropology, participant observation and the journalistic sociological research tradition of Robert Park. The intellectual link to this tradition was Goffman's tutor, Everett Hughes, who first coined the term 'moral career' and initiated an interest in the underdog on the principle that 'sociologists could learn as much about doctors by studying plumbers and about prostitutes by studying psychiatrists' (Burns 1992: 11). Goffman's PhD was supposed to be an anthropological account of the social structure of the island community in Shetland, but he quietly switched the emphasis to an examination of the rituals characterising the relationship between islanders and visitors from the mainland. During this period he also published papers 'Symbols of class status' (1951) and 'On cooling the mark out' (1952), both of which can be seen as precursors of his satirical style. Lemert has argued that Goffman's critical stance was a reaction to the intolerant and self-satisfied atmosphere of postwar McCarthyism and that his debunking of conformist America should be seen as part of a growing mood of social criticism which united rock and roll music, civil rights activism, the humour of Lenny Bruce and radical social comment. In this sense, Lemert refers to Goffman as 'an undercover social critic of post war society' whose sociology was 'based on the premise that world reality was fragile, changing, uncertain, vulnerable and always, always mediated' (Lemert and Branaman, 1997: xxxiv, xxxvii).

While Lemert regards Goffman as a sociologist of genius others are not so sure. Tom Burns (1992: 1–5) notes that literary critics could be fulsome in their praise of Goffman but also dismissive of the value of his overdetailed analysis of everyday social life. Not only does Goffman dwell upon the commonplace and the familiar but he does it from an individualistic stance which reduces his sociological contribution to little more than a 'sideshow'. Burns, however, argues that Goffman may write well enough to impress literary critics but that does not prevent him from being a great sociologist. It may be true that Goffman pillages the work of novelists and playwrights to illustrate his ideas, but 'whatever he read was read with a sociological eye and an eye for sociology' (Burns 1992: 4).

Even if we can agree that Goffman was a sociologist, it is almost impossible to get agreement on what kind of sociologist he was. Sociology is a discipline which agonises over defining its terms and classifying its content and, as every student of the subject knows, there are conventional pigeon-holes into which theorists must be slotted. Unfortunately, life is not quite like that and Erving Goffman is one of those square pegs that refuse to be forced into a neat hole that someone else has prepared. There are clear links to the work of Simmel and James, Mead and Blumer, but the influences of Marx, Durkheim and Spencer also appear in his work. Consequently, Burns has warned against any attempt to attach Goffman to a particular school of thought, preferring instead to identify three related themes as central to his work: the micro-sociology of social interaction, the individual self and, finally, social structure. As if to reinforce the point, Lemert and Branaman (1997) organise Goffman's contribution to social theory under four headings: the production of self, the confined self, the nature of social life, and frames and the organisation of experience. For the purposes of this brief review we simplify the task with the use of two headings: social interaction and the self, and the self and social order.

Social interaction and the self

Although Goffman was aware that people as individuals had to be placed in the context of the groups and institutions to which they belong and returned to the issue of macro-sociological influences later in his career, his early work is primarily concerned with the social interaction that occurs between individuals as they are involved in the processes which simultaneously maintain social life and confirm their own identities. In the grand order of things it may be attractive to talk of the ways in which groups, classes, institutions and organisations interact with one another, but at the level of everyday observation these abstract relationships are not evident. The point at which 'most of the world's work gets done' is that which involves the interaction of individuals and the social rituals involved in the games they play with one another as part of these daily encounters.

For this reason Goffman makes a distinction between belonging to social groups and the actual encounters which take place within them. Whether the social group is our family, school, workplace or an amorphous crowd, Goffman's attention is on the face-to-face interaction which occurs there between individuals. Such inter-action can take two forms. Firstly, unfocused interaction in which individuals are aware of the presence of others but avoid direct communication with them. We devote much time to this kind of encounter and there are strict rules attached to it which assist us in the simultaneous recognition and avoidance of others without appearing rude. Through the use of what Goffman calls 'civil inattention' we per-form rituals of politeness whereby we acknowledge the presence of someone else without upsetting them or embarrassing ourselves. If we do not indicate our aware-ness of others through eye contact, we may be seen as being shifty, arrogant or rude. On the other hand, our interest in others must not be intrusive; it is not only 'rude to stare' it may be seen as provocative ('What you looking at?'). Proper behavi-our in such encounters is therefore circumscribed by the individuals' 'right to civil inattention' and the social rules which govern the balance between normal social surveillance in public places and staring.

> Perhaps the clearest illustration both of civil inattention and of the infraction of this ruling occurs when a person takes advantage of another's not looking at him, and then finds that the object of his gaze has suddenly turned and caught the illicit looker looking. The individual caught out may then shift his gaze, often with embarrassment and a little shame, or he may carefully act as if he had merely been seen in the moment of observa-tion that is permissible, in either case we see evidence of the propriety that should have been maintained.
>
> (Goffman 1963: 87)

As we have already noted, however, 'much of the world's work gets done' through direct interaction, not by avoiding it. Goffman therefore concentrates upon the words and gestures which occur in 'focused interactions' where people effect-ively agree to sustain for a time a single focus of cognitive and visual attention, as in a conversation, a board game or a joint task sustained by a close face-to-face circle of contributions. Within such encounters, what people say and the way that they say it are vital, but the range of facial and other gestures which constitute body language are equally important for transmitting or reinforcing messages. Again, the glances people give one another may be used to initiate a face-to-face encounter or to end it, while nods and smiles are often devices for maintaining a focused encounter. There may be cultural variations in the significance of certain gestures, but all societies require their members to engage in 'face work' which is both uni-versal and social but operates through the successful engagement of individuals:

> If persons have a universal human nature, they themselves are not to be looked to for an explanation of it. One must look rather to the fact that societies everywhere, if they are to be societies, must mobilise their members as self-regulating participants in social encounters. One way of mobilising the individual for this purpose is through ritual; he is taught to be perceptive, to have feelings attached to self and self expressed through face, to have pride, honour, dignity, to have considerateness, to have tact and a certain amount of poise. These are some of the elements of behaviour which must be built into the

person if practical use is to be made of him as an interactant, and it is these elements that are referred to in part when we speak of universal human nature.

Universal human nature is not a very human thing. By acquiring it, the person becomes a kind of construct, built up not from inner psychic propensities but from moral rules that are impressed upon him from without. These rules, when followed, determine the evaluation he will make of himself and of his fellow participants in the encounter, the distribution of his feelings, and the kinds of practices he will employ to maintain a specified and obligatory kind of ritual equilibrium. The general capacity to be bound by moral rules may well belong to the individual, but the particular set of rules which transforms him into a human being derives from requirements established in the ritual organisation of social encounters.

(Goffman 1967: 45)

In this passage Goffman not only manages to provide a sociological rendition of the notion of human nature but also establishes the idea of the self as central to the maintenance of the interaction order. In his early paper 'On cooling the mark out' (1952), Goffman had already begun to look at the impact of failure on self-esteem and the techniques which are employed to deflect or dissipate such damage. The title is taken from the practice of con artists to help their victim (the 'mark') come to terms with the fact that they have been taken for a ride. Such 'repair work' allows the victim to 'save face' and get on with life. Goffman uses this analogy with reference to competitive societies such as his own where the 'win at all costs' mentality ensures a high proportion of failure. To avoid the corrosive impact of such failure upon the self-image, potential victims must be given opportunities to 'cool out' by avoiding the blame and thereby adapt to their failure. Hence a porn queen may be dubbed a 'sex therapist', an incompetent member of staff 'promoted' to a position where they can do the least damage, and a professional footballer told he is being 'rested' to avoid the humiliation of being 'dropped'.

Discussion questions

1 Why should it be embarrassing to be caught in the act of looking at a stranger?

2 What tactics do you use if you are caught?

3 What excuses might you give?

4 When students fail their exams what strategies of adaptation may be used to repair the damage done to the self by:
(a) their tutor,
(b) fellow students,
(c) themselves?

In his next major work, Goffman takes these ideas a stage further. The self is not simply a potential victim but an active agent in the dramatic performance of social roles. In *The Presentation of Self in Everyday Life*, first published in 1959, the idea of society as drama and individual behaviour as a performance is established along with the possibility that we are all confidence tricksters of some sort. Through the various social roles we are expected to perform and the situations in which they have to be acted out, the individual establishes a relatively firm identity through a process of successful negotiations with a variety of audiences. This involves the actor in more than simply fulfilling the audience's expectations of what constitutes a role; it requires a performance of the role with such poise that the presented self becomes involved in an act which Goffman calls 'impression management'.

Just as the theatre comprises its front-stage where the drama is acted out and a backstage which is concealed from view, so our lives can be seen as operating somewhere between the two. Backstage is where we rehearse the parts we play but it is also where we can relax and be more like our real selves. Hidden from the audience we are able to conceal aspects of the self which would otherwise damage the public impression. Front-stage, however, we must stick more closely to the script, attend to the details of our appearance and ensure that the necessary props are in place if the performance is to be convincing.

These theatrical analogies apply to all walks of life and to the social roles we are expected to play. One of the best examples (and probably a better analogy) is that of the restaurant where 'front-stage' everything is serene, effortless and charming but backstage resembles Basil Fawlty's kitchen. Just as that famous TV series relied for its comic tension on the disaster which would befall Fawlty Towers should the secrets of the kitchen (drunken chefs, dead guests, poisoned food) leak out into the restaurant, so the 'front regions' of our public performances (as doctors, teachers, waitresses, parents) require development of 'impression management' skills in order to confine to the 'back regions' of our social space those aspects of our lives which threaten to disrupt credible presentations of the self. Goffman borrows the following extract from Monica Dickens to illustrate the point:

> The said maid – her name was Addie, I discovered – and the two waitresses were behaving like people acting in a play. They would sweep into the kitchen as if coming off stage into the wings, with trays held high and a tense expression of hauteur still on their faces; relax for a moment in the frenzy of getting the new dishes loaded, and glide off again with faces prepared to make their next entrance. The cook and I were left like stagehands among the debris, as if having seen a glimpse of another world, we almost listened for the applause of the unseen audience.
>
> (in Goffman 1972: 124)

Discussion questions

The restaurant/kitchen illustration is both a description of dramatic performance in the real world of work but it is also intended as another analogy. The metaphors of front-stage (restaurant) and backstage (kitchen) also refer to the social spaces we inhabit.

1 What areas of your social space occupy front-stage?

2 What spaces do you regard as backstage?

3 Think of a recent encounter in which you had to switch from one to the other. How did you achieve this? Why?

A superficial interpretation of Goffman's theatrical analogy can lead to the conclusion that the presentation of the self and its successful accomplishment is a purely individualistic activity; some individuals have the personal qualities (poise, confidence, charm) and skills (verbal ability, manual dexterity, intellect) required to perform particular roles better than others. Such a reading, however, would ignore his clear references to the social aspects of such qualities and, in particular, access to the resources necessary for the achievement of successful performances. These resources (possessions, accent, attire, manners and so on) are clearly related to one's position in the status hierarchy where the opportunities for access to resources are greater for some than for others. A convincing performance is a matter not simply of defining the situation, and negotiating it but also of the availability of the support materials (props, wardrobe or teamwork) necessary to conduct the 'art work of impression management'.

> The degree to which an individual is able to sustain a respectable self image in the eyes of others depends on access to structural resources and possession of traits and attributes deemed desirable by the dominant culture . . . access to such resources varies immensely with social status. Not only does self depend on structural props associated with power and status, but . . . sustaining a viable self also depends upon possession of traits and attributes deemed by the dominant society to be requisite of full-fledged humanity.
>
> (Lemert and Branaman 1997: xiv)

In his later work on the stigmatised self (1970) and the moral career of the mental patient (1975), Goffman demonstrates that limited access to resources and power will seriously restrict the control that an individual has over the image they portray. In these writings Goffman turns his attention to the constraints which are placed upon some individuals in their struggle to assert themselves by those who have the power and resources to define who they are. This 'framing' of the experiences of the powerless by those in positions of authority and control led Goffman to examine the relationship between the self and wider society.

The self and social order

If *The Presentation of Self in Everyday Life* is a celebration of the chameleon-like power of the individual to adapt and transform his or her identity, then *Stigma* (1970, first published in 1963) is the reverse. In this examination of spoiled identities Goffman examines the ways in which those who are blemished physically or socially also suffer damage to their social identity as a consequence of the treatment they receive at the hands of those around them. In this sense, someone who has a physical disability or deformity also has to face the prospect of being discriminated against by 'normal' society; the physical disfigurement is taken as a sign that the soul, the intellect or the personality are defective too.

In the past, physical stigmata were often associated with moral worth, a punishment visited upon the child for the sins of the parents or a sign of God's approval. In more secular times, however, the stereotypical responses to physical deformity are almost wholly negative.

For Goffman, this stigmatisation of physical disability is a metaphor for a whole range of social prejudices. Skin colour, gender, age, criminality and mental illness are all possible sources of condemnation. To use a term coined by Everett Hughes (1945), the negative label (be it cripple, mental defective, criminal or whatever) achieves a 'master status' against which the stigmatised individual finds it impossible to lay claim to any alternative status. An important distinction can be made, however, between those who are discredited and those who are discreditable. In the former category are those who cannot avoid discrimination because they cannot conceal the physical trait which marks them out, while the latter refers to individuals with hidden desires and secret lives who know only too well the cost of revealing these aspects of the self to 'normal' society and therefore conceal stigmatising aspects.

Coming to terms with stigmatisation is a learning process with identifiable phases of socialisation. This process may be handled well or badly, but it results in the stigmatised individual undergoing a transformation of the self which, to use another term borrowed from Everett Hughes, is a form of 'moral career'. Just as any other career is a matter of adjusting to the professional and organisational demands placed upon the self, so the stigmatised self is forced to accommodate the attempts by others to discredit it.

In *Asylums* (first published in 1961) Goffman examines the idea that those placed in institutional care have a 'moral career' ahead of them. A mental hospital shares with prisons, boarding schools and concentration camps the defining features of a 'total institution'. The goals of such institutions may be laudable (education, mental welfare, rehabilitation) but in practice they become self-serving bureaucracies whose smooth running requires the control of inmates via batch living, routinisation of tasks and binary management. The impact upon the recipient of such care is often the reverse of its original intention. Through a range of deliberate and unconscious procedures, the institution achieves the 'mortification of the self' through the routine and systematic destruction of those aspects of the personality which made the inmate unique or special. The inmate is forced to adopt the 'inmate role', and through a series of humiliations and degradations becomes depersonalised. Name, personal possessions and clothing are removed denying access to the 'identity kit' which is taken so much for granted in the outside culture. In their place, the inmate receives a number, a uniform and a routine haircut as a reminder that they are 'the same as everyone else'.

Inmates will adapt to these pressures to conform in various ways, but in extreme cases of 'institutionalisation' the self is 'colonised' and full 'conversion' to the inmate role so successfully achieved that the individual is rendered incapable of returning to an independent lifestyle outside the walls of the institution. In common parlance, the inmate is institutionalised.

By drawing attention to the institutional and organisational factors which constrain the development of the self, Goffman was addressing an issue which he is often accused of avoiding.

In his later work Goffman attempts to go beyond the face-to-face activity which characterises the 'interaction order' to examine the ways in which such activity and experience is 'framed' by the 'social order' – the social structures and institutions whose rules and rituals define situations and thereby shape the meanings which individuals attach to the situations they find themselves in.

> My aim is to try to isolate some of the basic frameworks of understanding available in our society for making sense out of events and to analyse the special vulnerabilities to which these frames of reference are subject . . . I assume that definitions of a situation are built up in accordance with principles of organisation which govern events – at least social ones – and our subjective involvement in them; frame is the word I use to refer to such of these basic elements as I am able to identify . . . My phrase 'frame analysis' is a slogan to refer to the examination in these terms of the organisation of experience.
>
> (Goffman, quoted in Lemert and Branaman 1997: 155)

Consequently, Layder (1994) argued that Goffman is not to be regarded simply as a micro-sociologist, but as one who had equal regard for the personal and the public aspects of social interaction and who achieves a 'loose coupling' of both worlds. Burns has suggested that this shift to the more structured aspects of social life, reveals a Durkheimian side to Goffman's work in which 'the lives, feelings and behaviour of individuals are not only like language, an essentially social construct but are subjected to the order imposed upon them by the collective moral consciousness of society' (Burns 1992: 370–1).

However, this should not be taken as some sort of theoretical about-face; Goffman, according to Burns, was basically interested in observing and classifying social encounters and not in broad theories of social order:

> There is hardly any discussion in his writings of the way in which the traffic of social interaction, which is the stuff of social order, organises itself, or is organised, so as to constitute society, which we ordinarily conceive of as populated by organisations and social institutions . . . while he believed that links between social interaction and social structure, social organisation and social order itself must somehow exist, they have to be regarded as attenuated, extremely variable in duration and difficult to determine.
>
> (Burns 1992: 359)

In response to those critics who accused him of conservatism and a failure to expose the contradictions of modern capitalism, Goffman makes clear that his perspective is not supposed to offer a theory of society or to suggest courses of action but is concerned only to start where people find themselves, no matter how much we might think we know what is good for them:

> The analysis developed [in *Frame Analysis* 1974] does not catch at the differences between the advantaged and the disadvantaged classes and can be said to direct attention away from such matters. I think that is true. I can only suggest that he who would combat false consciousness and awaken people to their true interests has much to do, because the sleep is very deep. And I do not intend here to provide a lullaby but merely to sneak and watch the way the people snore.
>
> (Goffman, in Lemert and Branaman 1997: 157–8)

HOWARD BECKER AND THE 'LABELLING PERSPECTIVE'

Becker studied at Chicago after the war and, as a peer of Goffman, was influenced by Blumer and Hughes. Theoretically his work leans towards Blumer's emphasis upon the interpretation of meaning and the symbolic nature of interaction, but his research interests and methods are drawn from the urban anthropology of Everett Hughes. Hughes encouraged Becker's interest in the seamier side of life and the direct observation of those involved in 'lowly' occupations and deviant careers. Under the patronage of Hughes, Becker's research interests were encouraged and he taught in the sociology department for two years following the award of his PhD. In a career very different from those he studied, Becker has held posts and lectureships around the world as well as being elected president of the Society for the Study of Symbolic Interactionism in 1977.

Becker's interests have been varied but he is best known for his groundbreaking work in the 1960s which introduced readers and students to the study of social problems and the sociology of the underdog. Although derided by some as the study of 'nuts, sluts and deviated preverts [*sic*]' (Liazos 1972), Becker managed to energise sociology through his deliberate choice of the novel and the deviant. In keeping with the 'oral tradition' of the Chicago School he was attempting to break the academic and theoretical stranglehold on sociological debate by taking it back to the streets and making it socially relevant.

In particular this approach was designed to get away from rigid models of social order to explore the meanings by which individual actors make sense of social action:

> It is all too easy to impose an alien explanatory scheme that obscures vision, ignores problems and pre-empts solutions . . . analysis must grasp the meaning that animates and shapes social activity. Consequential meaning is that employed by the social actors themselves not by the sociologist, and interactionism is designed to take the observer and audience inside the actors own perspectives on selves, acts and environments.
>
> (Downes and Rock 1996: 189–90)

Two aspects of his early and most popular work are important here: the social construction of social problems and the labelling of deviant behaviour.

The social construction of social problems

In the mainstream of empirical social science, the identification of 'social problems' was often taken for granted in that it reflected the official definitions of those who sponsored the research or collated the official data. One of the lasting contributions of the interactionist approach was its critique of the official categories employed to classify data and the assumption that the underlying definitions represented something real and commonly understood. By treating definitions of crime, suicide and deviance as problematic and by drawing attention to the human processes of interpretation and interaction involved in the application of definitions (as 'tags' or 'labels'), writers such as Erikson (1962), Kitsuse (1962) and Douglas (1967) raised fundamental problems for sociological research which are now seen as commonplace but at the time were a radical challenge to mainstream sociology. In the forefront of this critique can be found the young Howard Becker attacking the premise that social problems are some easily diagnosed expression of social pathology over which there is common agreement.

As far as functionalist writers such as Parsons and Merton were concerned, social order depends upon a common value system. This consensus view of the normative order not only informs members of society on what is good for society but also indicates that social problems are anything which challenges the core values of society and disrupts social order. In what Becker refers to as a 'social pathology' model, society is seen as an organism which remains healthy so long as its functioning parts are well maintained; social scientists see themselves as doctors capable of diagnosing the 'objective conditions' which may threaten this equilibrium. Because laypeople and social scientists share the same values, they tend to agree on what constitutes social problems in much the same way as a doctor and patient may agree on a diagnosis and a course of treatment. Becker disagreed fundamentally with this approach, arguing that it ignored the subjective aspects of defining social activities as problems and the possibility that, as people have different interests, they are likely to have different ideas on what is both good and bad for society. As Matza later pointed out: 'One man's deviation may be another's custom' (1969: 11). Hence, the identification and prosecution of an activity as a social problem is, in Becker's terms, a 'political process' in which some forms of social behaviour are treated as 'normal' and useful while others are branded as 'social problems'. In this process he identified three clear stages.

The first stage involved the identification by 'some person or group' of 'a set of objective conditions [which are seen as] problematic, posing a danger or containing the seeds of future difficulties' (Becker 1963: 13–14). Clearly the original step of identifying something as a social danger is anything but straightforward. Which groups have identified the 'problem' and how did it come to their attention? Why are some problems seen as more threatening than others and why do some people feel more threatened by particular problems?

These questions indicate that the 'objective conditions' which define 'social problem' are subjective, relativist and highly problematic; and Becker asks us to think about the kinds of people who involve themselves in defining what other people do as cause for public concern and legislation. These people he calls 'moral entrepreneurs' because they are in the business of constructing rules for others which benefit themselves and the interests they represent. In his own work (1963) and the work of others this idea of the moral entrepreneur plays an important part in understanding the social construction of rules and social problems.

The next stage in defining a social problem involves the raising of awareness so that the private concerns of a few become the public concerns of the many. By mobilising support for their worries, particularly through the media, these moral campaigners ensure that their concerns become 'shared and widespread'. By emphasising the social role played by the media in any moral crusade which creates a social problem and identifies new groups of 'outsiders', Becker was instrumental in drawing attention to the danger that moral crusades can quickly turn into 'moral panics' which demonise some groups and reinforce the power and authority of others. The work of Cohen (1972), Pearson (1975) and Hall *et al.* (1978) are among the best known examples of studies inspired by this important concept.

The final stage of establishing the credentials of a social problem is to identify an appropriate agency for dealing with it. The problem may become the responsibility of an existing body or a new one will be created to deal with it. Either way, once 'widespread concern has been aroused, it must be embodied in an organisation or institution if the problem is to achieve lasting existence as a defined social problem.' By colonising a particular problem, professional bodies set themselves up as the experts in the field and become the 'rule enforcers' (Kitsuse preferred the term 'legitimate labellers') and as such discover that they have a vested interest in maintaining public concern over 'their' social problem. This places social control agencies in contradictory positions of providing solutions to social problems while agitating at the same time for their continued existence on the public agenda. If, as Becker argues, 'social problems are what people think they are', then the experts (police, psychiatrists, educationalists) become the 'moral entrepreneurs' of the next generation in order to maintain high levels of public concern and thereby remain in business.

In Small's account of the criminalisation of narcotics in Canada in the first quarter of the twentieth century (see Hester and Eglin 1992: 32–6) Becker's insights are applied to a specific social problem: the 'dope fiend'. By identifying the use of opium, cocaine and marijuana by the Chinese as a threat to family life and social order, groups of politically motivated moral crusaders mounted a public campaign against the use of narcotics which drew support from the clergy, the Department of Health, the Anti-Opium League of Vancouver and the Mounted Police. Despite the fact that some of the professional groups and business interests involved had clear vested interests in criminalising particular drugs (and not others), their work as moral entrepreneurs depended upon the defence of the core values of Canadian society against an alien culture and in particular those standards threatened by drug abuse. Becker (1963) had already identified the three key values under such threat as individual responsibility, sobriety and humanitarianism, and it was in defence of these values that the Canadian campaign was mounted:

> From a social constructionist perspective, values . . . are not regarded as determinants of behaviour but rather as resources which have uses in social action. Thus criminal law creation in general and drug laws in particular involve the use by their creators of values which it is claimed justify, warrant, demand and otherwise make desirable the criminalisation of certain behaviours.
>
> (Hester and Eglin 1992: 36)

Becker's work on the social construction of social problems can be applied to a range of social issues but he is best known for his application of these ideas to social deviance in particular and the impact of social reaction on the development of 'deviant careers'.

The labelling of deviant behaviour

In Mead's theory of the self, much is made of the importance of social factors for the development of identity and the process of distinguishing between those regarded as 'conventional' and those who are 'condemned'. In the former case it may be said that if the key figures in the socialisation process ('significant others') direct and reward behaviours which coincide with the expectations of society (the 'generalised other') the individual learns to appreciate and derive pleasure from conformity to conventional career patterns. For example, in Rosenthal and Jacobson's (1970) study of self-fulfilling prophesies in school, it was claimed that teacher expectations had a direct bearing on performance.

Where teachers were encouraged to believe that they had children of untapped potential (called 'spurters' by Rosenthal and Jacobson) in class, this led to an overall improvement of academic performance and a subsequent heightening of expectation which led Rosenthal and Jacobson to conclude that 'teachers may not only get more when they expect more; they may also come to expect more when they get more' (Rosenthal and Jacobson, quoted in Stones 1970: 419). It was not clear how this 'halo effect' had been achieved but in a variety of ways which would make clear sense to Cooley, Mead and Goffman, the self appeared to respond to positive expectations placed upon it:

> We may say that by what she said, by how and when she said it, by her facial expressions, postures and perhaps her touch, the teacher may have communicated to the children of the experimental group that she expected improved intellectual performance. Such communications together with possible changes in teaching techniques may have helped the child learn by changing his self-concept, his expectations of his own behaviour and his motivation, as well as his cognitive style and skills.
>
> (Rosenthal and Jacobson, quoted in Stones 1970: 422)

Conversely, if our 'significant others' direct us away from the approved values of the community, they will not become incorporated in our notion of self and more marginalised identities emerge which are condemned by wider society. It was this alternative career route that interested Becker.

In *Outsiders* (1963), Becker debunks conventional definitions of deviance and the associated notion that the cause of deviance is an inherent part of the personality (or social background) of the individual. Rather the key to understanding deviance is to give up the search for the 'common factors of personality or life situation' which indicate its cause and to focus upon the processes of social reaction which contribute to its construction as a form of deviance. In one of the most quoted phrases in the sociology of deviance, Becker makes it clear that society does not cause deviant behaviour, it 'creates' it:

> I do not mean this in the way it is ordinarily understood, in which the causes of deviance are located in the social situation of the deviant or in 'social factors' which prompt his action. I mean, rather, that social groups create deviance by making the rules whose infraction constitutes deviance, and by applying those rules to particular people and labelling them as outsiders. From this point of view, deviance is not a quality of the act the person commits, but rather a consequence of the application by others of rules and sanctions to an 'offender'. The deviant is one to whom that label has successfully been applied; deviant behaviour is behaviour that people so label.
>
> (Becker 1963: 8–9)

What appears at first glance to be a truism (if we had no rules there would be no opportunity to break them) was in fact a serious attack upon the commonsense assumptions about deviance to be found in society at large and among those employed to study it. Becker insists that we re-examine the nature of deviant acts and the assumption that the explanations for it may be located in the nature of the individual deviant:

> Deviance is not a simple quality, present in some kinds of behaviour and absent in others. Rather, it is the product of a process which involves responses of other people to the behaviour . . . Deviance is not a quality that lies in behaviour itself, but in the interaction between the person who commits an act and those who respond to it.
>
> (Becker 1963: 14)

This is not an attempt to diminish the importance of anti-social behaviour or to relativise it out of existence or to shift the blame on to society, but a genuine reminder that, in the real world, simplistic medical and legalistic notions of deviance have severe limitations. Whether an act is treated as a serious crime or dismissed as a prank will involve a range of cultural and situational factors as well as the relative power to label (and resist labels) that particular groups in society have. By employing the teachings of his mentors at Chicago, Becker is not trying to avoid the serious issues of crime and deviance; he is confronting them. Through a serious application of interpretive sociology, Becker is saying that deviant behaviour and deviant careers involve processes of interaction and interpretation:

> All behaviour, deviance included, is an interactional product, its properties and impact cannot be known until we understand how it is defined, conceptualised, interpreted, apprehended and evaluated; in short what it means to participants and relevant observers alike. Labelling theory is not a separate theory at all, but an application of symbolic interactionism to deviant phenomenon.
>
> (Goode 1997: 103)

Discussion questions

> [The] same behaviour may be an infraction of the rules at one time and not at another; may be infraction when committed by one person, but not when committed by another; some rules are broken with impunity, others are not. In short, whether a given act is deviant or not depends in part on the nature of the act . . . and in part on what other people do about it.
>
> (Becker 1963)

The well known Liverpool streaker [Mark Roberts] has been banned from attending football matches following a 'streak' at the Cup Final in May 2001.

Using nudity as the form of deviance, answer the following questions on the conditions under which the rules on nudity are applied or withheld.

1 In what conditions are rules applied?

2 Who is subjected to the rules and who are the exemptions (and why)?

3 How flexible are the rules?

4 Who made the rules and whose interests do they serve?

5 What are the reactions to deviation from these rules?

Until now, Becker's analysis has focused upon the social reaction to 'deviant' acts and the processes by which those who commit them are labelled, but he was also concerned with the reaction of 'outsiders' to the labels which were applied to them by others. The first attempt to use this kind of analysis can be found in the work of the historian Frank Tannenbaum (1938) who was primarily interested in the ways in which the normal and everyday behaviour of boys cooped up in slum districts was defined as delinquent by those in authority. In a process he called 'tagging', the 'troublemakers' were identified and punished but often became involved in a spiral of criminal behaviour exacerbated by the institutional attempts to correct their behaviour. The first sociologist to examine these ideas was Edwin Lemert (1951), who made an important distinction between primary and secondary deviance. Primary deviance refers to the widespread practice of rule-breaking which may be the result of some biological defect, psychological trauma or social crisis. Lemert, however, is interested not in the factors which led to the initial act of deviance but in the reaction of wider society and the impact that this reaction might have on identity formation.

It is relatively easy to rationalise the odd act of primary deviance and to deflect any attempt by others to label us deviant, but a continuous assault upon the self by those in positions of authority can establish secondary deviance in which the self and the deviant role become one and the same:

> Secondary deviants . . . not only centre their lives around the facts of their deviance, they also consider themselves to be a deviant kind of person. Their deviance is the most central or organising feature of their identity . . . social control creates problems such as community rejection, stigmatism, discrimination, economic difficulties and police surveillance; the solution for these problems may be found in the commission of further deviant acts. It is in that sense that the deviance becomes 'secondary'; that is, a deviant response to social reactions to earlier deviant behaviour.
>
> (Hester and Eglin 1992: 112)

By bringing together Lemert's concept of secondary deviance and Everett Hughes's notions of moral career and master status, Becker was able to develop a perspective within which the deviant identity and the deviant career are explained via the process of labelling. There are at least three steps in the process of secondary deviance:

- *Getting caught.* We all break rules at some time or other, but getting caught and labelled by those in authority is crucial.
- *Accepting the label.* Over time, the episodes of being apprehended become more frequent and a 'master status' emerges which is reinforced by the labelling process. It becomes increasingly difficult to lay claim to any other status position and the self becomes defined primarily in terms of the label.
- *Dropping out.* If the outsider is prevented from participating in other roles because of the exclusive nature of the master status then it is likely that the deviant will be attracted to the subculture of those similarly labelled and pursue a lifestyle which confirms the status of 'outsider'.

In this way, the alternative moral career of the 'outsider' goes through stages similar to those enjoyed by the conformist. There is no instant or automatic conversion to a deviant identity as a consequence of labelling, rather it is a slow process in which the individual drifts into a deviant lifestyle with which they will identity.

> It is one thing to commit a deviant act e.g. acts of lying, stealing, homosexual intercourse, narcotics' use, drinking to excess, unfair competition. It is quite another thing to be charged and invested with a deviant character, i.e. to be socially defined as a liar, a thief, a homosexual, a dope fiend, a drunk, a chiseler, a brown-noser, a hoodlum, a sneak, a scab, and so on. It is to be assigned to a role, to a special type or category of persons. The label – the name of the role – does more than signify one who has committed such and such a deviant act. Each label evokes a characteristic imagery. It suggests someone who is normally or habitually given to certain kinds of deviance; who may be expected to behave in this way; who is literally a bundle of odious or sinister qualities. It activates sentiments and calls out responses in others: rejection, contempt, suspicion, withdrawal, fear, hatred.
>
> (Albert Cohen 1966: 24)

In a paper published in 1953, Becker charted the moral career of the marijuana smoker and noted six stages in the progression, from beginner to regular user.

- A general and vague interest in the drug is aroused.
- The opportunity to try it is offered and accepted.
- The techniques of dope smoking are learned – types, cost, sources, amounts to use, how to use.
- Recognising the effects of using the drug – the psychical effects and getting 'high'.
- Interpreting the experience – the social and personal meaning of using the drug usually in discussion with other users.
- The connoisseur. The individual user is now an expert in using the drug; can distinguish different types, knows where to get the stuff and introduces others to its use and helps them interpret its effects.

Discussion questions

1 Just as marijuana users had to go through a process of learning to enjoy and control their use of the drug, so legal drugs (coffee, tobacco, alcohol) involve the user in a career. If you are a regular user of one of these stimulants, think back over your own career as a user and see how closely it fits the six-stage career outlined above.

2 Choose a conventional career (becoming a student, a nurse, a trainspotter or a parent, for instance) and try to identify the stages through which you learn to become a member.

3 Now try the same thing with a deviant career (such as prostitute, criminal, football hooligan). It helps if you choose one that you are familiar with!

Becker was criticised from several quarters for suggesting that deviance was in the eye of the beholder and for his failure to explain where deviant behaviour comes from in the first place. His response (Becker 1974) pointed out that those looking for the causes of primary deviance were bound to be disappointed, as the interactionist approach was concerned only with the interaction of all those actors (both 'normal' and 'deviant') who are involved in the process of secondary deviance because 'the study of deviance [is] essentially the study of the construction and reaffirmation of moral meanings in everyday social life'. From this perspective, deviance is 'not motivated by mysterious, unknowable forces' but part of 'the drama of moral rhetoric and action in which imputations of deviance are made, accepted, rejected and fought over'. In this drama the key players are the moral entrepreneurs and the legitimate labellers because they are the people who have the power to make their definitions stick. Rather than suggesting some simplistic link between label (as cause) and deviant behaviour (as effect), Becker argues that the interactionist approach provides 'a complex theory that takes into account the actions and reactions of everyone involved in episodes of deviance'.

The interactionist approach also represents a challenge to empirical methods for studying deviance based on official records because 'a closer look at people acting together has made us aware that records are also produced by people acting together and must be understood in that context'. In other words, the samples and statistics upon which empirical sociologists base their research conclusions are socially constructed in the same way that deviance is.

CRITICISM OF INTERPRETIVE SOCIOLOGY

Is it sociology?

Despite the fact that American sociology is founded upon the work of early social action theorists and ethnographic researchers, one of the biggest criticisms is that it is not really sociology. There are three possible reasons for saying this and we will consider each in turn.

Firstly, the subject matter of this micro approach is not recognisable as the raw material of sociological study, concentrating upon the interaction between individuals, the mind games they play and the labels they attach to one another may be an interesting form of 'navel gazing' but it detracts from the wider picture of social life. To many, symbolic interactionism has more in common with social psychology than the normal stuff of sociological enquiry and it is noticeable that the early contributors were not trained sociologists but philosophers and psychologists. By shifting attention away from the general to the particular, from the social to the personal and from society to the self, this perspective 'pays too much attention to the transient, episodic and fleeting aspects of interaction rather than the more durable structural features . . . [and] fails to connect the face to face aspects of behaviour to their structural ones' (Layder 1994: 72–3).

Secondly, symbolic interactionism and the labelling perspective associated with it are often criticised for not providing a consistent social theory. Its insights might highlight problems in other perspectives but there is no recognisable theory of society developed as an alternative. Writers such as Mead and Goffman do acknowledge the necessary existence of society in their exploration of the self and the processes by which it is constructed, but they do not advance any theory on the nature of society itself. As we have already noted, one of the strongest criticisms of 'labelling theory' was its failure to explain why deviant behaviour occurs in the first place. The vague nature of symbolic interactionism reinforces the criticism that it cannot provide a sound conceptual basis for a proper theory (Ritzer 1992: 368), but Layder has argued that by avoiding speculative theorising in favour of generating ideas from empirical data, symbolic interactionists offer a form of 'grounded theory' which develops out of their research. However, in comparison with other approaches, it is probably true to say that interpretive sociologists are far more interested in observing the fragilities of everyday encounters than building theoretical models of society.

The third criticism of interpretive sociology is that if the core concepts of symbolic interactionism are incapable of providing the basis of convincing theoretical models of society they are also too 'confused and imprecise' to provide testable hypotheses for conventional research (Ritzer 1992: 368). In this sense the concerns of symbolic interactionism fall outside the 'scientific frame of reference' and in some instances offer a clear critique of the use of the scientific method in sociological research. The more ideographic methods preferred by ethnographic researchers (life histories, personal documents or participant observation, for example) are commonly regarded as 'soft' social science in contrast to the 'hard science' derived from statistical data. For all the insights he provides into the human condition, Goffman, for example, cannot be regarded as a social scientist in the conventional sense; his work is an eclectic mixture of his own observations and illustrations drawn from literature. Anyone looking for a systematic template for conducting social research will be sorely disappointed if they turn to his work for guidance. It would no doubt please Robert Park to hear the sociological work of his disciples dismissed as journalism.

What – no structure?

While some writers in this tradition make concessions towards the idea of social structure, there is a thread running through this form of social action theory which is strongly resistant to notions of social structure to the extent that some writers have argued that the social structure is nothing more than the invention of sociologists and has no substance outside of sociological discourse (see Collins 1981). No one likes to be told that what they think they are studying is a figment of the imagination, and structuralist writers resent the humanist and voluntaristic tendencies of symbolic interactionism; the emphasis upon the creative subject is seen as a form of psychological reductionism which ignores social structure, inequality and power altogether.

The 'obsession with identity', which is the most interesting aspect of interpretive sociology, may be regarded as nothing less than a luxury when most of the inhabitants of the global economy are more concerned about where their next meal is coming from. Conversely, the apparent choices available in the pluralistic capitalism of the West contrast awkwardly with the 'choices' available to child labourers in the sweatshops of Indonesia. People may appear to make choices but that does not put them in control of their lives; choices are severely constrained by the social and political environment in which individuals find themselves.

Is it just conservative ideology?

Directly linked to the previous criticism is the political implication that any social perspective which ignores the unequal nature of the social structure, and the processes of stratification and discrimination which are built into it, diverts attention away from these important social issues and reinforces the status quo. Overlooking the context within which meaning is constructed and interaction takes place in favour of analysing the microscopic features of everyday life could be seen as a political manoeuvre which renders invisible the inequalities of wealth and power embedded in the interaction order long before individual encounters actually occur. Writers such as Goffman may make vague references to the importance of the 'ritual order', but they take the order for granted and fail to question the essentially conservative nature of 'impression management' techniques which are aimed simply to please.

By emphasising the cooperative aspects of the rituals and expectations surrounding social interaction, this approach tends to ignore conflict between significant interest groups in society at large. Gouldner's critique of American sociology (1971) drew attention to the ways in which sociological research was used to examine the poor and the powerless for tendencies which the powerful might regard as 'social problems'. Despite the claims to be 'radical', Goffman and Becker were singled out for criticism because of their emphasis upon the deviant and the underdog:

> By being generally sympathetic to powerless groups without either discriminating between greater or less suffering, or indeed responding with any real passion to the problem of suffering itself, Chicago sociology promoted a positive sympathy convenient to those in power and comforting to guilt ridden liberal academics.
>
> (Fisher and Strauss 1979: 482)

In addition, the work of symbolic interactionists is seen as essentially ideological. Firstly, the fact that the meaning attached to action is taken for granted, without questioning where meanings come from, is a matter of concern for radical sociologists and structuralists alike; the ideas, and therefore the meanings which people attach to their actions (and the behaviour of others), originate in their cultural experiences and the social positions which they inhabit in the social structure. To treat meaning as the raw material of social analysis without raising the question of how it is formed by powerful interests ignores the power of ideology (especially through the media) and is itself ideological. Secondly, this question of cultural power in the formation of meaning systems is taken a stage further by structuralist writers, such as the Marxist Louis Althusser, who argue that the fetishisation of the individual which we find encouraged by American sociology is nothing more than a form of 'bourgeois ideology' because it falls into the trap of foregrounding the interests of the individual and marginalising any structural account of how they come to take these interests for granted in the first place.

Is it just radical ideology?

If Becker and Goffman are simply apologists for capitalism, what do we make of Lemert's assertion that such writers represented a threat to the establishment? In postwar America it did not take much to be regarded as an agent of protest and change. In a world where communist sympathisers were hounded out of their jobs and 'liberal' remains a term of abuse, it is not hard to imagine why anyone who focused attention upon the fragility of the social order and proclaimed the viewpoint of the underdog as valid was regarded with distrust. Certainly the work of writers such as Goffman, Becker, Matza and Scheff explored aspects of American life which were potentially embarrassing and from a standpoint which did not find favour with those members of the American Sociological Association who supported the dominant functionalist paradigm. Writers such as Merton firmly believed that American society was based upon a value consensus in which competition and success were highly prized; deviance was a condition produced by anomic separation from this value system and deviants were an estranged group whom he considered 'non-productive liabilities' (Downes and Rock 1996: 141).

If we follow Matza's relativist arguments on social norms and deviation, the cultural certainties of a consensual value system are undermined and the deviant is simply someone who undertakes a different career path but is victimised by the moral entrepreneurs and legitimate labellers of society who impose their moral and political prejudices on others. On the one hand this approach can be seen as an attack upon the hypocrisy of those in power, on the other a defence of the prostitute, the mental patient and the drug addict. In any event, the underlying message of tolerance and understanding encouraged the belief that these writers were the gurus of student radicalism which became associated with civil rights activism and the protest movement of the 1960s.

Where am 'I' in all of this?

Critics on the left and right of the sociological spectrum seem to agree on one thing: by emphasising the psychology of social interaction, American micro-sociologists fail to recognise the significance of social structure. However, there are critics from the disciplines of psychology and psychiatry who argue that symbolic interactionism does not go far enough in its treatment of the personal aspects of human behaviour. By emphasising the conscious and rational features of impression management this approach overlooks the more emotional, irrational and unconscious aspects of personality. In other words, the exaggerated concern with the objective social self and the ways in which we manipulate its performance excludes the more unpredictable and subjective elements of the 'I' and the deeper forces of the individual psyche which may explain irrational behaviour.

Adopting a 'psychoanalytic view of the self', Jessica Evans (2000) criticises the Meadian view of the self popularised by Goffman because it focuses attention upon 'the part [of the self] which comes alive in a social situation where display is an issue' (2000: 40). This overly rational concern with the rules governing social interaction and the interpretation of others' behaviour gives a one-sided view of personal identity which concentrates upon role performance and ignores the deep-seated feelings which exist prior to and outside of social interaction:

> Symbolic interaction, in its sole concern with the presentation, management and artificial construction of emotions through the contexts of social interaction, assumes that the self can only ever be a 'false' self.
>
> (Evans 2000: 41)

In order to get a fuller picture of the self it is therefore necessary to go beyond 'encounters' with others to explore 'the irrational, the repressed and conflictual dimensions of emotional life' (Evans 2000: 42). If there is a core to the real self hiding behind the performances of everyday life, it remains hidden from view because social action theorists are not looking for it; psychoanalysis begins where social constructionism ends.

SUMMARY

The interpretive approach was a direct challenge to the positivist tradition in sociology. It shunned the armchair theorising which reified society as a prior structure determining behaviour and shaping history according to immutable laws. It also dismissed the idea that the hidden structure of the social order could be revealed through analysis of social facts. By adopting a different empirical approach it was suggested that direct observation of people as they go about their lives would take us beyond the quantifying of behaviour to engage with people at the point at which they construct and interpret the rules of social behaviour. This idea that the viewpoint of the actor is important is markedly different from one which takes 'society' as its starting point. By shifting attention to the definitions, interpretations and interaction of individuals, this strand of humanist sociology returned the active and creative subject to centre stage and raised important questions over the theoretical and methodological principles of mainstream sociology.

We have seen that interpretive sociology in general and symbolic interactionism in particular have attracted a range of criticisms which reflect the contradictory nature of the enterprise. Not sufficiently interested in structural issues to be accepted as proper sociology, interpretive sociology is also dismissed by psychologists for providing a theory of the individual which is too heavily influenced by social processes. Attacked by conservatives for being too radical, this stance is decried by radical sociologists as a pose. As a theoretical position it is taken to task for lumping together a range of ill-defined concepts which do not constitute a unified body of knowledge, while its journalistic attempts to observe everyday life from close quarters are pilloried as unscientific. However, for all its shortcomings and inconsistencies this general perspective has touched a raw nerve somewhere within the body of knowledge which calls itself sociology. It may be true that it does not offer a strong alternative to some of the better-defined theoretical perspectives, but it has provided the basis for a critique of those more established positions and a range of sensitising concepts which have enabled a more humanistic sociology to develop.

EXERCISES

The self and stigma – applying Goffman's analysis

1 Read the extract from Louis de Bernieres' *Captain Corelli's Mandolin* (1995) and answer the questions that follow. Remember that Carlo is growing up in Catholic Italy before the war.

> I, Carlo Piero Guercio, write these words with the intention that they should be found after my death, when neither scorn nor loss of reputation may dog my steps nor blemish me. The circumstance of life leaves it impossible that this testament of my nature should find its way into the world before I have drawn my last breath, and until that time I shall be condemned to wear the mask decreed by misfortune.
>
> I have been reduced to eternal and infinite silence, I have not even told the chaplain in confession. I know in advance what I will be told; that it is a perversion, an abomination in the sight of God, that I must fight the good fight, that I must marry and lead the life of a normal man, that I have a choice.
>
> I have not told a doctor. I know in advance that I will be called an invert, that I am in some strange way in love with myself, that I am sick and can be cured, that my mother is responsible, that I am an effeminate even though I am as strong as an ox and fully capable of lifting my own weight above my head, that I must marry and lead the life of a normal man, that I have a choice.
>
> What could I say to such priests and doctors? I would say to the priest that God made me as I am, that I had no choice, that He must have made me like this for a purpose, that He knows the ultimate reasons for all things and that therefore it must be all to the good that I am as I am, even if we cannot know what that good is. I can say to the priest that if God is the reason for all things, then God is to blame and I should not be condemned.
>
> And the priest will say, 'This is a matter of the Devil and not of God,' and I will reply, 'Did God not make the Devil? Is He not omniscient? How can I be blamed for what He knew would occur from the very commencement of time?' And the priest will refer me to the destruction of Sodom and Gomorrah and tell me that God's mysteries are not to be understood by us. He will tell me that we are commanded to be fruitful and multiply.
>
> I would say to the doctor, 'I have been like this from the first, it is nature that has moulded me, how am I supposed to change? How can I decide to desire women, any more than I can suddenly decide to enjoy eating anchovies, which I have always detested? I have been to the Casa Rosetta, and I loathed it, and afterwards I felt sick. I felt cheapened. I felt I was a traitor. I had to do it to appear normal!'
>
> And the doctor will say, 'How can this be natural? Nature serves its interests by making us reproduce. This is against nature. Nature wants us to be fruitful and multiply.'

This is a conspiracy of doctors and priests who repeat the same things in different words. It is medicinal theology and theological medicine. I am like a spy who has signed a covenant of perpetual secrecy, I am like someone who is the only person in the world that knows the truth and yet is forbidden to utter it. And this truth weighs more than the universe, so that I am like Atlas bowed down forever beneath a burden that cracks the bones and solidifies the blood. There is no air in this world that I am fated to inhabit, I am a plant suffocated by lack of air and light, I have had my roots dipped and my leaves painted with poison. I am exploding with the fire o' love and there is no one to accept it or nourish it. I am a foreigner within my own nation, an alien in my own race, I am as detested as cancer when I am as purely flesh as any priest or doctor . . .

I, Carlo Piero Guercio, testify that in the Army I found my family. I have a father and mother, four sisters, and three brothers, but I have not had a family since puberty. I had to live among them secretly, like one who conceals leprosy. It was not their fault that I was made into a thespian. I had to dance with girls at fiestas, I had to flirt with girls in the playground of the school and when taking the evening passeggiata in the piazza. I had to answer my grandmother when she asked me what kind of girl I would like to marry and whether I wanted sons or daughters. I had to listen with delight to my friends describing the intricacies of the female pudenda, I had to learn to relate fabulous histories of what I had done with girls. I learned to be more lonely than it ought to be possible to feel.

In the Army there was the same gross talk, but it was a world without women. To a soldier a woman is an imaginary being. It is permissible to be sentimental about your mother, but that's all. Otherwise there are the inmates of the military brothels, the fictitious or unfaithful sweethearts at home, and the girls at whom one catcalls in the streets. I am not a misogynist, but you should understand that to me the company of a woman is painful because it reminds me of what I am not, and of what I would have been if God had not meddled in my mother's womb.

(a) Why does Carlo write this in a secret diary ?

(b) What reactions does he expect to get if he reveals his secret ?

(c) What impact are these reactions likely to have on his self concept ?

(d) What strategies of 'impression management' does Carlo use to appear 'normal'?

2 In Goffman's work on stigmatisation (Goffman 1970) he makes a clear distinction between discredited and discreditable forms of stigma. Where the evidence of difference is clear, e.g. facial disfiguration or criminal record, the individual is stigmatised by their appearance or public knowledge and consequently labelled as deviant; but where the form of deviance is based upon behaviour which is concealed then we refer to discreditable evidence. This involves a potentially damaging secret which the individual may well seek to hide because they can predict the nature and extent of public reaction to its revelation. Homosexuality is a good example, not only because it clearly involves secretive behaviour and denial but also because it has recently led to a debate within the gay community over the enforced 'outing' of gays in public life.

In Humphreys' (1975) study of what is euphemistically referred to in the USA as 'the tearoom trade' – the use of public toilets by men for sex – he revealed the extent to which homosexuality is a discreditable activity. In Humphreys' sample only 14 per cent saw themselves as homosexual and openly identified with a homosexual subculture. These were referred to as 'gay'. Twenty-four per cent recognised their homosexuality but identified themselves as bisexual. They lived a dual existence: one which was publicly heterosexual and often expressed through marriage, and a secret life within the gay subculture. These were classified as 'ambisexuals'. The largest group in the sample (38 per cent) were identified as 'trade'; these men had jobs and families and showed no interest in pursuing a homosexual lifestyle. For them the 'tearoom' provided the opportunity for instant and impersonal sex with no complications. Conversely, the 'closet queens' (24 per cent) recognised their homosexual identity but could not afford to take the risk of 'coming out' or making a commitment to a gay lifestyle no matter how much they were attracted to the gay subculture. Sexual satisfaction for them came through extremely secretive and lonely one-night stands.

(a) What percentage of the sample did not involve themselves in the gay subculture?

(b) What percentage kept their homosexuality a secret?

(c) Using Goffman's terms, which of the four groups are 'discredited' and which are 'discreditable'?

(d) What changes since the 1970s may affect homosexuals prepared to move from discreditable to discredited status?

Chapter 7

Contemporary theorising – postmodernism

DAWN JONES

> Subject, Meaning, Truth, Nature, Society, Power and Reality have all been abolished in the transformation of industrial-commodity society into a post-industrial mediascape.
>
> (Sarup 1993: 167)

That we live in 'postmodern times' is, for many social theorists, an observation that has transformed the ways that sociologists theorise about the social world. Just as society has dramatically transformed in ways that would have been unrecognisable to sociologists writing, for instance, in the times of Durkheim and Weber, so too sociology as a discipline must change in its approaches and frameworks to reflect the immensity of these changes. Indeed, such changes have raised questions as to whether it is still possible to apply sociological frameworks to make sense of and 'understand' society. To put it another way, is it still *desirable* to reach beneath the surface of the social world and ask the 'why' and 'how' questions that 'pre' postmodern social theory has been characterised by? Do we need social theory at all now that the 'traditional' concerns of the modernists are, quite literally, 'post-ed' in the past? Or has social theory simply 'evolved' with the emergence of a 'postmodern' social theory as a distinctive type of theoretical framework mirroring the historical evolution of society as a whole? Does 'postmodern' society require a break with approaches that sociologists have formally applied in their study of society? Or can the (alleged) social, political, cultural and economic changes with which postmodernism is associated be theorised quite adequately within existing 'modernist' theoretical approaches to the social world?

The focus of this chapter is to define postmodernism (and its variant forms of postmodernity and the postmodern) and to explore the consequences of the claimed social, cultural and economic shifts in our society for sociological theory.

In so doing, the questions raised above will be investigated. The chapter is structured as follows:

- The debates surrounding the definition of the postmodern will be explored in some depth in order to convey to the reader the confusion and disagreement among postmodern theorists and commentators. It will be suggested that any attempt to reach a consensus on what postmodernism is (and is not) is a futile and ultimately self-defeating project; indeed, it is suggested that more can be gained for the reader from an acknowledgement of the *lack* of consensus over what postmodernism is: a state of affairs which can in itself be seen to be significant for an understanding of sociological theory today.

- Having explored the debates surrounding the label 'postmodernism', the chapter goes on to explore what have been seen by theorists to be the implications of the emergence of postmodern society for the development and status of sociological theory.

- In conclusion, some of the wider implications of a postmodern sociology are considered, reflecting specifically on some of the theoretical and political consequences of such approaches for the enterprise of sociology as a whole.

DEFINITIONS AND CONTROVERSIES – WHAT IS POSTMODERNISM?

> I once heard it said that postmodernism is like jelly, not at all easy to nail down.
>   (Postmodern-Christian archives 1998)

At its simplest, the phrase 'postmodernism' has been used by social theorists to refer to a break or 'epochal shift' from modernity, with the emerging postmodern society characterised by a distinctive, 'new' social totality (Featherstone 1988:198). Within this new postmodern society, distinguishable in so many ways from what has gone before it, we see the emergence of postmodern social and cultural practices, defined by some as representing a new 'cultural logic'. Such a shift is said to have emerged in the late 1960s and early 1970s, a period where concerns of the 'modernists' have been seen by some to be increasingly irrelevant in the new age of the postmodern (Baudrillard, cited in Smart 1993: 54). Rather than being characterised by the search for truth and progression towards an 'ideal', rationally organised society, it is suggested that the quest for the modern has been lost. Large-scale multinational economic, political and social changes have necessitated a move away from the grand narratives of modernism (see Chapters 4 and 5) with its all-encompassing 'macro' focus on 'society'. The postmodern is, by contrast, said to represent a fissure with modernism, with the emergence of a fragmented, 'disorganised' set of social arrangements oriented around a culture that no longer privileges the search for a single truth or logic. Indeed, as will be seen later when discussing the approach of the postmodern theorist Baudrillard, it has even been premised that postmodernism implies the death of the social and of society *per se*. In its place we have a depthless space in which certainties, truths and defined realities blur, even disappear, in a rapidly changing global milieu.

Reflecting the immensity of the postmodern moment, Featherstone defines post-modernism as referring to:

> [*an*] epochal shift or break from modernity involving the emergence of a new social totality with its own distinct organising principles.
>
> (Featherstone 1988: 198)

To say that theorists of postmodernity have reached a consensus about what, precisely, postmodernism is, would, however, be incorrect. While writers such as Lyotard (1984) and Baudrillard (1983) suggest that the social system is in the midst of a very real social, cultural, economic and political transformation, defined by the emergence of social structures and identities that are decidedly postmodern in nature, others posit a more ambiguous interpretation of the postmodern. Before exploring how certain writers, such as Smart (1993), have interpreted the postmodern, it is important to consider in more detail precisely *what* the postmodern can be said to refer to, and how it can be said to differ from the modern.

From modernism to postmodernism – definitions and debates

Before an attempt is made to represent sociologists' attempts to delineate how the postmodern social formation is 'different' from (or 'post') that which has gone before it, it is useful to acknowledge that *when* postmodernism is said to have come about (and what area or 'level' of the social experience it is said to refer to) is itself highly contested among social theorists. Some writers see postmodernism as strongly linked to the economic sphere, as an emergent system of accumulation that embodies a 'postmodern' way of organising capitalism – for instance, Lash and Urry's (1987) 'disorganised capitalism' and regulation theory's focus on flexible accumulation in 'post-Fordist' times (Jessop 1987; Tickell and Peck 1992). Others, such as Mort (1994), prefer to focus on the emergence of the postmodern *mood* or climate, addressing how postmodern culture affects the way that, as a society, we have come to think about and make sense of the world as individuals. Postmodernism as *lifestyle* then, is one way in which the postmodern experience has been appropriated within social and cultural theory. One step on from this we have Jameson's understanding of postmodernism not merely as a 'style' but as a *cultural dominant*, allowing for the 'presence and coexistence of a range of very different, yet subordinate features' (Jameson 1991). Whether the existence of a postmodern style, or indeed dominant 'ethic' derives from a society-wide epochal shift, or whether the existence of such a mentality is simply indicative of a crises of modernity (Smart 1993: 27), is yet another area of debate among contemporary social theorists. Before exploring the variety of standpoints on the postmodern, it is helpful to consider in greater depth some of the notions of the modern that have been provided by theorists.

Modernism and modernity

In general terms, the phrase 'modernism' can be used broadly to refer to a social organisation and/or style and cultural logic of western society from as early as the late fifteenth century, 'peaking' in the late seventeenth century when the 'new' or 'modern' age was said to have dawned (Smart 1990). As with postmodernism, however, there has been a great deal of disagreement not only over *when* modernism commenced, but also concerning the elements that can be identified as making up the modern spirit and era.

The specification of when modernity ended and postmodernity took over as the dominant hegemonic culture and/or societal formation is an equally fraught area of debate. Indeed, while some would say that the times we are living in might best be classified as 'late modernity' (Lash and Urry 1987), others would say that post-modernism has itself been superseded by an indefinable sense of something new, perhaps what one might confusingly label 'post-postmodernism'. Leaving aside for now such debates, modernism/modernity can be defined as referring to a social arrangement and/or style of living that is very much encapsulated by the spirit of the Enlightenment. Such a spirit can be seen to have occurred across a variety of social formations – art, science, literature, architecture, archaeology, music, consumption, politics and economics. It stressed the importance of rationality, social and political progress, and the need to develop or 'move away' from old, restrictive practices. Modernity embodied a faith in the future. It involved a vision of and belief in a new social order that would provide lasting, stable and predictable foundations on which individuals could base their actions and choices.

The 'natural' social formations that accompanied such 'modern' faith can be seen, for example, in the rise of the modern nation state that shaped its citizens towards rationally ordered lives, driven by the desire for fulfilment, certainty and cohesion. While uncertainty about one's place in society and the meaning of one's life can be said to be a key theme in modernist accounts of identity in the modern world, the 'escape' from uncertainty through a drive to create a better life/society/ world is the defining motivation for the modern citizen. While recognising that life can be meaningless, empty and at times frightening, the spirit of modernity stresses a desire or longing to escape to a more stable, equal and protected social environment.

The modern individual, then, might be characterised as rational, calculating (in a self-reflexive way) and having some awareness of their position in society. The importance of a sense of growth and progression would also form a central part of the modern psyche. While 'angst' might exist in the modern world, fuelled in no small part by the growth of the classically modern 'bureaucratic' system of organisation (Weber 1968), the modern pursuit of 'escape' from stagnation is linked by modernists to the very modern faith in new technologies, science and the role of the nation state. Modern culture, while encompassing a variety of formats (art, sculpture, dance), might be characterised by its fascination with the human condition: of the desire to say something about society that recognises the existence of lifestyle differences (in terms of class and gender, for example), while at the same time reaching across social groupings by drawing on the commonality of humanity.

Discussion question

We have suggested that modernity is characterised by the need to progress and live a life of fulfilment. Think about your own life. In these *post*modern times can you identify any occasions on which your life has followed a modernist path? Can you find any evidence to support the claim that modernism has demised?

That modern society is characterised by the drive to progress is reflected in the guiding philosophies and sociological theories that have dominated modern academia. Modernism is characterised by the dominance of *grand narrative* or *rationalistic theories* such as Marxism, functionalism and Weberian social theory. Such theories are grand or all-encompassing in a number of related ways. Firstly, they attempt to say something about society *as a whole* and are, as such, macro rather than micro in focus. As with Talcott Parsons' theory of structural functionalism (Parsons 1951), grand theories have a particular understanding of how society 'hangs together' as a whole. The grand theoretical framework can be applied, with equal validity, to explain areas as diverse as the criminal justice system and the organisation of conjugal roles in modern society. Secondly, modernist grand narratives can be defined by a view of societies as following a specific historical path, the end-point of which represents the highpoint of civilisation (for example, Marx's theory of capitalist society's inevitable historical progression towards the state of communism). That society is following a logic of development, with the ultimate destination always in mind, can be seen for example in the work of sociologists in the 1960s and 1970s (e.g. Rostow 1971), and is reflected in, for example, postwar political drives towards the 'better society', premised on the principles of growth, modernity and an improved standard of living for all. Finally, the narratives of modernity can be seen as driven in a sense by a moral logic of 'betterment': of the need to act as a force for change, whether that change be directed towards a more equal society within, for example, Marxist-inspired theories (in terms of class, gender, ethnicity), or towards a truly consensual, structurally functional society (perhaps most notably in work of Parsons).

Having outlined briefly some of the main characteristics of modernity and modernism, it should now be possible to sketch an outline of what a *post*modern society would entail. Surely postmodernism can, at its simplest, be understood as the next stage in the progression of human evolution: the embodiment of a mood, culture, even social arrangement that has gone beyond the modern, and yet is in some ways strongly linked to that which has passed? To some extent, it is correct to think of the postmodern as *relationally* defined. Writers such as Smart have in fact promoted the postmodern as a mood or spirit of an age that has at last come to terms with the perilous and unstable nature of the modernist project, as a way of 'living with the realisation that the promises of modernity remain unfulfilled' (Smart 1993: 27). Smart thus sees postmodernism as having a close association with the modern, defined as a way of dealing with the unfulfilment of modernist dreams and desires. Postmodern culture, social organisation, political arrangements and economic practices can, as such, all be seen as a means of 'coping' with the outcome of modernist machinations. Writers such as Lash and Urry (1987) also view the postmodern as constituting, to some extent, the outcome, as opposed to the antithesis, of modernism, linking its emergence to the rise of disorganised society in the 'late' stages of capitalism.

Others claim that to categorise postmodernity as simply one facet of modernism and modernity is to vastly underplay the significance of its distinctiveness. Jameson, for example, supports the idea of there having been a radical break with the philosophies and assumptions of modernity. It is this break away from modernity that he sees as the starting point in the search for an understanding of the postmodern; a break that is best understood as deriving from the changing economic conditions of western societies from the early 1960s onwards. In reflecting on the relation between the two 'isms', he argues:

> even if all the constitutive features of postmodernism were identical with and coterminous to those of an older modernism . . . the two phenomena would still remain utterly distinct in their meaning owing to the very different positioning of postmodernism in the economic system of late capital and, beyond that, to the transformation of the very sphere of culture in contemporary society.
>
> (Jameson 1984: 57)

What characteristics, then, does the postmodern condition have that modernism does not? In contrast to modernism, postmodernism – as a cultural logic, mood, or entire socio-political system – is said to be characterised by lack of depth, loss of certainty and the shift away from modernism's relentless search for fixed meanings, truths and certainties. The idea of progress, of a path that can be followed that will lead to societal improvement, is entirely absent in postmodern culture, logic and discourse. In its place we see a plurality of models for living, understanding and relating to each other that manifest themselves across a range of social and cultural phenomena: from politics to art, to pop music, sexuality, architecture and engineering. Modernism's obsession with stability, certainty and purity is countered by the emergence of a ruleless, schizophrenic life, of a disorganisation that, for writers such as Lyotard and Baudrillard, reflects the loss of society as we know it, and the emergence of lives lived on the 'surface' of things.

Grand narratives with their logical models of social evolution no longer have a relevance. There is nothing resembling modern society that needs, or indeed *can* be explained by an all-encompassing macro-sociological theory. In the words of Fukuyama (1989), we have reached the 'end of history', with an accompanying loss of emancipatory projects so beloved of modern political and sociological politics. The view of history 'ending' relates to a notion of history as a great rationalistic project that is directed towards some ultimate destination and is driven by some form of totalising logic. The end of history, then, is seen as merging with the termination of modernism and the emergence of a postmodern society.

With a loss of faith in social progress, writers have suggested that 'society' (the very concept of which is challenged by some postmodern writers) has redrawn the agenda – an agenda that social theorists interpret differently. Zygmunt Bauman sees the demise of the modern as accompanied by the emergence of a loss of hope and vision. Without the belief in progression, individuals are morally and psychically lost in a society that increasingly detaches itself from any fixed logic or guiding philosophy:

> the dominant sentiment is the feeling of uncertainty – about the future shape of the world, about the right way of living in it, and about the criteria by which to judge the rights and wrongs of one's way of living.

> (Bauman 1997: 50)

While uncertainty and disillusionment were certainly defining characteristics of modernity (e.g. Munch's *The Scream*), Bauman argues that we have gone beyond the stage of modern angst, a sense of fearfulness that carried with it the antidote of societal progress, of a better society that could, somehow at least, be achieved with a sense of vision and commitment. Postmodern times lack the 'temporary' nature of modern fears; they are characterised by the permanent nature of uncertainty, panic and fearfulness.

Other writers *celebrate* the emergence of the postmodern social formation, with its accompanying 'anything goes' mood. Advocates of the postmodern such as Hebdige (1989) and Stacey (1993) suggest that a postmodern culture allows the views of minority groups to flourish, with a fragmentation of dominant modernist political and cultural dogma. Unfettered by modern desires for rational, ordered cultural expression, the postmodern ushers in an age of the free spirit, of an eclectic, unorthodox mix of tastes, lifestyle choices and cultural identities.

Before expanding on the different contributions of standpoints on the postmodern by social theorists – and examining the implications (political, cultural and theoretical) of such approaches – we firstly consider briefly some examples of postmodern economic, social and cultural practices. Only then can the significance of the shift from the modern to the postmodern be fully understood.

Living the postmodern – what does the postmodern look like?

In attempting to apply abstract understandings of what postmodernism *is* to 'real' examples, theorists have focused on a wide variety of areas to illustrate their claims. The examples that postmodern theorists use often reflect their field of interest, with the result that particular writers have tended to privilege certain spheres – popular culture; new information technologies; sexualities – as central to an understanding of postmodern society. Indeed, as may befit the shift away from modernist grand narratives and totalising theoretical frameworks, theories of postmodern society are, almost exclusively, characterised by partial, sometimes specialised, investigations into certain *aspects* of society. Where theorists have made pronouncements of a more totalising nature, these have tended to be grounded in frameworks which have some association with the modern theoretical tradition – such as Jameson's Marxist-inspired account that sees postmodernism as the cultural logic of late capitalism (pp. 244–8).

As a result, postmodern writers have employed a rich plurality of case study focuses to ground their theoretical claims. The areas that are introduced in this section relate to (a) industrial production, (b) media culture and identity, and (c) politics.

From industry to information – new technologies and new mentalities

For many postmodern theorists, the immense changes that have occurred in the economic sphere since the 1970s symbolise the end of modern production-based industry and the emergence of something 'new': of a postmodern shift towards flexible production, the growth of the service sector and the huge growth of information technologies (Harvey 1989). In essence, it is claimed that the postmodern marketplace is a very different trading sphere from that of the modern factory system, not least because of the technological revolution that has permitted a 'new mode of development – informationalism' (Castells 1996: 14). Whereas the modern age is said, by theorists such as Bell (1973, 1976), to be associated with the logics of growth, production and technological progress, resulting in the emergence of 'mass production' often based around the factory assembly line, the postmodern economic experience is quite different.

Indeed, observers such as Castells have written of the shift away from modernist production techniques as heralding the dawn of a 'new socio-technological paradigm', strongly linked to the growth of new information technologies. Furthermore, information systems – which include telecommunications, computers, the Web, microelectronics – function as highly integrated networks, with knowledge itself a 'product' of such systems (Castells 1996). In contrast to modernist Wallerstein's writings on the capitalist world economy, what we now have in existence is a qualitatively different 'global economy', a distinctive characteristic of postmodern society:

> The information economy is global. A global economy is a historically new reality, distinct from a world economy . . . it is an economy with the capacity to work as a unit in real time on a planetary scale. While the [modernist] capitalist mode of production is characterised by its relentless expansion, always trying to overcome limits of time and space, it is only in the late twentieth century that the world economy was able to become truly global on the basis of the new infrastructure provided by information and communication technologies. This globality concerns the core processes and elements of the economic system.
> (Castells 1996: 92–3)

Accompanying these global, structural shifts in production, we have the development of a postmodern organisational logic. Such a workplace logic can be described as an approach that stresses the importance of post-Fordist flexibility, innovation and adaptability, as opposed to the Fordist regime that promoted ideals of tight control, mass production, reliability and conformity. In addition to structural and ideological shifts, the growth of the postmodern information network is also said to influence culture and lifestyle among the workforce: the flexible, fast-moving, unpredictable nature of the post-Fordist workplace is said to inhibit the development of a strong workplace culture and the growth of class-related identities. For Castells, we have in place of bourgeoisie and proletariat the development of a core labour force of 'networkers' (decision-makers), those who are 'networked' (key to the organisation but with little power to influence decisions), and the 'switched-off workers' defined primarily by the tasks they perform, often working at the bottom of the power hierarchy and defined by their relative powerlessness.

The global networks that Castells defines can be seen to exist across a variety of enterprises, and are not restricted to the information and service sectors. Indeed, accompanying the new dynamic, flexible and creative firm of the 1980s – such as Saachi and Saachi – and seen by Castells as the embodiment of the 'multidirectional network model' – the network paradigm is apparent in larger production-based corporations such as McDonald's. While the McDonald's global corporation may be said to contain many of the features that characterise Fordist production practices and ethics of the modern age – mass production of products that are identical in terms of size, taste and appearance, instantly recognisable by the globally resonant golden arches – McDonald's, too, has been characterised as epitomising the new organisational logic (Ritzer 1993). We have, then, the opening of franchises across the globe – albeit with the occasional cultural tweaking as a concession to local tastes and culture – and the incorporation of networking cross-industry with film, television and toy corporations (for example Disney; Beanie babies).

Discussion question

Do postmodern networks of production (e.g. the McDonald's Corporation) encourage post-modern patterns of consumption? In other words, in what ways can Castells' network society encourage a postmodern mood of uncertainty, fragmentation and diversity?

It is important to recognise that Castells is not suggesting that the growth of the network society in any way represents a decline of capitalist civilisation, nor a reversal of the power-laden nature of capitalist relations of production. As well as new networking arrangements continuing to differentiate between the powerful and the powerless, albeit in a different context from that found in the typically Fordist factory system, Castells is keen to highlight that information technologies themselves are not freely available to all (Castells 1996). Postmodern economic arrangements do not necessarily usher in equality in the workplace and the end of poverty (i.e. typically modernist concerns). Rather, the restructuring of the capitalist system creates a (typically postmodern) era of contradiction and conflict – of a combination of flexibility, diversity and creativity in the workplace, alongside uncertainty, powerlessness and fear in one's working environment:

Our world, and our lives, are being shaped by the conflicting trends of globalisation and identity. The information technology revolution, and the restructuring of capitalism, have induced a *new form of society, the network society*. It is characterised by the globalisation of strategically decisive economic activities. By the networking form of organisation. By flexibility and instability of work, and the individualisation of labour. By a culture of real virtuality constructed by a pervasive, interconnected and diverse media system. And, by the material foundations of life, space and time, as expressions of dominant activities and controlling elites.

(Castells 1997: 1)

Postmodern culture and identity 1 – the global and the local

In attempting to provide some indication of what the postmodern 'looks like', analysts have been particularly prolific in their discussion of postmodern culture and identity. Alongside the shifts in the economic and industrial landscape outlined above, theorists such as Morley and Robins (1995) and Featherstone (1991) have written at length about the development of 'cultural globalisation', a term that implies a degree of convergence and commonality across diverse geographical areas, with a decline in internationally based cultural allegiance. Stemming from the growth of new media technologies (satellite television and the Internet) Morley and Robins (1995) talk about a new 'global arena' of culture. In contrast to the modernist attachment to the national state, with an individual's geographical identity relatively fixed, national forms of cultural identity have been weakened, with a strengthening of identities 'beyond' the level of the nation state. The 'global postmodern' (S. Hall 1992, 1996) works alongside the growth of a global consumerism – meaning and identity can be seen to derive from a common cultural resonance and identification with the lifestyles promoted by the new communications network. Identities thus become, for writers such as Hall, subject to a process of 'containment' or cultural homogenisation through the global capitalist system. While cultural identities have become detached from a fixed place in space (for example one's local village hall), exposing each of us to a plurality of lifestyles, cultures and traditions, the effect of the global 'cultural supermarket' is to make the distinctive and specific understandable and contained:

The more social life becomes mediated by the global marketing of styles, places and images, by international travel, and by globally networked media images and communications systems, the more identities become detached – disembodied – from specific times, places, histories and traditions, and appear 'free-floating'. We are confronted by a range of different identities, each appealing to us, or rather to different parts of ourselves from which it seems possible to choose. It is the spread of consumerism, whether as reality or dream, which has contributed to this cultural supermarket effect. Within the discourse of global communication, differences and cultural distinctions which hitherto defined identity become reducible to a sort of international lingua franca or global currency into which all specific traditions and distinct identities can be translated. This phenomenon is known as 'cultural homogenisation'.

(S. Hall 1992)

While it may appear that such cultural homogenisation implies a simple replication of the 'mass' culture of modernism, albeit on a larger scale, it is the tension among the local, national and global in the creation of cultural attachment that makes contemporary culture in some ways distinctive for the postmodern theorist. One can now, to a far greater extent than ever before, simultaneously enjoy a soap opera based in one's own country, attend a local council meeting about town planning issues, and sign a petition to support the expulsion of a dictator in a country that one has never heard of. While mass culture has certainly not disappeared – seen, for example, in the popularity and 'meaningfulness' of entertainment corporations such as Disney and continued global screening of soap operas such as 'Dallas' – the postmodern condition throws into question the fixed, stable nature of an individual's relationship to cultural practice.

However, it should be noted that even writers who acknowledge the emergence of a postmodern global culture advise a certain degree of caution (Robins 1996; Massey 1997). In particular, it must be remembered that globalisation is essentially a western process. As Robins puts it:

> global capitalism has in reality been about westernisation – the export of western commodities, values, priorities, ways of life . . . Globalisation, as it dissolves the barriers of distance, makes the encounter of colonial venture and colonised periphery immediate and intense.
>
> (Robins 1996: 25)

The same 'power geometry' that has been recognised, by theorists such as Wallerstein, to have defined the *modern* 'capitalist world system' can therefore be said to have been replicated, albeit on a different scale, within the new postmodern global community. Furthermore, while theorists of the postmodern look to the consequences of homogenisation, there has also been a growth in the number of analysts who have simultaneously associated postmodern culture with a celebration of cultural difference, distinctiveness and diversity. While writers such as Hall have tended to concentrate on the relation *between* local and global identity, others have displayed a fascination through their work with the emerging new forms of cultural identities within the postmodern era.

Postmodern culture and identity 2 – the dissolution of the self

Postmodern theorists identify the occurrence of a shift away from the relative certainties of the modern perspective, a time in which the necessity of achieving a sense of unity and attachment for the individual, albeit in a world of disillusionment and alienation, was acknowledged. Theorists such as Baudrillard, Deleuze, Guattari and Foucault (the latter being more strongly associated with the post-structuralist movement) claim that the notion of the self-constituting subject – an individual who is autonomous and self-reflexive – is rapidly disappearing in postmodern society. In its place the individual is exposed to a myriad of disjointed and discontinuous experiences, resulting in identities that are 'disintegrated into a flux of euphoric intensities' (Foucault 1980). Anxiety – a state associated with the modern self's sense of isolation and detachment – no longer means anything in postmodern culture. One's state as an individual becomes decentred, pleasurably schizophrenic, in a constant state of formation and reformation. The loss of a centralised authority structure (perhaps, for instance, with the decline of the traditional family) in postmodern society has, for writers such as Plant and Healey (1994), an emancipatory effect on one's gender identity. With the loss of centralised structures such as local communities and traditional families, Plant suggests that we have a 'privileging of instability', in which there is a recognition of the necessity of the plural self, 'free to shift, redefine and to re-emerge' into new spaces that offer a degree of autonomy. We are each free to embrace 'lifestyle transgression', whether this be in the sphere of sexuality, gender or indeed within the broader sphere of everyday 'lived' culture (e.g. rave culture, New Age travelling). Such a positive plurality is to be applauded, representing a form of resistance against the fixed, orthodox practices of patriarchy and heterosexuality (Mort 1994). As Plant suggests, however, it may be that underneath the constant search to repackage the self there still lingers the modernist pretension to *define*, to be part of something that is solid, fixed and constant, albeit only for a short while. Further complexities derive from the contention within 'standpoint feminism' that postmodernism as an academic enterprise is but one more way of white, middle-class 'male' sociology detracting attention away from the political underpinnings of the feminist emancipatory project (Skeggs 1991; Marshall 1994).

Postmodern politics – a contradiction in terms?

Modernist society and culture has been defined by theorists in terms of a struggle for truth, progress and the end of inequality. Accompanying such a condition is a rise in social movements that increasingly look towards mass organisation and protest as a form of mobilising individuals in the quest for improvement of one's life. Modernism has been associated by theorists with the primacy of a particular type of political action, that of *class-based politics*, organised around the recognition that the working class shared, to some extent at least, common working conditions and consequent lifestyles. Politics in modernist society can be defined primarily through an individual's relationship to the social structure, with status and life chances theorised by analysts as stemming, to different degrees, from location in the social strata. The shift away from unitary forms of identity within modernism, and the postmodern shift towards the growing multiplicity of social groups and organisations through which the individual is able to 'live out' his or her own specific experience of social organisations, raises the important question of what the implications for political culture might be. The theorist Frederic Jameson, whom we return to later, has written extensively on the political implications of the postmodern condition. Jameson suggests that the postmodern can be defined in part through the plurality of power-bases and interests in society. Class formation and class consciousness is in crisis, through the

> global restructuring of production and the introduction of radically new technologies,
> that have flung workers in archaic factories out of work, displaced new kinds of industry

to unexpected parts of the world, and recruited work forces different from the traditional ones in a variety of features, from gender to skill and nationality.

(Jameson 1991: 319)

Alongside this – and to some degree stemming from the crisis of class – is the emergence of 'new social movements', based around the growth of feminism, environmental movements, sexuality, ethnicity and locality, and the disability movement, to name but a few. A consequence of the dispersion of political action away from a unified core of class has been a type of politics that is typically dispersed and fragmented. No longer can the individual look to unite in a combined struggle with their workplace peer: with the growth of flexible labour practices, and the accompanying rise of 'new' forms of political allegiance, politics takes on a disjointed indefinable nature. Who, now, can easily be identified as the ruling class, or indeed as a member of the working class? Is an individual's gender, sexuality, race or occupation the defining element in the choice of struggle and protest? What are the grounds on which people unite in common protest?

Discussion questions

Look at the extracts on the anti-capitalism demonstrations of 1 May 2001 and the fuel crisis of 2000.

> But far more significant in the longer run than apportioning blame for yesterday's clashes is the fact that 10 years after the end of the cold war and the supposed global triumph of liberal capitalist ideas, the international workers' day has again become a focus of international protest, animated yesterday by a common political agenda from London to Sydney, Moscow to Seoul: rejection of neo-liberal globalisation, opposition to the eclipse of democracy by corporate power and demand for international action to tackle the ecological crisis. Even by simply making the slogan of anti-capitalism common currency, the movement has raised the possibility of a systemic alternative, derided as a nonsense for most of the past decade.
>
> And far from being a minority cause, the central concerns of the anti-corporate movement are becoming mainstream, finding support far beyond the ranks of environmentalists, animal rights activists and global economic justice campaigners on the streets of London and other British cities yesterday. This week's NOP poll for Channel Four found most people believe multinational companies have more power over their lives than Tony Blair's government and that the corporate giants care 'only about profits and not the interests of the people in the countries where they operate'.
>
> (*Source*: Seumas Milne, 'Special Report: May Day 2001', *Guardian*, 2 May 2001)

> The fuel protests are a ragbag of different interests. Their cause – 'cheaper fuel' – is actively unpopular with people concerned about the environment. This is not the stuff of popular revolution. It has only become so because it has tapped into something potent; the feel bad factor.
>
> If the government is relying on polls to gauge public support, it will be very confused. They don't add up. MORI has 58 per cent supporting protest action, while the RSPB found 51 per cent believing petrol should be taxed for environmental reasons and 46 per cent wanting taxation to limit greenhouse gas emissions. Away from number crunching though, the feel bad factor is unmissable. Everyone is fed up about something, whether it's stealth taxes, the risk of bankruptcy, commuter chaos, extreme weather or fears about contamination of food.
>
> . . .

I would despair if I thought this support was because the majority believe cheap petrol is a basic human right and are either indifferent to or ignorant about its disastrous environmental impact. But it is obviously more complex. The majority say they would use public transport if it was reliable and cheap. London voted for Ken Livingstone, who explicitly calls for congestion charges and reducing car dependency. Many people say they would support higher fuel tax if the money were ring-fenced for public transport. And no parent is in any doubt that safe streets for children are more important than cheaper fuel.

Yet, the fuel protest has articulated wider and deeper grievances: about stealth taxes driving up living costs without any public pay-offs; about unfair advantages for European hauliers and farmers; about British uncompetitiveness with the high pound; and general hostility to a government which seems pre-occupied with abstract 'human' rights and indifferent to the difficulties of ordinary citizens. Other targets might have focused some of this discontent: supermarket chains have undermined British farming by over-reliance on imports and have driven up the cost of living with expensive foods. But only fuel protests symbolise all the elements of current dissatisfaction.

(*Source*: Ros Coward, 'Special Report: The Petrol War', *Guardian*, 7 November 2000)

1 To what extent can class identity be said to have driven these recent political protests?

2 Has Tony Blair's 'Third Way' style of politics in which 'rights and responsibilities' override, for example, class-based forms of political identification, resulted in the development of a postmodern style of politics? In what ways can politics today be considered modernist in style?

For writers such as Jameson, and the post-Marxists Laclau and Mouffe (1985), there is no denying the reality of protest groups organised around non-class-based issues. For Jameson, however, such movements lack the depth and authenticity of the class movement; dispersed around the globe, and, with action directed towards several 'enemies', solutions to struggles are often defined by local concerns and conditions. The (modernist) meta-narrative of class will, however, emerge as victorious for Jameson, through a merging of existent political protests in a unified movement:

> I'm convinced that this new post-modern global form of capitalism will now have a new class logic about it, but it has not yet reconstructed itself on a global scale, and as such there is a crisis in what classes and class consciousness are.
>
> (Jameson 1991: 31)

Other writers such as Mort applaud the postmodern move away from fixed class identification as a basis for political identity and action. The mobilisation of politics around identity (or 'structures of subjectivity') that is not exclusively class-based, but which recognises that attachments to the social structure are diverse, plural and changing, has, for Mort, an 'autobiographical relevance' (Mort 1994). A postmodern politics would recognise that we each have different narratives according to the 'dimensions of our subjectivities and the contours of self-identity'. Whether or not this new type of politics, based very much around identities, represents a shift away from modernist notions of equal rights and fairness, is, however, a concern shared by theorists such as Moore. While recognising that politics in postmodern society means a great deal more than class, and supersedes even the aims of the liberal feminist movement, Moore claims that the demands of 'traditional' politics have yet to be met. Writing in Cherrie Smythe's *Lesbians Talk Queer Notions* (1992) around the rise of the politics of sexuality, Moore makes the following point:

> I don't think I could claim Queer. While I want to embrace Queer politics, some of the very basic demands of the Women's Movement have to be met, like childcare. But that's not very Queer is it? Not very exciting.
>
> (Moore, cited in Smythe 1992)

To say that the postmodern represents the decline of one type of political identity and action and the emergence of another would be to overstate the case. From the work of analysts in this area, it would appear that while politics is changing, in part a reflection of the very real changes that are taking place in society, by no means does this suggest that older forms of political identity no longer have a relevance. Certain postmodern theorists (for example Jameson) believe that socio-economic location is, today, more important than ever in defining an individual's life chances and status. Rather, it is perhaps clearest if the postmodern is associated with a freeing up of the political arena, an opening of a formally exclusive 'club' to a plurality of groups, ideas and challenges to political orthodoxies.

POSTMODERN THEORISTS – THEORISING THE UNTHEORISABLE

Just as the postmodern is a contested and shifting notion, so too do we find a good degree of variation, even disagreement, among social theorists who have, to differing degrees, been labelled in some way as theorising the postmodern. For instance, there are those writers such as Jameson who, while commenting on the 'cultural logics' of postmodernism or 'late capitalism' still seek to address the relations between culture and material practices. Others such as Jean Baudrillard, however, suggest that so pervasive is the 'postmodern shift' that any reference to 'modernist' notions such as 'reality', the 'material' and 'truth' are meaningless within the context of postmodernism. The implications of such a shift away from traditional, modernist sociological concerns for social theory as an enterprise will be addressed later. For now it is important to appreciate the diversity of postmodern theory. While theorists are certainly 'linked' by a similar concern to explicate what can, in general terms, be defined as a shift towards depthlessness, diversity and loss of certainty, the *ways* in which this shift is conceptualised, and the political, economic, social and cultural consequences that are said to stem from such practices, clearly differ from theorist to theorist.

Below, three key theorists associated with the postmodern tradition are examined.

Jean Baudrillard – postmodern simulations

> Determination is dead, indetermination reigns. We have witnessed the ex-termination (in the literal sense of the word) of the reals of production and of the real of signification . . . This historical and social mutation is readable at every level. The era of simulation is henceforth opened everywhere through the commutability of terms once contradictory or dialectically opposed.
>
> (Baudrillard 1973)

The writings of Jean Baudrillard represent what is arguably the most radical attempt to theorise postmodernism in its entirety. In presenting what is an all-encompassing exposition on postmodern life, Baudrillard critiques modernist attempts to 'rationalise' postmodernity (see *On Seduction*, 1979). Just as modernist notions of truth, essences and factual realities are no longer valid, so it is suggested must the social theorist move away from the rational procedures of 'depth analysis', of delving beneath appearances in order to reveal the 'answer' to a question. In seeking to investigate, instead, the 'surface' of social life, we have our first insight into Baudrillard's view of postmodern social, political and cultural practices. Baudrillard's work has itself shifted in focus from a 'realist' critique of capitalist communication and commodification (*The System of Objects*, 1968; *La Société de Consommation*, 1976) towards what is unequivocally concerned with appearances as opposed to 'realities' (*Simulacra and Simulation*, 1981). It is in his later writings that the foundations of his radical and very distinctive approach can be found, the key themes of which are as follows:

- The order of the world has shifted, from an order based on material com-modification to one based upon *models, codes and simulations*.
- Action is determined not by 'hidden' or latent social structures (e.g. the capital-ist mode of production), but by surface appearances (the '*code* of production').
- Claims to truth and reality are, for Baudrillard, nonsensical in postmodern life. Life is made up of images and signs – the hyperreal – that has no reality other than its own.

The notions of hyperreality and the simulacrum have been seen as the chief con-tributions of Baudrillard's work, and for this reason are worth exploring in some depth. Both terms operate at a high level of abstraction, and refer to a 'hyperreal' society in which dichotomies between reality and appearance, surface or depth, life and art have been dissipated. In their place we have a model of society in which 'simulations' (surface images or codings) dominate, resulting in a social order that comprises not 'real' social problems and practices, but 'simulacra' (reproductions of objects or events). This notion of social life as a series of simulacra is developed further, and given an historical significance, through Baudrillard's notion of *orders of simulacra*. In classifying various types of 'reproductions' chronologically, an account of changing social orders – from the modern through to the postmodern – is pro-vided. Whereas, in the feudal era, codes or 'signs' were relatively fixed (e.g. social rank and status easily signified by the clothes worn by a person), and in the modern

age codes were mass produced and marketed, *post*modern society is to be characterised by 'third-order simulation', or 'simulation proper' (Kellner 1989). The world
does not operate with a notion of an 'original' that is being simulated – simulation
is, quite simply, all there is, now having finally 'devoured' representation.

One example that Baudrillard gives to illustrate the notion of 'hyperreality' is that
of Disneyland in the USA. Disneyland, through its representations of imaginary places,
stories and realities is, for Baudrillard, presented as imaginary in order to make us
believe that America is real, whereas in fact

> all of Los Angeles and the America surrounding it are no longer real, but of the order of
> the hyperreal and of simulation . . . It [Disneyland] is meant to be an infantile world, in
> order to make us believe that the adults are elsewhere, in the 'real' world and to conceal
> the fact that real childishness is everywhere, particularly amongst those adults who go here
> to act the child in order to foster illusions as to their real childishness.
>
> (Baudrillard 1981: 25)

Albeit in a rather confused and exaggerated fashion, Baudrillard is making the
point that society is more and more dominated by the construction of imaginary
images, these images often being reproductions of other images and so on. Extending this point to the organisation of social life in general, the model now dominates,
structures and controls: from the power of the interior design· programme, the representation of USA elections, even the coverage of a fashion show in a magazine,
our understandings about the world and our place in it are formed through and
by the image. Our very identities are simulations, reinforced and contested by other
simulations, resulting in a social order that is precoded and 'pre-organised', despite
an apparent multitude of simulation choices. Our lives may gain meaning and
identity by the kinds of clothes we wear (chain store or designer), the food we eat
(junk food or 'low fat'), the holidays we take (package holiday or backpacking trip)
or the colleges we attend (elite university or local technical college).

Discussion questions

1 In what ways can your life be said to be made up of simulations? To what extent does
the image dominate reality?

2 What are the factors that shape your choice of clothing/cuisine/entertainment/college?
Are these determined by the 'real' or the hyperreal?

The codings that are taken from such lifestyle choices are, it must be remembered,
preset, with Baudrillard stressing how a society of simulations comes to shape and
structure an individual's range of choices and options in the first place, however
diverse these choices may turn out to be. The controlling nature of the hyperreal is
suggested by Kellner:

> Models and codes . . . come to constitute everyday life, and modulation of the code comes
> to structure a system of difference and social relations in the society of simulations. The

codes send signals and continually test individuals, inscribing them into the simulated order. Responses are structured in the binary system of affirmation or negation: *every ad, fashion, commodity, television program, political candidate and poll presents a test to which one is to respond. Is one for or against? Do we want to or not? Will we choose X or Y? In this way, one is inserted in a coded system of similarities and dissimilarities, of identities and programmed differences.*

(Kellner 1989, emphasis added)

With no depth or 'substance' to the simulacrum, modernist questions about power and resistance become meaningless. Indeed, the only kind of resistance that Baudrillard writes about is through a refusal to delve beneath the surface in a search for answers and insights. 'Accept the surface, reject the meanings' appears to be the advice that Baudrillard gives when confronted with claims that this model of the postmodern is overly pessimistic, albeit with the additional claim that even this supposedly threatening gesture is itself functional to the society of simulations (Baudrillard 1981: 82).

The implications of a model of society that refuses meaning, the 'real' and indeed talks about the 'end of the perspective space of the social' (Smart 1993) will be considered in the following sections. It is useful at this point to consider briefly some of the critiques that have been applied to the work of Baudrillard, before moving on to consider other writers of the postmodern tradition.

Critiquing Baudrillard

Although Baudrillard himself has rejected the label of postmodernist for his own approach (categorisation of thought being a modernist practice), it cannot be denied that his notions of simulation, the simulacrum and hyperreality characterise perfectly the postmodern mood of illusion and unreality, albeit in a radical way. While Baudrillard's work has indeed been applauded by many academics as epitomising the shift away from cultural certainties and towards the multiplication of means and codes in social life, his work has also received strong criticism, not least from the academic left. The main criticisms that Baudrillard's work has received are summarised below.

Baudrillard's work is a form of 'moral and political nihilism' (Norris 1993)

It has been suggested by writers such as Norris (1992, 1993) and Kellner (1989) that Baudrillard's writing represents a surrender to the forces of moral apathy. With the loss of the distinction between truth and falsity, how can judgements on, for example, the behaviour of governments, be permitted as valid and meaningful? How, for instance, would it be possible to distinguish between the legitimacy of anti-racist and racist argumentation? Is one more 'true' than the other? And what are the consequences for social, political and cultural practices if we remove the rules and fall for the seduction of sensation and the imaginary? As writers such as McLennan (1992) argue, if social theory is to accept that the nature of the social order has fundamentally changed, to the extent that there is no longer any differentiation between good and bad, and right and wrong, there is no longer any basis in the social sciences for a critique of practice and recommendations for change.

Baudrillard's work ignores issues of power and inequality

By ignoring the fact that some 'realities' (e.g. poverty, unemployment) may be more real for some groups in society than for others, it could be suggested that Baudrillard's approach fails to capture the fundamentally uneven nature of social life. Do all groups in society have equal access to the simulacrum? And who determines which simulations dominate in any one historical period? For if there is no 'reality' then there can be no propaganda, misrepresentation or plain 'unreality' in, for example, political and media discourse. In other words, while Baudrillard's account of the changing social structure may well alert the reader to transformations that have occurred in the realm of culture – not least through reference to the implosion of rules and realities (Kroker and Cook 1988: 167) – it is not clear from his work who or what has the power to participate in the new hyperreal, and who does not. Furthermore, if we accept Baudrillard's premise that the 'mode of production' no longer guides the logic of capitalist consumerism, questions about resources, life chances and even issues relating to discrimination are not only irrelevant but totally meaningless.

Baudrillard's vision of society is true only for a privileged few

However pessimistic a case Baudrillard makes for the state of contemporary society and the position of the individual in it, his vision of a society seduced by imagery and little else is a departure from modernist writers' concerns with self-improvement and resistance of the dominant order. For Baudrillard, the image stupefies and 'resists' resistance by the subject, who in turn is left to find meaning(lessness) in a world that fragments the individual, leaving them detached from self-certainty and a clear, definable identity. Kellner, however, has argued that Baudrillard's notion of the self-reflexive subject for whom change and diversification is part and parcel of the postmodern, is, in the main part, a fallacy. While, for a privileged few, the luxury of a self-reflexive adjustment to a notion of 'self' may indeed occur, for the majority of people identities and indeed realities are still stable, subscribing to a certain set of norms, values and rules:

> Identities are . . . still relatively fixed and limited, though the boundaries of possible identities and of new identities, are continually expanding.
>
> (Kellner 1995: 231)

While it cannot be denied that contemporary social life offers the individual a greater degree of movement between identities (e.g. cultural, political, sexual) this is not to deny that there still exist certain rules and boundaries that to some extent police the types of identities that some groups in society can and cannot take. The categories of age, gender and class may indeed be shifting in meaning, but nonetheless continue to shape, in a relatively fixed way, the expectations and judgements we make about individuals according to their membership of such groups.

Baudrillard's own theoretical framework is self-defeating and ultimately redundant

It has been suggested by writers such as Kellner (1995) that Baudrillard's critique of modernist theories or 'depth models' – those theoretical frames that attempt to reach 'beneath' the surface in a quest to reveal the 'real' conditions of social, political and cultural life – is but another attempt to impose his own version of truth and reality on the academic audience. For if distinctions between the rational and irrational, and between that which is 'true' and that which is 'false' have disappeared, how and why does Baudrillard himself have grounds upon which to critique other writers' attempts to make sense of the social and cultural world? Why, for instance, would Baudrillard feel that it is more valid to speak of the society of the hyperreal, if there is no basis to believe that this is the case? Is not Baudrillard's work simply a means of diverting the academic community away from an uncomfortable but necessary return to modernist concerns about inequalities and power differences? As Jameson argues (pp. 244–8), it is possible to see postmodern controversy and debate as an instance of cultural and symbolic class struggle, just as is found in other areas of society – with Baudrillard's particular position as 'true' and 'real' to Baudrillard himself as Marx's theory of historical materialism was to Marx.

Knowing the postmodern – Jean-François Lyotard and the rejection of modernity

The work of the French social theorist Jean-François Lyotard can be considered, along perhaps with that of Baudrillard, to be one of the most radical and exciting attempts by a social philosopher to explore the consequences of the postmodern shift in social and cultural practices in contemporary society. One of the key figures in the postmodern camp, Lyotard is perhaps best known for his book *The Postmodern Condition* (1984), in which he argues that the defining characteristic of postmodernity is the ways in which the status of knowledge, or our understandings of the world and our place in it, is fundamentally different from the types of knowledge and understanding that can be said to have characterised the modernist era. Put simply, the status of knowledge in the postmodern era displays, for Lyotard, characteristics that distinguish it from modernist knowledge in two ways.

The first is that the whole process of collecting, disseminating and communicating knowledge has changed significantly as societies have entered the post-industrial age. Technological transformations – computerisation, the World Wide Web, satellite and cable television, to take just a few examples – have led in part to a world in which knowledge is the principal force of production, a commodity in the global, economic and political community. As Lyotard himself puts it:

> Knowledge in the form of an informational commodity indispensable to productive power is already, and will continue to be, a major – perhaps the major – stake in the worldwide competition for power. It is conceivable that the nation-states will one day fight for control of information just as they battled in the past for control over territory, and afterwards,

for control of access to and exploitation of raw materials and cheap labour. A new field is opened for industrial and commercial strategies on the one hand, and political and military strategies on the other.

(Lyotard 1984: 6)

With the rise of the information age, Lyotard argues that the 'senders' and 'receivers' of knowledge enter into a new 'pragmatic' relation of communication. In the postmodern age of information transmission, knowledge is strategically directed towards targeted audiences, just as goods and services are aimed at specific consumer groups in the marketplace. According to Lyotard, this results in the development of networks of 'language games', each individual viewing knowledge as a commodity, something that can be used for a specific social purpose.

It is the *effect* of this process by which information and 'language networks' are seen as pragmatically used resources that leads Lyotard to his second point. Lyotard claims that, in the modernist era, at least some forms of knowledge can be characterised as objective, rational, universal and broadly progressive (McLennan 1992: 330). The Enlightenment, for example, can be characterised as concerned with the search for forms of knowledge that can morally 'prescribe' the path that modern societies should take: the growth of science, and indeed the social sciences, as concerned with the promotion of truth, progress and self-realisation, can be seen as forms of knowledge, and epitomise the modernist quest for liberation and political and social improvement. It is alongside the development of modernist knowledge-types that Lyotard identifies the key defining characteristic – indeed condition – of modernist knowledge: the appeal within such knowledge types to *meta-narratives* that legitimate and ground modernist discourses. Meta-narratives can be understood as legitimising discourses or myths that provide justifications for the pursuit of modernist knowledge – the appeal of science to industrial and social development, or Marxism's recourse to the liberation of the human spirit. Lyotard claims that such meta-narratives exist simply as ideological rationalisations for the pursuit of certain types of knowledge – without 'proof' of objectivity. He states that any such claims should be treated sceptically in terms of their special status as 'truth' (McLennan 1992: 333).

So how does knowledge in the postmodern age differ from that which has been identified as characterising modernism? For Lyotard, the very condition of post-modernity can be defined as incredulity towards meta-narratives *per se*. It is not one particular legitimating discourse or another that is problematical for Lyotard; rather, it is the very process of legitimisation and justification through recourse to grand meta-narratives that is rejected. In contrast, postmodern knowledge is defined by a new epistemology, with a rejection of objective, universal and totalis-ing thought and an embracing of plurality, heterogeneity, innovation and prag-matically agreed upon 'rules for understanding' (Best and Kellner 1991: 165). The rejection of definitive truth claims within academic disciplines such as the sciences and social sciences, epitomises the postmodern condition for Lyotard. Searches for truths, answers and progress have been replaced, he argues, by a focus on non-totalising, pragmatically directed information, with knowledge losing its 'privileged' modernist status as the exclusive property of elites. As McLennan puts it, for Lyotard:

> the reality of knowledge today is a huge array of 'moves' within pragmatic 'discourses' or 'language games', all targeted towards very specific audiences, each having its own criteria of accreditation and each increasingly treated in practice as an economic commodity to be bought and sold according to its market demand.
>
> (McLennan 1992: 333)

With postmodern knowledge and the discourses or 'language games' contained within such knowledge seen by Lyotard as transient and provisional, it is almost as if knowledge has been subjected to a process of 'hollowing out' – not only with the disappearance of the meta-narrative, but through fundamentally rewriting the relationship between knowledge and power. To have knowledge today is not to have a privileged relation to the 'truth', enlightenment or reason, but is simply a means by which people communicate and 'live out' their relation to the world. Whereas modernist meta-narratives *exclude* other truth claims both inside and outside of their specific community of knowledge, and attempt to impose a degree of *conformity* and *consensus* in the process of universalising the 'truth', postmodern narratives for Lyotard differ quite dramatically. The postmodern condition is characterised by its specific notion of knowledge as *non-prescriptive* and heterogeneous. Removing knowledge creation from its modernist 'ownership' by elite communities, the process of acquiring, disseminating and contesting knowledge is freed from the constraining influence of modernism. Diversity and dissent are the order of the day in these postmodern times, a feature that Lyotard positively relishes:

> Consensus does violence to the heterogeneity of language games. And invention is always born of dissension. Postmodern knowledge is not simply a toll of the authorities; it refines our sensitivity to differences and reinforces our ability to tolerate the incommensurable.
>
> (Lyotard 1984: 75)

As we move from the modern to the postmodern, then, knowledge for Lyotard loses its intrinsic association with the Enlightenment: no longer an exclusive tool of the powerful, but a 'game' within which all of us 'play' at making sense of ourselves in this ruleless, unpredictable world. Every contribution, or 'move' that we make in the game contributes in some way to the creation of knowledge – although, as Lyotard points out, this is one game where there are no rules, no winners and consequently no losers. This is not to deny that some degree of personal satisfaction can be achieved from partaking in communication processes in society. Whether replying to an e-mail, listening to a radio programme or watching a satellite TV news broadcast, it becomes clear to all who are involved that certain groups have a closer relationship to the 'types' of language code that are being produced – be these politicians, journalists, editors or indeed media audiences. However, what makes postmodern knowledge production so distinctive for Lyotard is its temporary, shifting, and ultimately non-deterministic nature. What might one day appear to be controlled by one group may well shift unpredictably into the hands of others the next, the very process of receiving information endowing one with a stake in the language game. Power and its relation to knowledge does not disappear, but becomes transient, opening the playing-field to all.

Discussion questions

Knowledge production, be it through our communications with the media, our tutors, friends or family, is a fact of everyday life. Thinking of a recent situation in which you were subject to a 'language game', reflect on the following points:

1 Did the 'game' have an obvious 'sender' and 'receiver' of knowledge, or was it a mutually creative exchange?

2 Were there 'winners' or 'losers' in the exchange?

3 Did some in the game appear to have more power than others? Were 'meta-narratives' used in any way as part of an attempt to convince or legitimise certain 'truth claims'? If some have more power than others in the game, where does this power come from?

(An example of language game might be found in a doctor's surgery, where issues of power, knowledge and control could be drawn out and reflected upon.)

Critiquing Lyotard

Lyotard's work has been widely considered as epitomising the postmodern turn within social and philosophical theory (Bauman 1992; McGuigan 1999) and for this reason has been the subject of a great many debates and interrogations. Indeed, so often is it the case that Lyotard's work has been presented as representative of postmodernism *per se*, that it is tempting, though in many ways inaccurate, to see critiques of Lyotard's work as synonymous with wider critiques of postmodern social theory as a whole. While the critiques that follow are specific to Lyotard's own 'brand' of postmodernism, many of the issues that stem from such critiques do raise bigger questions about the status of postmodernism as a valid 'replacement' for modernist social theory.

Lyotard's work caricatures modernist knowledge in order to present a convincing postmodern alternative

It has been suggested by writers such as McGuigan (1999) that Lyotard's approach presupposes that modernist discourses can be classified together in a homogeneous 'mass' through their reliance on grand narratives that legitimise their proponent's pursuit of a particular path of reason and logic. While it is clearly the case that modernity is characterised by approaches to knowledge that can be broadly identified as truth-seeking, traditional and potentially liberating, it is equally clear that there is, arguably, as much conflict and dissent within modernist discourses as there are between them: for example the debates within Marxism in the 1970s regarding the emancipation of the subject; the numerous ongoing self-critiques within feminist social theory (see Chapter 8). In failing to acknowledge that forms of modernist knowledge are frequently associated with a high degree of dissent and self-reflexivity, it could be argued that Lyotard is guilty of doing precisely what he accuses the modernist of doing: producing an image of knowledge as consensual and totalising where no such model of understanding actually exists in the day-to-day work of 'doing' modernist social theory.

Lyotard's version of the postmodern mood or 'condition' itself embodies a modernist epistemology

As has been seen, Lyotard's work is notable for its rejection of the meta-narrative as an accompanying legitimising 'story' to modernist knowledge. However, as Best and Kellner (1991) argue, Lyotard's attack on the process of grounded critique is itself a critical, ontological position that carries its own legitimising meta-narrative: the supremacy of irrationality and dissensus as a basis for knowledge production.

> His [Lyotard's] 'war on totality' rejects totalising theories which he describes as master narratives that are somehow reductionist, simplistic, and even 'terroristic' by providing legitimations for totalitarian terror and suppressing differences in unifying schemes. Yet Lyotard himself is advancing the notion of a postmodern condition which presupposes a dramatic break from modernity. Indeed, does not the very concept of postmodernity, or a postmodern condition, presuppose a master narrative, a totalising perspective, which envisages the transition from a previous stage of society to a new one . . . precisely the sort of epistemological operation and theoretical hubris which Lyotard and others want to oppose and do away with?
>
> (Best and Kellner 1991: 45)

It would appear that certain versions of the grand narrative are subject to critique in Lyotard's work, yet the idea of legitimising discourse *per se* is actually an intrinsic part of Lyotard's very notion of the postmodern condition, without which his position would be meaningless (and thus truly postmodern?). Furthermore, an integral part of Lyotard's modernist critique is the inbuilt assumption that postmodern forms of knowledge are infinitely more accurate, valid and 'truthful' than their modernist cousins – epistemological assumptions that the most ardent modernist would be proud of.

Lyotard's position is, at best, politically relativist, and, at worst, potentially ideological

The political consequences of Lyotard's work have been commented upon by several writers, seen not least in Rorty's essay 'Habermas and Lyotard on postmodernity' (Rorty 1985). While the work of Habermas (1981) pays very little attention to the ideas of Lyotard (McGuigan 1999), the two writers are frequently juxtaposed through their vastly differing views on liberation and knowledge. While Habermas writes at length about the emancipatory potential of what he sees to be the unfinished modernist problematic, arrived at through the reaching of a consensus about society's political and ethical goals, Lyotard's commitment to social change, even the recognition of relations of domination based on class, race and gender, is obscure. While it could, quite reasonably, be suggested that a postmodern knowledge would, by design, have little concern with following the modernist tract of broad-based political critique (having no grounds upon which to claim certain versions of truth over others), there is some evidence from Lyotard's work that questions of power and domination *are* considered.

Writing in *The Differend*, Lyotard (1988) suggests that postmodern discourses have the potential to give minority discourses a voice. We are told that meta-discourses 'suppress minority discourses', while the plurality of discursive practices under conditions of postmodernity encourage a 'freeing up' of those types of knowledge that were, supposedly, formally excluded as valid types of knowledge. That the presence of a 'plurality of reason' should itself be seen as reflective of any wider deconstruction of power relations is, however, questionable. Lyotard's work may open up the possibility of a politics of language – perhaps, ironically, along the lines of Marxist-inspired critical discourse analysts such as Fairclough (1989, 1995) and Hodge and Kress (1979) – and yet the structural basis upon which certain discourses come to have greater power, authority and legitimacy over others is never developed in Lyotard's work. While the postmodern condition may create more 'players in the game', with a greater diversity of voices available to speak, any focus on the uneven, power-ridden nature of the playing-field itself is absent. As feminist writers Fraser and Nicholson (1988) argue, there is no place for a critique of broad-based relations of domination in Lyotard's work. Rather, Lyotard privileges an approach to knowledge that is local and ad hoc in nature, replacing any foray into the world of depth models and 'essences' of reality with a conception of playful deconstruction and textual gaming (Sarup 1993).

Politically, then, Lyotard's approach is indeed rather limiting. Questions of power, inequality and social justice may occasionally appear in and through his critique of modernist meta-narrative domination, yet any account of the material conditions that may be seen to underpin such a transformation of knowledge and the holders of knowledge in these postmodern times is, perhaps inevitably, lacking. What Lyotard's rejection of all matters of empirical truth and falsehood implies for the development of social theory is a matter that will be returned to later (see pp. 253–4).

Frederic Jameson – postmodern Marxist or 'having his cake and eating it'?

The theorists that have been examined so far in this chapter have, without doubt, been regarded within philosophy and the social sciences as in many ways personifying the postmodern approach. The work of Frederic Jameson, by contrast, is not quite no clearly categorised as such: Jameson has variously been categorised as postmodern cultural theorist, neo-Marxist and dialectical materialist (McGuigan 1999). Indeed, the reason that Jameson is such a fascinating theorist to examine in a chapter on postmodernism is precisely because of the potentially contradictory nature of his work, of the crossing over from Marxism to postmodernism and back again in a way that may anger the postmodern purist, yet which ironically represents what is arguably one of the most lucid yet simultaneously problematical accounts of postmodernity today. While Jameson's credentials as a postmodernist may be questioned, what is not in doubt are the contributions that his work has made as a theorist *of* the postmodern. As the title of his seminal 1984 essay, 'Postmodernism or the cultural logic of late capitalism' makes explicit, for Jameson the term 'postmodernism' principally refers to the 'cultural logic of late capitalism'. Accompanying the growth of late or 'third-stage' capitalism is an 'explosion' of culture that is itself an integral part of the production process. In short, the development of postmodern culture represents a *commodification* of cultural forms, judged not in modernist terms of high or low but, in a similar way to Lyotard's focus on communication, in aesthetic or purely economic terms. As Jameson puts it:

> What has happened is that aesthetic [*cultural*] production today has become integrated into commodity production generally, the frantic economic urgency of producing fresh waves of ever more novel-seeming goods (from clothing to airplanes), at ever greater rates of turnover, now assigns an increasingly essential structural function and position to aesthetic innovation and experimentation.
>
> (Jameson 1984: 56)

Incorporating postmodern cultural aesthetics alongside a Marxist-oriented focus on 'real' socio-economic 'shifts', the term 'postmodern' is applied not simply to cultural production, but is seen by Jameson as a 'multinational' economic and cultural 'space' that has 'genuine historical reality as a third great original expansion of capitalism around the globe' (Jameson 1991: 49). This reference to the postmodern as signifying both 'real' and symbolic transformations blurs in many ways the much lauded distinction between the modernist sphere of historical materialism and Marxist meta-narrative, and a postmodern focus on the cultural consequences of aesthetic transformation for the human subject. And yet by locating what writers such as Lyotard see as the defining surface phenomenon of the postmodern age – cultural aesthetics – as an integral part of the development of a real socio-economic historical development, Jameson's argument about the effects of postmodernity develop an epistemology which suggests that cultural practices do not have an autonomy from the 'real'. This is not to say, however, that Jameson's cultural forms and images are but a straightforward reflection of the economic infrastructure, working to 'distort' the proletariat away from the 'real' economic realities of society. As Connor argues: 'Here styles and representations are not the promotional accessories to economic products, they are the products themselves' (1989: 46).

With culture having, in a sense, a 'lived' reality, functioning to differing degrees as a commodity in late capitalist times, our lives take on a distinctly postmodern mood and sensibility. No longer having any emotional identification with the angst-ridden experience of anxiety, yearning and anomie that is seen to characterise the modern human condition, the postmodern individual is defined for Jameson as a symbol of 'depthlessness, flatness and apathy' (1991: 11). With there no longer being any referential condition or experience within postmodern culture that can be 'reached out' to, one's life is but a series of empty recycled signs, similar to the experience of 'generalised zapping between television channels' (McGuigan 1999:

71). For Jameson, the condition of postmodernity is best represented as a 'crises of historicity', with the forces of material history being trapped in a schizophrenic succession of 'perpetual presents in a scrambling of signifiers and images' (Jameson 1991: 72). Disoriented by the lack of attachment, the postmodern individual or 'subject' is exposed to a crisis of identity and location. In order to 'reattach' and reorient oneself in the 'world space of multinational capital', Jameson calls for a 'new aesthetic of cognitive mapping' – quite simply, a new way of 'making sense' of oneself and one's location in a social world which increasingly refuses sense, order and logic. The immensity of this task is not lost on Jameson:

> An aesthetic of cognitive mapping – a pedagogical political culture which seeks to endow the individual subject with some new heightened sense of its place in the global system – will necessarily have to respect this enormously complex representational dialectic and invent radical new forms to do it justice . . . The political form of postmodernism, if there ever is any, will have as its vocation the intention and protection of a global cognitive mapping on a social as well as a spatial scale.
>
> (Jameson 1991: 54)

Ironically, it is within the very realms of popular culture – in David Cronenberg's *Videodrome* – that Jameson discovers the type of cognitive mapping that allows us to 'glimpse the grain of postmodern urban life more vividly than any documentary or social drama' (Jameson 1992: 32–3). In a world of simulated screen culture, then, we have the potential to 'see' and realign meaning to our lives, albeit existences in which meaningless and disorientation are the defining qualities.

Discussion question

Jameson, like many other theorists of postmodernity, writes about the depthlessness and lack of attachment to the 'real' that we experience in society today. From your own life(style), can you think of any evidence to support or refute these claims?

(Think about the role of the media – soap operas, magazines, film, the Internet – in your experiences of life.)

Critiques of Jameson's postmodernism

Jameson overplays the dominance of postmodern culture in contemporary society

While Jameson recognises that the transition to postmodernity may contain within it 'countervailing logics' and tendencies that may disrupt the 'pure' emergence of a postmodern hegemony (Best and Kellner 1991: 186), he is insistent that the cultural logic that he identifies as postmodern be conceived of as the *dominant* cultural space of late global capitalism. It has been suggested, however, that Jameson is guilty of exaggerating – perhaps like many other theorists of the postmodern – just how pervasive and all-encompassing the culture of postmodernism actually is. Without providing specific, local instances of the shift away from the Enlightenment premises of, for example, progress, logic and rationality, and towards the depth-lessness and de-centredness of postmodern existence, Jameson leads us to conclude that the latter constitutes social experience to the exclusion of modernist forms of cultural expression. This criticism is clearly attested to by Best and Kellner:

> We find Jameson's claim that postmodernism is a cultural dominant to be overly totalis-ing in the sense that it exaggerates some tendencies – such as hyperrality or schizophrenia – which may only be emergent rather than dominant. Like extreme postmodernists, Jameson tends to inflate insights that apply to limited sectors of contemporary social life into overly general concepts representing all social spheres, thereby failing to analyse each sector in its specificity.
>
> (Best and Kellner 1991: 188)

The possibility that the occurrence of fragmentation and dissolution of self-identity, alongside a sense of depthlessness might also have been pertinent features of the modern experience (albeit experienced as part of a modernist search for mean-ing and ceremony – see, for example, Sartre's account of existentialist angst in *Nausea* (1969) is not considered by Jameson. Furthermore, despite the progress of global capital accumulation, it is clear that similar social, political and economic con-ditions as existed in less advanced capitalist times may still be dominant features in the day-to-day experiences of many in society (poverty, threat of unemployment, aspirations for a 'better' life) – something that is, in the main part, ignored by Jameson as a significant feature of the postmodern experience.

Jameson's blend of Marxism and postmodernism is fundamentally immiscible

In even attempting to theorise the postmodern within the modernist context of a Marxist project, it could be suggested that Jameson's theoretical account of the contemporary social world fails to fulfil the epistemological requirements of either of the two traditions he is working with. That is, in working with a Marxist meta-narrative that identifies the very real 'depth' processes of global capitalism, while at the same time wholeheartedly expounding, in the manner of Baudrillard, the 'hyperreal' sphere of visual screen culture, it could be suggested that we get a partial insight into, on the one hand, postmodern culture and, on the other, late capitalist economics, but *not* a totalising picture or theory of the corresponding moment whereby each are in articulation. In short, evidence of a Marxist meta-narrative is lacking when addressing, for example, film culture in the 'third machine age', just as any consideration of the potential effects of postmodern discourses on 'real' global capitalist practices are absent. As Robins (1996) argues, there is a tendency, in bringing together two unlikely bedfellows in an attempt to provide a totalising theory of contemporary global society, that one will tend to be privileged over the other. Does, for example, Jameson's aforementioned focus on *Videodrome* – seen by some (e.g. Turkle 1997) as postmodern cultural deconstruction *par excel-lence* – represent a means of gaining true consciousness of one's location in the progression of global capitalism? Is Jameson's enthusiasm for the self-realisation that *Videodrome* brings equal to the kind of consciousness (class or otherwise) that an exploration of one's position in the real, 'non-virtual' world might promote? Is Jameson stretching the point a little by equating postmodern screen culture (which might itself be regarded by many as an elitist, privileged pastime) with the formation of a radical, anti-capitalist standpoint?

Jameson's account results in a pluralist, de-radicalised notion of political action

Following on from the above point, it has been suggested that Jameson's partial accounts of culture and economics do not provide an adequate foundation for the development of a genuinely radical form of political opposition to late capitalism. Indeed, Jameson himself suggests that such politics can follow only from an account of the social sphere that is able to grasp the 'interconnectedness' of its disparate parts: 'Without a conception of the social totality (and the possibility of transforming the whole system) no socialist politics is possible' (Jameson 1988: 355).

Nonetheless, leaving aside the criticism of 'partiality' made above, can Jameson's proffered notion of cognitive mapping, discussed above, provide a political resource that is capable of engendering a 'new, radical culture politics' (Jameson 1984: 89)? Such cognitive maps that individuals would use to chart their place in the depthless, schizoid world on a journey to 'reality' are to be found when Jameson provides some illustration through certain postmodern 'cyberpunk' films (*Videodrome*, *Bladerunner*) and through the politically illuminating effects of the third world novel (Jameson's *Third World Literature in the Era of Multinational Capitalism*, 1986). How accessible, or indeed politically effective, such sources might be to Jameson's global proletariat is, however, unclear, with such materials more likely to be found on a postgraduate sociology or cultural studies' reading list than the average person's shopping list. Radical cultural politics may stem, for oppressed groups such as women, lesbians and gay men, ethnic minority communities and disabled groups, from the discoveries of cultural mapping: indeed, an *alliance* of such groups stemming from a realisation of their common map 'coordinates' is precisely what Jameson hopes for. With reference to the task that lies ahead of cultural politics, Jameson suggests that such a politics must act to

> make an inventory of the variable structures of 'constraint' lived by the various marginal, oppressed, or dominated groups – the so-called 'new social movements' fully as much as the working classes – with this difference, that each form of privation is acknowledged as producing its own specific 'epistemology', its own specific view from below, and its own specific truth claim.
>
> (Jameson 1988: 71)

However worthy such sentiments, the possibilities of ever reaching a common consensus *within* movements such as, for example, feminism and class politics, with increasing evidence here of divisions and differences, must surely be one area that needs further analysis, let alone the consideration of how such a 'realisation' be converted into practical political action.

POSTMODERN SOCIOLOGY, OR A SOCIOLOGY OF POSTMODERNISM?

> Reducing social critique to ironic commentaries does not remove the social structures which position and limit us as we are – it simply reduces our ability to do anything about them. The inability to address the real, and to change it, is implicit in the post-modern vision – what is its resort to irony, other than the gallows humour of the politically impotent?
>
> (Philo and Miller 1999)

In rejecting the essence of modernity – the search for truth, emancipation and human progress – it could be suggested that postmodern discourses provide little in the way of a recognisable social theory. In relation to the orthodox sociological pursuit of social research, for instance, the sociologist would, as part of his or her investigations, produce 'data' that would provide an insight into real, 'empirical' social facts. Insights provided from respondents – say in the form of an open-ended questionnaire – would provide information that would take the sociologist some way towards the formation of statements that would provide an 'answer' of sorts to the research questions that would have guided and structured the research. Once published, the sociologist may have to defend his or her findings against the 'truths' that others produce from their own research, with possible critique of methods, mobilisation of hypothesis, even the research question itself. The research procedures of the postmodernist, however, may appear to bear little resemblance to our orthodox sociologist. While the traditional theorist may unwittingly be promoting their 'discourse' as having something valuable to say about the changing social environment – as is indeed seen in the many heated debates among postmodern theorists – this may be where the similarity would end. For the postmodern theorist would rarely incorporate traditional research methods into their research programme. Textual or discursive analysis of some kind may be attempted, perhaps in the spirit of post-structuralist linguistic 'deconstruction', but any attempt to 'measure' social opinions, estimate the 'true' picture or even explore the reasons why something is as it is, are almost entirely absent from postmodern research. A fragmented social world, in which there are no truths, no 'depth' to social practices and no 'reality' with which to ground one's research, can, at the most, produce a focus on 'micro-events'; to attempt to grasp what is going on in society *as a whole* would be to turn the postmodern project on its head (Kroker 1988).

This leads to a contemplation of whether such a sociology can be said to be the natural and inevitable descendent of modern social theory. Is the move away from logic, discovery and rationality, towards a diverse, fragmented, even contradictory, social theory perhaps just a reflection of a changing social order that can only be analysed by 'surface theory'? In this section, two opposing perspectives on this issue are examined. The first suggests that the social system is so completely transformed that the tools of social theory must receive a 'long-awaited overhaul' (Giddens 1987). The second suggests that while there has indeed been some dramatic social and cultural changes in recent times, this is not to deny the continued validity of modern sociology, albeit under changing social conditions (Bauman 1988). While postmodernism has taught us that there are no set answers and no guaranteed truths, this is not to say that the sociologist cannot continue to distinguish between the acceptable and the unacceptable (Hirst 1990: 19). Whether or not such a middle road – a radical pluralism as Stuart Hall calls it – is possible, or even desirable, is an issue that will be returned to in the concluding section of the chapter.

From social structure to fragmented simulation – postmodern sociology

Just as society has been increasingly characterised by fragmented and rapidly changing 'realities', so too is it argued that social theory must employ radical changes to the way it investigates the world if it is to remain a viable discipline for the analysis of society. As Baudrillard argues, with the end of any fixed 'external' referent for sociologists to focus their investigations on (for example, social class formation), we are seeing the end of the 'perspective space of the social' (Baudrillard 1983). With the loss of a distinction between the 'real' and the 'ideal', with nothing substantive left to analyse, explain and perhaps change, it can be suggested that the very underpinnings of modern society have been extinguished: 'Theory can no longer be reconciled with the real, cannot be the reflection of the real, or enter into a relation of critical negativity with the real' (Smart 1993).

Sociology as a discipline, then, must evolve if it is to survive, with no place in intellectual circles for theoretical analysis of social structures, relations and realities that no longer exist. So how might a postmodern social theory look? To say that all theory of 'society' *per se* is now redundant would, ironically, invalidate the very existence of postmodern writings which are, in the last instance, but an attempt to promote to readers a particular way of seeing the social world. Nonetheless, it cannot be denied that a 'new' postmodern sociology has emerged; it implies a totally new direction and focus for the theorist, with new social space requiring radically new tools for the job of analysis. Likewise, with the loss of the search for truth, certainty and social progression that is said to characterise the postmodern society, theoretical tools that are designed to reveal, expose and 'mend' must be abandoned. As the writings of theorists such as Smart and Giddens imply, an acceptance of the necessity of a new type of sociological enterprise requires a philosophical and ontological shift in the way that the social theorist sees the world, suggesting two criteria for the 'new' social theory: to challenge the idea of 'hidden' or 'deep' structures, and to observe and question, but not to prescribe, the way that society should go.

To challenge the idea of hidden or deep structures

With the loss of 'manifest' or 'deep' social realities that modernist sociology sees as underpinning social structures and practices, sociology must now work to shift its focus towards the new immediacy of social experiences. In short, a refocus on the new 'reality' of surface appearances, without anything beneath, is necessary for the postmodern theorist. This new 'cognitive mapping' (Jameson 1988) forms the essential underpinning of postmodern theory, with investigative topics such as media simulations, screen culture, lifestyle and identities, and fragmented sexualities increasingly replacing the modernist focuses on, for example, social class, power and industrial society. While the latter may still form the focus of the postmodern investigation – though with increasingly limited application in a world in which such features are, for the postmodernist, less and less in evidence – it is, above all, the *approach* to the social that epitomises the postmodern theorist. Simulations replace social realities, hyperreality replaces reality, with the ephemeral, transitory and unclassifiable increasingly forming the objects for sociological study.

To observe and question but not to prescribe the way society should go

With no certainties in the social world, no 'plan' to which societies and individuals are working, and no meta-narrative which either theorists or the 'layperson' can appeal to, the modernist desire to transform and direct, through research and invest-igation, must similarly be abandoned. With no reality to be 'fixed', the motivation to transform and 'make better' must be replaced by a postmodern detachment from attempts to change the world. With the loss of any guiding notions or narratives of what a 'better' society might look like and, indeed, the social structure resem-bling a fragmented and disjointed set of simulations, subject to the shifting 'play' of meanings, codes and significations, any grand plan to 'change society' appears now to be misguided and impossible.

In essence, then, sociology should simply track and trace the shifting progression of social forms, with no attempt to question, provide answers or 'reasons' for why things are as they appear to be. For writers such as Baudrillard, it is enough for social theorists to reflexively explore the provisional and circular nature of social knowledge, with a recognition that sociological knowledge itself is no less transit-ory, fixed and secure than any other postmodern enterprise. To ask 'why' questions is of little interest, as 'answers' are themselves so fluid, variable and provisional. Smart, while politically uncomfortable with the consequently limited nature of post-modern sociological questioning, agrees:

> Answers are permitted, as long as they have a relatively provisional, conditional, and even at times contentious status . . . [and we question] in a context where there are no epi-stemological or political guarantees to which we can appeal.
>
> (Smart 1993: 125)

A postmodern sociology, then, is one that is almost entirely unrecognisable from its modern ancestry. The postmodern theorist investigates only the manifestations, or 'surfaces', of social life and may raise questions yet never seek to provide answers other than those which are unstable and provisional. Indeed, it has even been suggested that so different is postmodern social analysis from 'orthodox' social theorising, that it is better seen as a form of 'lifestyle and cultural politics', than as a theory *per se* (Mort 1996). No longer exterior to the objects it seeks to explore, postmodernism as a social theory becomes understandable only in terms of its place in the broader social and cultural transformations occurring within society as a whole.

A sociology of postmodernism

Re-engaging the social

Writers who argue for the development of a radically new 'postmodern' sociological approach to the exploration of the social world do so with the assumption that the object of their investigation ('society') has fundamentally changed from that which is seen to have characterised the modern social world. With social practices and experiences more and more defined through the nature of appearances and simulations, it makes sense to approach the study of such forms from a radically different angle. A second approach within social theory argues, however, that such a radical overhaul of the sociological enterprise – with implications for both social theory and methodology – is premature to say the least (Bauman 1988).

Before 'postmodern sociology' can be established as the new 'orthodoxy' within social theory, a number of questions need to be addressed, the first of which might be: do claims that we are living in postmodern times refer to 'real' shifts in the social and cultural organisation, or simply a 'mood' or sensibility? As writers such as Bauman (1988) have argued, the *nature* of the postmodern shift – if it can be said to have occurred at all outside of academia – will affect the extent and direction towards which social theory will grow and develop. If, for example, closer economic, political and cultural analysis reveals evidence to suggest that, despite the presence of certain postmodern features, the social structure can best be identified as exhibiting a late, or 'hypermodern' formation (Lash and Urry 1987), the abandonment of modernist-inspired sociological approaches may be deemed inappropriate. Similarly, it could be appropriate to regard the emergence *within* social and cultural theory, and in society as a whole, of postmodern 'sensibilities' as simply a manifestation of yet another way of trying to make sense of increasingly complex and frequently perplexing social experiences. Indeed, writers such as Alex Callinicos (1982) go so far as to suggest that the postmodern 'mood' – to which the academic community have, in no small way, contributed – is but itself a form of ruling class ideology. By diverting attention away from processes at work beneath 'surface' appearances, questions of power, control and concealment disappear from view. As a last attempt by intellectuals to impose a 'new' regime of truth in the sociocultural sphere, and to foreclose critical investigative debate, postmodernism for Callinicos is but an ideological smokescreen for the continued perpetuation of capitalist class relations.

A second question that would need to be addressed is: are the modernist tools of the sociological enterprise now redundant? According to writers such as Touraine (1989), orthodox sociological images of social life have little explanatory value in postmodern times. As Lemert (1997) argues, however, it is not always clear to see within the work of writers such as Baudrillard why it should be the case that a critical, investigative and self-reflexive approach – which is arguably a defining feature of the 'sociological imagination' – is of little relevance for the analysis of the postmodern social world. Furthermore, it could be argued that sociology has always sought to question, in a postmodern way, the status of knowledge, cultural formations and social groups in a way that *is* questioning, fluid and often representative of a challenge to orthodox understandings and meta-narratives (from Durkheim's *Suicide* (1963), to Firestone's *Dialectic of Sex* (1979)). That a study of the postmodern be seen as but an additional 'object' of *sociological* thought – with postmodern theory representing an extra 'level' of analysis reflective of the shift within modernist sociology towards a greater acceptance of the plurality and contingency of social life – is one possible way in which the sociological enterprise can be strengthened, rather than rendered obsolete.

CONCLUSION – MODERNIST POSTMODERNISM OR POSTMODERN MODERNISM?

This chapter has been concerned to provide the reader with an understanding of what postmodernism is and who its main protagonists are; and to draw out some of the complexities, contradictions and implications of the postmodern project for the social theorist in contemporary society. That there are no clear answers to these questions should by now be apparent to the reader – if indeed 'clear answers' are what the reader still requires in these supposedly postmodern times. To finish, it is useful to make some concluding observations about postmodernism, drawing upon what others in the field, particularly Bauman and Giddens, see to be the utility of postmodern theory in present times. Firstly, it can be suggested that a final definition of postmodernism is impossible. While certain features and characteristics of postmodernism can be observed again and again in the literature – such as the rise of virtual realities, consumer culture *par excellence* and increased interactive political communication *vis-à-vis* new media technologies – there is much disagreement as to which areas of society such practices can be located in. Some writers see the postmodern as referring to changes occurring in the 'symbolic' sphere, and others to a state of mind, or even to macro changes at the level of the economy and state. Evidence for the existence of postmodernism, then, may be sought at a number of different levels, or simply accepted as representing a subtle 'shift' in the way that we see the world. Perhaps were it not for the publicity accorded to postmodern within sociology, such an 'ism' would not have been evident to most at all.

With little agreement among theorists as to these matters, it could be suggested that there exists the potential to apply a 'pick and mix' approach to contemporary theorising, selecting what appears useful and relevant to one's particular social project. Indeed, with the desire to avoid 'labelling' and 'classifying' so fashionable at the moment within the social sciences, some may even wish to develop a fusion or 'middle way' between the contributions of postmodern and modern theorising. As Bauman argues, the distinction that has been made by postmodern theorists between modernist and postmodernist claims perhaps understates the degree of interdependency between each framework. Writers such as Lyotard may dismiss modernist theorising, and yet many of its premises appear to have a degree of centrality within postmodern theorising. For example, the process of societal critique, so alien to the postmodern writer, is nonetheless a striking feature of the postmodern project. Indeed, it could be argued that the critique of modernism (based upon a postmodern 'meta-narrative') and the promotion of a particular 'regime of truth', form a central part of postmodern social theorising, just as modernist theory promotes other types of societal critique (Bauman 1988: 121).

In understanding that modernist and postmodernist thought do not differ widely in, for instance, their desire to promote certain understandings of the social world over others, it has been suggested by some authors (including writers such as Bauman, Featherstone and indeed Jameson) that one 'mutually enriching' compromise for social theory would be the promotion of a sociology that continues to address 'modern concerns under postmodern conditions' (Bauman 1988). To put it another way, it has been argued that it is more than feasible to combine a recognition of the rapidly changing social and cultural practices that increasingly come to characterise social life, with a continued desire to critique, question and search for 'better' ways of making sense of such practices. How such a proposition is received by theorists, of both the modern and postmodern persuasions, does of course depend in no small part upon how each of us understand – both personally and as sociologists – precisely what postmodernism represents. As Sarup argues:

> Obviously each position on or within postmodernism is marked by our political interests and values. How we conceive of Postmodernism is central to how we represent the past, the present, and the future to ourselves and others.
>
> (Sarup 1993: 183)

What can be stated with some certainty is that as long as postmodernism continues to occupy the mind of the social theorist, so will it demand attention, debate and critique. And that its presence continues to provoke powerful reactions among theorists perhaps tells us more about the times that we live in than any social theory can ever do.

EXERCISES

1

Determination is dead, indetermination reigns. We have witnessed the extermination (in the literal sense of the word) of the reals of production and of the real of signification . . . This historical and social mutation is readable at every level. The era of simulation is henceforth opened everywhere through the commutability of terms once contradictory or dialectically opposed. The same 'genesis of simulacra' is apparent everywhere: commutability of the beautiful and the ugly in fashion, of the Left and the Right in politics, of the true and the false in every message from the media, of the useful and the useless in objects, of nature and culture at every level of signification. All the grand humanist criteria of value, those of an entire civilisation of moral, aesthetic and practical judgement, are wiped out in our system of images and signs. Everything becomes undecidable – this is the characteristic effect of the domination of the code which is based everywhere on the principle of neutralisation and indifference. This is what the generalised brothel [*bordel*] of capital is, not a brothel of prostitution, but a brothel of substitution and commutation.

(Baudrillard 1976: 20–1)

(a) In your own words, summarise what Baudrillard is trying to say about postmodern culture and society.

(b) Do you agree with Baudrillard that this new universe made up entirely of images and signs is an accurate representation of the society you live in? Give reasons for your answer.

(c) In what ways can, and cannot, Baudrillard's approach be seen as a theoretical framework with which to analyse society? In what ways does it represent a departure from modernist social theories?

2

We're a left-of-centre party pursuing prosperity and social justice – Polly Toynbee, Michael White and Patrick Wintour

Poised at the start of the new political season, the prime minister in this first interview since the election, looked less grizzled and frazzled after his month-long holiday. At ease in his shirt sleeves, there was less of that edginess in answering criticism as he settles into the security of a second term.

He was more emphatic and clear-cut on where he stands – even if it is not always where some in his party might wish him to be. What once was the Third Way has hardened into a resolute set of propositions – pro-capitalism in virtually all its aspects, anti-poverty and all its causes, strong on making public services work for all. There is a more adamant take-me-as-I-am jut to his jaw, less keenness to please than in his early days: a second victory breeds new certainty.

'The last election was a watershed,' he said. 'Because for the first time in my adult political life-time, in the battle of tax cuts versus public services, the public services won. This is something to celebrate. Let's be clear, there are certain people in the Labour party who never agree with the direction we take . . . and my job is to make sure we stick to the position we are in.'

This was no-turning-back, no u-turn talk. Those who hoped for some radical new departure in the second term were given firm notice that this is it – but, he suggested, they have nothing much to complain about.

'We are a left-of-centre party, pursuing economic prosperity and social justice as partners and not as opposites.'

He sometimes sounds mildly exasperated. 'Heavens above – public services are social justice made real! The child who didn't get a decent education? There can be nothing more unjust than that. The pensioner that didn't get a decent standard of service in the NHS, what greater injustice can there be? . . . It goes to the heart of what the Labour party believes, the values of solidarity and community and society. We are trying to change the public services to make sure people have confidence in them. They are the bringer together of people in society. They are the visible expression of the principle of solidarity.'

In the name of that conviction, he will use whatever it takes, public or private means – but he suggested that media hype had overexaggerated his private sector plans. 'The notion that the government has gone anti-public service or is privatising public services is fatuous.'

As ever the list of all that was done in the first term rolls off the prime ministerial tongue with some impatience that his own people people take too much for granted – the minimum wage, trade union recognition, House of Lords reform, devolution to the nations.

Emollience

All these, he says, have been Labour ambitions since the dawn of the party in 1900 – all now achieved. Add to that Sure Start, nurseries, urban regeneration, halving youth unemployment and much more. On the eve of his speech to the TUC, there was emollience in his words, but no question of headlines suggesting he was caving in to anyone.

That also included a refusal to be tempted into populist anti-business sentiment, even business at its least acceptable. So Lord Simpson's pay-off from Marconi and the average 28 per cent pay increase for FTSE 100 directors last year drew no word of reproof: 'The government has got to be careful of its own role, but I think it's important that an example is set. I am not commenting on individual cases.'

Pressed again he would only say: 'I don't think it is my job to get involved in determining pay between one person and another. I choose my own words, but I do think it is important that there is some correlation between the rewards that people get and the performance of the company. Some shareholders are actually beginning to flex their muscles . . . and it is really for them to do.'

Does he not think any change in the law is needed? 'I don't.' But he added, as if it barely concerned him: 'Isn't there some review of corporate governance going on at the moment?' Killing the subject dead, he only said: 'Well, I've said what I feel.'

What of the gap between rich and poor, which grew so sharply in the last 20 years? Here his party may prefer his answers, which were markedly more egalitarian than in interviews before the election. 'The Labour party stands for a more equal society,' he said without hesitation. Is that a goal to narrow inequality? 'Yes, of course it is.'

But when it came to the means, he firmly ruled out any consideration of wealth or incomes at the top, concentrating entirely on lifting up living standards at the bottom. 'It can't be done by saying let's take the top lot of earners and wallop them, because all our experience has been that that is not a sensible way to proceed.

'Instead of introducing children's tax credit or the working families tax credit, we could have lopped more off the top rate of tax, but we didn't. You've got to be extremely pragmatic these days, particularly with the very top earners because of the international market in which most of them work. The other point is that you've got families on reasonable, modest incomes who will pay some of their income in the top tax rate, so you've got to be careful.'

He would not be drawn on the question of how exactly he could reach his target of abolishing child poverty, when the measure of poverty itself requires closing the gap between rich and poor, only pointing out that 'there are a million children who have been taken out of poverty in the last four or five years.'

Source: The *Guardian*, 11 September 2001, p. 7

Sarup argues that 'thinkers like Lyotard . . . are neo-conservatives. They take away the dynamic upon which liberal social thought has traditionally relied' (Sarup 1993).

(a) Describe what you think a postmodern politics might look like?

(b) Does the extract from the *Guardian* (above) contain a meta-narrative? Is politics possible without one?

Chapter 8

Feminist theory – a question of difference

JAYNE RAISBOROUGH

> Feminism is not one set of struggles: it has mobilised different women in different times and places, who are all seeking transformations, but who are not necessarily seeking the same thing, nor even necessarily responding to the same situation.
>
> (Ahmed *et al.* 2000: 1)

The above definition of feminism emphasises difference. Feminism, it is argued, speaks to different women at different times for different reasons and for different political aims. It is usual for chapters in textbooks such as this to discuss difference by stating that feminism is not a single theory or a united political movement, rather that feminism is a rhetorical term that speaks to diverse political theories that seek to end gender oppression. Textbooks often then identify and compare different *strands* within western feminist theory: liberal feminism with its emphasis upon equality is distinguished from Marxist feminist critiques of capitalism, which are in turn contrasted with radical feminist's theories of patriarchy and sexuality, and so on. Listing the different strands in feminism theory like this may serve as a useful illustration of the diversity of feminist thought, but comparing and contrasting the various feminist strands encourages us to learn almost by rote the differences *within* feminism and then use these to generate rather static and dated definitions of feminism *as a whole* (Maynard 1995).

Feminism, however, is far from static; it is in a constant state of movement, critique and development, and this resists neat classification into discrete strands. Not only do debates within feminism cut across the various strands, but also feminist theorists draw from a wide range of ideas and influences (Stanley and Wise 1993; Bryson 1999). Furthermore, feminism responds to outside influences (such as postmodern theories) and is also challenged through its own internal critique to seek out more sophisticated analyses of engendered power relations (Aitchison 2000). Feminism is, therefore, dynamic and volatile (Beasley 1999) and is best described as 'a theory in the making' (hooks 2000: 144).

To introduce you to the dynamism of feminist theory, this chapter explores how the recognition of differences among women has changed feminist conceptualisations of gender and gender relations. We take the period described as second wave feminism (1960s to the 1980s) as our starting point because at this time the political imperative of feminism was to unite women into a sisterhood, identify the cause of women's oppression and strive to bring about the necessary political, social and cultural changes to eradicate it (Barrett and Phillips 1992). Underpinning the notion of sisterhood was a conceptualisation of women as a homogeneous group. Criticisms of this conceptualisation have encouraged more recent feminist theorists to approach 'woman' as a social category that houses an array of differences. The question of difference has not just meant an understanding that women of various racial, ethnic, class, sexual and ability groups may experience gender oppression in different ways, but in addition led feminism to rethink how engendered power relations and inequalities are reproduced and challenged. In particular, it has encouraged feminist theories of gender to explore how gender may well intersect with other forms of social oppression such as 'race', sexuality and class.

This has not been a mere matter of adding 'race' and class to gender to produce an 'improved' model of power relations; the reconceptualisation of gender marked a dramatic theoretical shift within feminism (Walby 1992). Feminist theories have often looked to structural determinants to explain women's subordination; however, the plays and intersections of gender with other forms of oppression focus attention upon the specific contexts in which these power relations are realised and experienced. This has necessitated a closer exploration of the cultures of women's agency and subjectivity, for instance, and in ways that were not possible through structural theorisations (Brooks 1997; Green 1998).

The reconceptualisation of gender and accompanying theoretical shifts from structural analyses towards analyses of culture and agency have created new debates within feminism. Many feminists are concerned that, in our celebration of difference (different women in different contexts, positioned within unique intersections of different power relations), we have undermined the political impulse of feminism to effect social change. The purpose of feminism is arguably then less clear-cut (Scraton 1994; Jeffreys 1997) than during the second wave. The problem now facing feminism is how to forge politics for social change while recognising that women have different needs and concerns (Fawcett 2000).

We start our overview of the shifts and changes within feminist theory by discussing a feminist politics of sisterhood. Sisterhood assumed that gender oppression shaped the lives of all women, regardless of their race, class and sexual differences, and used this sense of shared oppression to bring about social and cultural changes.

TRANSCENDING DIFFERENCE – THE POLITICS OF SISTERHOOD

The solidarity of sisterhood

It is important to recognise that the traditional location of women in the home and in the private spheres of social life has shaped feminist campaigns to highlight and oppose women's oppression. At the start of second wave feminism, feminists had to contend with two major effects of women's position in the private sphere. Firstly, women were still considered the possessions of their husbands or fathers and, secondly, women's experiences of the private sphere were regarded as private matters. Cultural taboos ensured women's experiences of sex, sexuality, violence, domestic labour, motherhood and the like were often left unspoken and were considered private matters that were not suitable for public political debate (Ahmed *et al.* 2000).

The silence around many aspects of women's oppression encouraged women to adopt individualist explanations and solutions to their everyday lives. Betty Friedan's (1963) now classic text, *The Feminine Mystique*, spoke of women struggling by themselves with the 'problem with no name'. Speaking of the middle-class, suburban American housewife in the 1960s, Friedan wrote:

> As she made the beds, shopped for groceries, matched slip cover material, ate peanut butter sandwiches, chauffeured Cub Scouts and Brownies, lay beside her husband at night, she was afraid to ask even of herself the silent question 'Is this all?'
>
> (Friedan 1963: 11)

For some women the 'problem' included systematic domestic abuse, for which they felt a responsibility:

> 'When I came to, I wanted to die, the guilt and depression were so bad. Your whole sense of worth is tied up with being a successful wife and having a happy marriage. If your husband beats you, then your marriage is a failure, and you're a failure. It's so horribly opposite of how its supposed to be.'
>
> 'I actually thought if I only learned to cook better or keep a cleaner house, everything would be okay.'
>
> (Testimonies of battered women cited in Sheffield 1999: 57)

For feminists, the problem was not the fate of a particular hapless or dissatisfied woman, but a manifestation of the systematic oppression of all women. One of the biggest successes of feminism at this time was to identify and name the forces that oppressed women. Patriarchy, the rule of the father, and its ideological justification, sexism, explained how men and their social structures exploited and subordinated women. Rich's (1979) definition of patriarchy below clearly indicates how feminists identified patriarchal organisation as working to exclude women from full societal participation:

> [Patriarchy is] any kind of group organisation in which males hold dominant power and determine what part females shall and shall not play, and in which capabilities assigned to women are relegated generally to the mystical and aesthetic and excluded from the practical and political realms.
>
> (Rich 1979: 78)

The naming of oppression and the identification of the oppressor were both politically significant as they rendered oppression visible (Thomas and Kitzinger 1997). Once named, feminists could work to expose and then oppose the various machinations of patriarchal structures. Women's own personal narratives were key factors in exposing the forms and degrees of patriarchal power, as feminists encouraged oppressed women to make the personal political by abandoning individualistic explanations of their lives for a recognition that their daily experiences were shaped by patriarchy:

> We discover oppression in learning to speak of it as such, not as something which is peculiar to yourself, not as something which is an inner weakness . . . but as something which is indeed imposed upon you by the society and which is experienced in common with others.
>
> (Smith 1977: 10–11)

Discovering oppression involved realising the cultural myths surrounding many aspects of women's lives. Cultural myths explaining sexual violence worked to position women as culpable for their own sexual attack, rape and incest. Some of these myths, listed by Sheffield (1999) below, could provide justifications for sexual violence:

- All women want to be raped.
- She asked for it.
- When she says no she means yes.
- Some women need and like to be beaten.
- She must have done something to provoke him.
- She was seductive.
- She misunderstood.

These myths operate to suggest that women are deserving victims by fostering a climate of self-blame (Richardson and May 1999). By identifying sexual violence as key to the reproduction of patriarchy, feminists provided women with a political vocabulary and shifted the blame from the self to patriarchal socio-political structures.

As patriarchal oppression was 'experienced in common' with other women, early second wave feminism strove to unite women in a political quest to eradicate patriarchal discriminatory practices, structures and violence (Weedon 1999). McNeil (1985) remembers how the sharing of experiences led women towards a collective action to 'fight back' against sexual harassment:

As woman after woman cited incidents, we breathed out a sigh of relief. We had (almost all) been so isolated. Felt nutty almost in complaining, blamed ourselves for reactions we 'had provoked' or suffered in confused silence. Now we knew it was a common problem . . . We must begin to collectively fight back.

(McNeil 1985: 85)

Feminism used the concept of sisterhood to represent this unity and its political intent. Described by Daly (1978: 8) as 'an authentic bonding of women', sisterhood had rhetorical resonance with the brotherhood of the trade union movement, as it represented political solidarity in the face of exploitation and a commitment to transformatory action. The power and resourcefulness of the sisterhood fuelled an activist impulse, which tackled the various sites of oppression identified by women's own testimonies. Alongside grassroots initiatives that established rape crisis centres, women's refuges and consciousness raising groups, feminism challenged social and political structures by initiating 'a wide range of political campaigns directed at issues as diverse as equal pay, pornography, sex shops, lesbian rights, nuclear weapons and abortion' (Weedon 1999: 1–2).

The main objective of sisterhood was to achieve equality. Based upon liberal notions of equality and inclusion, the politics of sisterhood measured women's oppression in terms of the economic and social inequalities between men and women and sought to remove them (Weedon 1999). As women workers at Ford's Dagenham plant in Essex took industrial action for equal pay, the first British Women's Conference met at Ruskin College, Oxford, in 1970 to make four demands: equal pay, equal education and opportunity, twenty-four hour child care and free contraception including abortion on demand (Thornham 1999).

Sisterhood, then, represented women's unity and operated as a political strategy against various manifestations of patriarchal oppression to achieve equality. While the emphasis was upon *all* women facing a shared enemy, the feminist move- ment in the 1960s and 1970s was not oblivious to the differences between women. Women of various ethnic, sexual, class and religious locations were involved in the fight against patriarchy. Indeed, McNeil (1996: 53) remembers the 'heated, angry, painful' discussions of the time as women argued across their differences. How- ever, the political imperative to forge solidarity in the face of patriarchy compelled women to subsume differences into a feminist agenda that purported to represent all. Gregson *et al.* (1997) emphasise that the stress upon the common experiences of women was a deliberate political strategy:

Choosing to emphasise women's common experiences and needs is a strategic choice because it unites women as one group working for social, political and economic advance. In this position, difference, although recognised, is suspended in favour of a strategic alliance seeking political, social and economic change.

(Gregson *et al.* 1997: 74)

By subsuming differences between women into a homogeneous front, feminists were attempting a politics of inclusion. Recognising that women from various racial, ethnic and class locations were politically marginalised, sisterhood absorbed them into the campaign for equality for all. Differences between women were, therefore, assimilated into an impression of a homogeneous sisterhood working in consensus to identify and resolve issues concerning all women (Beasley 1999)

It is possible to distinguish three theoretical assumptions underpinning the politics of sisterhood:

- The cause of women's oppression could be identified.

- Women's equality would result from their increased participation in the public sphere.

- The politics of sisterhood could speak for, and gain equality for, all women. (Barrett and Phillips 1992; Scraton 1994; Weedon 1999)

Discussion questions

Consider the following passages and then address the questions below.

You Are Not Alone
Woman, crouched down low in the corner
Woman, feeling blood pour from your mouth
Woman, watching the man you love, the man you hate, the man you
    love and hate
Watching the man you hate, the man you love, the man you hate to love
Beat you and abuse you
Woman, the pain you feel is the pain of many generations.
The pain you share with so many other souls.
The pain which you feel doomed alone to know.
Lying to your family, lying to your friends, lying to yourself.
Woman, your tears can nurture growth of spirit.
Your blood can feed the strength so deep inside.
Break the chain that holds you locked within 'that woman'.
Swing from the chain and gather your pride.
You are not alone
You are not to blame
Your shame is all of our shame
Your blame is all of our pain.

Child see your mother/father beat you
Child you are also not to blame
Your pain is their shame, is our pain and shame and blame.
Child, just hold to the promise not to repeat the cycle and remember
You Are Not Alone.
                (Lennie St Luce 1989, cited in Sexwale 1994: 218–19)

At the United Nations Fourth Women's Conference held in Beijing in 1995, Hillary Clinton invoked a sense of global sisterhood when she stressed that women shared common concerns.

However different we may be, there is far more that unites us than divides us. We share a common future.
                (Clinton 1995, cited in Sum 2000: 134)

As Sum observes, Clinton's speech shows recognition of the various racial, economic, geographical and sexual differences between the world's women, but simultaneously places these differences secondary to the similarities shared by all women. Sum (2000) argues that this practice of naming and dismissing difference masks the power relations that exist *within* the feminist movement itself. Simons' (1995) critique of the Beijing conference illustrates this. Simons argues that rather than use the Beijing conference as a means to tackle the most urgent problem facing most women – poverty – western feminists dominated the agenda with their own concerns around domestic violence. While there is no disputing the importance of addressing domestic violence, Simons questions the prioritising of this issue over that of poverty. She cites the case of the western feminist organisation, Womankind Worldwide, who directed massive resources to help finance a hotline telephone service for women experiencing domestic violence in Peru. The inappropriateness of this to women living in dire poverty was not lost on Simons:

> What this can mean to the millions of impoverished Peruvian women living in shanty towns without access to a telephone is anyone's guess.
>
> (Simons 1995: 34)

1 What advantages are there to establishing a political movement based on unity?

2 Can the politics of sisterhood represent the interests of all women?

3 What does the extract from Simons suggest about the problems of assimilating differences into a feminist movement based on unity?

Contemporary feminists criticise the politics of sisterhood on two related grounds. Firstly, some argue that by encouraging women to identify their lives as shaped by patriarchal oppression, feminism has produced images of women as victims of outside forces, and has consequently denied their critical agency (Wolf 1993). Secondly, by assimilating the differences between women into a sisterhood of common, shared experiences, power relations between women are undertheorised (Beasley 1999). Both produce a limited and distorted analysis of gender.

Victimhood and agency

It is fashionable for some contemporary feminists to criticise the second wave's politics of sisterhood for its promotion of women as victims. The thrust of this critique is a frustration at the perceived inability of second wave feminists to explore and celebrate women's agency, instead presenting women solely as the victims of male oppression; hence the description of second wave feminism as 'victim feminism' (Wolf 1993). This criticism is not misplaced: Sum (2000: 133) notes that stressing women's shared status as victims plays a 'key rhetorical role' in generating notions of unity and sisterhood. In her analysis of Hillary Clinton's speech to the Beijing Women's Conference, Sum argues that Clinton downplays the various racial and geographical differences between women to invoke their shared status as victims:

Clinton referred to baby girls being 'denied food, or drowned, or suffocated'; 'girls [being] sold into the slavery of prostitution'; 'women [being] doused with gasoline, set on fire and burned to death'; and 'women . . . subjected to rape as a tactic or prize of war'.

(Sum 2000: 133)

Clinton uses victimhood as a political strategy, yet contemporary feminists, and some at the heart of the politics of sisterhood, realise its limitations. Political constructions of women as victims 'eliciting pity and sorrow' (Barry 1979: 44), may be useful in highlighting the plight of women to prompt political and social action, but they deny the complexity of women's lives, notably women's critical agency in negotiating, colluding, resisting and subverting oppressive gender relations.

The complexity of women's lives is illustrated by LaSpina's (1998) accounts of her own disability. LaSpina argues that the power relations involved in the medical care of disabled women and girls can create a context for sexual abuse and violence, which many disabled women are expected to passively accept:

Disabled women may . . . put up with abuse because we feel that our bodies do not belong to us. We are forced to get used to strangers touching us, handling us, manipulating us, inflicting pains on us. Many medical procedures and treatments are undoubtedly forms of violence and abuse. In these hospitals I put up with waking suddenly in the middle of the night because I felt a man's hand on my breast or having a penis pushed in my face while being pushed down to therapy. The same way as I put up with the surgeon's scalpels, the body casts, the braces, the learning to walk, the falling and breaking of knees and ankles. Until my polio legs were wrecked beyond repair and had to be amputated at the knees.

(LaSpina 1998: 6)

Yet, far from identifying women as victims, LaSpina celebrates women's agency in fighting against the internalised social and medical discourses that teach women to hate their disability and which work to encourage a passive and grateful response to their treatment and social marginalisation. She argues that the communities of disabled women, brought together by a feminist concern with gender, are key to women finding a pride and strength in all aspects of their identities. She discusses disabled artists who celebrate their bodies, citing Mary Duffy, born without arms, who makes her body into performing art by posing like the Venus de Milo. She quotes Duffy as saying:

By confronting people with my naked body, with its softness, its roundness and its threat, I wanted to take control . . . I wanted to hold up a mirror to all those people who stripped me bare previously . . . The general public with naked stares and more especially the medical profession.

(Duffy, cited in LaSpina 1998: 9)

The resistance to the medical and public gaze allows disabled women to rewrite their femininities, sexualities and bodies in a way that reclaims them. Far from describing the pitiful image of disability, LaSpina speaks of the vibrancy, confidence and creativity of disabled women:

I am proud to be disabled. I am proud that we are a people that has endured centuries of oppression – isolation, poverty, incarceration . . . In spite of the indoctrination we all received to hate our disabilities and hate ourselves and each other . . . today we love ourselves and we love other. Today our community is flourishing, even though the struggle is far from over . . . our people are giving voice to the disability experience, telling their stories, writing books, making films, creating beautiful poetry, creating beautiful art. We are building culture . . . Disability Culture.

(LaSpina 1998: 12–13)

The key critique, therefore, of the politics of sisterhood is the lack of critical attention paid to forms of women's agency that LaSpina describes. However, it is important to note Drake's (1997) observation that such critiques of second wave feminist politics of sisterhood can be overemphasised. While second wave feminism did critically expose how patriarchal structures, practices and violence worked to constrain and exclude women (thereby positioning women as victim to these forces), it also began to conceptualise how women negotiated and resisted these constraints. Feminist theories of leisure, for example, explored how women negotiated the time, money and space for leisure activities even in the face of family and work responsibilities (Scraton 1994). However, the focus upon women's agency *was* limited. Scraton explains this as consequence of the structural analysis that shaped sociological endeavours in the 1980s and which feminism adopted:

Women's lives are seen to be structured by gender within a society structured by patriarchal relations.

(Scraton 1994: 252)

This structural emphasis combined with a political intent to chart the different means through which patriarchy subordinated and exploited women did necessarily invoke political images of women as victims of male oppression. By replacing self-blame with the collective status of victim, feminism provided a political platform for women to challenge those now visible oppressive forces. This also enabled feminist researchers to map the material realities of women's lives with a proliferation of empirical research not yet surpassed (Scraton 1994). It is helpful, then, to think of the politics of sisterhood as a timely political strategy, but one that leads feminism into a theoretical impasse through undeveloped explorations of women's agency.

The assimilation of difference and the limitation of theory

The second and related critique of the politics of sisterhood revolves around its treatment of difference. McNeil (1996) makes it clear that women of various class, race and sexual locations were engaged in second wave feminism, yet the political imperative to produce a solidarity encouraged differences to be subsumed into the common experiences of the sisterhood. However, by assimilating differences, early second wave feminism clearly defined gendered power relations solely in terms of the differences between men and women and by-passed the power relations that existed *between* women and *between* men (Brooks 1997). This produces three weaknesses within feminism. Firstly, Beasley (1999) observes that a reluctance to deal with difference, such as race, leads us to a very limited understanding of the ways in which gender operates and how it is experienced. If, she argues, we focus upon the power inequalities between the two homogeneous gender groupings of men and women, we cannot see how race, sexuality, class and disability are gendered, or indeed how gender shapes our experiences of race, class, etc. Secondly, by ignoring the power relations between women, second wave feminism can avoid the suggestion that women can oppress other women, or that feminism through its internal racism and homophobia can oppress some groups of women (Hill Collins 1990). This leads us to the third point, which questions the construction of 'normative' and 'different' definitions of women's experiences. This concerns us here, for if differences are subsumed into a 'normative' set of women's experiences, then whose experiences are set as the norm from which differences are defined?

Spelman (1988) is clear that normative experiences of sisterhood, and consequently of the generic 'woman' for whom second wave feminism speaks, are white, middle-class women. Scraton (1994) further observes that this description is also of *heterosexual*, *able-bodied*, white, middle-class women. The reproduction of these hegemonic (culturally dominant) locations produces a feminist politics of white, middle-class and heterosexual interests, which denies the historical and cultural diversity of women's experiences and, as a consequence, reduces the scope of feminist debate (Ahmed *et al.* 2000). Huggins (1987), for example, was clearly aware of the dominance of white, middle class interests when she described this period of feminism as a family quarrel between white, middle-class women and their men. Lorde (1996) outlines the limitations of the family quarrel by acknowledging that while women may share *some* experiences of gender oppression, women in non-hegemonic race locations face materially different realities which the politics of sisterhood is incapable of addressing:

> Some problems we share as women, some we do not. You fear that your children will grow up to join the patriarchy and testify against you, we fear our children will be dragged from a car and shot down in the street, and you will turn your backs upon the reasons they are dying.
>
> (Lorde 1996: 222)

Lorde further argues that the denial of race, class and sexual differences makes 'pretence to a homogeneity' of women's experiences that sisterhood purports to represent. Aziz (1997), for example, notes how white women and black women's experiences of reproductive health are radically different. She observes that while white women campaign for freer access to contraception and abortion, black women fight for the right to refuse the same:

> The pro-abortion feminist stance of the 1970s did not take into account the fact that many Black women's reproductive struggles were around the right to keep and realise their fertility. For these women, abortions, sterilizations and Depo-Provera, were all-too-easily available and were often administered without adequate consultation.
>
> (Aziz 1997: 70)

Similarly, feminists concerned with disability have noted with some irony that while the politics of sisterhood campaigned against the restrictions imposed by the normative feminine roles of mother and wife, women with disabilities were fighting to be accepted within these roles:

> Mainstream feminists have battled limited gender roles for non-disabled women; sex object, wife and mother. But as disabled women, we've had the opposite problem; we've been denied sexual, spousal or maternal roles when we wanted them.
>
> (Waxman and Saxton 1997: 60)

Lloyd (1995), for example, notes how important the status of motherhood is to hegemonic definitions of femininity, yet disabled women are constructed as unsuitable mothers, and are expected to forgo motherhood in the interests of the child. In some cases, the choice of motherhood is taken from disabled women, who may be denied reproductive health, forcibly sterilised or coerced into abortions (Waxman and Saxton 1997). The negative discourses constituting disabled mothers as unsuitable reinforce notions of disabled women as needy and unable to cope, and also reflect a eugenics-influenced concern that disabilities may be reproduced as they are passed on to the child.

As Cole notes, the complexity of women's lives suggests that oppression does not operate in the linear and uniform way that the politics of sisterhood appears to assume:

> Patriarchal oppression is not limited to women of one race or one particular ethnic group, women in one class, women of one age group or sexual preference, women who live in one part of the country, or women with certain physical abilities or disabilities. Yet, while oppression of women knows such limitations, we cannot, therefore, conclude that the oppression of all women is identical.
>
> (Cole 1986: 1)

The politics of sisterhood quickly become unworkable as women from marginalised locations such as Carby (1997: 52) asked 'what exactly do you mean when you say "WE"?', and argued for a theory and politics of gender that placed the difference and diversity of women's experiences centre stage (Bryson 1999). The next section briefly outlines how women, excluded from the sisterhood of middle-class, white, heterosexual interests, used their location at the margins of feminism and feminist theory to develop a series of theoretically challenging critiques of feminism. Before we discuss these, it is important to note that these critiques not only highlight the failure of sisterhood to speak for all women, but also challenged the theoretical assumptions upon which early second wave feminism was based. By arguing that their experiences of gender and gender oppression are shaped and structured by their race, ethnicity, disability and sexuality, women in these locations demonstrate that gender cannot be divorced from other forms of oppression (Spelman 1988). This has three consequences:

■ It forces a reconceptualisation of power relations. It is no longer viable to argue that women are solely and uniformly oppressed by men/patriarchy. If gender relations and identities are shaped by, or constitute race, sexuality, ability and so on, then feminist theories of gender have to be rethought.

- It encourages feminism to think critically about the ways in which oppressive power relations such as racism and homophobia are reproduced, even within a self-proclaimed inclusive and liberatory project such as feminism.

- It provides a useful theoretical awareness for feminism to challenge other sociological theories that purport to speak for or represent social groups.

The question of difference, then, leads to a radical transformation in feminist theorisations of the social world.

VOICES FROM THE MARGINS – DECONSTRUCTING THE NORM

This chapter has indicated that challenging and contesting normative and naturalised power relations is a key feminist strategy. We have already discussed the success of second wave feminism in naming and making male oppression visible. By identifying sexist oppression and outlining the ways in which patriarchy extracted reproductive and domestic labour from women, feminists disputed the natural status of male dominance and demonstrated that women's supposed inferiority came not from within but was imposed from without. Through this work, feminists became all too aware that patriarchy and sexism operate more effectively when they are deemed the natural order of everyday social life. As 'natural', male oppression escapes definition and identification, and as a consequence becomes invisible. Feminists, then, realise that normative locations, assumptions and beliefs are sites of oppressive power relations, and work to challenge their natural status by unmasking, naming and making oppression visible (Frankenburg 1993).

As the politics of sisterhood mapped out the consequences of naturalised male dominance, women marginalised from the white, middle-class, heterosexual norm upon which the politics of sisterhood was based, argued that normative assumptions, beliefs and understandings about 'women' and male power were being reproduced in feminist theory and politics (hooks 1984; Spelman 1988; Sum 2000). Marginalised women argued that the construction of white, middle-class, heterosexual, able-bodied women as the norm, and the projection of their interests as the political concerns of feminism, have played a key role in denying the different experiences of women, the reproduction of racism, and class and sexual discrimination within feminism. As a result, they are responsible for producing limited theories of gender oppression. Accordingly, the naturalised hegemony of white, middle-class women came under attack.

Fuelling this critique was standpoint theory, a means through which women who were not the 'norm' could critically theorise the power of normative locations (Hill Collins 1990). By arguing that their marginalised position gave them a clearer vision of power relations, feminists excluded from the norm of sisterhood used standpoint theory to demonstrate how oppression was reproduced within feminism and how this restricted feminist insights into the complexities of gender identities and gender relations. These critiques alerted feminism not only to the ways in which power relations were reproduced within feminism itself but also to 'the means by which power relations are constituted and sustained in wider social life' (Ahmed *et al.* 2000).

Standpoint

Standpoint is premised upon the argument that differences in our material lives afford us different perspectives and understandings of our social world (Maynard 1998). Originally developed from the work of Hegel by Marx in his thesis of capitalist class relations, standpoint argues that those who are oppressed have a clearer understanding of the workings and consequences of oppression than those who benefit from such oppression. Two pivotal themes in standpoint theory are vision and privilege. Hartsock (1983), who adapted standpoint theory for feminism, claims that subordinated women can see and know the operations of sexism in ways that are largely closed to men. She explains this by following Marx's argument that those who gain privilege from the everyday oppression of other groups are often blinded to the means of their privilege:

> The concept of standpoint rests on the fact that there are some perspectives on society from which, however well intentioned one may be, the real relations of humans with each other and with the natural world are not visible.
>
> (Hartsock 1983: 117)

Women's ability to see the 'real relations' of power is possible as their lives and daily experiences are shaped by sexism in ways that men's lives are not. Men who benefit from sexism and patriarchy may not realise their privileges as they are quickly built into the fabric of their expected, normal daily reality. Maynard claims:

> Women and men lead lives that have significantly different contours and boundaries. It is the material oppression experienced in women's daily lives which gives them a different standpoint from that of men, and so access to different knowledge of the relations involved in their subordination.
>
> (Maynard 1998: 123)

While standpoint theory argues women may have a clearer vision of patriarchal oppression then men, it also suggests that their own privileges and subsequent lack of vision may well blind them to the realities of other women. Sykes, for example, highlights the privileges of white women over Aborigine women:

> White women have less power and control than white men. I do not doubt that white women experience this state acutely, but in comparison to both black women and black men, white women are extremely powerful and have control over many resources.
>
> (Sykes 1984: 63)

Power and privilege differentials also exist between heterosexual and homosexual women, women of different economic classes and those of different physical and mental abilities. Yet hooks (1984) notes that women in normative locations are often unaware of the privileges that shape their everyday lives and of the real costs involved – hence the ease with which some white women can declare a sisterhood of common experiences.

As privilege can be blinding, standpoint suggests that feminist theory and politics cannot solely rely upon the vision of white, middle-class women, who, through their normative positions, may well not see the many different aspects of engendered power relations that other women face on a daily basis (Hill Collins 1990). There is, then, a political necessity to deconstruct privilege in feminist thought, and standpoint theory suggests that this is best achieved by those pushed to the margins of feminism. Privilege, however, is elusive and it may be difficult for us to acknowledge our privileges and their accompanying blindspots.

Discussion questions

Consider McIntosh's reflections upon her own whiteness and the extract from Prendiville, below.

> I think whites are carefully taught not to recognize white privilege, as males are taught not to recognize male privilege. So I have begun in an untutored way to ask what it is like to have white privilege. I have come to see white privilege as an invisible package of unearned assets that I can count on cashing in each day, but about which I was 'meant' to remain oblivious. White privilege is like an invisible weightless knapsack of special provisions, maps, passports, code books, visas, clothes, tools and blank cheques.
>
> (McIntosh 1988: 1)

> If I am heterosexual can I? If I am lesbian or gay can I?
> Walk down the street holding hands with my partner?
> Rent a house together with my partner?
> Attend family events with my partner?
> Have a romantic candle-lit dinner in a restaurant?
> Book a room in a hotel?
> Adopt or foster a child?
> Buy a house with my partner?
> Discuss my 'love life' at work/university?
> Kiss my partner in public?
> Get life insurance and a pension plan?
>
> (Adapted from Prendiville 2000: 27)

1 What privileges do you associate with whiteness?

2 Are the options listed by Prendiville equally open to people who identify as heterosexual or lesbian/gay? Use this questionnaire to reflect upon the everyday nature of sexual privilege.

3 Reflect upon your responses, emotional and academic, to these discussions of privilege. Consider how your identity shapes the way that you see and know the world.

Feminists concerned with race and ethnicity have used their standpoint to analyse the processes of racial marginalisation. Their critiques aim to demystify the hegemony of the white norm in western feminism by highlighting the ways in which whiteness is constructed as normative and privileged, and the political consequences of this construction. These critiques have provide key theoretical platforms and the critical momentum for feminists marginalised on other grounds (such as sexuality or disability) to place the question of difference centre stage in feminist theories and politics, and with it a critical focus on culture and agency (Maynard 1994). It can be said, therefore, that the thrust of changes marking contemporary feminism have their origin here.

A success of feminists marginalised on the grounds of race was in analysing the ways in which racial differences are constructed and conceptualised *dichotomously*. It is to dichotomous thinking that we now turn.

Revealing white hegemony – the power of dichotomous either/or thinking

bell hooks (1984), using her standpoint produced by racial marginalisation, revealed the major role that dichotomous thought plays in the maintenance of racial privilege, its elusiveness and the reproduction of racism within feminism. She claims that all forms of oppression require ideological justifications that operate to provide a rationale for that oppression while simultaneously undermining the resistance of the oppressed group. The most powerful justifications lie, she argues, within the creation of the norm and the association of the norm with natural superiority and privilege. She extends this insight to claim that beliefs in the natural superiority of one group over another are reflected and constituted in western language, philosophy and theorising by what she describes as dichotomous either/or thinking.

Dichotomies have traditionally dominated western thought as a means to classify and understand the social world (Gatens 1992). They create 'hard and fast distinctions' between two terms set in a mutually exclusive relationship (Oakley 1998: 715). Man/woman, white/black, straight/gay, able/disabled are all examples of dichotomies. These identities are presented as either/or: one is *either* a man *or* a woman, *either* white *or* black and so on. The mutual exclusivity involved here is presented with its own natural logic as irrefutably defined and biologically destined (Fuss 1991). Furthermore, dichotomies arrange terms in such a way that our identities are understood and defined in contrast to their opposite: for example, masculinity is defined in terms of its distance from femininity; white from black and so forth. There is, then, an intimate and powerful relationship between dichotomous terms and the identities they represent, to the extent that Jackson (1999: 173) observes that dichotomous identities, 'can only exist in relation to the other, neither makes sense without its other'.

However, as may be already clear, dichotomies are not neutral classifications of the social world. Since the philosophy of Descartes established a hierarchical relationship between the mind and body, dichotomies, as Gatens (1991: 93) argues, 'contain a set of implicit assumptions that assign a prominence and a dominant value to one side of the dichotomy'. Prokhovnik (1999) extends this observation to argue that identities on one side of the dichotomy are accorded social worth, respect and authenticity *at the expense of the other*. Those who inhabit the social locations on one side of dichotomous pairings (for example 'man', 'heterosexual', 'white') are presented as 'normal, healthy, mature' and are accorded political, material and social privileges (Wilton 1995: 9). However, people who are identified with the opposite pairings (for example 'woman', 'homosexual' 'black') are presented in pathological, caricatured, stereotypical ways which not only work to deny them social and economic privileges but may well position them as unsuitable or undeserving of such privileges (Hill Collins 1990).

Dichotomies can, then, be defined by the following features:

- An opposition between two identities.
- A hierarchical ordering of two identities.
- The idea that between them this pair sum up and define a whole (Prokhovnik 1999: 23).

Feminists concerned with race and ethnicity have related these insights to the maintenance of white hegemony in feminist theorising. In particular, Glenn's analysis of racial dichotomies offers a useful way to discuss the relationship between dichotomous thought, white hegemony in feminism and the resultant limitations these produce for feminist theories of gender (Glenn 1999). Glenn's analysis flows from the concept of *relationality*, which she identifies as the operating principle of dichotomous thought. By relationality Glenn refers to ways in which white identity is accorded dominance through its relation to its opposite:

> The dominant group's self identity (e.g., as moral, rational and benevolent) depends on the casting of complementary qualities (e.g., immoral, irrational, and needy) onto the subordinate 'other'.
>
> (Glenn 1999: 10)

Glenn uses the relationality of dichotomous thought to make two observations, which frame our discussion below. Firstly it highlights the socially constructed nature of difference. There is, for example, nothing intrinsically moral or immoral in skin colour, rather, as Ahmed *et al.* (2000) argues, skin colour is *invested* with cultural meanings. This states that the hegemony of whiteness is conferred through social processes not through natural dictates. Secondly, as identities are defined through their opposition, there exists an intricate yet fundamental relationship between white people and black people, between privilege and oppression, which entraps all people into racist relations:

> A White person in the United States enjoys privileges and a higher standard of living by virtue of the subordination and lower standard of living of people of colour, even if she or he is not personally exploiting or taking advantage of any person of colour.
>
> (Glenn 1999: 11)

Glenn's first point concerns the socially constructed nature of racial differences. Feminist insights into the workings of dichotomous thinking reveal the social mechanisms that construct racial differences and privileges. Young (1992), for example, has argued that dichotomous racial differences are produced through social processes of 'othering', a means by which differences are constructed through the investment of shifting meanings designed to protect the purity, exclusivity and privileges of one racial group. Hill Collins (1999) stresses that othering is an expression of social and economic power, functioning simultaneously to reproduce dominance and to construct it:

> In order to exercise power, elite white men and their representatives must be in a position to manipulate appropriate symbols concerning Black women.
>
> (Hill Collins 1999: 142)

Hill Collins (1990, 2000) has provided an historical account of stereotypical images of African American women. She found that images of black women rebound with presumptions of 'sexual promiscuity, lower morals, inferior intelligence and heightened fertility'. Carby (1997: 50) adds that black women are represented as primitive and pathological through reductionist associations with 'footbinding, clitoridectomy, female circumcision'. There are striking similarities here with the ways that Aotearoa's Maori women are represented by Pakeha (New Zealand's white) as primitive, 'sexually promiscuous and wanton' (Johnson 1998: 31). These images of black women are contrasted with the purity and innocence, moral superiority and civilised status of white women (Brittan 1997).

Weedon (1999) reminds us that stereotypes of black women are not just found in the racist's vocabulary, but are built into societal structures, determining the allocation of material and cultural resources. Stereotypes, she argues, permeate every aspect of social life and organisation:

> They surface in common-sense thinking, popular and 'high' culture and help structure the everyday practices of institutions ranging from education and policing to social welfare and medicine.
>
> (Weedon 1999: 15)

What is often left unsaid is that commonsense thinking, culture and institutional practices, that Weedon marks as sites of black women's oppression, are also sites of relative privilege for white women. That privileges are often unseen and 'unthought', and that whites can only glimpse them by listing the manifestations of racial discrimination and realising that they themselves escape the 'hassle' of oppression (Crawford 1993: 44), signals the ability of whiteness to render itself and its privileges invisible. Glenn attributes invisibility to the power of dichotomies whereby:

> The dominant category is rendered 'normal' and 'transparent', whereas the other is the variant and therefore 'problematic'. Thus White appears to be raceless.
>
> (Glenn 1999: 10)

What is of specific interest to us here is the way in which whiteness becomes the invisible site of enunciation, that speaks of and for other groups and in so doing defines other groups, and their social reality to white advantage. Thus Mirza (1997) identifies whiteness as a 'powerful place' through its power to name and define others:

> Whiteness that powerful place that makes invisible, or re-appropriates things, people and places it does not want to see or hear, and then through misnaming, renaming or not naming at all, invents the truth – what we are told is 'normal', neutral, universal, simply become the way it is.
>
> (Mirza 1997: 3)

The construction and maintenance of white hegemony in western thought, including western feminism then, rests in its ability to name and define the other while escaping identification and recognition. Marginalised feminists have therefore suggested that the way forward is to name whiteness and remove it from its 'unmarked, unnamed status that is itself an effect of its domination' (Frankenburg 1993: 6). In so doing, the real relations of privilege and oppression are made apparent to those who benefit from them, thus forcing racial differences into the centre of feminist conceptualisations of engendered power.

We have already touched upon Glenn's second observation which stresses the interconnections between white and black identities. Such emphasis is needed as the progressive invisibility of white renders it 'raceless' while effectively constructing 'race' and racism as the problems of black women and black men (Maynard 1994; Glenn 1999). Yet, as we have seen in our discussions of both standpoint theory and the relationality of dichotomous identities, there exists a fundamental relationship between white and black and between their respective privileges and oppressions.

McIntosh (1988), discussing her own whiteness, argues that whites are socialised to see racism as 'individual acts of meanness' not as 'invisible systems' which daily confer privilege and discrimination. As a beneficiary of such systems, McIntosh recognises with some unease the role that she, as a white woman, plays in the oppression of non-whites. Aziz draws out the implications of this:

> Whiteness is every bit as implicated as blackness in the workings of racism. Thus whether or not they are aware of it, *racism affects White women constantly.*
>
> (Aziz 1997: 71, original emphasis)

One way of exploring the effect that racism has upon white women is to examine the normative standards and behaviours of femininity that are produced through systems of 'othering'. In contrast to the supposed immorality of black women, whiteness presents its own code of femininity, which stresses morality and sexual fidelity and neatly positions women in subordinate relations to men. This can be illustrated by Leonard's (1982) account of the symbolism of the traditional white bridal dress. Here she clearly demonstrates how white femininity is monogamously heterosexual and is inextricably embedded in the home and its labours:

Wedding dresses tend to be not just white but lustrous and shiny. This connection of white and light suggests a radiance and spirituality in the bride, a radiance that comes from her inner happiness, tranquillity and purity of heart. She, as maker and physical symbol of the home, will provide a home which is a refuge and retreat from the depressing, corrupt and hurried world of work for her husband and children.

(Leonard 1982: 133)

Mary Daly is quick to point out that such norms place severe restrictions upon the ways that women can express and experience their femininity and humanity. She argues that the norm promotes 'lobotomised and tame behaviour which is in fact man-made femininity', which becomes an unspoken expectation of ideal feminine behaviour (Daly 1978: 287). As white femininity is constructed through racist stereotypes, there is a strong relationship between racism and sexism. Thus Smith alerts white women to the fallacy of developing a feminist politics that divorces gender relations from race relations:

You have to comprehend how racism distorts and lessens your own lives as white women – that racism affects your chances for survival too, and that it is very definitely your issue.

(Smith 1979: 49)

Glenn draws upon these observations to argue that, as racial differences are socially constructed through the investment of cultural meanings, there is room for resistance through the construction of new meanings. Differences can therefore be rethought from the antagonistic relations that dichotomous thinking places them in, to ways of seeing and conceptualising difference that relies upon respect and non-exploitation (hooks 1984). This creates a struggle over meanings of difference which are 'meaningful, appropriate and empowering' for marginalised women (Johnson 1998: 29), for not only are the many diversities within the categories white and black realised (i.e. cultural, geographical and economic) but the effect of internalised stereotypes have to be countered (Aziz 1997). hooks (2000), however, welcomes the struggle, seeing the 'diversity of voices, critical dialogue and controversy' as the only means to resist hegemonic domination of feminism:

We resist hegemonic dominance of feminist thought by insisting that it is a theory in the making, that we must necessarily criticise, question, re-examine and explore new possibilities.

(hooks 2000: 144)

The feminist critique of dichotomous thinking provides mainstream feminism with a sophisticated model of power relations while recognising women's agency in redefining or reproducing the meanings of difference. Its success lies in recognising that the difference is not natural but a product of social and cultural processes. Gatens emphasises this shift:

The crux of the issue of difference . . . is that difference does not have to do with biological 'facts', so much as with the manner in which culture marks bodies and creates specific conditions in which they live and recreate themselves.

(Gatens 1991: 133)

She further adds that differences have meaning 'only in so far as they are constructed as possessing of lacking some socially privileged quality or qualities' (1991: 135).

These insights have enabled other marginalised voices to speak out against the erasing abilities of the hegemonic norm in feminist theory. Feminists marginalised on the grounds of sexuality have explored the dichotomy of heterosexual/homosexual to explain how heterosexuality, like whiteness, becomes an invisible yet powerful place of enunciation and privilege. Their aim is to demonstrate that women's lives are not determined solely by gender relations but rather that gender intersects with sexuality in powerful and dramatic ways. Their critique concludes that sexuality cannot be marginalised if feminism is to achieve a meaningful politics of gender.

Normative heterosexuality and gender

As whiteness attempted to mould the direction of feminism, normative assumptions of heterosexuality were also silently shaping the contours of feminist theories of gender. Feminists whose experiences of sexuality were not recognised by the politics of sisterhood used their marginal standpoint to make the influence of heterosexuality upon gender visible, apparent and accountable. They did this by interrogating the heterosexual/homosexual dichotomy to produce two arguments. Firstly, that far from being naturally dominant, normative heterosexuality is a social phenomenon, accorded socially privileged status, and, secondly, that normative heterosexuality works in stubbornly persistent ways to influence gendered identities of masculinity and femininity and the relations between men and women in the interests of patriarchy (Jackson 1999; Dunne 2000).

The impact of heterosexuality upon gender is often unseen owing to the pervasive assumption that heterosexuality is biologically natural, universal and a stable aspect that transcends historical and cultural changes. The logical conclusion is that 'natural', heterosexuality has little bearing upon the social and cultural inequalities that the concept of gender alerts us to. Certainly the bulk of social theory falls prey to this assumption:

> Heterosexuality is rarely acknowledged, or even less likely, problematised. Instead most of the conceptual frameworks we use to theorise human relations rely implicitly upon a naturalised heterosexuality.
>
> (Richardson 1996: 1)

However, Carabine (1996) reminds us that the naturalised status of heterosexuality is an effect of the dichotomous categorisation of sexual identities as either normal or abnormal:

> Normalising judgement compares and contrasts, differentiating between individuals according to a desired norm. It establishes the measure by which all are judged and deemed to conform or not. The normalising effect is a means by which appropriate and acceptable sexuality . . . is enforced and regulated. The normalising effect is such

that sexuality is understood in terms of what is 'natural' and 'normal', 'unnatural' and 'abnormal'.

(Carabine 1996: 61)

Classifying sexual identities as normal/natural or unnatural/abnormal not only disguises the ways in which heterosexuality has been variously shaped under the pressures of cultural and historic forces, but also works to target prejudice, oppression and hatred against the sexual identities labelled 'other'.

A horrifying example of this is provided by Wilton's (2000) recollections of the aftermath of the 1999 Soho nail bombing that killed, maimed and wounded those frequenting a gay public house in London.

As the debris was being cleared and the families and friends began to weep and the wave of shock turned into despair and loss, the calls started coming in . . . 'We're so sorry', 'Is there anything we can do?' Tears on the switchboard . . . But then 'I've got a box of nails here, shall I send them to you', 'They should have bombed every pub in the street' . . . 'Gas the queers'. They go on and on. Twenty five calls by lunchtime. These words are second cousin of the bomb.

(Fenshaw 1999: 2, cited in Wilton 2000: 2)

Wilton (2000: 5) notes that other forms of prejudice and oppression are rightly deemed irrational, yet homophobia is in many cases 'actually felt to be morally praiseworthy and socially sanctioned'. Central to this is the construction of maledictory stereotypes that present gay men and lesbians as predatory, seeking converts, sexually promiscuous, immoral and perverted, who, as such, present a serious threat to the vulnerable and innocent (Wallis and Vanevery 2000). Lesbians are further presented as dysfunctional women who are incapable of attracting men or too immature to sustain a heterosexual relationship. As 'other', lesbians are considered to be deserving of anti-lesbian harassment which ranges from 'murder, rape, torture and other forms of physical attack through to defamation, intimidation, ostracism and verbal abuse' (Kitzinger 1994: 125). Kitzinger cites the experiences of Kathleen Sarris to demonstrate the extent of homophobic violence:

Kathleen Sarris appeared at a press conference as an 'out' lesbian. The next day she began receiving threatening telephone calls and letters, and two weeks later (after seeking help from the police who told her that there was nothing they could do) she was held captive in her office by a man, who for three hours beat her with his fists, his gun, and his belt. He sexually molested and raped her, saying repeatedly throughout the assault that he was acting for God.

(Kitzinger 1994: 125)

There are two related consequences of the virulent and vilifying representations of homosexuality. Firstly, as Carabine has already indicated, social processes of othering idealise heterosexuality as natural, unproblematical and trustworthy. Wilton (2000: 25) emphasises this relationship by stating that 'negative sanctions imposed on homosexuality have the effect of enforcing the status of heterosexuality as the desirable norm'. Secondly, heterosexuality is presented as the only

authentic expression of sexuality and sexual identity. This presentation of heterosexuality attempts to close off the possibility of sexual diversity and distract from
its own social construction (Jackson 1999).

Discussion question

The constructed norm of heterosexuality is demonstrated by reversing the questions normally
asked of gay men and lesbians. What assumptions and beliefs about sexuality are found
here?

(a) What do you think caused your heterosexuality?

(b) When and how did you first decide that you were heterosexual?

(c) Is it possible your heterosexuality is just a phase you'll grow out of?

(d) Is it possible your heterosexuality stems from a neurotic fear of people of the same sex?
Maybe you just need a positive lesbian experience.

(e) If heterosexuality is normal, why are a disproportionate number of mental patients
heterosexual?

(f) To whom have you disclosed your heterosexual tendencies? How did they react?

(g) Your heterosexuality doesn't offend me as long as you leave me alone, but why do so
many heterosexuals try to seduce others into that orientation?

(h) Most child molesters are heterosexual. Do you consider it safe to expose your children
to heterosexuals? Heterosexual teachers particularly?

(i) Heterosexual marriages have total social support yet the divorce rate continues to
spiral. Why are there so few stable heterosexual relationships?
(Adapted from Prendiville 2000: 28–9)

Feminists concerned with sexuality have used these insights to redefine heterosexuality, not just as sexual practices or sexual orientation, but as a set of social
relations and social practices which work to make heterosexuality *compulsory* for
women with the explicit intention of tying women into subordinate relations to men
(Rich 1983; Valentine 1993).

Heterosexuality operates in this way by creating a (constructed) desire between
masculine and feminine identities. The significance of this is understood when we
recollect that masculinity and femininity are defined and understood dichotomously, with normative masculinity defined through the socially favoured attributes
of agency, rationality and strength, and ideal femininity as lacking these 'masculine'
traits. Heterosexuality can, therefore, be understood as the logic that brings gender
opposites together into a hierarchical and unequal relationship (Jackson 1999;
Dunne 2000).

Part of the logic of heterosexuality is love, romance and marriage. Frye (1983),
however, shrugs off any romantic idealisations to state that love operates to secure
women's collusion to their own subordination:

Under the name of love, a willing and unconditional servitude has been promoted as something ecstatic, noble, fulfilling and even redemptive.

(Frye 1983: 72)

Jeffreys (1983) continues this theme to argue that heterosexuality is the logic of the unequal, and, she argues, erotised power relations that are directly related to the interests of patriarchy:

Without heterosexuality, it would be difficult for individual men to extract unpaid sexual, reproductive, economic, domestic and emotional servicing from women.

(Jeffreys 1983: 174)

Valentine (1993) emphasises the relationship of heterosexuality and patriarchy through the term heteropatriarchy:

Heterosexuality, in modern Western society can therefore be described as hetero-patriarchy that is, a process of sociosexual power relations which reflects and reproduces male dominance.

(Valentine 1993: 396)

These critiques serve to direct our critical attention to the ways in which hetero-sexuality establishes a politicised context in which gender identities and gender relations are played out (Kehily and Nayak 2000).

Discussion questions

'They're for a friend!' Shrieked Dot, as she dropped the flavoured condoms into her bag.

Cartoon 'Dot' by Daphne David copyright Paperlink Ltd, London, UK, 1994.

1 (a) Why is Dot embarrassed?

(b) Are there different standards, beliefs and assumptions around men and women's sexuality?

(c) Do different standards affect how women and men approach safe sex?

It is at the intersections of normative heterosexuality and normative femininity that sexual beliefs and sexual practices are constructed. Feminist research into sexual practice is concerned mainly with safe-sex practices and women's ability to protect themselves against HIV (Miles 1993; Holland *et al.* 1998). This research has demonstrated that young women are often unable or unwilling to suggest either condom use or an alternative to penetrative sex.

> Young women spoke, for example, of having unprotected sexual intercourse; of not using condoms even when they were at hand; of making no protest at rape; of accepting violence; of coming under pressure to have unwanted vaginal penetrative intercourse rather than non-penetrative sex. The majority were able to practice safe sex at times but, whether they intended or expected, they tended to be unable to do so consistently.
>
> (Holland *et al.* 1998: 6)

2 Holland *et al.* explain this by examining the ways in which normative femininity is constructed as 'sexually unknowing, aspire to a relationship, to trust love and to make men happy' (Holland *et al.* 1998: 6). These constructions are maintained by judging women either as 'respectable' or as 'slags'. Respectability, as Skeggs argues, accrues cultural capital, for not only do 'respectable' women have more power in the marriage market, but they can access other institutional privileges (Skeggs 1997: 10). Marriage and long-term heterosexual relationships also signal 'proper' social assimilation by invoking notions of 'commitment' and 'responsibility'.

(a) When have you heard or used the term 'slag'? What does it mean to you?

3 Kitzinger (1995) notes that 'slags' are defined as women who allow themselves to be (sexually) used by men, yet she also observes that as appropriate femininity is defined in terms of love and relationships, young women may be placed in the position of having to engage in male-defined sexual behaviour in order to keep their male partner and their respectability.

> The line between acceptable femininity and unacceptable slaggishness was easily crossed if women were dumped after sleeping with their boyfriend, if women slept with men who convinced them of love, or because they were drunk.
>
> (Kitzinger 1995: 191)

(a) Are all women concerned with their respectability in the same way? If women have access to cultural and economic capital in other ways than marriage or stable long-term heterosexual relationships, would this affect the way that their sexuality is policed and experienced?

(b) Consider this discussion in terms of heterosexual power relations and gender power relations. Is it appropriate to argue that heterosexuality shapes and polices normative ways of doing and being feminine and masculine?

Returning to standpoint and rethinking oppression

As the critiques from feminists marginalised on the grounds of race and sexuality demonstrate, standpoint theory, with its focus upon the political vision of the marginalised, has been utilised to radical effect to undermine the white, heterosexual hegemony of feminism and its accompanying partial theories of gender. It is clear that there are different sites for women's oppression (i.e. race, sexuality and gender), and therefore different sites of women's resistance and struggle (Brooks 1997). Gender is, then, more complex and multifaceted than the politics of sisterhood could yet realise.

That said, there is a strong resistance to the logical conclusion of standpoint that opines that the more marginalised and oppressed a group, the clearer and truer their vision and knowledge of power relations. This leads to what Bryson (1999) calls an additive model of oppression, whereby all women are positioned as experiencing sexism, but women are doubly oppressed if they experience racism, and triply so if they experience homophobia and so forth. Those who can demonstrate the greater amount of oppression can, through the dictates of standpoint, have greater insight into the relations of power than those less so.

Harding (1993) and others have demonstrated the futility of different groups of feminists each battling to prove their oppression as greater. Not only would this deny the 'diversity of voices' that hooks (2000) had hoped would contribute to feminist theory, because the only voices heard would be from the demonstrably most oppressed, but it would bear little resemblance to the lived experiences of women's identities. Women, like men, have different aspects to their identities that reflect their simultaneous location along the lines of race, class, sexuality, age or ability. (Kitzinger 1994). Women's lives, then, are not compartmentalised into those of race and those of gender, but their racial and gender locations are experienced as *intersecting and interlocking*. Laurie *et al.*, speaking of race locations and sexual identities, argue:

> An individual is not a woman and white in any simple sense. She does not have one set of experiences that stem from her gender to which is added one stemming from her 'race'. Rather these subject positions are shaped together producing a racialised femininity or a feminized ethnicity.
>
> (Laurie *et al.* 1999: 28–9)

Kitzinger (1994) takes up the notion that our subject positions and their sites of oppression 'are shaped together' to argue that oppressions intersect to produce experiences and conditions that we then experience against us as a *whole*:

> We are harassed as a whole people: we don't ever stop being all of whom we are. When anti-Semitic comments are made because of my surname, being a lesbian may not be irrelevant . . . My friend who is subjected to racist taunts as she walks through a hostile environment late at night is certainly harassed because she is black, but the opportunity for the harassment arises as she returns home late at night from a lesbian bar. We do not experience our oppressions as fragmented according to discrete identity categories, nor

should we have to label what happens to us as though it could be neatly categorised into mutually exclusive or competing oppression.

(Kitzinger 1994: 132)

These arguments signal two profound advances within feminist theory. The first concerns women's multiple identities. As women are simultaneously positioned within different subject positions, they can be both 'oppressed' and 'oppressor' (Bryson 1999). There has been some resistance to conceptualising women as anything other than an oppressed group (Carby 1997), yet understanding that women can be both the oppressed and the oppressor reveals the interconnections of gender with other forms of oppression and destabilises hegemonic relations which reproduce oppression within feminism. The awareness that women may well oppress others has sparked a radical self-evaluative project in feminism that has not only led to heightened reflexivity within feminist research (indeed reflexivity is one of the defining features of feminist research), but has also prompted critical attention on to the processes of feminist theory production. This is best illustrated by Skeggs's (1995) *Feminist Cultural Theory: Process and Production*, in which feminists reflect upon the power relations involved in their own writing and theorising of women's lives. Feminism theory needs now to make clear who is speaking for whom and to constantly think about blindspots caused by unthought and unconscious privileges: in short to display the place and processes of enunciation. Parmar concludes:

Critical self-evaluation is a necessary pre-requisite for all of us engaged in political struggle if there is to be any movement from intransigent political positions to tentative new formulation.

(Parmar 1997: 67)

Secondly, and what may now seem obvious, feminism moves from conceptualising women's oppression as emanating from one single source. This is not to deny male dominance but suggests that economics, race and (hetero)sexual relations are also fundamentally implicated. The sisterhood focus on 'equality' is then somewhat problematised, while a more complex vision of women's oppression and lived realities emerges. Bryson (1999: 21) neatly sums this up as a shift from liberating women from structural inequalities, to exploring the key questions of 'how power is exercised, how conformity works' and how we come to inhabit the subject positions that we do. This necessarily focuses feminist attention upon the cultures and contexts of doing femininity and gender. It is fair to say, then, that these questions mark contemporary feminism.

RECONCEPTUALISING GENDER – PERFORMANCE AND PROCESSES

The questions that Bryson (1999) raises reflect the increased feminist interest in the *processes* that produce difference and oppression. While a concern with the consequences of oppression remains, charting and analysing the social processes that leads to them has greater political import if feminism is to generate a theory and politics for social change. The shifts within feminism are clearly reflected (and are constituted) through the ways in which gender is conceptualised within feminism.

Feminism is commonly defined by its concern with gender (Luff 1999). However, how gender is understood and how feminists use it is subject to change. At the start of second wave feminism, gender was conceptualised mainly as social constructions of masculinity and femininity that were read from biological sex differences (Oakley 1972). Gender therefore conceived of two static and homogeneous groupings of men and women, and was used to measure the economic, political and social inequalities between them. Underpinning this use of gender was the notion of socialisation. Socialisation explained how men and women were channelled into gendered behaviours and identities through society's main institutions (the family, education, mass media and so forth). However, this approach produced rather descriptive analyses of gender relations (Green and Cassell 1996) and struggled to provide adequate theorisations of the diverse ways in which gender operated and was experienced.

Brooks (1997) argues that the 'most significant challenge' presented to such notions of gender comes from the work of Judith Butler. Butler (1990) argues against the theory of an essential or natural basis for gender identity, stating that gender is the effect of a performance. This is not, as Brook (1999) is keen to emphasise, suggesting that gender is a 'custom or role that can be put on and off at will' but rather that 'a stylized repetition of acts' produces gender as either male or female. For Butler there is no essential or authentic gender that prompts performance, rather performativity produces the gender just as it purports to represent it;

> Because gender is not a fact, the various acts of gender create the idea of gender, and without these acts, there would be no gender at all.
>
> (Butler 1990: 140)

She moves on to claim that our performances are so successfully regulated by societal rewards and sanctions that gender has no ontological reality beyond the performances that constitute it:

> Gender is thus a construction that regularly conceals its genesis; the tacit, collective agreement to perform, produce, and sustain discrete and polar genders as cultural fiction is obscured by the credibility of those productions – and the punishments that attend not agreeing to believe in them.
>
> (Butler 1990: 140)

There are two points arising from Butler's work as they concern us here. The first lies in recognising women's agency. The theory of performativity suggests that gender is produced through our own actions, behaviours and interactions with others. Kvande (1999) understands this to mean that we are 'co-creators' of our gender identities and gender relations. The second and related point lies in Butler's recognition of the possibility that we can perform gender in different ways. If there is no 'fact' to gender then we can, she argues, 'trouble' the hegemony of existing gender relations by performing alternative and transgressive gender and sexual identities. However, Butler is keenly aware that the permutations and possibilities of our performances are limited; an exploration of why and how these limitations are imposed and of the varying degrees to which they are accepted or contested reveals the operations of gender.

Jones (1993), for example, questions why women conform in lesser or greater degrees to expected and socially approved performances of normative (hetero) femininity, when such performances secure their oppression. Skeggs (1997) asked a similar question in a different context and concluded that some women may have very little choice. Jones explains that degrees of conformity are ensured by the cultural and social values placed upon hegemonic identities. Heterosexuality, as we have seen, is constructed as 'normal' through shifting sets of meanings that valorise heterosexuality while vilifying homosexuality. This, argues Jones, makes hetero-sexuality a more attractive identity *prima facie*, and of course has the benefit of social privileges. She concludes that discursive constructions of normality shape the availability and possibility of women's identities and the performances that con-stitute them:

> It is not a choice between being liberated and being oppressed. Rather it is a choice between being 'okay' or 'normal' and being 'weird', between being on the margins or in the centre – albeit the marginalised centres reserved for women.
>
> (Jones 1993: 162)

Here, Jones is arguing that the hegemonic value of heterosexuality and femininity may encourage women's investment in certain practices and performances and dis-courage them from others. Therefore, although alternative performances of gender may be possible, women may not necessarily take them up, or may take them up to varying degrees at different times.

The work of Joan Acker (1992, 1998) furthers feminist insight into the work-ings of gender. Her main concern is the ways in which gender inequalities are reproduced in the workplace. By studying the day-to-day working practices of an organisation, Acker argues that gendering, the means by which masculine and feminine identities are constructed and defined are normalised through four sets of interrelated processes.

The first set operates within the daily routines of organising workers and alloc-ating labour. Brittan's (1997) study of prison officers, for example, demonstrates how assumptions of women's physical strength and their ability to handle difficult situations in dangerous situations shapes prison work rotas, which often assign women desk jobs. The routine allocation of work is shaped by a second set of processes that operate through the imagery and symbolism of an organisation. Brittan found that women officers were constantly battling against an ingrained organisational image of the prison officer as male. She argued that prison work was symbolically constructed as 'men's work'. The third set of processes revolves around the daily interactions and networks that develop between workers. Acker notes the way that friendship networks can build up around the sharing of certain tasks and responsibilities.

Male prison officers, then, develop strong networks of trust that emerge from the perceived dangers of their duty. As women are excluded from dangerous duties, they are also excluded from the networks that are forged around them. The fourth set of processes relates to the worker's gender performances within the organisation. These may involve adopting male behaviour in order to 'fit in' to an organisation (Kvande 1999) or adopting a 'sexual self' in order to cope with the flirtation and/or sexual harassment that is an informal but expected aspect of some women's jobs (Adkins 1995).

> **Discussion question**
>
> In the text the four processes of gendering were related to the role of the prison officer. Think of another occupational role that is conventionally seen as masculine and relate it to these four processes.

As Acker and others have noted, these gendered processes do not appear to be actively shaping gender for they operate through commonsense assumptions and daily routines. As such, many experience them as 'the way things are done' (Benschop and Doorewaard 1998; Dunne 2000). However, the 'way things are done' can change between organisations, suggesting that feminism should also be looking at gender in different sites, locales and spaces. Differences may therefore lie not just in our identities, but also in the spaces that we experience and perform them.

Women, therefore do not perform their femininities in isolation. Jones and Acker both demonstrate Butler's extended argument that gender performances, whether normative or transgressive, are in a constant state of negotiation between the structure, culture and symbolic processes that operate in different sites. This is realised only as we move from thinking of gender in static terms and conceptualising gender in terms of situated processes and practices. Gender, then, is best seen not as something that is, but as something we do (West and Zimmerman 1987).

Butler's and Acker's work suggests the following:

■ Our gender identities are an effect of a repeated performance.

■ Our performances are informed, shaped and regulated by normative idealisations of racialised, heterosexualised gender that encourage us to invest in hegemonic performances and practices. There is, however, room for resistance: we can cause 'gender trouble' by performing transgressive gender identities.

■ Normative ideals of gender operate through gendering processes that work at different levels (structural, cultural and symbolic), which vary between different sites, contexts and spaces.

These points suggest a strong relationship between our performances of gender and the sites and space that we inhabit. Accordingly, feminist attention is directed towards the difference that space makes to our performances of gender.

THE DIFFERENCE SPACE MAKES – FEMINISM, GENDER AND SPACE

The question of difference in feminist theory has not just led to a critical exploration of the intersection of gender relations with other power relations, but also
encouraged feminists to closely examine the specific contexts and settings in which
women experience these intersections of power. By focusing upon the diversity of
women's lived realities, feminists have recognised that engendered power relations
vary in their forms and degrees over different social spaces. This recognition has
led to a theoretical concern with space and its different configurations of power
relations (Sayer 2000).

Feminist theories of space both contribute to and are informed by cultural
geography (Massey 1994). By blurring the traditional disciplinary boundaries
between geography, sociology and cultural studies, cultural geography marks a
radical departure from geography's traditional concern with measuring and mapping physical spaces, by arguing that spaces are socially constructed (McDowell
1993). The socially constructed nature of space is expressed through the term 'spatiality', which 'emphasizes the socially produced and interpreted nature of space'
(Aitchison 1999: 29). Spatiality reminds us that spaces are not innocent backdrops
to our social interactions, but are sites of localised power relations that work to
both enable and constrain our interactions and behaviours (Mowl and Towner 1995;
Sayer 2000).

If we accept the argument that spaces contain varying and different power relations, which may enable women to perform their femininity in different ways, the
issue of access to different spaces then becomes a key focus for feminist research.

Accessing space

Fenster's (1999) study of Bedouin women presents an ideal starting point for our
discussion of gender and space. She argues that Bedouin women's movement through
different spaces and their interactions therein are governed by the cultural division
of space into forbidden spaces and permitted spaces. Forbidden and permitted
spaces are marked by cultural norms of appropriate femininity that are *projected*
into spaces. Fenster claims that cultural norms include notions of honour, shame
and modesty, and that these work to police women's access to certain spaces. Within
Bedouin cultures, the male stranger poses a threat to women's modesty and honour, and, accordingly, spaces where women may meet male strangers are forbidden. For the most part, then, spaces outside the home are forbidden to Bedouin
women. However, forbidden and permitted spaces are not etched on to the physical landscape in any absolute sense; when a stranger enters the Bedouin tent, this
once permitted space for women becomes forbidden, forcing women to retreat. Fenster
also notes how women can access forbidden places by using a veil to protect
their modesty. The veil, although regarded by western feminists as a symbol of

women's oppression, is used strategically by women to enter otherwise forbidden spaces:

> Veiled women feel less exposed to verbal or physical male abuse when using public transport or when moving anywhere in a public space.
>
> (Fenster 1999: 232)

Fenster's work clearly demonstrates the relationship between space and gender. Her study not only suggests that cultural norms projected into space create the conditions of women's use and access to different spaces, but also indicates that women's visibility and presence in some spaces serves as a marker of a woman's modesty and respectability. Women who break with spatial and gender conventions are forced to negotiate the 'verbal and physical abuse' that is designed to police not only their spatial presence but also their performances of (modest) gender within that space.

There are strong parallels between Fenster's research of Bedouin women in southern Israel, and other research conducted in Britain's cities. Green *et al.*'s (1990) study of women's access to public space in Sheffield concluded that constructions of respectable femininity operated to encourage women into private, domestic spaces by forging a cultural equivalence between normative femininity and the caring, nurturing, sexual labour of the home. The association between respectability and the private space of the home was such that unescorted women in some public spaces (bars, cafés and nightclubs) were perceived by both men and women as sexually available. Valentine's (1992) research in Reading, and Scraton and Watson's (1998) in Leeds, both suggest that notions of spatialised appropriate femininity and fear of violence curtail women's mobility in public spaces to varying degrees. While the actuality of physical attack is statistically greater for young men than women, women's fear of sexual assault actively shapes their movement through public spaces. Both studies demonstrate that women construct mental maps of safe areas and no-go zones, to which they constantly refer as they negotiate their way through public spaces (Valentine 1992; Scraton and Watson 1998). We should, however, be attentive to Deem's (1996) observation that some women may well include the perceived risks of public spaces as part of the fun and excitement of a night out.

However, Fenster's concern with the ways in which norms are projected into spaces reminds us to question the ways in which spaces are perceived as safe or as no-go. Aitchison (1999) emphasises that cultural processes of othering underpin perceptions of space. Certainly Day's research of white, black and Hispanic women's perceptions of space in California revealed that spaces considered risky were also those spaces deemed 'other' (Day 1999). White women's perceptions of space and risk were heavily racialised, with no-go zones being, in the main, identifiably black and Hispanic communities. However, Hispanic and black women perceived their own communities to be safer then identifiably white spaces, which contained for them the risk of racially motivated sexual attacks.

As Day's (1999) research shows, while perceptions of risky spaces may change, the home is consistently constructed as a desirable and safe space for women. Skeggs (1999) stresses that programmes like *CrimeWatch* and the disproportionate press attention given to 'stranger attacks' than to those of domestic violence play a key role in constructing public space and the 'stranger' as dangerous. This construction runs counter to the reality that most women run more of a risk of sexual assault and other forms of mental and physical abuse in their own homes or familiar spaces than they do at the hands of a stranger in public spaces (Radford *et al.* 2000). While there is a 'mismatch' between the actual incidence of violence in public space and women's perceptions of it (Valentine 1992), the fear of stranger sexual assault or harassment undermines women's assurance in their legitimate right to use and occupy some public spaces. Skeggs (1999) claims that women learn 'that they do not belong in many public spaces, that many spaces are not for them'. Women's presence in public space is therefore a politically contested and negotiated one, and this has consequences for the types of femininity they can express and experience.

Discussion question

Larkin and Popaleni (1994) identify three challenges to women's physical presence in public spaces: diminishment (this may include joking and verbal assault); intimidation (threats and surveillance) and force (assault and rape). These work to engender public spaces and create the context in which women must negotiate their access to and presence in public spaces. How do women negotiate these challenges?

Work space

Studies of women entering the spaces of the labour market and organisations suggest that despite the increasing numbers of women now in the public domain, women enter as gendered and sexual 'others' (Adkins 1995; Henwood 1998). Kvande (1999: 309) argues that women upon entering an organisation are confronted by a 'dilemma of difference'. Kvande's dilemma of difference refers to how women manage their difference (their 'otherness') in order to participate in organisational life:

> It is women who have been considered to be more or less different from men, not men from women. Differences between men and women do not mean that men have to 'reject' or tone down their gender status.
>
> (Kvande 1999: 306)

Maddock continues this theme to stress the centrality of care in the construction of women as 'other', arguing that women are, to varying degrees, faced with a 'caring conundrum'. The conundrum is how women can be considered 'credible in a male world' (Maddock 1999: 199). Caring presents a conundrum because it reproduces gendered stereotypes of femininity that rarely receive reward or remuneration (Taylor and Tyler 2000), yet, by 'not caring', women run the risk of being positioned as 'unfeminine', or unprofessional (Perriton 1999; Tretheway 1999). Perriton neatly discusses the problems in escaping the stereotypical caring role without damaging her professionalism. What frustrates her is that her professionalism and her competence are constantly evaluated in terms of her caring ability. She fumes over descriptions of her as 'nice'.

In facing the dilemmas and conundrums created by normative constructions of femininities, women are required to engage in subjectivity work; that is to say, they perform femininities which enable them to be part of that work space (Kvande 1999). This suggests that women are not passively positioned in the public spaces of work, but rather the femininities they perform are due to their active practices. Yet the possibilities open to them are in many ways regulated by the work space:

> The organisation creates possibilities and places restrictions on which forms of femininities can be negotiated among the organisational members.
>
> (Kvande 1999: 306)

However, in her study of female service workers in a large university, Holmer-Nadesan (1996) suggests that women can identify, counter-identify or dis-identify with dominant notions of femininity circulating in an organisation. Women who identify are those who uncritically identify with constructions of hegemonic femininity. They may judge gender differences as natural, and conform to a large degree with their position as other. For these women there are few and limited means to perform different constructions of femininity, simply because these women do not recognise an authentic alternative. Women who counter-identify recognise how they are positioned as other but do not actively position themselves in an alternative (and subversive) performance of femininity. Women who dis-identify are those who take this extra step and actively construct alternative subjectivities that work to oppose and subvert those constituted through the plays of normalising discourses in the work space. As Jones (1993) notes, there are certain risks attached to strategies of dis-identification, as normalising discourses carry the rewards of acceptance and belonging. However, these can be as invigorating and exciting as they are stressful. The key, then, to identifying, counter-identifying or dis-identifying with the subjectivities and practices of the organisation is whether women recognise that alternatives exist and then take them up.

Holmer-Nadesan's typology is useful in highlighting the range of women's agency. This emphasises that women do not uniformly conform or uncritically accept their gendered positions in organisations. Her typology offers a useful means to explore women's agency within the work spaces. However, the typology does present a rather static view of women's agency. It may be the case that women shift between different identifications over the time they inhabit a specific work or organisational space. Gherardi writes:

> This situation is well illustrated by the story of a young woman engineer who joined an entirely male research team. For a whole year she was marginalised and teased as the 'angry feminist' because she repulsed the advances made by her colleagues. The situation changed dramatically one day when the boss, in the presence of everyone praised her work and as a sign of appreciation gave her a hearty slap on the back – something famously not done to a woman but to 'one of the boys'.
>
> (Gherardi 1994: 603)

While women's reactions to the slap on the back are mixed, Gherardi (1994) notes with some interest that women who do not subscribe to expected performances of femininity may then be assimilated into an organisation as an 'honorary man', thereby defusing the threat that non-conforming femininity presents. A new set of challenges arises then, to challenge women's presence in the public spaces of work, suggesting that our performances are constant, repetitive acts of 'doing' gender within the possibilities that spaces contain. Lorber (2000) reminds us that 'gender is a constant performance, but its enactment is hemmed in by the general rules of social life, cultural expectations, workplace norms and laws'.

Discussion questions

'Femininities may be constituted differently within particular types of spaces, such as workplaces or domestic spaces and may vary between different work or domestic environments' Laurie et al. (1999: 12).

1 Consider how your gender performances change over different spaces.

2 What gender performances are possible in particular spaces? Consider what enables or constrains the means by which you express and perform masculinities or femininities.

CONCLUSION – THE QUESTION OF DIFFERENCE

The critique from women marginalised from the sisterhood of early second wave feminism has sparked a series of explosive reactions within feminism that have still to run their course. The certainties that second wave feminists could rally around – those of an identifiable oppressor and oppressed and the linear, objective-led politics borne from this vision of power relations – have given way to uncertainties and complexities which stem from the question of difference. Where, once, women were oppressed in a uniform way by an identifiable oppressor, now we must recognise that men and women are both located within processes, practices and performances that locate them as simultaneously both oppressors and oppressed (New 2001). 'In this sense difference is expanded from man versus woman, to the mutliplicities of sameness and difference among women and among men and within individuals as well' (Lorber 2000: 85).

The notion that each us has a 'piece of the oppressor . . . planted deep within' (Lorde 1984: 123) has prompted a dramatic reflexive project within feminism, with a stress upon 'confronting our investments and positioning, listening and learning' to differences wherever and whenever they are realised, thought and expressed (Ahmed *et al.* 2000). Feminism is thus engaged in an introspective deconstruction that involves envisioning and enacting new forms of communication and processes of inclusion in order to avoid locking feminism into the limitations of static categorisations and models of power and identity which may unwittingly exclude and marginalise (hooks 1989).

While the question of difference has sparked off new debates and insights, there is, however, a real concern that the increasing focus on the differences between women, each realising and negotiating their agency in specific and localised spaces, will prevent the construction of a meaningful theory and politics that recognises that these specific sites and spaces are shaped and influenced by wider social–political forces (for example, capitalism), and prevent feminism from speaking of, and opposing, the common oppression of women. (Maynard 1994; Scraton 1994; Deem 1999).

Maynard (1994) voices her concerns around the emergence of difference in feminist theory. Firstly, the endless differences realised when we deconstruct broad categories such as 'woman' into their constitutive identities, and then discuss the individual as multiply situated, confuses feminist theorisation of identity in terms of power and inequality. This is of grave political concern, as power differentials and inequalities still shape women's lives as women (Deem 1999; Lorber 2000). Her second concern is that an overemphasis upon the differences between women masks any similarities that they share as 'women'. She argues that 'since cultural differences are not absolute, the similarities as well as diversities need to be acknowledged' (Maynard 1994: 18).

Scraton (1994) also stresses the similarities between women that are forged through their relationship to structural inequalities:

Difference and deconstruction can be important aspects of the politics of resistance, and as such should be very much a part of feminist understanding and theorising. But we must not lose sight of the economic, social, political and physical reality for many women that *does* continue to produce a shared oppression.

(Scraton 1994: 256)

Both theorists are careful not to be misread as suggesting a return to notions of women's universal oppression, but both make sober appeals for a balance to be struck between agency and structure, between difference and similarities. Lorber reflects this concern in her vision of a feminist theory for political change that incorporates 'structural analyses of the social and psychic processes and practices that maintain the gender order, combined with analyses of where individual agency can undo gender' (Lorber 2000: 86).

But this is ongoing work; the question of difference has initiated processes of 'troubling questions' (Ahmed *et al.* 2000: 19) and has ignited starbursts of transformations within feminist theories and politics to the extent that the shape of its future and directions are hotly debated.

It is, then, a solely misguided and reductionist reading of feminism to state that feminism is a matter of women's equality – yet this definition is stubbornly persistent in the popular imagination (Winter 2000). Notions of 'equality', the category 'woman' and the assumptions of liberatory politics are unpacked and analysed to reveal the nuances and niches, the reverberations and reproductions of multifaceted, volatile and shifting power, and its overt and invisible shaping of our life chances and lifestyles. That feminism is now highly complex, confusing and seemingly contradictory, speaks volumes about the nature of the oppression(s) it is trying to eradicate. This does not mark the demise or failure of feminism, but is rather a characteristic of feminism as a constantly shifting, emerging, contesting 'theory in the making' (hooks 2000: 144).

EXERCISE

1

Read the article below by Dea Birkett (The *Guardian* 28 July 1998).

Voyage of self-discovery – Dea Birkett

Going on holiday? Planned your itinerary yet? Received any recommendations from friends? Checked the guidebooks? Been to the travel agents? Still deciding? Then let me give you some advice. Don't listen to anyone. Go anywhere you'd like to go. Just go.

Like many of you, I'm planning my summer break. And like approximately half of you, I'm being continually told that there are certain places I should not go. The reason given is stark – my biology. A man's potential destination is only curtailed by cash or character. But because I'm a woman, I'm told huge expanses of the globe are simply unsuitable for me.

Brittany and Tuscany, as pretty as girls' names, are appropriate, but I mustn't consider more far-flung adventures, especially on my own. I'm sure to get mugged at best, raped and murdered at worst. Don't I realise that I'm an easy target, more vulnerable and less able to defend myself than a man?

Sometimes awful things do happen to women who venture abroad. These harrowing reports encourage the belief that the best place for us to be is inside, in front of the telly, and preferably in the protective arms of a man. But all these dire warnings are wrong.

Over and over again, dry statistics prove that within your own four walls is the most perilous place for a female. The location in which you're most likely to be molested, beaten up, raped and even murdered is not under a tent pitched in the Asian wastes or in the lightless back allies of Marrakesh, but in your own sitting room. It's your brother or your best friend who's going to steal your wallet, sexually abuse you or even, in the most extreme circumstances, batter you to death – not that frisky Malawian you met when bicycling from Lilongwe to Livingstonia.

Despite incontrovertible evidence that it is safer to be Bhutan-bound than homebound, the advice women still receive is to lock themselves up and throw away the key. Each time I announce that I'm setting out for distant climes, the response is 'take care of yourself', accompanied by a wary shake of the head. It's made quite clear that my actions are frowned upon and foolhardy. The risks I'm taking are unacceptable.

When I report back on my travels, the question I am most frequently asked is: 'How many times were you attacked?' Like the old, tired and objectionable joke about the man beating his wife, the presumption of this question is obvious. I am a women who sometimes travels alone; I must have been molested abroad on several occasions. But the answer to this question is not what my interrogator wants to hear: 'Only once. At home, on my own doorstep.'

I suspect that the fervour with which stay-at-home advice is given to women is rooted in something other than concern for our safety. Away from home we might trespass, not only on new physical ground, but into the far more threatening landscape of fresh and thwarted desires. Abroad, we might do – and be – anything.

Abandoning old emotional baggage has always been recognised as part and parcel of travel. As long ago as the turn of the century, desert traveller Gertrude Bell wrote from the Middle East that, venturing far afield, she "felt the bands break that were riveted around my heart." Thousands of miles away from the watchful eye of family and friends, we might get ideas.

Unfortunately, too many women continue to be influenced by the continental-sized lies we're fed about foreign lands and foreign men. Although statistics are hard to come by, you only need to open your eyes to see that there are far fewer lone women travellers than men. A major deterrent to women wandering is this fear of being a victim of violence. It's hardly surprising. Scare stories are legion. Remember when we were all going to get raped if we went to Greece? The message was ubiquitous and chillingly clear: if you fancy your first foray to an Aegean island, don't. It's far too dangerous for someone like you. Try La Baule or Bournemouth instead.

But when a male tourist comes to harm abroad, the warnings issued are somewhat different. It isn't suggested that men shouldn't travel. Instead, the country in which the crime took place is held responsible. When British holiday-maker Gary Colley was fatally shot in his car in Miami five years ago, Florida was deemed to have a serious problem with violent crime. Rental companies were told to remove identifying signs from their vehicles. New road signs were erected.

Quite rightly, in no way was the man himself held to blame. No general warning was issued advising men not to stray from home turf. I don't recall hearing it said that people with willies shouldn't wander west of 30 degrees longitude. The idea is faintly ridiculous. But if a women treads off the beaten track and is then attacked, the problem identified is that she dared to roam. Advice is smartly issued: if you happen to be female and foreign, don't go there.

We women also scare ourselves. At a women travellers seminar I attended, the female participants reported stories of friends of friends who had been robbed in South America and sexually assaulted in Burma. Surely these were not safe places for women? But I have a friend who had her passport stolen while shopping in London department store, yet I do not consider the lingerie department dangerous territory. When incidents occur close to home, we simply take more caution. We don't lock our doors and never go out.

No one is immune from this sexist stay-at-home attitude. Even the right-on Rough Guides warn women about destinations as seemingly unthreatening as Cyprus. For men, they advise that Nicosia's and Limassol's red light districts are 'more ridiculous than threatening'. But the the advice to women is: 'Avoid these areas.' What's a laugh to a lad is treated as unnecessary risk-taking for one of us.

You will search in vain for a guide that treats male and female globetrotters with anything like equality. The Lonely Planet's Morocco guide has two sections – Women Travellers and Men Travellers. The women's section talks exclusively about potential risks; the men's doesn't even mention them. Ironically, the men's section is all about how you should treat your female travelling companion. 'You must play very protective and jealous,' it warns. 'If you don't, some Moroccans will assume that your friend or wife is available for all to appreciate.' The irony would be wonderful if it wasn't so sad: even the men's section is all about the dangers to women.

I'm afraid this condescending advice, which presumes a slight brush on the knee will send a woman reeling and leave her blubbering into her Kleenex travel pack, has the opposite effect to that intended. As soon as I'm told my sex should stop me going somewhere, I get out the map and locate the spot. Why should the fact that I'm female make me stay at home fearful? Why should women be no more than armchair travellers to the less accessible, unpackaged areas of this huge and wonderful world?

I'm wondering whether to pack my bags for some sun in the Philippines. The entry in the Lonely Planet section for women warns to ignore drunken Filipino men pestering you, never accept a cigarette as it might be drugged, and run your hand over your hotel wall, checking for peepholes. All of these warnings may well be right. But if I never left my South London home, would I really be any safer?

Source: The *Guardian*, 28 July 1998

(a) List the dichotomous differences between (a) men and women, and (b) space or locations highlighted by Birkett.

(b) Describe the construction of masculinity and feminity and home and away that these differences indicate.

(c) What are the consequences of this construction for our perception of risk? How does our perception of risk shape our perception and use of space?

(d) If Birkett were to travel abroad and be molested/raped, where might the blame be seen to lie? Why do you think this is? What does this say about the relationship of space and femininity?

Bibliography

Acker, J. (1992) 'Gendering organisational theory', in A.J. Mills and P. Tancred (eds) *Gendering Organisational Analysis*. London: Sage.

Acker, J. (1998) 'The future of gender and organisations: connections and boundaries', *Gender, Work and Organisations* 5(4): 195–206.

Adkins, L. (1995) *Gendered Work: Sexuality, Family and the Labour Market*. Buckingham: Open University Press.

Afshar, H. and Maynard, M. (eds) (1994) *The Dynamics of 'Race' and Gender: Some Feminist Interventions*. London: Taylor & Francis.

Ahmad, A. (1992) *In Theory: Classes, Nations, Literatures*. London: Verso.

Ahmed, S., Kilby, J., Lury, C., McNeil, M. and Skeggs, B. (2000) *Transformations: Thinking Through Feminism*. London: Sage.

Aitchison, C. (1999) 'New cultural geographies: the spatiality of leisure, gender and sexuality', *Leisure Studies* 18: 19–39.

Aitchison, C. (2000) 'Poststructural feminist theories of representing "others": a response to the "crisis" in Leisure Studies Discourse', *Leisure Studies* 19: 127–44.

Aldridge, A.D. (1974) *Age of Reason*. Oxford: Basil Blackwell.

Anderson, P. (1992) *A Zone of Engagement*. London: Verso.

Arnold, M. [1869] (1960) *Culture and Anarchy*, edited by J. Dover Wilson. Cambridge: Cambridge University Press.

Aziz, R. (1997) 'Feminism and the challenge of racism: deviance or difference?', in H.S. Mirza (ed.) *Black British Feminism: A Reader*. London: Routledge.

Back, L. (1996) *New Ethnicities and Urban Culture*. London: UCL Press.

Barker, E. (1984) *The Making of a Moonie: Choice or Brainwashing?* Oxford: Blackwell.

Barrett, M. and Phillips, A. (1992) (eds) *Destabilizing Theory: Contemporary Feminist Debates*. Cambridge: Polity Press.

Barry, K. (1979) *Female Sexual Slavery*. New York: Avon.

Baudrillard, J. (1968) *The System of Objects*. London: Verso.

Baudrillard, J. (1973) *The Mirror of Production*. St Louis: Telos Press.

Baudrillard, J. (1976) *La Société de Consommation*. Paris: Gallimard.

Baudrillard, J. (1979) *On Seduction*. Paris: Éditions Galilée.

Baudrillard, J. (1981) *Simulations*. New York: Semiotext(e).

Baudrillard, J. (1983) *Simulacra and Simulation*. Ann Arbor: University of Michigan Press.

Baudrillard, J. (1987) *Forget Foucault and Forget Baudrillard*. New York: Semiotext(e).

Baudrillard, J. (1988) *The Ecstasy of Communication*. New York: Semiotext(e).

Bauman, Z. (1987) *Legislators and Interpreters: On Modernity, Postmodernity, and Intellectuals*. Cambridge: Polity Press.

Bauman, Z. (1988) 'Is there a postmodern sociology?' *Theory, Culture and Society*, 5(2–3).

Bauman, Z. (1992) *Imitations of Postmodernity*. London: Routledge.

Bauman, Z. (1997) *Postmodernity and its Discontents*. Cambridge: Polity Press.

Beasley, C. (1999) *What is Feminism? An Introduction to Feminist Theory*. London: Sage.

Beck, U. (1992) *Risk Society: Towards a New Modernity*. London: Sage.

Beck, U. (1997) *The Reinvention of Politics: Rethinking Modernity in the Global Social Order*. Cambridge: Polity Press.

Becker, H. (1953) 'Becoming a marihuana user', *American Journal of Sociology* 59 (November): 235–42.

Becker, H. (1963) *Outsiders: Studies in the Sociology of Deviance*. New York: Free Press.

Becker, H. (1964) *The Other Side: Perspectives on Deviance*. New York: Free Press.

Becker, H. (1973) *Outsiders*, 2nd edn. New York: Free Press.

Becker, H. (1974) 'Labelling theory reconsidered', in P. Rock and M. McIntosh (eds) *Deviance and Social Control*. London: Tavistock.

Bell, D. (1973) *The Coming of Post-Industrial Society: A Venture in Social Forecasting*. New York: Basic Books.

Bell, D. (1976) *The Cultural Contradictions of Capitalism*. New York: Basic Books.

Bellah, R. (1973) *Emile Durkheim, On Morality and Society*. Chicago: University of Chicago Press.

Benschop, Y. and Doorewaard, H. (1998) 'Covered by equality: the gender subtext of organisations', *Organizational Studies* 19(5): 787–805.

Berger, P.L. and Luckmann, T. (1966) *The Social Construction of Reality*. London: Lane.

Berlin, I. (1976) *Vico and Herder: Two Studies in the History of Ideas*. London: Hogarth Press.

Bernière, L. de (1995) *Captain Corelli's Mandolin*. London: Minerva.

Best, S. and Kellner, D. (1991) *Postmodern Theory: Critical Interrogations*. London: Macmillan.

Beynon, H. (1973) *Working for Ford*. Harmondsworth: Penguin.

Bierstedt, R. (1979) 'Social thought in the eighteenth century', in T. Bottomore and R. Nisbet (eds) *A History of Sociological Analysis*. London: Heinemann.

Blumer, H. (1969) *Symbolic Interactionism*. Englewood Cliffs, NJ: Prentice Hall.

Bocock, R. (1976) *Freud and Modern Society*. Walton-on-Thames: Nelson.

Booth, C. (1902) *Labour and Life of the People of London*. London: Macmillan.

Bottomore, T. and Frisby, D. (eds) (1978) *An Introduction to George Simmel*. London: Routledge.

Bottomore, T. and Nisbet, R. (eds) (1979) *A History of Sociological Analysis*. London: Heinemann.

Bottomore, T. and Rubel M. (eds) (1963) *Karl Marx: Selected Writings in Sociology and Social Philosophy*. Harmondsworth: Penguin.

Bourdieu, P. (1990) *The Logic of Practice*. Cambridge: Polity Press.

Bourdieu, P. (1992) *An Invitation to Reflexive Sociology*. Cambridge: Polity Press.

Boyne, R. and Rattanski, A. (eds) (1990) *Postmodern and Society*. London: Macmillan.

Brandell, G. (1979) *Freud: A Man of his Century*. Brighton: Harvester Press.

Brittan, D.M. (1997) 'Gendered organisational logic: policy and practice in men's and women's prisons, *Gender and Society* 11(6): 796–818.

Brook, B. (1999) *Feminist Perspectives on the Body*. Longman: London.

Brooks, A. (1997) *Postfeminisms: Feminism, Cultural Theory and Cultural Forms*. London: Routledge.

Bryson, V. (1999) *Feminist Debates*. London: Macmillan.

Bull, R. (1988) *The Social Psychology of Facial Appearance*. New York: Springer.

Burns, T. (1992) *Erving Goffman*. London: Routledge.

Butler, J. (1990) *Gender Trouble: Feminism and the Subversion of Identity*. London: Routledge.

Calhoun, C.J. (1995) *Critical Social Theory: Culture, History and the Challenge of Difference*. Oxford: Blackwell.

Callinicos, A. (1982) *Is there a Future for Marxism?* London: Macmillan.

Callinicos, A. (1989) *Against Postmodernism: A Marxist Critique.* Cambridge, Polity Press.

Callinicos, A. (1999) *Social Theory: A Historical Introduction.* Cambridge: Polity Press.

Carabine, J. (1996) 'Heterosexuality and social policy', in D. Richardson (ed.) *Theorising Heterosexuality: Telling it Straight.* Buckingham: Open University Press.

Carby, M.V. (1997) 'White women listen! Black feminism and the boundaries of sisterhood', in H.S. Mirza (ed.) *Black British Feminism: A Reader.* London: Routledge.

Castells, M. (1994) *Technopoles of the World: The Making of 21st Century Industrial Complexes.* London: Routledge.

Castells, M. (1996) *The Rise of the Network Society.* Oxford: Basil Blackwell.

Castells, M. (1997) *The Power of Identity.* Oxford: Basil Blackwell.

Cohen, A.K. (1966) *Delinquent Boys: The Culture of the Gang.* New York: Free Press.

Cohen, S. (1972) *Folk Devils and Moral Panics.* Oxford: Martin Robertson.

Cohen, S. and Taylor, L. (1972) *Psychological Survivor: The Experience of Long-term Imprisonment.* Harmondsworth: Penguin.

Cole, J.B. (ed.) (1986) *All American Women: Lives That Divide, Ties that Bind.* New York: Free Press.

Collins, R. (1981) 'On the microfoundations of macrosociology', *American Journal of Sociology* 86: 984–1014.

Comte, A. (1853) *The Course of Positive Philosophy. Book VI: Social Physics.* London: John Chapman.

Comte, A. (1858) *The Catechism of Positive Religion.* London: Chapman.

Comte, A. (1863) *A General View of Positivism.* London: Trubuer.

Comte, A. (1970) *Introduction to Positive Philosophy.* Indianapolis: Bobbs Merrill.

Comte, A. (1974) *The Essential Comte.* Edited with Introduction by S. Andreski. London: Croom Helm.

Condorcet, M.J.A.N. Marquis de (1955) *Sketch for a Historical Picture of the Progress of the Human Mind.* London: Weidenfeld & Nicolson.

Connor, S. (1989) *Postmodernist Culture: An Introduction to Theories of the Contemporary.* Oxford: Basil Blackwell.

Cooley, C.H. (1902) *Human Nature and the Social Order.* Schoken Books.

Coser, L. (1977) *Masters of Sociological Thought, Ideas in Social Context,* 2nd edn. New York: Harcourt Brace Jovanovich.

Coser, L. (1979) 'American trends', in T. Bottomore and R. Nisbet (eds) *A History of Sociological Analysis.* London: Heinemann.

Craib, I. (1984) *Modern Social Theory.* Brighton: Harvester Wheatsheaf.

Crawford, M. (1993) 'Identity, "passing" and subversion', in S. Wilkinson and C. Kitzinger (eds) *Heterosexuality: A Feminism and Psychology Reader.* London: Sage.

Cuff, H., Sharrock, W. and Francis, D. (1998) *Perspectives in Sociology.* London: Routledge.

Daly, M. (1978) *Gyn/Ecology: The Metaethics of Radical Feminism.* Boston: Beacon Press.

Davis, K. and Moore, W. (1945) 'Some principles of stratification', *American Sociological Review* 10: 242–9.

Dawe, A. (1970) 'The two sociologies', *British Journal of Sociology* 21: 207–18.

Day, K. (1999) 'Embassies and sanctuaries: women's experiences of race and fear in public space', *Environment and Planning D: Society and Space* 17: 307–28.

Deem, R. (1996) 'Women, the city and holidays', *Leisure Studies* 15(2): 1–15.

Deem, R. (1999) 'How do we get out of the ghetto? Strategies for research of gender and leisure for the twenty-first century', *Leisure Studies* 18: 161–77.

Dilthey, W. (1988) *Introduction to the Human Sciences: An Attempt to Lay a Foundation for the Study of Society and History*. London: Harvester Wheatsheaf.

Douglas, J. (1967) *The Social Meaning of Suicide*. Princeton: Princeton University Press.

Downes, D. and Rock, P. (1996) *Understanding Deviance: A Guide to the Sociology of Crime and Rule Breaking*. Oxford: Oxford University Press.

Drake, J. (1997) Review essay 'Third wave feminisms', *Feminist Studies* 23(1): 97–108.

Dunne, G.A. (1998) 'Add sexuality and stir: towards a broader understanding of the gender dynamics of work and family life', *Journal of Lesbian Studies* 2(4): 1–8.

Dunne, G.A. (2000) 'Lesbiana as authentic workers? Institionalised heterosexuality and the reproduction of gender inequalities', *Sexualities* 3(2): 133–48.

Durkheim, E. (1933) *The Division of Labour in Society*. New York: Macmillan.

Durkheim, E. (1938) *The Rules of Sociological Method*. Chicago: University of Chicago Press.

Durkheim, E. (1963) *Suicide: A Study in Sociology*. London: Routledge.

Durkheim, E. (1971) *The Elementary Forms of the Religious Life*. London: George Allen & Unwin.

Durkheim, E. (1972) *Selected Writings*, edited by Anthony Giddens. Cambridge: Cambridge University Press.

Engels (1971) *The Conditions of the Working Class in England*, translated and edited by W. Challoner. Oxford: Basil Blackwell.

Erikson, K. (1962) 'Notes on the sociology of deviance', *Social Problems* 9(4): 307–14. Reprinted in Becker (1964).

Evans, J. (2000) 'Psychoanalysis and psycho social relations', in *Identity in Question*. Buckingham: Open University Press.

Fairclough, N. (1989) *Language and Power*. London: Longman.

Fairclough, N. (1992) *Discourse and Social Change*. Oxford: Polity Press.

Fairclough, N. (1995) *Critical Discourse Analysis*. London: Longman.

Falk, J. (2000) 'Ferdinand Tönnies', in H. Andersen and L.B. Kaspersen (eds) *Classical and Modern Social Theory*. London: Basil Blackwell.

Fawcett, B. (2000) *Feminist Perspectives of Disability*. London: Longman.

Featherstone, M. (1988) *Postmodernism*. London: Sage.

Featherstone, M. (1991) *Consumer Culture and Postmodernism*. London, Sage.

Featherstone, M. (1998) 'In pursuit of the postmodern: an introduction', *Theory, Culture and Society*, 5(2–3).

Fenster, T. (1999) 'Space for gender: cultural roles of the forbidden and the permitted', *Environment and Planning D: Society and Space* 17: 227–46.

Ferguson, A. (1767) *An Essay on the History of Civil Society*. Edinburgh.

Feyerband, P. (1975) *Against Method: Outline of an Anarchistic Theory of Knowledge*. London: NLB.

Firestone, S. (1979) *The Dialectic of Sex: The Case for Feminist Revolution*. London: The Women's Press.

Fisher, B. and Strauss, A. (1979) 'Interactionism', in T. Bottomore and R. Nisbet (eds) *A History of Sociological Analysis*. London: Heinemann.

Foucault, M. (1977) *Discipline and Punishment*. London: Allen Lane.

Foucault, M. (1980) *Power/Knowledge – Selected Interviews and Other Writings 1972-1977*, edited by C. Gordon. Brighton: Harvester Press.

Fowler, B. (1997) *Pierre Bourdieu and Cultural Theory: Critical Investigations*. London: Sage.

Frankenburg, R. (1993) *White Women, Race Matters: The Social Construction of Whiteness*. London: Routledge.

Fraser, N. and Nicholson, L. (1988) 'Social criticism without philosophy: an encounter between feminism and postmodernism', in A. Ross (ed.) *Universal Abandon? The Politics of Postmodernism*. Edinburgh: Edinburgh University Press.

Freud, S. (1963a) *The Ego and the Id*, in J. Strachey (ed.) *The Complete Psychological Works of Sigmund Freud*, Vol. 21. London: Hogarth Press.

Freud, S. (1963b) *Civilization and Its Discontents*. Harmondsworth: Penguin.

Freud, S. (1973) *Thoughts for the Time on War and Death*, in Pelican Freud Library. Harmondsworth: Penguin.

Freud, S. and Breuer, J. (1955) *The Complete Psychological Works of Sigmund Freud*, Vol. 2. London: Hogarth Press.

Freund, J. (1979) 'German sociology in the time of Max Weber', in T. Bottomore and R. Nisbet (eds) *A History of Sociological Analysis*. London: Heinemann.

Friedan, B. (1963) *The Feminine Mystique*. New York: W.W. Norton.

Frisby, D. and Featherstone, M. (eds) (1997) *Simmel on Culture: Selected Writings*. London: Sage.

Fromm, E. (1980) *Greatness and Limitations of Freud's Thought*. London: Cape.

Frye, M. (1983) *The Politics of Reality: Essays in Feminist Theory*. New York: The Crossing Press.

Fukuyama, F. (1989) 'The end of history?', *The National Interest*, 16.

Fuss, D. (ed.) (1991) *Inside/Out: Lesbian Theories, Gay Theories*. London: Routledge.

Garland, D. (1990) *Punishment and Modern Society: A Study in Social Theory*. Chicago: University of Chicago Press.

Gatens, M. (1991) *Feminism and Philosophy: Perspectives on Difference and Equality*. Cambridge: Polity Press.

Gatens, M. (1992) 'Power, bodies and difference', in M. Barrett and A. Philips (eds) *Destabilizing Theory: Contemporary Feminist Debates*. Cambridge: Polity Press.

Gay, P. (1966) *The Enlightenment: An Interpretation*. London: Weidenfeld & Nicolson.

Gellner, E. (1992) *Postmodernism, Reason and Religion*. London: Routledge.

Genosko, G. (1998) *Undisciplined Theory*. London: Sage.

Gerth, H.H. and Mills, C. Wright (1948) *From Max Weber: Essays in Sociology*. London: Routledge.

Gherardi, S. (1994) 'The gender we think, the gender we do in our everyday organisational lives', *Human Relations* 47(6): 591–610.

Giddens, A. (1984) *The Constitution of Society: Outline of the Theory of Structuration*. Cambridge: Polity Press.

Giddens, A. (1987) *Social Theory and Modern Society*. Cambridge: Polity Press.

Giddens, A. (1990) *The Consequences of Modernity*. Cambridge: Polity Press.

Giddens, A. (1996) *In Defence of Sociology: Essays, Interpretations and Rejoinders*. Cambridge: Polity Press.

Giddens, A. (1998) *The Third Way: The Renewal of Social Democracy*. Cambridge: Polity Press.

Gilbert, N. (1993) *Researching Social Life*. London: Sage.

Glenn, E.N. (1999) 'The social construction and institutionalisation of gender and race: an integrative framework', in M.M. Ferree, J. Lorber and B.B. Hess (eds) *Revisioning Gender*. London: Sage.

Goffman, E. (1951) 'Symbols of class status', *British Journal of Sociology* 11: 294–304.

Goffman, E. (1952) 'On cooling the mark out: some aspects of adaptation to failure', *Psychiatry* 15: 451–63.

Goffman, E. (1963) *Behavior in Public Places: Notes on the Social Organization of Gatherings*. New York: Free Press.

Goffman, E. (1967) *Interaction Ritual: Essays on Face-to-Face Behavior*. New York: Basic Books.

Goffman, E. (1970) *Stigma: Notes on the Management of Spoiled Identity*. London: Pelican. First published 1963.

Goffman, E. (1972) *The Presentation of Self in Everyday Life*. London: Pelican. First published 1959.

Goffman, E. (1974) *Frame Analysis: An Essay on the Organisation of Experience*. London: Harper.

Goffman, E. (1975) *Asylums*. London: Pelican. First published 1961.

Goldberg, D. (1993) *Racist Culture: Philosophy and the Politics of Meaning*. Oxford: Basil Blackwell.

Goode, E. (1997) *Deviant Behaviour*. Englewood Cliffs, NJ: Prentice Hall.

Gouldner, A. (1968) 'The sociologist as partisan: sociology and the welfare state', *The American Sociologist* 3 (May): 103–16.

Gouldner, A. (1971) *The Coming Crisis of Western Sociology*. London: Heinemann.

Green, E. (1998) 'Women doing friendship: an analysis of women's leisure as a site of identity construction, empowerment and resistance', *Leisure Studies* 17: 171–85.

Green, E. and Cassell, C. (1996) 'Women managers, gendered cultural processes and organisational change', *Gender, Work and Organisation* 3(3): 168–78.

Green, E., Hebdron, S. and Woodward, D. (1990) *Women's Leisure, What Leisure?* Basingstoke: Macmillan.

Gregson, N., Kothari, U., Cream, J., Dwyer, C., Holloway, S., Maddrell, A. and Rose, G. (1997) 'Gender in feminist geography', in Women and Geography Study Group (ed.) *Feminist Geographies*. Harlow: Longman.

Habermas, J. (1981) 'Modernity versus postmodernity', *New German Critique*, 22.

Hall, C. (1992) *White, Male and Middle Class*. Cambridge: Polity Press.

Hall, S. (1992) 'The west and the rest – discourse and power', in S. Hall and B. Gieben (eds) *Formations of Modernity*. Cambridge: Polity Press.

Hall, S. (1996) 'Who needs "identity"?' in S. Hall and P. du Gay (eds) *Questions of Cultural Identity*. London: Sage.

Hall, S., Critcher, C., Jefferson, T., Clarke, J. and Roberts, B. (1978) *Policing the Crisis*. London: Macmillan.

Hall, S., Held, D. and McGrew, T. (1992) *Modernity and its Futures*. Cambridge: Polity Press.

Halsey, A.H. (1996) *No Discouragement: An Autobiography*. Basingstoke: Macmillan.

Haralambos, M. and Holborn, M. (1995) *Sociology: Themes and Perspective*, 4th edn. London: Collins Educational.

Harding, S. (1987) *Feminism and Methodology: Social Science Issues*. Bloomington: Indiana University Press.

Harding, S. (1993) 'Rethinking standpoint epistemology: what is "strong objectivity"?', in L. Alcott and E. Potter (eds) *Feminist Epistemologies*. New York: Routledge.

Hartsock, N. (1983) 'The feminist standpoint: developing ground for a specifically feminist historical materialism', in S. Harding and M. Hintikka (eds) *Discovering Reality. Feminist Perspectives on Epistemology, Methodology and the Philosophy of Science*. Dordrecht: Reidel.

Harvey, D. (1989) *The Condition of Postmodernity*. Oxford: Basil Blackwell.

Hebdige, D. (1983) *Subculture: The Meaning of Style*. London: Methuen.

Hebdige, D. (1989) 'New times: after the masses', *Marxism Today*, January.

Hegel, G.W. [1821] (1967) *The Philosophy of Right*. London: Oxford University Press.

Heilbron, J. (1995) *The Rise of Social Theory*. Cambridge: Polity Press.

Henwood, F. (1998) 'Engineering difference: discourses on gender, sexuality and work in a college of technology', *Gender and Education* 10(1): 35–49.

Hester, S. and Eglin, P. (1992) *A Sociology of Crime*. London: Routledge.

Hill Collins, P. (1990) *Black Feminist Thought: Knowledge, Consciousness, and the Politics of Empowerment*. London: Routledge.

Hill Collins, P. (1999) 'Mammies, matriarchs and other controlling images', in J. Kournay, J.P. Sterba and R. Tong (eds) *Feminist Philosophies*, 2nd edn. Englewood Cliffs, NJ: Prentice Hall.

Hill Collins, P. (2000) 'The social construction of Black feminist thought', in J. James and T.D. Sharpley-Whiting (eds) *The Black Feminist Reader*. Oxford: Blackwell.

Hirst, P. (1990) 'An answer to relativism?' *New Formations*, Spring.

Hobsbawm, E. (1989) *The Age of Revolution 1789–1848*. London: Cardinal.

Hodge, R. and Kress, G. (1979) *Language as Ideology*. London: Routledge & Kegan Paul.

Hodge, R. and Kress, G. (1988) *Social Semiotics*. Oxford: Oxford University Press.

Hof, U. Im. (1997) *The Enlightenment: An Historical Introduction*. Oxford: Basil Blackwell.

Holdaway, S. (1983) *Inside the British Police*. Oxford: Blackwell.

Holland, J., Ramazanoglu, C., Sharpe, S. and Thomson, R. (1998) *The Male in the Head: Young People, Heterosexuality and Power*. London: Tufnell Press.

Hollingdale, R.J. (1973) *Nietzsche*. London: Routledge.

Holmer-Nadesan, M. (1996) 'Organizational identity and spaces of action', *Organization Studies* 17(1): 49–81.

hooks, b. (1984) *Feminist Theory: From Margin to Centre*. Boston: South End Press.

hooks, b. (1989) *Talking Back: Thinking Feminist, Thinking Black*. Boston: Southend Press.

hooks, b. (2000) 'Black women: shaping feminist theory', in J. James and T. Sharpley-Whiting (eds) *Black Feminist Reader*. London: Blackwell.

Huggins, J. (1987) 'Black women and women's liberation', *Hecate* 13(1).

Hughes, E.C. (1945) 'Dilemmas and contradictions of status', *American Journal of Sociology*, 50 (March): 353–9.

Hughes, S. (1958). *Consciousness and Society: The Reorientation of European Social Thought 1890–1930*. New York: Alfred A. Knopf.

Hume, D. (1953) *David Hume's Political Essays*, edited with an Introduction by C.W. Hendel. New York: Liberal Arts Press.

Hume, D. (1966) 'Of national character', *Essays*. London.

Humphreys, L. (1975) *Tearoom Trade: A Study of Homosexual Encounter in Public Places*. London: Duckworth.

Ionescu, G. (1976) *The Political Thought of Saint-Simon*. Oxford: Oxford University Press.

Jackson, S. (1999) *Heterosexuality in Question*. London: Sage.

Jacob, M. (2001) *The Enlightenment: A Brief History with Documents*. Boston: St Martins Press.

Jacobs, M. (1992) *Sigmund Freud*. London: Sage.

James, W. (1890) *Principles of Psychology*. Henry Holt.

Jameson, F. (1984) 'Postmodernism or the cultural logic of late capitalism', *New Left Review*, 146.

Jameson, F. (1986) 'Third world literature in the era of multinational capitalism', *Social Text*, 15 (Fall): 65–89.

Jameson, F. (1988) 'Cognitive mapping', in C. Nelson and L. Grossberg (eds) *Marxism and the Interpretation of Culture*. London: Macmillan.

Jameson, F. (1992) *The Geopolitical Aesthetic: Cinema and Space in the World System*. London: British Film Institute.

Jeffreys, S. (1983) 'Consent and the politics of sexuality', *Current Issues in Criminal Justice* 173–83.

Jeffreys, S. (1997) *The Idea of Prostitution*. Melbourne: Spiniflex.

Jenkins, R. (1992) *Pierre Bourdieu*. London: Routledge.

Jenkins, R. (1997) *Rethinking Ethnicity: Arguments and Explorations*. London: Sage.

Jessop, B. (1987) 'The economy, the state and the law: theories of relative autonomy and autopoietic closure', Florence: European University Institute Working Paper 87.

Jessop, B. (1990) 'Regulation theory in retrospect and prospect', *Economy and Society*, 19(2), 153–216.

Johnson, P.M.G. (1998) 'Maori women and the politics of theorising difference', in R. Du Pliess and L. Alice (eds) *Feminist Thought in Aotearoa New Zealand*. Auckland: Oxford University Press.

Jones, A. (1993) 'Becoming a "girl": post-structuralist suggestions for educational research', *Gender and Education* 5(2): 157–66.

Jones, H. (1997) *G.H. Mead: A Contemporary Re-examination of his Thought*. Cambridge, Mass.: MIT Press.

Kehily, M. and Nayak, A. (2000) 'Schoolgirl frictions: young women, sex education and school experiences', in G. Walford and C. Hudson (eds), *Genders and Sexualities in Educational Ethnography*. Oxford: JAI Press.

Kellner, D. (1989) *Jean Baudrillard: From Marxism to Postmodernism and Beyond*. Cambridge: Polity Press.

Kellner, D. (1995) *Media Culture: Cultural Studies, Identity and Politics between the Modern and the Postmodern*. London: Routledge.

Kitsuse, J. (1962) 'Societal reaction to deviant behaviour: problems of theory and method', *Social Problems* 9(3): 247–56. Reprinted in E. Rubington and M. Weinberg (eds) (1987) *Deviance: The Interactionist Perspective*. London: Macmillan.

Kitzinger, C. (1994) 'Anti-lesbian harassment', in C. Brant and Y. Lee Too (eds), *Rethinking Sexual Harassment*. London: Pluto Press.

Kitzinger, J. (1995) 'I'm sexually attractive but I'm powerful: young women's negotiating sexual reputation', *Women's Studies International Forum* 18(2): 187–96.

Kroker, A. (1988) *The Postmodern Scene: Excremental Culture and Hyper-Aesthetics*. New York: St Martin's Press.

Kroker, A. and Cook, D. (1988) *The Postmodern Scene: Excremental Culture and Hyper-Aesthetics*. London: Macmillan.

Kumar, K. (1993) 'Modernity', in W. Outwaite and T. Bottomore (eds) *The Blackwell Dictionary of Social Thought*. Oxford: Basil Blackwell.

Kvande, E. (1999) 'In the belly of the beast: constructing femininities in engineering organisations', *European Journal of Women's Studies* 3(6): 305–28.

Laclau, E. and Mouffe, C. (1985) *Hegemoney and Socialist Strategy*. London: Verso.

Larkin, J. and Popaleni, K. (1994) 'Heterosexual courtship, violence and sexual harassment: the private and public control of young women', *Feminism and Psychology* 4(2): 213–27.

Lash, S. and Urry, J. (1987) *The End of Organised Capitalism*. Cambridge: Polity Press.

LaSpina, N. (1998) 'Disabled woman: the forging of a proud identity', Keynote address at Women's Studies Conference 'Fulfilling Possibilities: Women and Girls with Disabilities', Southern Connecticut State University, 2 October.

Laurie, N., Dwyer, C., Holloway, S. and Smith, F. (eds) (1999) *Geographies of New Femininities*. Harlow: Longman.

Layder, D. (1994) *Understanding Social Theory*. London: Sage.

Lazarsfeld, P., Berelson, B. and Gauder, H. (1944) *The People's Choice*. New York: Duck, Sloan and Pearce.

Lemert, C. (ed.) (1993) *Social Theory: The Multicultural and Classic Readings*. Oxford: Westview.

Lemert, C. (1997) *Social Things: An Introduction to The Sociological Life*. Oxford: Rowman & Littlefield.

Lemert, C. and Branaman, A. (1997) *The Goffman Reader*. London: Blackwell.

Lemert, I.L. (1951) *Social Pathology: A Systematic Approach to the Study of Sociopathic Behaviour*. New York: McGraw-Hill.

Leonard, D. (1982) *Sex and Generation: A Study of Courtship and Weddings*. London: Tavistock.

Lepenies, W. (1988) *Between Literature and Science: The Rise of Sociology*. Cambridge: Cambridge University Press.

Liazos, A. (1972) 'The poverty of the sociology of deviance nuts, sluts and preverts' [deliberate misspelling] *Social Problems* 20: 103–20.

Lloyd, M. (1995) 'Does she boil eggs? Towards a feminist model of disability', in M. Blair, J. Holland and S. Sharpe (eds) *Identity and Diversity: Gender and the Experience of Education*. Buckingham: Open University Press.

Loomis, C.P. (trans.) (1955) Preface to *Community and Association*. London: Routledge & Kegan Paul.

Lorber, J. (2000) 'Using gender to undo gender: a feminist degendering movement', *Feminist Theory* 1(1): 79–95.

Lorde, A. (1984) *Sister Outsider*. Freedom. Calif.: The Crossing Press.

Lorde, A. (1996) 'Age, race, class and sex: women redefining difference', in L. Harne and E. Miller (eds) *All the Rage: Reasserting Radical Lesbian Feminism*. London: The Women's Press.

Luff, D. (1999) 'Dialogue across the divides: "moments of rapport" and power in feminist research with anti-feminist women', *Sociology* 33(4): 687–703.

Lukes, S. (1973) *Emile Durkheim: His Life and Work*. Harmondsworth: Penguin.

Lyotard, J.F. (1984) *The Postmodern Condition: A Report on Knowledge*. Manchester: Manchester University Press.

Lyotard, J.F. (1988) *The Differend: Phrases in Dispute*. Manchester: Manchester University Press.

Maddock, S. (1999) *Challenging Women: Gender, Culture and Organization*. London: Sage.

Magee, B. (1987) *The Great Philosophers*. London: BBC Publications.

Mahon, M. (1992) *Foucault's Nietzchian Genealogy*. New York: University of New York Press.

Malik, K. (1996) *The Meaning of Race*. London: Macmillan.

Marcuse, H. (1964) *One Dimensional Man: The Ideology of Industrial Society*. London: Routledge.

Marshall, P. (1994) *Lacanian Theory of Discourse: Subject, Structure and Society*. New York: New York University Press.

Martindale, D. (1960) *The Nature and Types of Sociological Theory*. London: Lowe & Brydon.

Marx, K. (1958) *The Eighteenth Brumaire of Louis Bonaparte*. Moscow: Progress Publishers.

Marx, K. (1959) *Economic and Philosophical Manuscripts 1844*. Moscow: Foreign Languages Publishing House.

Marx, K. (1963) Preface to a contribution to the *Critique of Political Economy*, in T. Bottomore and M. Rubel (eds), *Karl Marx: Selected Writings in Sociology and Social Philosophy*. Harmondsworth: Penguin.

Marx, K. (1976) *Capital*. Harmondsworth: Penguin.

Marx, K. and Engels, F. (1959) *Manifesto of the Communist Party*. Moscow: Foreign Languages Publishing House.

Marx, K. and Engels, F. (1963) *The German Ideology*. New York: International Publishers.

Massey, D. (1994) *Space, Place and Gender*. Cambridge: Polity Press.

Massey, D. (1997) 'A global sense of place', in A. Gray and J. McGuigan (eds) *Studying Culture*, 2nd edn. London: Arnold.

Matza, D. (1969) *Becoming Deviant*. New Jersey: Prentice Hall.

Maynard, M. (1994) ' "Race", gender and the concept of "difference" in feminist thought,' in H. Afshar and M. Maynard (eds) *The Dynamics of Race and Gender: Some Feminist Interventions*. London: Taylor & Francis.

Maynard, M. (1995) 'Beyond the big three: the development of feminist theory into the 1990s', *Women's History Review* 4(3): 259–81.

Maynard, M. (1998) 'Feminists' knowledge and the knowledge of feminisms: epistemology, theory, methodology and method', in T. May and M. Walters (eds) *Knowing the Social World*. Buckingham: Open University Press.

McDowell, L. (1993) 'Space, place and gender relations. Part 2: Identity, difference, feminist geometries and geographies', *Progress in Human Geography* 17(3): 305–18.

McGuigan, J. (1992) *Cultural Populism*. London: Routledge.

McGuigan, J. (1998) 'What price the public sphere?', in D. Thussu (ed.) *Electronic Empires: Global Media and Local Resistance*. London: Arnold.

McGuigan, J. (1999) *Modernity and Postmodern Culture*. Milton Keynes: Open University Press.

McHugh, P. (1968) *Defining the Situation: The Organisation of Meaning in Social Interaction*. Indianapolis: Bobbs-Merrill.

McIntosh, P. (1988) 'White privilege: unpacking the invisible knapsack', www.spokanehumanrights.org/ccrr/packet/article.htm

McLennan, G. (1992) 'The Enlightenment project revisited', in S. Hall, D. Held and T. McGrew (eds) *Modernity and its Futures*. Cambridge: Polity Press.

McNeil, S. (1985) 'Sexual harassment at work', in D. Rhodes and S. McNeil (eds) *Women against Violence against Women*. London: Onlywoman Press.

McNeil, S. (1996) 'Identity politics', in L. Harne and E. Miller (eds) *All the Rage: Reasserting Radical Lesbian Feminism*. London: Women's Press.

Mead, G.H. (1934) *Mind, Self and Society*. Chicago: University of Chicago Press.

Mead, G.H. (1982) *The Individual and the Social Self: Unpublished Work of George Herbert Mead*, ed. A. Strauss. Chicago: University of Chicago Press.

Merton, R.K. (1948) 'The position of sociological theory', *American Sociological Review* 13.

Merton, R.K. (1967) *Social Theory and Social Structure*. New York: Free Press.

Merton, R.K. (1976) *Sociological Ambivalence and Other Essays*. New York: Free Press.

Middleton, C. (1997) 'Sociology, social reform and revolutions', in C. Ballard, J. Gubbay and C. Middleton (eds) *The Students' Companion to Sociology*. London: Blackwell.

Miles, L. (1993) 'Women, Aids and the power in heterosexual sex: a discourse analysis', *Women's Studies International Forum* 16(5): 497–511.

Milgram, S. (1974) *Obedience to Authority: An Experimental View*. London: Tavistock.

Miller, D. (1982) Introduction, in *The Individual and the Social Self: Unpublished Work of George Herbert Mead*, ed. A. Strauss. Chicago: University of Chicago Press.

Mills, C. Wright (1959) *The Sociological Imagination*. London: Oxford University Press.

Mills, C. Wright. (1970) *The Sociological Imagination*. Harmondsworth: Penguin.

Mirchandani, K. (1999) 'Feminist insight on gendered work: new directions in research on women and entrepreneurship', *Gender, Work and Organization* 6(4): 224–35.

Mirza, H.S. (1997) (ed.) *Black British Feminism: A Reader*. London: Routledge.

Morley, D. and Robins, K. (1995) *Spaces of Identity: Global Media, Electronic Landscapes and Cultural Boundaries*. London: Routledge.

Mort, F. (1994) Postmodern Times – taped essays from the BSA Conference, 'Sexualities in Social Context', March 1994.

Mort, F. (1996) *Cultures of Consumption*. London: Routledge.

Mosse, G.L. (1978) *Toward the Final Solution: A History of European Racism*. London: Dent.

Mouzelis, N. (1997) 'In defence of the sociological canon: a reply to David Parker', *Sociological Review* 45.

Mowl, G. and Towner, J. (1995) 'Women, gender, leisure and place: towards a more humanistic geography of women's leisure, *Leisure Studies* 14: 102–16.

Nakana, G.E. (1999) 'The social construction and institutionalisation of gender and race', in M.M. Ferre, J. Lorber and B.B. Hess (eds) *Revisioning Gender*. London: Sage.

New, C. (2001) 'Oppressed and oppressors? The systematic mistreatment of men', *Sociology* 35(3): 729–48.

Nietzsche, F. [1901] (1968) *The Will to Power*, translated and edited by W. Kaufman and R.J. Hollindale. London: Weidenfeld & Nicolson.

Nietzsche, F. (1983) *The Gay Sciences*, in R. Schacht, *Nietzsche*. London: Routledge & Kegan Paul.

Nisbet, R. (1965) *Durkheim, with selected essays*. Westport, Conn.: Greenwood Press.

Nisbet, R. (1973) *The Sociological Tradition*. London: Heinemann Educational.

Norris, C. (1992) *Uncritical Theory: Postmodernism, Intellectuals and the Gulf War*. London: Lawrence & Wishart.

Norris, C. (1993) *The Truth about Postmodernism*. Oxford: Basil Blackwell.

Oakley, A. (1972) *Sex, Gender and Society*. London: Temple-Smith.

Oakley, A. (1974) *Housewife*. London: Lane.

Oakley, A. (1981) *From Here to Maternity*. Harmondsworth: Penguin.

Oakley, A. (1998) 'Gender, methodology and people's ways of knowing: some problems with feminism and the paradigm debate', *Social Science Sociology* 32(4): 707–31.

Olson, R. (1993) *The Emergence of the Social Sciences, 1642–1792*. New York: Twayne Publishers.

Ørnstrup, H. (2000) 'George Simmel', in H. Andersen and L.B. Kaspersen (eds) *Classical and Modern Social Theory*. London: Basil Blackwell.

Paine, T. (1937) *The Rights of Man*. London: Watts.

Pampel, F.C. (2000) *Sociological Lives and Ideas*. New York: Worth Press.

Parker, D. (1997) 'Why bother with Durkheim? Teaching sociology in the 1990s', *Sociological Review* 45.

Parmar, P. (1997) 'Other kinds of dreams', in H.S. Mirza (ed.) *Black British Feminism: A Reader*. London: Routledge.

Parsons, T. (1937) *The Structure of Social Action*. New York: Free Press.

Parsons, T. (1948) 'The position of sociological theory', *American Sociological Review* 13.

Parsons, T. (1951) *The Social System*. New York: Free Press.

Pearson, G. (1975) *The Deviant Imagination*. London: Macmillan.

Peel, J.D.Y. (1971) *Herbert Spencer: The Evolution of a Sociologist*. London: Heinemann.

Perriton, L. (1999) 'The proactive and evocative gaze upon women in management education', *Gender and Education* 11(3): 295–307.

Philo, G. and Miller, D. (1999) *Cultural Compliance*. London: Glasgow University Media Group/Longman.

Plant, S. and Healey, P. (1994) 'Essays 2 & 3', in F. Mort, Postmodern Times – taped essays from the BSA Conference, 'Sexualities in Social Context', March 1994.

Popper, K. (1934) *The Logic of Scientific Discovery*. London: Hutchinson.

Popper, K. (1963*) Conjectures and Refutations: The Growth of Scientific Knowledge*. London: Routledge & Kegan Paul.

Porter, R. (2001) *The Enlightenment*, 2nd edn. Basingstoke: Palgrave.

Prendiville, P. (2000) *Lesbian Information and Resource Pack*. Dublin: LOT (Lesbians Organising Together).

Prior, P. (1995) 'Surviving psychiatric institutionism: a case study', *Sociology of Health and Illness* 17(5): 651–67.

Prokhovnik, R. (1999) *Rational Woman: A Feminist Critique of Dichotomy*. London: Routledge.

Radford, I., Friedberg, M. and Harne, L. (eds) (2000) *Women, Violence and Strategies for Action*. Buckingham: Open University Press.

Ray, L. (1999) *Theorizing Classical Sociology*. Milton Keynes: Open University Press.

Ribbens McCarthy, J. and Edwards, R. (2001) 'Illuminating meanings of "the private" in sociological thought. A response to Joe Bailey', *Sociology* 35(3): 765–77.

Rich, A. (1979) *On Lies, Secrets and Silence: Selected Prose 1966–1978*. New York: W.W. Norton.

Rich, A. (1983) *Powers and Desires*. New York: Monthly Review Press.

Richardson, D. (ed.) (1996) *Theorising Heterosexuality: Telling It Straight*. Buckingham: Open University Press.

Richardson, D. and May, H. (1999) 'Deserving victims? Sexual status and the social construction of violence', *Sociological Review* 47(2): 308–31.

Ritvo, H. (1997) *The Platypus and the Mermaid, And Other Figments of the Classifying Imagination*. Cambridge, Mass.: Harvard University Press.

Ritzer, G. (1992) *Sociological Theory*. New York: McGraw-Hill.

Ritzer, G. (1993) *The McDonaldization of Society*. Newbury Park, Calif.: Pine Forge Press.

Ritzer, G. (1994) *Sociological Beginnings*. New York: McGraw-Hill.

Ritzer, G. (1996) *Classical Sociological Theory*. New York: McGraw Hill.

Robins, K. (1993) 'The war, the screen, the crazy dog and poor mankind', *Media Culture and Society*, 15(2): 321–7.

Robins, K. (1996) *Into the Image: Culture and Politics in the Field of Vision*. London: Routledge.

Rock, P. (1979) *The Making of Symbolic Interactionism*. Basingstoke: Macmillan.

Rock, P. and McIntosh, M. (eds) (1974) *Deviance and Social Control*. London: Tavistock.

Rorty, R. (1985) 'Habermas and Lyotard on postmodernity', in R. Bernstein (ed.) *Habermas and Modernity*. Cambridge: Polity Press.

Rose, D. and Sullivan, O. (1993) *Introducing Data Analysis for Social Sciences*, 2nd edn. Milton Keynes: Open University Press.

Rosenhan, D.L. (1973) 'On being sane in insane places', *Science* 179: 205–8.

Rosenthal, R. and Jacobson, L. (1970) 'Levels of expectancy and self-fulfilling prophesy', in E. Stones (ed.) *Readings in Educational Psychology*. London: Methuen.

Rostow, W.W. (1960) *The Stages of Economic Growth: A Non-Communist Manifesto*, Cambridge: Cambridge University Press.

Rostow, W.W. (1971) *The Stages of Economic Growth: A Non-Communist Manifesto* (2nd edn). London: Cambridge University Press.

Rousseau, J-J. [1762] (1968) *The Social Contract*. Harmondsworth: Penguin.

Rubington, E. and Weinberg, M. (eds) (1987) *Deviance: The Interactionist Perspective*. London: Macmillan.

Runciman, W. (1978) *Max Weber: Selections in Translation*. Cambridge: Cambridge University Press.

Said, E.W. (1980) *Orientalism*. London: Routledge & Kegan Paul.

Saint-Simon, Henri, Comte de (1952) *Selected Writings*, edited by F.M.H. Markham. Oxford: Basil Blackwell.

Sartre, J-P. (1969) *Nausea*. Harmondsworth: Penguin.

Sarup, M. (1993) *An Introductory Guide to Poststructuralism and Postmodernism*, 2nd edn. Hemel Hempstead: Harvester Wheatsheaf.

Sayer, A. (2000) *Realism and Social Science*. London: Sage.

Schacht, R. (1983) *Nietzsche*. London: Routledge & Kegan Paul.

Schimdt, J. (1996) *What is Enlightenment? Eighteenth Century Answers and Twentieth Century Questions*. Berkeley: University of California Press.

Schutz, A. (1932) *The Phenomenology of the Social World*. Evanston: Northwestern University Press.

Scraton, S. (1994) 'The changing world of women and leisure: feminism, "postfeminism" and leisure', *Leisure Studies* 13(4): 249–61.

Scraton, S. and Watson, B. (1998) 'Gendered cities: women and public leisure space in the postmodern city', *Leisure Studies* 17: 123–37.

Sexwale, B.M.M. (1994) 'Violence against women: experiences of South African domestic workers', in H. Afshar and M. Maynard (eds), *The Dynamics of 'Race' and Gender: Some Feminist Interventions*. London: Taylor & Francis.

Sheffield, C.J. (1999) 'Sexual terrorism', in J.A. Kourany, J.P. Sterba and R. Tong (eds), *Feminist Philosophies*, 2nd edn. Englewood Cliffs, NJ: Prentice Hall.

Simmel, G. (1978) *The Philosophy of Money*. London: Routledge & Kegan Paul.

Simmel, G. (1979) *The Metropolis and Mental Life*, in D. Frisby and M. Featherstone (eds) *Simmel on Culture: Selected Writings*. London: Sage.

Simons, H. (1995) 'A hidden agenda', *Living Marxism* July/August: 32–5.

Skeggs, B. (1991) 'Postmodernism; What is all the Fuss About?', *British Journal of Sociology of Education*, 12: 2.

Skeggs, B. (1994) 'Refusing to be civilized: "race", sexuality and power', in H. Afshar and M. Maynard (eds) *The Dynamics of 'Race' and Gender: Some Feminist Interventions*. London: Taylor & Francis.

Skeggs, B. (1995) (ed.) *Feminist Cultural Theory: Process and Production*. Manchester: Manchester University Press.

Skeggs, B. (1997) *Formations of Class and Gender: Becoming Respectable*. London: Sage.

Skeggs, B. (1999) 'Matter out of place: visibility and sexualities in leisure spaces', *Leisure Studies* 18(3): 212–32.

Smart, B. (1990) 'Modernity, postmodernity and the present', in B. Turner (ed.) *Theories of Modernity and Postmodernity*. London: Sage.

Smart, B. (1993) *Postmodernity: Key Ideas*. London: Routledge.

Smith, A. [1776] (1986) *The Wealth of Nations*, Books I–III. London: Penguin.

Smith, B. (1979) 'Racism and women's studies', in G.T. Hull, P. Bell Scott and B. Smith (eds), *But Some of Us are Brave*. New York: The Feminist Press.

Smith, D. (1977) *Feminism and Marxism*. Vancouver: New State Books.

Smythe, C. (1992) *Lesbians Talk Queer Notions*, cited in F. Mort, Postmodern Times – taped essays from the BSA Conference, 'Sexualities in Social Context', March 1994.

Solomon, R. (1985) *Reading Nietzsche*. Oxford: Oxford University Press.

Spelman, E. (1988) *Inessential Woman: Problems of Exclusion in Feminist Thought*. London: The Women's Press.

Spencer, H. (1880) *The Study of Sociology*, 9th edn. London: Williams & Northgate.

Spencer, H. (1885) *The Man v. the State*. London: Williams. (Reprinted essays from the *Contemporary Review*.)

Spencer, H. (1967) *The Evolution of Society: Selections from Herbert Spencer Principles of Sociology*, edited by R.L. Carnerio. Chicago: University of Chicago Press.

Spencer, H. (1969) *Principles of Sociology*, edited by Stanislav Andreski. London: Macmillan.

Stacey, J. (1993) 'Untangling feminist theory', in D. Richardson and V. Robinson (eds) *Introducing Women's Studies*. London: Macmillan.

Stanley, L. and Wise, S. (1993) *Breaking Out Again: Feminist Ontology and Epistemology*. London: Routledge.

Stern, J.P. (1977) *Nietzsche*. London: Fontana.

Stones, E. (1970) *Readings in Educational Psychology*. London: Methuen.

Sum, N. (2000) 'From politics of identity to politics of complexity: a possible research agenda for feminist politics/movements across time and space', in S. Ahmed, J. Kilby, C. Lury, M. McNeil and B. Skeggs (eds) *Transformations: Thinking Through Feminism*. London: Sage.

Swingewood, A. (1991) *A Short History of Sociological Thought*. Basingstoke: Macmillan.

Sykes, B. (1984) Untitled article in R. Rowland (ed.) *Women who Do and Women who Don't Join the Feminist Movement*. London: Routledge.

Tannen, D. (1994) *You Just Don't Understand: Women and Men in Conversation*. London: Virago.

Tannenbaum, F. (1938) *Crime and the Community*. New York: Columbia University Press.

Taylor, S. and Tyler, M. (2000) 'Emotional labour and sexual difference in the airline industry', *Sociology* 14(1): 77–96.

Thomas, A.M. and Kitzinger, C. (eds) (1997) *Sexual Harassment: Contemporary Feminist Perspectives*. Buckingham: Open University Press.

Thomas, C. (1999) *Female Forms: Experiencing and Understanding Disability*. Buckingham: Open University Press.

Thomas, W.I. (1923) *The Unadjusted Girl*. Boston: Little Brown.

Thomas, W.I. and Znaniecki, F. (1927) *The Polish Peasant in Europe and America*. New York: Dover.

Thompson, H. (1985) *Hell's Angels*. Harmondsworth: Penguin.

Thompson, J.B. (1984) *Studies in the Theory of Ideology*. Cambridge: Polity Press.

Thornham, S. (1999) 'Second wave feminism', in S. Gamble (ed.) *Feminism and Post-feminism*. Cambridge: Icon Books.

Tickell, A. and Peck, J. (1992) 'Accumulation, regulation and the geographies of post-Fordism: missing links in regulationist research', *Progress in Human Geography*, 16(2).

Tocqueville, Alexis de (1955) *The Old Regime and the French Revolution*. New York: Doubleday.

Tönnies, F. (1955) *Community and Association*, translated by C.P. Loomis. London: Routledge & Kegan Paul. First published in German in 1887.

Touraine, A. (1989) 'Is sociology still the study of society?', *Thesis Eleven*, 23.

Tretheway, A. (1999) 'Disciplined bodies: women's embodied identities of work', *Organization Studies* 20(3): 423–50.

Turkle, S. (1997) *Life on the Screen: Identity in the Age of the Internet*. London: Phoenix.

Turner, B.S. (1996) *For Weber: Essays in the Sociology of Fate*. London: Sage.

Valentine, G. (1992) 'Images of danger: women's sources of information about the spatial distribution of male violence', *Area* 24(1): 22–9.

Valentine, G. (1993) '(Hetero) sexualising space: lesbian perceptions of everyday spaces', *Environment and Planning D: Society and Space* 11: 395–413.

Veblen, T. (1919) *The Place of Science in Modern Civilization*. New York: Huebsch.

Walby, S. (1992) 'Post-post-modernism? Theorising social complexity', in M. Barrett and A. Phillips (eds) *Destabilizing Theory: Contemporary Feminist Debates*. Cambridge: Polity Press.

Wallis, A. and Vanevery, J. (2000) 'Sexuality in the primary school', *Sexualities* 3(4): 409–24.

Warde, A. (1994) 'Consumption, identity-formation and uncertainty', *Sociology* 28: 4.

Watier, P. (1998) 'George Simmel', in R. Stones (ed.), *Key Sociological Thinkers*. London: Macmillan.

Waxman, B. and Saxton, S. (1997) 'Disability feminism: a manifesto', *New Mobility* October: 60.

Weber, M. [1902] (1930) *The Protestant Ethic and the Spirit of Capitalism*. London: Allen & Unwin.

Weber, M. (1947) *The Theory of Social and Economic Organisation*. New York: Oxford University Press.

Weber, M. (1948) 'Bureaucracy', in H.H. Gerth and C. Wright Mills (eds) *From Max Weber: Essays in Sociology*. Oxford: Oxford University Press.

Weber, M. (1949) *The Methodology of the Social Sciences*. New York: Free Press.

Weber, M. (1968) *Economy and Society*. New York: Bedminister Press.

Weber, M. (1983) *Max Weber on Capitalism, Bureaucracy and Religion: A Selection of Texts*. London: George Allen & Unwin.

Weedon, C. (1999) *Feminism. Theory and the Politics of Difference*. Oxford: Blackwell.

West, C. and Zimmerman, D. (1987) 'Doing gender', *Gender and Society* 1: 125–51.

Wheen, F. (2000) *Karl Marx*. London: Fourth Estate.

Whyte, W. (1943) *Street Corner Society: The Social Structure of an Italian Slum*. Chicago: University of Chicago Press.

Wilson, E. (2001) *The Contradictions of Culture: Cities Culture and Women*. London: Sage.

Wilton, T. (1995) *Lesbian Studies: Setting an Agenda*. London: Routledge.

Wilton, T. (2000) *Sexualities in Health and Social Care: A Textbook*. Buckingham: Open University Press.

Winter, B. (2000) 'Who counts (or doesn't count) what is feminist theory? An exercise in dictionary use', *Feminist Theory*, 1(1): 105–11.

Wolf, N. (1993) *Fire with Fire*. London: Chatto & Windus.

Wood, A. (1975) *Europe 1815–1945*. London: Longman.

Young, I.M. (1992) 'Together in difference: transforming the logic of group political conflict', *Political Theory Newsletter* 4: 11–26.

Zimbardo, P.G. (1972) 'Pathology of imprisonment', *Society* 9: 4–8.

Index